Overwhelming Terror

D1563210

War and Peace Library
Series Editor: Mark Selden

Overwhelming Terror

Love, Fear, Peace, and Violence among Semai of Malaysia

Robert Knox Dentan

ROWMAN & LITTLEFIELD PUBLISHERS, INC.
Lanham • Boulder • New York • Toronto • Plymouth, UK

ROWMAN & LITTLEFIELD PUBLISHERS, INC.

Published in the United States of America
by Rowman & Littlefield Publishers, Inc.
A wholly owned subsidiary of The Rowman & Littlefield Publishing Group, Inc.
4501 Forbes Boulevard, Suite 200, Lanham, Maryland 20706
www.rowmanlittlefield.com

Estover Road, Plymouth PL6 7PY, United Kingdom

British Library Cataloguing in Publication Information Available

Library of Congress Cataloging-in-Publication Data
Dentan, Robert Knox, 1936–
  Overwhelming terror : love, fear, peace, and violence among Semai of Malaysia
/ Robert Knox Dentan.
    p. cm. — (War and peace library)
  Includes bibliographical references and index.
  ISBN-13: 978-0-7425-5329-3 (cloth : alk. paper)
  ISBN-10: 0-7425-5329-9 (cloth : alk. paper)
  ISBN-13: 978-0-7425-5330-9 (pbk. : alk. paper)
  ISBN-10: 0-7425-5330-2 (pbk. : alk. paper)
  eISBN-13: 978-0-7425-5728-4
  eISBN-10: 0-7425-5728-6
  [etc.]
  1. Senoi (Southeast Asian people)—Psychology. 2. Senoi (Southeast Asian
people)—Wars. 3. Senoi (Southeast Asian people)—Social conditions. I. Title.
  DS595.2.S3D45 2008
  305.895'93—dc22

                              2008030714

Printed in the United States of America

⊗™ The paper used in this publication meets the minimum requirements of
American National Standard for Information Sciences—Permanence of Paper
for Printed Library Materials, ANSI/NISO Z39.48-1992.

Contents

Preface

In the nineteenth century there was a tradition whereby novelists, story-tellers and even poets offered the public an historical explanation of their work, often in the form of a preface. Inevitably a poem or a story deals with particular experience: how this experience relates to developments on a world scale can and should be implied within the writing itself—this is precisely the problem posed by the "resonance" of language . . . ; nevertheless it is usually not possible in a poem or story to make the relation between particular and universal fully explicit. . . . Hence the writer's desire to write an explanation *around* the work or works he is offering the reader. The tradition became established in the nineteenth century precisely because it was a century of revolutionary change in which the relation between the individual and history was becoming a conscious one. (Berger 1975:195)

"I am a rather elderly man. The nature of my avocations, for the past thirty years, has brought me into more than ordinary contact with what would seem an interesting and singular set of men," writes Herman Melville (1974:901–2), whose view of the world pervades this book. I too am a rather elderly man. The nature of my avocations, for the past half-century, has brought me into more than ordinary contact with what would seem an interesting and singular set of people, people whose lives may hold a lesson for all of us, the traditionally peaceable Semai Senoi of central peninsular Malaysia. At a time when my own country is struggling to formulate an effective response to terrorism, there may be something to learn from a people whose whole way of life seems to embody a response to terror. Let me introduce them—as they used to be because, like everyone else, their lives are changing rapidly. Their current situation deserves attention, which I've often tried to give elsewhere. But their enormous achievement deserves attention too, not just their present struggles.

But first I need to admit that when you live for a long time with people, your memory starts to blur them together. Not all of them, of course: but the ones who didn't like you well enough to hang around with you, who had more pressing business elsewhere, or whom you for some reason didn't make the extra effort necessary to "know." Joseph Brodsky (1997), an exile whose life forced him to travel a lot, wrote a sad, funny essay, "A Place as Good as Any," about how cities blend in memory into a single generic city. When teachers think about "students," women about "men," or adults about "children," most of what they remember is this background blur. The fragments of Semai I'm trying to cobble together in this book stick together in part because, in my memory, the experiences they represent are embedded like raisins in rice pudding, in a background notion of "Semai." That's the context that makes sense of the stories, if sense can made.

And that's all the introduction to the people is for. An "ethnographic summary" like this is about as accurate as an equally short introduction to Americans would be: vapid and oversimplified. It's just a starting point. What you need to know at the outset are two things: individually Semai are a lot like you and me, and collectively they managed to develop a way of life that may be the most peaceable ever documented.

The second part discusses the book itself and how it came to be offbeat and erratic, "experimental" in current jargon. There's a method in the weirdness, and I try in the second part of this introduction to give a reason for it, though I've left the bulk of this discussion on the website that accompanies this book (http://www.rowmanlittlefield.com/isbn/ 0742553302). I put most of the bibliography, theoretical explorations, methodological details, and ethnographic minutiae there in a scholarly shadow ethnography that accompanies and "documents" this one.

A LETTER TO MALAYS AND MALAYSIA

I know that some people—particularly Malaysians, who tend to see social problems through an ethnic glass, darkly—will read this book as anti-Malay or anti-Malaysian. That saddens me, because on a personal level I love the people and the country as I love my own. I remember with pleasure long conversations I've had with ordinary Malays, filled with warmth, and with my Malay colleagues, almost all of whom would endorse the wonderful Malay expression of tolerance, *lain padang lain be-*

lalang, different fields, different grasshoppers = different places, different customs. Ironically, I have in different contexts also been called anti-American, anti-White, and the like, for the same sort of analysis.

The problems I'm addressing here are human, not local. One reason for all the epigraphs from various places and times that I've included in the text is to show that the experiences I'm talking about aren't peculiarly Malaysian but common or even universal. I'm counting on readers to pick up the similarities. Any evil I describe comes not from problems with Malay character or Malaysian "culture," but from disparities in power. At the end of *The Second Sex,* Simone de Beauvoir remarks that a colonial judge *cannot* do justice; to do justice he would have to cease being a judge. And, she adds, a general *cannot* treat his troops fairly, as long as he is a general. It's easy to conflate "Americans" with powerful Americans, or "Malays" with ruling-class Malays, and therefore seem to criticize the whole people. But it's the power, not the people, that's the problem.

Most people in "advanced" societies are unaware of the historical or present conditions that underpin their current innocence. They can't imagine what it's like always to have, inside your mind, an avatar of the people who control your lives, always watching what you do with faint contempt; most African-Americans and Semai can. The majorities don't understand why anyone would reflexively try to become like that watcher, if only to be whole.

Most New Yorkers, until the dawn of casinos, were unaware there were any Native Americans in New York state; most Malaysians know nothing much about Semai. The behavior of the Bureau of Indian Affairs and the Jabatan Hal Ehwal Orang Asli toward their "clients" is mind-bogglingly similar: an American anthropologist keeps thinking, "My God, they're making exactly the same mistakes we did" (see, e.g., Colin Nicholas's letter of 20 September 2008 to the *New Straits Times*). Similar power relations, similar results. The situation is no different in China, as I once said to a Chinese audience in a talk titled "Putting the Fox in Charge of the Henhouse."

The evil, if that's even the right word, lies not in the peoples or their countries or their cultures but in the structures of power within which, often completely unawares, we all try simply to get through the day.

Thanks

I visited Semai in 1961–1963, 1975–1976, and 1991–1992 with permission from the Jabatan Hal Ehwal Orang Asli or JHEOA, the Malaysian "Bureau of Indigenous People's Affairs." The Malaysian Prime Minister's Office paid my way to a conference on indigenous peoples in 1993 (Dentan 1993b), and I visited as a tourist in 2006. Hood Salleh of the Universiti Kebangsaan Malaysia and Tan Chee Beng, formerly of Universiti Malaya but now at the Chinese University of Hong Kong, were my official sponsors during my first research, without being responsible for any of my conclusions. The American Museum of Natural History and the Ford Foundation supported my early work. The Harry Frank Guggenheim Foundation supported research in Malaysia on Semai violence in the 1990s and gave me a semester's support to write this book. They are wonderful people to work with, and I especially want to thank Karen Colvard. Much that follows comes from talks with Ngah Hari, Kin-Manang, Risaaw, Sudeew, and Mrlooh (memorialized in Dentan 1993b). Conversations with and writings by Juli Edo and his grandfather, Mat Ariff, Colin Nicholas, Bah Tony (Anthony) Williams-Hunt, and Hasan Mat Noor have been helpful, encouraging, and corrective. In the past few years, I've coauthored papers with Tony and Juli. But I'm solely responsible for errors in this book.

I learned how to think about Semai not just from Semai but partly from colleagues in the old Department of American Studies at the University of Buffalo, especially the late Larry Chisolm, Charles and Angeliki Keil, Oren Lyons, John Mohawk, and Barry White. Charlie and Angie persuaded me to resuscitate this book after I'd abandoned it, following a rejection by the University of Chicago Press. Arthur Redding, then of Central European

University, and Lee Wilson, then of Cambridge University, encouraged me. I have looked for and received help, as always, from my wife, Leta, and from present and past students I have been lucky enough to know: Alexandra Bakalaki, Nneka Black, Dan Cadzow, Christine Eber, the late Wanda Edwards, the late Celia Ehrlich, Nathaniel Galletta, Daniel I. Grover, Eva Hulse, Ronald Houston, Grant Ingram, Liz Kish, Thomas Lechner, Laura McClusky, Jennifer Malicher, Peter Morrow, Michael Niman, Deirdre Newell, Barbara S. Nowak, Fred Rawski, Jennifer Randall, Lucille Sherlick, Matthew Smith, Louise Tokarsky, Vincent Wan, Charles Weigl, and Zoe Zacharek; Laura and Fred helped me far more than students owe their advisers. I also thank my departmental colleague Carol Berman, who shares the uneasiness of many biological anthropologists about particularistic literary-interpretive ethnography but approved this effort; Keith Otterbein and Douglas Fry, genial and sobering influences who know a lot about violence and peace; Andrew Shryock, who always makes me think; Carol Laderman, the expert on Malay shamanism; James Scott, whose work I find wonderful; and Cuthbert Simpkins, former director of the Erie County Center for the Study and Prevention of Violence.

The book would have never got off the ground without Emilie Broderick, who checked the bibliography, and the patient and long-suffering staff at Rowman & Littlefield, notably Susan McEachern, Jessica Gribble, Alden Perkins, and Bruce Owens.

A remarkable thing about ethnographers who work with Malaysian indigenes (Orang Asli) is how rarely you encounter the stupid unproductive backbiting that pervades so much academic activity. We've speculated that maybe the cooperative and loving people with whom we work influenced how we deal with each other. Besides the people already mentioned, I particularly want to thank Clayton and Carole Robarchek, who have concentrated on explicating Semai peaceability and who shared their field notes with me; Colin Nicholas, whose work on the current plight of Semai is invaluable (e.g., Nicholas 1990, 1994) and who not only supplied information to me but actually sought it out; and Alberto Gomes, Juli Edo, and Hasan Mat Noor, whose Semai research deepened my own. Geoffrey Benjamin of the National Technological University of Singapore, Rosemary Gianno of Keene College, Barbara Nowak of many places lately, and Kirk Endicott of Dartmouth University, longtime colleagues and friends, have been a great help, especially in moderating my responses to events in Malaysia. Lye Tuck-Po, then of the World Wildlife Fund, shared her "struggles" (*pompous word!* as she says, but it does feel like a struggle) to write up her material on Batek (e.g., 2004), which led her independently to decide that maybe "eclecticism is the key."

I've mostly used pseudonyms for Semai who worked with me. But some people wanted to be known and deserve my thanks: Ngah Hari and

Kin-Manang of Mncaak were my family and mentors in more than just ethnography. Without them and Bah Sudeew, their son; Mat Ariff, Juli Edo's uncle; and Risaaw and Mrlooh, Jambu's children, of the Tluup River, there would be no book. I have other Semai friends whose loyalty and warmth over the last half-century is a grace for which no thanks could be adequate, notably Wa' Saiyah, Kin-Sima and the late Bah Bluuk of Mncaak. I'm always surprised, when totting up the number of people I consider friends, people who seem glad to see me when I arrive unexpectedly, how many are Semai. The affection seems so improbable, across the gaps of time and space and culture. I am inexpressibly grateful to them, and that has little to do with helping me write books. Special thanks to Phyllis Hartrich for her support over many years.

Another set of folks who have helped me a lot are children, especially Elizabeth Meimei Dentan, Terence Dolan, Alex Schaffner, Gordon Buchanan Simpson, Kenneth Simpson, and David Gavin Simpson, who helped me understand Bah Rmpent, Bah Tkooy, and Wa' Prankuup—and everyone else, in fact. Their analyses of their own lives kept me thinking about power, love, and terror, and what they do to children and adults.

* * *

I had just finished the first draft of this book when Sudeew, my *mnaang*, wrote to say that his mother Kin-Manang had died: my mother too, that's how Sudeew and I became siblings, *tne'-mnaang*. Many people have been kind to me, but she was the kindest person I have ever known, not just to me but to everyone.

Kin-Manang was small and easily flustered, even for Semai, with a long, homely, thin face and wispy hair. Last time I saw her, her cataracts were bad, and her deafness was getting worse, and she looked very small and frail until she spoke, and the love she managed to have for me once again bridged all our mutual weirdness and increasing decrepitude. Love was just matter-of-fact for her, not a big deal, not something you talked about, just like her nose, just *there*. She wasn't a "good informant," not brilliant or charming. All she knew how to do well was to love misfits and bumblers. She did that wonderfully, with

> A faith that we have something yet to share
> Though all the universe's atoms move
> Toward regions desolate of human love

> (Carper 1991:8)

Introduction

Writing Someone Else's Life

Objectivity, of course, is the motto of every historian, and that's why passion is normally ruled out—since, as the saying goes, it blinds.

One wonders, however, whether a passionate response, in such a context, wouldn't amount to a greater human objectivity, for disembodied intelligence carries no weight. Moreover, one wonders whether in such a context the absence of passion is nothing but a stylistic device to which writers resort in order to emulate the historian or, for that matter, the modern cultural stereotype, a cool, thin-lipped, soft-spoken character inhabiting the silver screen for the better part of the century in a sleuthing or slaying capacity. If that's the case—and all too often the imitation is too convincing to feel otherwise—then history, which used to be the source of ethical education in society in society, has indeed come full circle.

In the end, however, most of these thin-lipped folk of the silver screen pull the trigger. A modern historian doesn't do anything of the sort, and he would cite science as the explanation for his reserve. In other words, the quest for objectivity of interpretation takes precedence over the sentiments caused by what is interpreted. One wonders, then, what is the significance of interpretation: Is history simply an instrument for measuring how far we can remove ourselves from events, a sort of anti-thermometer? (Brodsky 1997:127).

SEMAI AS "ORANG ASLI"

Semai are the largest group of "Orang Asli." Orang Asli are the indigenous people of peninsular Malaysia in the southeasternmost corner of Asia. Counting people in towns, there are about 100,000 Orang

Asli, divided into over a dozen language groups, each with its distinctive way of life. In 2008, about 30,000 were Semai. Orang Asli languages are or were related to the languages of Cambodia's Khmer and Thailand's Mon, unrelated to the languages of later-arriving immigrants like the politically dominant Malays.

Economy

In the old days, the times they call *manah ntvvm*, Semai were "agro-foresters." They also cleared fields, technically "swiddens," in the heart of the rain forest, usually targeting areas where trees were small enough to cut down easily. Two men take a day to fell a rain forest giant. So they usually cleared new swiddens in secondary forest, where they had cleared fields a dozen or more years earlier. They spared trees that produced valuable products, like fruit or blowpipe dart poisons. They also planted or tended such trees in their fields or in the forest. The result was a forest rich in valuable species of trees, with a greater variety of plants and animals than in untouched forest. This sustainable adaptation lasted for thousands of years.

When the possibility of joining the Malaysian mainstream economy emerged, Semai responded by adapting their traditional agroforestry. They began to grow trees as cash crops. But, as time went on, Malaysian governments "regrouped" most Semai into overcrowded "Regroupment Schemes" and turned their orchards and forests over to loggers and developers who had "connections" with local officials.

Social Life

Early European and Malay observers describe Semai as fearful. Although there were trade ties between Malays and Semai, Malay and Chinese "patrons" often exploited their Semai "clients." The difference between "clients" and slaves was blurry. Semai fearfulness was a reasonable response to their brutal political environment, which, especially as the British colonial government sought to develop the country after 1874, involved increasing displacement and enslavement by Indonesian "Malay" immigrants who had no ties with Semai and who exterminated other groups of Orang Asli. Slavers particularly targeted Semai children since they were easy to steal and domesticate as slaves, primarily for domestic work and sexual abuse. As a result, Semai became deeply distrustful of outsiders. In the early 1990s, the next-to-last time I visited them, people were still teaching children to fear and flee from strangers.

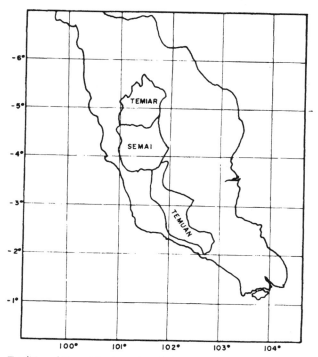

Traditional Semai territory in relation to Temiar and Temuan
Courtesy of the Department of Aborigines Federation of Malaysia.

Semai turned inward, elaborating an existing ideology in which loving one's friends and neighbors became a matter of survival and quarreling potentially lethal. A number of ways emerged to minimize violence and maximize cooperation within local groups (for a list, see Dentan 2004). Usually, Semai describe violence as ludicrous and stupid. Although the people can be violent when violence is safe and necessary or appropriate, they prefer peace. They deserve their reputation as one of the least violent people known to anthropology. But they do not much like that reputation. They know that most other Malaysians see Semai peaceability as cowardice, not as an extraordinary achievement.

Semai were egalitarians. They knew, however, that as people get older, they accumulate experience and become wiser and spiritually more adept.

Their age grade system distinguishes between children, sexually but not socially mature boys and girls (*litaaw* and *mnaleeh*), mature people, and old people. Any grown-up who is particularly knowledgeable about a particular activity—hunting or fish poisoning, say—and who can convince other people of his skill can be a leader as long as the activity continues. When the activity stops, however, the person stops being a leader. No one has a right to coerce anyone else. When a child refuses to follow a parent's order, the parent should accept the child's refusal. Trying to coerce children would damage them spiritually, maybe kill them, adults say.

This radical democracy is frustrating, particularly for administrators from outside Semai society. No Semai speaks for anyone else, and no one pays attention to you if they don't want to: "I'm not listening," people say to insistent unwelcome suggestions. At first, the outsiders, who came from relatively patriarchal and hierarchical societies, responded to the frustration of their designs for changing Semai into a more complaisant people by recognizing someone—a man brave or greedy enough not to flee from outsiders—as "headman." They then rewarded this man by giving him some power in their scheme of things, although at first his power within the community usually went away as soon as they did. Failure to respect these differences in political organization has led to many misunderstandings.

Religion

Traditional Semai theology resembles early Hinduism. Both religions may grow out of an ancient religion that once spread from southern China through Malaysia and into India. In Semai thinking, animals are people, though not human people. The souls of animals are *nyanii'*, "demons." They resemble the "evil spirits" of other peoples, but they're not always evil, and they're not always "spirits." They fall into the domain of the Thunder Lord—a vicious, ludicrous, and stupid tyrant—whom Semai both mock and fear. This God, male rather than ungendered like most other Semai deities, brought sickness into the world and so is an expert on disease.

Long ago, Semai say, they tricked the Lord into sharing his demonic power with "Humans," their word for themselves. Since then, an adept Human may gain a demon "lover." An adept's "lovers" appear in dreams, attracted by his (rarely her) beautiful body, and give him melodies. In séances the adept can then lure his demon lovers to help diagnose and cure patients. In some areas successful Semai hunters go through a ceremony to thank and placate their "hunting wives," who serve hunters the same way demonic "lovers" serve adepts. Midwives, the usually but not always female equivalent of the usually but not always male adepts, either have spirit guides of their own or appeal to the seven "Original Midwives." When an adept or midwife seems to have lost spiritual power, for example, if a child they have been caring for falls sick, they may be ritually bathed. Ritual bathing in fragrant cooling magical water is a cure for most spiritual illnesses.

When a settlement needs spiritual refreshment or several people are pregnant or sick, Semai hold séances in the dark of night, which is daytime to demons. The people still sometimes perform sanitized versions of these ceremonies in the daytime for tourists and government officials, being careful to cover their breasts with bras and to wear shorts under their palm leaf skirts lest they offend the prurient onlookers. But the séances themselves have become rare and secretive as people seek to avoid offending their Muslim neighbors and the government seeks to convert the people to Islam.

Semai singularity lies not just in the fact that, with some exceptions on which this book concentrates, they have been perhaps the least violent people known but also that, unlike people better known for nonviolence, restudy has not shown them more violent than first believed and that, unlike those peoples, who include some of their neighbors, they seem like Melville to have learned their nonviolence in the darkest places of the soul. Perhaps that's where we have to look, those of us who fear violence and love peace. And that means I have to write in a style unfamiliar to me, one that is in some ways harder than I've tried before.

INTRODUCING THIS BOOK: STYLE, ORGANIZATION, AND THEORY

[I want to] honour the plurality of perspectives, relish the varieties of intellectual experience, acknowledge the location and uncertainty of old knowledge itself. . . . Assert its *interestedness:* that what we believe we know is a consequence of the human interest which picks that out as worth knowing, and that human interest is of its nature broken and refracted by its inevitable genesis in distinct human groups (classes, nations, races, genders), each probably quarrelling with another. . . . At the same time these studies must teach a dependable method by which to see, count, and give a name to the recalcitrance of the facts and the truths which really are out there. (Inglis 1993:227, 232)

The website that accompanies this book (http://www.rowmanlittlefield .com/isbn/0742553302) includes a couple of sorts of information. For people who want to know more about Semai or the particular adaptation I'm talking about, there are further ethnographic, methodological, and linguistic details as well as the bibliography from which some of the ethnography and all the theory and poetry come—and pictures, if you want to see the characters and activities involved. There're also detailed accounts of why I picked a particular writing style for particular topics. That is, I talk about how I "constructed" particular narratives and say what the raw materials are.

Coming from America in the early 1960s and living with Semai made me think about peaceability and violence. Signe Howell, who has worked with a different group of Orang Asli, says that ethnographers came to Malaysia with all sorts of projects (mine was food taboos), but all wound up having to deal with peaceability and religion. That's how important these two concerns were in Orang Asli life. Individually, Semai never struck me as different from other peoples, including my own. They're certainly not incapable of violence. But somehow they manage to keep the peace most of the time.

Thinking about peace and learning about Semai made me work up a theory of "negative peaceability," the peaceful way of life that emerges from a fear of violence and fosters "positive peaceability," a peaceful way of life based on love and mutual respect. It also made me go back to Malaysia in 1991–1992 looking for instances of violence among Semai. The H. F. Guggenheim Fund, which sponsors studies of violence, supported my work, and the Malaysian Department of Orang Asli Affairs allowed me to pursue it. I wanted to "disconfirm" my theory if possible. That's how science is supposed to work. This book is a product of that research.

In brief, the theory, which you can read about elsewhere (Dentan 1992, 1994, 2004), runs like this. A powerful numerous people impinge on the borders of a smaller, less powerful one. In this book the powerful people are Mons, Khmers, Bengalis, and, for the past few centuries, Malays who were members of what became the "pasisir" Islamic coastal culture of Southeast Asia, a culture whose members always looked westward to Bengal, Afghanistan, Iran, and Arabia for inspiration. These people establish trading, patron–client, and slaving relationships with the indigenes, in this case Semai and other Orang Asli.

[Orang Asli] place themselves under bondage of debt, which in many cases ends only with life. In their dealings with these childlike people the Malays are most unscrupulous and practise all sorts of imposition; but the aborigines, though conscious of their own simplicity and alive to the roguery they suffer, are yet too honourable to throw off obligations into which they have voluntarily entered, no matter by what deceits they were induced to do so.

Their timid nature, however . . . [may] preserve the great bulk of the aborigines for a long time from this fatal contact. (Cameron 1865:124–25)

These relationships overlap: the safest trading partner is a debt serf (Malay "hamba"), and the difference between serfdom and utter enslavement (becoming a Malay-Arabic "abdi") is pretty abstract. Frontiers everywhere are brutal places, attracting sociopaths and other desperate deviants with little compassion; the first modern student of frontier society refers to frontiersmen as "that line of scum that the waves of advancing civilization bore before them."
In Malaysia

it would be unjust to the Malay to leave him to be judged by the influence which his contact has had and is likely to have upon the aboriginal tribes. The Malays, who have pushed their way into the recesses of the jungle to force a trade on its primitive people, are not a fair representation of the race. They are those who have themselves been badly corrupted by intercourse with the heterogeneous trading communities of European ports and who have had their avarice and cupidity excited to the exclusion of many good and amiable qualities. (Cameron 1865:125)

Even trading "partners" who remain free know about the threat of slave raids. The slavers scare off or kill adults, usually, at least adult men, because they are hard to transport and tame. The children become domestic slaves, a status not very different from that of other slaves and serfs and children. Traditional slavocrats train the kidnapped children for domestic service and sexual abuse. The motive for keeping slaves is prestige. For male aristocrats in precolonial Malay society, as for such men in most patriarchal regimes, the prestige comes in part from their power to coerce sex from attractive women. Thus, slaves occupy in Malay feudalism something like the position that land did in European feudalism. The revenue from land was less important to aristocrats than the revenue from piracy and trade, which went hand in hand. Having a bunch of serf/slave thugs at one's beck and call was better than having land. And the slave trade was the economic underpinning of the traditional economy.

Such slave populations rarely reproduce themselves. Descendants of traditional slaves usually become members of the lowest and most despised class of the dominant people. Hence, one Semai name for themselves is *maay miskin*, from a Malay-Arabic word meaning "poor and pathetic."

Responding to predation by slavers and maltreatment by "patrons," "refugee" peoples of the theory sought refuge in the rugged interior. Scattering into the steep heavily forested mountains that run down the center of peninsular Malaysia, Semai could protect themselves against invasion and occupation since the land was worthless to invaders. Brief sporadic raids to steal women and children, against which there was no protection, kept the threat of violence alive in people's minds. Refugee populations often became mixed, accepting fugitives from all ethnicities and all walks of life. This geographical transformation affected people's sense of who they were, not just the circumstances under which they live. So Semai sometimes call themselves *maay cnaan*, "people of the mountains." As their home country fell to the invaders and their refuge became their new country, the meaning of another Semai name for themselves, *maay sraa'*, apparently changed from "people of the [Khmer] realm" to "people of the hinterland forest." The slave raids, unpredictable and brutal, create a sense that the whole cosmos is unpredictable and brutal. As in the Semai case, they may give rise to feelings that love and peace within the local group are the only security people can have.

Many other responses are possible and historically available, although this is a common one. People under attack almost always have a choice: fight, flight, tend (children), and befriend—and what I'll be calling "surrender." What ethnographers need to study is not culture or individuals but the circumstances that make some choices more attractive than others.

> The dread some of these tribes entertain of contact with the Malays was lately illustrated in a peculiar manner. The Tumongong [Malay official] had to cut a road through the forest. . . . [T]he aborigines were the only people who could do it properly. . . . They commenced operations at once, without any bargain being made, but fled into the jungle on every attempt to approach them; they, however, marked the stump of a tree in a peculiar manner, and on this the reward of their labour was placed from time to time. It was always taken away in the night, no complaints being made of its sufficiency. (Cameron 1865:124n)

The idea of "double consciousness," first formulated by W. E. B. Du Bois in his account of African American life, helps explain the immanence of threat in the thought of Semai and people in similar circumstances. Malays are always present in Semai imagination, like whites in African American thinking or adults for children. The adaptation in the refuge to this sporadic slaving is a remarkably peaceable way of life, which Semai share with some other Southeast Asian hill farmers and foragers. Still, today's Semai, unlike African Americans, are the descendants of people who managed to escape the slavers, not of freed slaves. Semai slaves did not reproduce or ceased to be Semai in their own minds. So slavery has not had the crippling effect it has had on the descendants of American slaves and of American slaveholders.

Eventually, in the theory, outsiders invade and occupy the refuge area itself, thus destroying its function as a refuge and, with it, the demographic base of refugee peaceability. For example, the penetration of the interior by the Malaysian state, with its attendant landgrabs, displacement, dislocation, dispossession, and "regroupment," destroys the peaceable social ecosystem. Oppression becomes routinized and continuous, not vicious and sporadic. The outside threat becomes less brutal and more humdrum. Escape to areas outside the state becomes impossible on a peninsula dominated by a single colonial power. The shift from external colonialism by British to internal colonialism by Malays did not diminish incursions into Semai territory by the State and its "development" programs.

Studies of war suggest that the difference between state formation and criminal terrorism is more subtle than self-serving state propaganda makes it seem. The state need not actually commit violence to attain its end: it needs merely to threaten it. In olden times, state representatives were more frank than they are today. Take the Athenian general Alcibiades at the Melian "conference," an early dispute resolution meeting, after which the Athenians killed all the Melian men and took their women and children as slaves:

> When you speak of the favor of the gods, we may as fairly hope for that as yourselves, neither our pretensions or our conduct being in any way contrary to what men believe of the gods, or practise among themselves. For of the gods we believe, and of men we know, that by a law of their nature whenever they can rule they will. This law was not made by us, and we are not the first who have acted upon it; we did but inherit it, and shall bequeath it to all time, and we know that you and all mankind, if you were as strong as we are, would do as we do. (Thucydides 1951:334)

Routinized and in reserve rather than sporadic and actualized, state terrorism works by fear that makes double consciousness evolve into its starker sister defense mechanism, "identification with the oppressor," first documented by Bruno Bettelheim in the death camps and later as the "Stockholm syndrome." The similarity to protection rackets is clear. But also, of course, identifying with the powerful, as Freud says, is how children become adults.

The former refugees become rural lumpens, as Marxists say, disorganized day laborers, badly educated, tempted by the brief illusory comforts of alcohol, and deculturated. Peaceability falters, then fails.

The first section of this book is about the rise of this peaceable polity out of the cruelty of slavery and warfare. The second is about how Semai maintained it. The third deals with its destruction (for destruction, see also Dentan 1995, 1999a, 2004).

The perspective that pervades the following pages reflects not just my concerns but also my observations of other people's lives. What I need to do is present the kinds of observation that led me to the theory I've just sketched. But all we ever know of other people's lives are the fragments we see and the stories we hear them tell, always inaccurate, about the connections between the fragments. That's true even when we collect the fragments secondhand, from stories other people tell about them, as ethnographers usually do when describing violence. If we are obsessive or loving enough, we try to cobble these fragments and stories together to make some sort of sense, holding the resulting ramshackle elaborate construction together with the spit and glue of our own experience of life or our experiences of other people who we think are "like" the people we're trying to understand. Our pet theories usually generalize our own experience and tell us who is "like" whom. The constructions we make are flimsy and often collapse under the weight of the new fragments we try to fit onto them. And so we have to start all over again with our handful of shards.

Love and cruelty and fear and how they loop around each other as what I'm calling "surrender" are the main themes of this book. Children are a recurring topic because, as the weakest people, they are so often the objects of love and cruelty, so often tokens of love and cruelty and fear, and then they become us. Slaving is another theme because there is no worse cruelty than stealing and enslaving children, because it is so central to Semai political ecology and because historians' accounts of slaving generally ignore or dismiss what it does to children.

While I think the theory is correct, it rests on interpretation of what Semai experiences must have been like and felt like, and that's a matter of interpretation rather than theory. Theories, says Wittgenstein (1974:74) at the end of the *Tractatus*, are like ladders. You put them up to build something or to reach the roof, with an eye to taking them down after they have served their purpose. Trying to re-create those experiences is one way of trying to interpret them. That's what I'm trying to do here, and it raises problems of representation.

> . . . Now that my ladder's gone,
> I must lie down where all the ladders start
> In the foul rag-and-bone shop of the heart
> (Yeats 1962:184–85)

So I've tried to let the facts and my response to them dictate how I try to represent them, whatever format seemed appropriate, a midrash, taking the facts as sacred but subject to commentary and interpretation. But, like any person, I respond to those facts as a whole person, as myself, and that also has something to do with how I present them. Surprise. Sometimes I felt I was writing a lament, sometimes an elegy, an epic, Gothic horror, old-fashioned ethnography. I talk about that on the website. Here I want to say only that the whole thing feels to me like singing the blues: not just sad blues but happy blues and angry blues and defiant blues—still, blues throughout. Champion Jack Dupree or Fruteland Jackson would understand, I hope.

The blues are American, but Americans aren't supposed to think of themselves as having the blues. We "expect to be winners even as we lose, so we scream" (Feiffer 1995:3). The blues are bad; they discourage consumption and invidious striving:

> What point pessimism, the people who live in commercials cry, what have you contributed to the economy anyway? (Oates 1978:53)

But to understand the greatness of the Semai achievement, you have to understand the enormity of the forces that work against them, against all people. You have to understand that their achievement is transitory, like all human achievements, and that their future is bleak, like that of most minority peoples and maybe everybody else. That's blues material. A lot of folks prefer not to hear that song, but if you don't understand that peace has costs and is hard to keep, you'll never understand peace at all.

1

Spotted Doves at War: The Praak Sangkiil

"WE DON'T LIKE KILLING PEOPLE, AND WE HATE BEING KILLED"

If we keep moving, people will have a hard time getting at us. We don't like killing people, and we hate being killed. Settling down is just asking for trouble.

—Jraan, Tluup River headman, 1962

If the pressure of outside influence is too great, and their hereditary freedom is in jeopardy, their only defense lies in flight to the interior. But they will take counter action if the pressure is weak, or they think they are being imposed-on or cheated. There are many cases of Chinese and other traders, who, having penetrated up the main rivers, have tried to cheat the hill people, or molested their women. They bide their time, but one night the trader finds his house on fire and his goods destroyed. Such extremes, however, are only resorted to if the safety of the group thereafter can be assured; which means an overwhelming attack force, followed usually by flight. There are other examples of them succumbing initially to threats of violence, and even violence itself; but they have always taken swift retaliatory action if they think they can win. (Noone [1961:7–8] about Temiar, northern neighbors of Semai)

The theoretical series of events sketched in the last chapter move from a terror that overwhelms a people to a response by the people that overwhelms the terror, hence the punning title of this book. Before this development, Semai were probably egalitarian "simple swiddeners," with a

13

social organization based on sharing and manifesting relatively sparse violence, like other similar societies—but unlike, say, big-game hunters, pastoralists, or agriculturalists (Dentan 1992, 2004, 2008; Fry 2006; Otterbein 2004). Understand: Semai can be violent. Their nonviolence isn't a disease or incapacity but a reasonable response to a political economy based on slave raiding and coerced trade.

The sequence of events involved opens this way: an irruption of terrorism from outside, followed in turn by resistance, defeat, powerlessness, and internalized terror. This chapter and the next try to flesh out these abstractions. The story begins with the Semai version of the Praak Sangkiil, the only war of which they have a tradition, an account of organized invasions and successful resistance. But it concludes with gradual defeat due to the people's inability to resist unpredictable, vicious slave raids that target women and children and then tells how such persistent terrorism affected their lives.

The Praak Sangkiil

The Semai word *praak* comes from Malay *perang*, "war." Malays distinguish *perang* from *serang*, "raids." Similarly, some Semai distinguish "war," *praak*, from "raiding," *sngraak*. In *praak*, you're just following orders; in *sngraak*, you're fighting for personal reasons. Normally, Semai don't—and didn't—*br-praak* or *br-sngraak*, say most Semai.

Only one person I talked with, an old intellectual from Klubii' (Dentan 1995), had any idea what *sangkiil* meant. He said the term contrasts with *sabil*, an Arabic term associated with jihads, holy wars. The Malay homonym means something like "having a precise goal," so the equivalent might be a "limited war," like the U.S. Persian Gulf wars, as opposed to the "war on terrorism." In the Sangkiil War, the goal seems to have been to exterminate Semai or at least drive them from their lands, as had happened to other peoples. So it was different, people listening to our conversation said, different from slave raids, which went on all the time and involved slaughtering all the adult men and kidnapping the young women and children.

The title of this chapter comes from the metaphor of "spotted doves" in the text. Doves' Western reputation as birds of peace comes from the biblical narrative of Noah. That story in turn probably reflects the fact that doves were cheap sacrificial animals, as opposed to sheep or oxen, and thus the common medium for approaching Yahweh. In the natural world, mating doves engage in brutal bloody battles, often until the loser is pecked to death. In the story, fighting like doves means fighting mindlessly, without the rules which for Malays, as for other piratical feudal peoples like the English, set standards of propriety in the manner of contesting with equals or slaughtering defenseless people. The narrator's comparison of Semai guerrilla warfare to the battles of mating doves suggests the cold butchery that can accompany a state of dissociation Semai call "blood intoxication," *blnuul bhiip* (Dentan 1995).

There are lots of versions of the Sangkiil story. The following is a shortened and simplified version of the most accessible version in English, a scholarly article (Dentan 1999) you need to look at for ethnographic and linguistic details and comparisons. Another complete version, in Malay by Mat Ariff (Juli 1990), reflects Mat Ariff's sense of how Semai should react to the dominant ethnic group in the area, loosely called "Malays." The Semai leader, modeled on himself, repeatedly outwits the violent and stupid "Malays." In more widespread oral versions, Semai (sometimes led by Malays) overwhelm attacking "Malay" forces by magic or guerrilla warfare. Mahat China, a Semai author from the Erong (Iròk) area where the war took place, recently published a long version of this tradition (2008). The following account conflates these versions.

This essay is a fairly literal translation of a Semai version an old Waar River headman who asked for anonymity taped in 1991. Let's call him "Tataa' Manah," Old Elder. I've tried to keep his performance alive by punctuation. Italics are used for imitative sounds. Hyphens indicate long drawn-out words. Capitals and boldface are for loud. The invading Raweeys in the text speak Malay; I've turned their English *w*s into *v*s to indicate they're speaking a language unrelated to Semai, like Nazis in U.S. propaganda in my boyhood. When the narrator's gestures seem important, I've put them in brackets. Ellipses indicate where I've left part of the story out.

The Rawas attackers (Semai *Raweey*) come from the Rawas River in east Sumatra. They settled in south-central Perak sultanate, around Gopeng, in the eighteenth century, and retain their ethnic identity, although the government officially counts them as "Malays," as Semai do. A European describes them "of more open, lively and enlightened character than those I had anywhere encountered . . . altogether a more likeable people than any other in the Residency" (Forbes 1885:246). But he admits they despised and terrorized neighboring peoples the same way they despised and tried to terrorize Semai.

How the War Began

Fighting has its roots in defensive rather than offensive instincts, whilst warfare proper is a refinement of civilization. (Harrison 1929:9)

About the days of old I know that I don't know.
Although I don't know the whole [story],

a part I have preserved of Sangkiil,
the Sangkiil story from when olden days were new.

They were "MALAYS," we "HUMANS."

There really was no other reason.
They wanted to take us on, they said.

They weren't local Malays, not neighbors.
Their race was Raweey, Raweey Malays,
from inside Raweey,
from outside this country,
not this country.

No sign yet of Tapah town,
No sign yet of Bidor town,
No stores yet open in Tapah,
In ancient times when the Raweeys attacked us,
according to grampa,
according to gramma.

So that's how they came to attack us,
They challenged us to war, us Humans
WE DIDN'T WANT TO MAKE WAR

The Humans said
"We're not warriors.
"We have no equipment,
        "not enough weapons,
        "not enough stuff,
        "muskets have we none."

They said, "You haf to vage var.
        "because here VEE are,
        "you'll see how strong vee are,
        "see who loses."

"Well," mused the Humans,
        "we don't know how to make war,
        "but they're going to attack us.
        "so we have to attack them.
        "What's wrong with that?"

Then they attacked us, in olden times,
        they invaded the parish of Sungkeey
        they invaded the parish of Bidor,
        they invaded along the Waar River,
        three places.

The chief of Bidor was named Bah Mnra';
   of the Waar, "Vanishing Goblin"
   men who knew how to make war.

The Raweeys attacked us Humans,
   a war of EXTINCTION,
   a war everywhere against us Humans.

They had many weapons:
   swords,
   machetes,
   iron-tipped spears,
   olden type bows.

For weapons the Humans had
   just dart-quivers for weapons,
   just blowpipes for weapons,
   just darts for weapons.

"Zo, how many of you vant to fight, Human scum?"
"ALL RIGHT, we'll fight you. WE'LL TRY. But we're no warriors."

So, said the Malays, "Vee'll war on your RACE!
   "Vee'll see who's stronger
   "Vee'll see who's weaker.
   "Lose, Humans, vee'll exterminate you,
   "vee of the Malay race."

"O, now the cooking's over
   "what can we do?"
So answered the Humans.

So in those olden days began the war.
What weapons did the Raweeys carry?
   They carried their swords
   They carried their muskets
      old fashioned muskets
   Kan' kan' kan' tamped down their powder
   ploooonh the sound of the guns
      not like modern guns

So, back to the story, they attacked us.

"Ah, wait," cried the Humans. "Have mercy upon us, we can't fight a war.
   "now you make war upon us,
   "make war on our race,
   "we never make war.

Tataa' Manah in Shamanic Headman's Dress. Vanishing Goblin would have dressed like this on ceremonial occasions. Spiritual power, obtained in dreams from demon lovers, is an important qualification for traditional Semai headmen. Along the River Waar the special headband is a sign of that power, manifest in the yellow/red of the marigolds and beads, which suggests the power of blood (see chapter 4). The headband, with the crossbands of Czech trade beads, recalls costumes used in Semai séances and ancient Khmer court dances. The blowpipe and dart quiver are emblems of Semai identity. This formal picture was a memento for Wa' Lisbet, a.k.a. Elizabeth Dentan. Upriver Waar, in the Perak highlands, 1992. This photo, by R. K. Dentan, first appeared in a book edited by Razha and Wazir (2001:14).

"We don't know how to make war.
"Rajahs have we none, you folks have rajahs
"You have rajahs, you of the Malay race, you Raweeys."

Sneered the Raweeys arrogantly, "Vee don't think you're people eef
    you're not spotted doves,
      "[If you don't fight mindlessly and to the death].
      "Eef you're not spotted doves, you're dead!"

Of Raweeys, how many came up to this country?
    o, many!
    to places like this.

Hwiiiiii'iiiin' shrilled their war flutes.
    That's how they shrilled.

"Warlord kommandant, let's kill zem!
    "Attack!"

And the Humans TO THE LAST MAN fled away
    TO THE LAST MAN ran away
    o, were they afraid!

Take "were afraid" back,
    only half were afraid
    the other half slaughtered.

British Policy and the Sangkiil War

During the whole period between 1786 and 1867, the Malay states of the peninsula were hard at work committing political hara-kiri. The process had begun much earlier, but during the nineteenth century it speeded up. There were constant wars between the different sultans, and the states were also weakened by frequent civil wars between rival claimants to the throne. The power of the sultans decayed, till even petty rajas were able to set themselves up as independent local rulers, free to plunder and fight pretty much at will. Piracy flourished, and trade declined. With the breakdown of the central government, the vassals seized the opportunity to establish themselves in a position of local independence at the expense of their weaker neighbors and the peasantry. No man's life and property were safe unless he were strong enough to defend them (Mills 1925:203–4).

The Sangkiil War probably happened in the 1880s when the British already dominated the sultanate of Perak, the western of the two states where most Semai live. But neither British colonials nor local sultans could establish order. And neither chose to eliminate slavery.

The narrator explains the Rawas' motive for genocide: "Let's see who beats whom." But the invaders may have had the same motive as the British had in attacking the tiny Malay state of Naning, a war that the British leaders described as a "useless war for a worthless object" (Mills 1925:149) and that historians agree was "an egregious blunder" that "bordered on the farcical" (Mills 1925:137). Like Semai territory, Naning was "a poor unprofitable possession" (Crawfurd, quoted in Mills 1925:137). Naning Malays fought off superior numbers of British troops, using tactics like those of Semai against Rawas, and were finally defeated only by a force of peninsular Malays. Once committed to the war, the British felt they had to continue it despite their losses and the futility of victory because defeat would undercut the prestige that allowed them to loot the local economy without actually fighting.

Raweeys Fail a Halaa' Magic Challenge (at Cba' Tnloop)

A *halaa'* [adept/magician] where the Tnloop meets the Waar [rivers],
    "Vanishing Goblin" his name,
    [addresses the Raweeys].
    "You attacking the Humans, have mercy,
    "have pity a moment, pause in your war
    "COME UP my house ladder."

"COME DOWN," say the Raweeys.

"COME UP here," says the Human.

"COME DOWN to the ground."

At last they come up, come up into his house.
"Here, eat this pot of rice, you hundred men.
    "Here's a bamboo tube of water"
    [to drink from after eating]
    "one water bamboo."

"Can you drink down all the water
    "drink it down at one gulp
    "you hundred warriors?"

"If not, if you can't drink it all, I tell every man of Malay stock,
    "Get out, every last one of you,
    "you who make war on the Human stock.

"Eat eat eat eat all of this rice
    "and the squash that goes with it.
    [If you can't eat it all,] I tell every man of Malay stock,
    "you who make war on the Human stock."

All the Humans had fled, every last man,
    all his kin and descendants,
    all his children and townsmen,
    every last one.

Now here into his country [Raweeys had come]
    to chop up the trees
    for firewood,
    every last tree.

"Here, drink this water!"
    They started to drink.
    The hundred men drink from the bamboo,
    Goblin's ONE bamboo
    And it doesn't run out at all.

"So, you can't do what we do,
    best give way before us,"
    [says Goblin].

"Hai, take it easy!
    "Vee see how things are, don't attack us,
    "don't make var against us of the Malay race,
        vee can't vin."

"Win, lose, not ours to choose, not for us Humans.
    "You all, you made war against us Humans
    "We wouldn't have made war if you hadn't."

"O, all right. Vee command quick retreat,"
    [says the Raweey warlord commandant,]
    Strrrrrrraightaway they retreat downriver.

The line "the outsiders wanted to chop up every last tree" suggests one motive for the attack. The British wanted to turn rural Malaysia into a wet-rice growing area to feed the Chinese and Indian coolies they imported to mine tin and harvest rubber. Rawas were "ready to clear the jungle, cut down trees, plant, and generally prepare the land for a better state of things" (McNair 1972:133). British policy encouraged Rawas incursions by giving the immigrants tax breaks and titles to the land from which they had driven indigenous people. Most immigrants were young single men, the most violent and irresponsible cohort in any society.

The colonial government turned a blind eye to the brutality of Rawas warfare. In the nineteenth century, Rawas exterminated one group of Malaysian indigenes, the Mantra, and drove three others—Temuan-Belandas, Semelai, and Btsisi' ("Mah Meri")—far from their native lands with great loss of life. Colonial policy thus transformed a relatively static frontier between the expanding Malay Muslim population and the indigenous pagan Mon-Khmer–speaking peoples into an encroaching European-style one of the sort that devastated the indigenes of the Americas.

Raweeys Meet Poisoned Darts

> But a little bit later, a bit after that,
>> they invade again
>> shrilling *mwiiiiiiiis*
>> What's that *mwiiiiiiis*? What's that shrilling?
>> Bamboo "warflutes" they're called.

> "Any Humans round here?
>> If there are, vee're eager
>> to feed our sharp swords."

> What happened then?

> Bees! "*OOOOOOO*" instead of their victims
>> were loosed [on the Raweeys].
>> *Bzzzzzzzz* went the bees.
>> Every last man was stung,
>> the Malay horde was stung.

> But not really bees, not at all,
>> The stings were not bee stings but
>>> poisoned dart stings.
>> So they were exterminated,
>> every last one of them died.

> When they got home to their houses:
>> [they whisper] "They metamorphosed, those humans,
>> they turned into bees.
>> Aaiiiy, vee lost, vee Malays"

> "Okay, just bad luck, vee'll deal with it," said they.
>> "It's our turn now, not the Humans',

"Vee'll test their endurance
"Test it."

Raweeys Fail a Second Magic Challenge by the Halaa' Adept (at Cba' Tnloop)

So one day they come back
      How do they come back?
      [whisper] Come uphill quick and quiet.

Arrived at our homesteads, they start whooping "wooooooOOOOOOH!!"
      shriek everywhere,
      "C-o-m-e o-n! Let us kill them!
      "Attack! Vee of Malay stock! Vee Raweeys!"

"Have mercy, put down your weapons!"
      [cries the adept/magician]
      "C-o-m-e u-p [here to my house]."

Up they come, come up again.

He dumps out his dart-quiver.
      Look! Out the darts rustle.
      he counts them: one two three four f-i-n-g-e-r-n-a-i-l-s.
      leaving just one

"If I can pull out enough darts for you hundred warriors,
      you abandon this war."
      pull. pull. pull pull. pull pullpullpull.

One hundred his darts,
      darts made of his fingernails,
      darts made of his bones.
      He counts them: "One two three four five six seven eight-nine-ten . . ."

"OOOO mercy!" [cry the Raweeys]
      "Vee can't deal with this,
      his darts are so many."

"You're begging for mercy,"
      [whispers the adept]
      ["But] you're the attackers."

All aflutter they flee
      "Fleeing? O yes,
      O yes, vee give up."

Raweeys Baffled by Guerrilla Tactics (Cba' Tnloop)

But not much later
        one day in the morning
        back upriver they come

What's their objective?
        Where Tnloop meets the Waar, where Bah Tony now lives
        That place they surround

They break into two parties, fording the river,
        are blowpiped by Humans
        [ask each other in whispers]
"What rules apply to fighting in midriver?"

They blowpipe again, & again & again again again.
        Wiped out are the Malays,
        half of them flee,
        their resistance broken.

"Oooo vee cannot resist,
        instead the Humans are really strong,"
        say the Raweey, the story goes

"Still, never mind,
        "Yet again
        "in revenge I will kill
        "these Humans,
        "I'll exterminate them,
        "to the last man, woman and child."

Raweeys Baffled by Hnalaa' *Transformative Power (Cba' Lngkaa')*

One person, a Human,
        was building
        a fish weir
        b-u-i-l-d-i-n-g it thus in the river

as he was building it, checking each part,
        where the Lngkaa' meets the Waar River

Finally *WOOOooo!* go the war whistles
        "C-o-m-e o-n!
        "Vee vill kill you!
        "Let us attack!"

Weeeeeeee! [nasal sound of] whirling his sword
    "Vhat's that virling?"

Vanishes this Human
    into his weir
    becomes giant carp
    fish.

He's metamorphosing! This human!
    still metamorphosing
    when the Raweeys arrive.

"VHERE is [the man] who was here?"
    They search hard, cannot find him.
    "Oooooooo! Here he is!"

They SLASH at the fish here
    They slash he escapes he
    flops around, flipflop flipflop flipflop flipflop flipflop flipflop flipflop

He attacks the Malays ripslash ripslash ripslash
    ripslash ripslash ripslash
    his tail turned to sword!

This Human metamorphoses
    See, that Human has *hnalaa'* transformative powers
    So the Malays are wiped out,
    Pellmell they flee.

"Aiiiiy, these humans have a lot of magical skill.
    "Vee here cannot handle them
    "VHATEVER vill vee do with the Humans?"

"Vell, never mind.
    "Yet again
    "I vill once more start the var up again."

Raweeys Confront Halaa' *Sugarcane (Bidor)*

How did they once more start the war up again?
After attacking along the Sungkeey River

"Here comes that accursed Warlord Kommandant,"
        said one of the Humans there
        [in the choked voice of a trancing adept]
            Bah Mnra' by name.

He carried a stalk of sugarcane, this way [like a spear]
        carried his cane this way because it was metamorphosed into a spear.
        Not just a solid single thing his sugarcane.

Weeeeeeee! they shrill
        "C-o-m-e o-n!
        "Vee vant to vage var!
        "These swords [whistle] *weeeeeeee!"*

He grabs his sugarcane stalk/spear and stabs with it
        here there here there a hundred Malays.
        Half flee away.

Raweeys Ambushed

        So the Sangkiil War they tell about this way like this is its name.
                So half of the Humans
                after they fled to this place,

        Half of these Humans
                got their darts ready,
                Humans of our stock.

        "Women and children," said the Human magician,
                "Get lots of darts ready,
                "bags and bags full."

        They whittle and whittle, they smear on the poison
                night and day they are working. . .

        Whatever sort of attack the Malays try
                doesn't worry them,
                don't care if it's nighttime,
                don't care if it's day,
                they're still blowpiping.

        Look, they invade Cba' Tnloop
                caught by surprise
                scattered while shitting
                dead meat, buried Raweeys . . .
                a graveyard. . . .

[Omitted: Survivors of a massacre at Sungkeey ambushed the Raweeys at
Jirm Kawad and at the fourteenth milestone of the road between Tapah
and the Cameron Highlands. Semai cleared a steep slope of obstacles and
rolled boulders and heavy mortars down on Raweeys trooping below.

The Raweey onslaught continued, but Semai began to realize the advantage guerrillas have over regular troops.]

The War Is Routinized

We lived in the mountains
> They came up [from the lowlands]
> shrilling their warflutes . . .
> Me, I don't know the year

Who knows how many moons they made war?
> Who knows if there were moons or not? [grins]

They say in the war in the Jrnang lowlands Raweeys turned the place into a
> GRAVEYARD.
AGAIN they invaded
> AGAIN they were blowpiped
> AGAIN
> AGAIN they were blowpiped

again they attacked again they were blowpiped
anywhere at all ambushed in the evening ambushed in daytime ambushed in
> the at night
ambushed in the rain ambushed in the storm

In their latrines, so what?
While they're shitting, so what?
While they're pissing, so what?

Not a one-time blowpiping, blowpipes all the time
> blowpipes with *halaa'* magic darts

Blowpipetherejumpawayhere
Blowpipeherejumpawaythere
Blowpipeherejumpthere.

Theoutsiders chopthere, who'dtheystab?
Shottheirgunshere, who'dthey injure?

Asymmetric Warfare

This wasn't the sort of war Rawas and their aristocratic Malay allies
wanted:

The Malay race has not been known as an overtly acquisitive people. The
antecedents of Malay royalty were the pirate chiefs roaming the Malay

archipelago long before the arrival of Islam, trading influences and the colonising powers. The successful pirates established dominance, instituted control over their spheres of influence and manifested Sultanates. The Malay trait of acquisition was until then initially expressed as piracy and subsequently as feudal regimes to gain hegemony and subservience of their subjects. Trade as the alternative mode of acquisition was practised by the visiting Arabic and Indian merchants and later by the Chinese brought into the region by the mercantile Europeans. The acquisitive trading skills of all these other communities threatened the yet undeveloped Malay race used to the feudal practice of acquiring wealth through rent rather than trade. ("Pak Sanno" 1998)

Semai in this story aren't against war because of "cultural values." They just don't have the weapons or cultural experience to wage one. So they need cleverness or magic. But once committed to violence, they become dangerous. The mindless, no-holds-barred style of guerrilla warfare—"like spotted doves"—suits people who, lacking a tradition of war, have no rules for how to conduct one. This inexperience with organized violence may in part account for the extreme brutality of Semai at war, when they say they suffer *blnuul bhiib*, "intoxication by blood," and become ruthless killers of anyone they encounter (e.g., Dentan 1995). Only warlike people, I suspect, wage "civilized" wars; spotted doves don't understand Geneva Conventions. Undermine the self-discipline that daily Semai life requires, and you don't have any chivalric code, no cost–benefit analysis, no "no hitting girls or people with glasses." Anything goes.

So, Semai violently resisted incursions by Rawas and others, fighting what Otterbein (2004) describes as standard "primitive war," guerrilla ambushes with weapons, blowpipes, used primarily for hunting. Malays in south Perak also fought Rawas, they say. Tataa' Manah's version seems to amalgamate two different stories, one prosaic, stressing practical measures Semai guerrillas took against "Malay" (Rawas) invaders bent on genocide, and one magical, stressing the supernatural skills of their (indigenous) "Malay" leaders.

Semai Reject a Truce

> So after that they sued for peace
>> sued for peace and mercy in that peace
>> but our *sngii'*, "minds," were uneasy
>
> "We Humans didn't want this peace,
>> "we didn't seek this peace.
>> "This wasn't our war, not the Humans'.

"This is a war by your race, you Malays came to harry us.
 "Now you want peace,
 "but our *sngii'* is uneasy.

"So you wanted war, now you have it, FIGHT ON!
 "Bring on as many of your race as you can.
 "your race, Raweey race,

"Malay race,
 "however many millions,
 "however many thousands.

"Bring them on against us hill people,
 the Humans you wanted to harry."

After that AGAIN they attacked
 Finally, at long last,
 who knows how many thousand
 fought hard, to the last man,
 harried and blowpiped.

So now what do you know? Of what are you aware?
 In the war they tell about,
 the war with the Raweeys,

your fathers recount
 the war wasn't fought physically,
 was fought with *nhalaa'* [adept] power . . .

Semai Mock the Raweey Sultan

 Of a hundred attackers one day he spared one
 he s-p-a-r-e-d o-n-e
 [*rising tone*] set one aside . . .

 "Mercy! We can't fight you Humans, what we understand is war at seven o'clock eight o'clock twelve o'clock. But you Humans make war in dark and daylight you make war where we shit when we bathe you make war in the rivers you make war anywhere any time. All we can do now is beg for mercy."

 "Now you seek mercy. So what?
  "Unless the whole Malay race seeks mercy,
  "begs for mercy every man.

 "If they don't beg for mercy this is our sign,
  "we Humans."
  [*reaches into his dart quiver*]

"In days to come when you're considering war
"When you want to come harry us Humans,
        "guns have we none,
        "machineguns have we none,
        "bombs have we none,
        "landmines have we none,
        "swords have we none,
        "[military] science have we none.
        "martial arts have we none.
        "But this we have."

He ties a poison dart to the Malay's arm,
        slashes the arm he ties the dart to.

This symbolic act parodies the beliefs of Indonesian folks like Rawas, who used to slash their prepubescent sons' arms and insert a bezoar, a concretion found in the stomachs of certain animals or the internodes of certain plants. The father then bound up the wound so that, tradition had it, the boy would become immune to sword or spear wounds. The Semai gesture seems to mean, "You're immune to your weapons, not ours."

"This is the sign of us Humans at the end of the war
        you waged against Humans.
    "You here carry it to your war council.
    "Carry it straight to your chief.
    "Carry it to your Rajah.

"When you've brought it to him, say 'I want you to
            send as many men as your Malay
            race can into these hills.'
    "This I give you as a sign . . .

"You show up again, we don't care.
        "We'll harry you out of there right away,
        "back to your own country

"We don't care WHAT race you are,
        "Malay, Chinese, Raweey, European.
        "We don't care, we Humans.
        "We don't fight by rules,
        "We don't fight by custom."

Then, the dart bound in his left arm,
        he took it straight to his country.
        The Rajah saw it,

And HE stared and s-t-a-r-e-d and s—t—a—r—e—d and s—t—a—r—e—d.
    "O mercy.

"So against the Human race, our race, the Malay race, the Raweey race couldn't win, not against those HUMANS.

"DO NOT harass Humans,
    "the Miskin [Malay-Arabic "poor and pathetic"] People,
    "who don't make war by our rules.
    "They make war without even
            CONSIDERING propriety.

"They war on us at night they war on us in daylight then they war on us some more
    "When we make war we check
    "whether it's one o'clock
    "or two o'clock

"While at night when we're asleep they make war on us some more.
    "In days to come,
    "Don't you harass them.

"These Humans, what sign did they send us?
    "So if we harass them some more,
    "Though we have bombs.
        "And we have machine guns.
        "And we have mortars.
        "We have all kinds of weapons.

"We can't beat the Humans,
    "whatever we have,

"See how they make war:
    "rustlerustle here,
    "rustlerustle there,
    "rustlerustle everywhere.
    "bodies invisible.

"Since we can't beat the Human race,
    "DON'T you wage this war.
    "So now we FORESWEAR war,

"Since we foreswear war, this will be a zone of PEACE . . ."

The Peace Conference

Tniweey was patriarch
      among Raweey headmen
      in command in the old days.

He advised every person
      in every river basin
      throughout the area.

They come together in Tapah, they meet & confer to renounce war.
      "Outsiders cannot interfere
      "with the *Miskin* People.
      "Let us never molest them.

"The *Miskin* People make war like spotted doves. They don't understand the rules of war.
      "We're out of here, right away,
      "totally and completely,
      [whisper] "We're not kidding."

Geographical Colonialism

Most Semai in Perak and a good many in Pahang have heard some version of the story. They can identify the rocks on which the slavers whetted their swords (Batu' Cwiis), the spot near the Tnloop delta where people threw the corpses of the dead Rawas (Huuk Crlvvk Gòp), the places where the events in the story happened. These are "mnemonic sites" that help conserve memory and serve as symbolic markers. That's why the colonial dispossession and "relocation" of Semai that began with the British and continues today is not merely a cynical landgrab but also, inadvertently, a destruction of their geographized historical and ethnic consciousness and sense of home. The destruction began with relocating entire settlements during the Communist insurrection of the 1950s, while British and Malay surveyors were renaming the landscape without even asking the Semai names. The result not only devalued Semai history but also obscured their separate identity, "obliterat[ing] difference in a cosmographic reordering of the local geography through the power of naming" (Anagnost 1994:240).

The Aftermath

Thereafter we Humans cooperated.
If not, no paved roads in Tapah.
You [RKD] wouldn't be here, pal.
My dad said back then we were many, many of us.

We came in gramma's time from Teluk Anson [in lowland Perak state].
    That is our country.

During the war the others forced us out, retreated s-t-r-a-i-g-h-t there,
    jammed with Malays, Chinese, Tamils,
    under a durian tree in Teluk Anson,
    OUR hereditary land.

This place is our place, Teluk Anson,
    not a place for MALAYS,
    not a place for Chinese. . . .

When [Semai of olden times] went to Tapah, they went on foot.

They even wore LOINCLOTHS.
    No shirts did they wear,
    no, uh, trousers.

What they wore was loincloths of domestic jackfruit tree barkcloth,
    of wild jackfruit tree barkcloth.
    For them "clothing" was just this one thing,
    not cloth the way it is now.

And this name outsiders gave us in olden times:
    We were the "Sakai" [Nigger] people.
    That's what they stuck us with:

"MISKIN," [poor and pathetic,]
    as if we'd been DEFEATED.
    We never had enough.

For clothes we had, first, eaglewood barkcloth,
    second for us backbaskets,
    third for us blowpipes,
    fourth for us quivers,
    fifth for us headbands,
    that's all we had.

So we went down to Tapah, nobody bothered us.
    That's where your [European] race saw us, pal.
    So you never did bother us, knowing our history.
    If you thought of bothering us, you decided against it,
    decided against it because our history was known.

Since then it's not allowed to call Humans *"Miskin,"*
    nor to call them the Have-Nots."
    IT ISN'T ALLOWED.

> Even Malays who wanted to harass our race were afraid to.
> > Afraid because of the story of this war.
> > So finally after all that
> > For the very first time peace was established,
> > at the finish of the Sangkiil War . . .

To the degree that Semai have a military tradition, the Praak Sangkiil is it. People sometimes refer to it when talking about the possibility of violently resisting dispossession and impoverishment. For instance, in 1990, a young man used a Praak Sangkiil phrase while talking with other young men about organizing a self-defense force to ward off attack by supposed organ-nappers (chapter 7). But the story is less inspiring than reassuring. It does not glorify or prompt violence but simply asserts that successful resistance, violent or not, is possible.

OUTCOMES

The guerrilla tactics and mindless violence the story describes temporarily halted the invasion and conquest of the highlands by the slavocratic state and its British sponsors. Malays came to think of the rain forest and the blowpipe as fearsome. In the area around Teiw R'eeis, little Malay boys might hoot at a visiting Semai headman, ridiculing his accent, loincloth, loose-limbed walk, and so on; Malay adults were interested in Semai only as trading partners, assistant child stealers, or agents in clearing rain forest. But these adults would not invade the forest because they dreaded poisoned blowpipe darts "more than rifle bullets" (Swettenham 1880:59).

The highlands and foothills were difficult terrain, unattractive to the British and their native agents. Both Malays and British agents could get most jungle produce cheaper by trade, often coerced, with frontier Semai and other indigenous people than by trying to invade and occupy the steep highlands where Semai lived. In this sense, the Semai retained a geographic refuge.

But at the turn of the century, the British and their Malay sockpuppet sultan devised a nonviolent scheme to recruit Semai vassals under the pretext of pacifying them (Gomes 2004:33–34). The war had led to an upsurge of violence, and, a century later, many Semai from the area upstream from Tapah see the expansion of Malay-style justice as the bedrock on which Semai peaceability rests (Juli, Williams-Hunt, and Dentan 2009; but see chapter 6).

Meanwhile, Semai did have one resource frontiersmen could take without trading: their children. The children weren't valuable as slaves, too small and dark for Malay standards of strength and beauty, but they were useful for sexual abuse and household drudgery. And any slave, even a Semai child, raised the prestige of the Malay owner, an almost obsessive concern of the Malay ruling classes. Slave traders could bribe or intimidate people who lived on the frontier, Malay peasants or Temiar indigenes, to kidnap the children, if only to save their own children from enslavement. Semai lacked the numbers, technology, and military skills to mount punitive raids against the raiders' home base within the slaver state:

> Other people kill us, we don't kill other people. We never get so angry [-bl'aal] that we go to war. How could we? We lack the equipment. We're isolated, other peoples are many, it'd be futile. Malays and Pale People have many weapons, many people. Though we -bl'aal, there's nothing we can do. . . . We flee. Since we can't fight back, we flee, of course. (Headman of Pangkaad, Teiw R'eiis, 6 May 1992)

Neighboring indigenous Malay settlements often had friendly ties with the hill people so that raiding them would be counterproductive (Jumper 1997:33). And Semai egalitarianism militated against counterslaving.

So, from their sanctuary within the colonial state, slavers raided the settlements of Semai and other Malaysian indigenous people like Btsisi':

> Hunted by the Malays, who stole their children, they were forced to leave their dwellings and fly hither and thither, passing the night in caves or in huts . . . which they burnt on their departure. "In those days," they say, "we never walked in the beaten tracks lest the print of our footsteps in the mud should betray us." For wherever the Malay perceived any indication of their presence, he would build himself a small shelter, and never leave it until he had discovered the place of retreat where they generally spent the night. Accompanied by a few accomplices, he would then repair to the spot at nightfall, and the party, concealing themselves until dark, would wait until the "Hill-men" were asleep. The Malays would then fire several rifle shots, spreading terror and confusion in every family, whose breaking up made them an easy prey to their assailants, who would promptly rush to the spot where they heard the shrieks of the women and children . . . There is hardly a family that has not its own especial calamity to relate . . . Any act of vengeance, moreover, would be fatal to them, in view of their insignificant numbers and lack of means of defence. They prefer therefore to sacrifice the part for the whole, and this is certainly the only possible course open to them. (Skeat and Blagden 1906, II:532–33)

These raids, in which groups of five to twenty brutal attackers concentrated overwhelming force on particular settlements or isolated homesteads, left Btsisi' "a shy, unwarlike people who have accepted without resentment the wrongs inflicted on them by past generations of Malays. Ask any of them for his family history, and you will often be told a harrowing tale of the cold-blooded murder of some parent or relative" (Wilkinson 1971b:18). Traders found these raids useful as a way of intimidating their partners into supplying jungle produce cheaply and reliably: look what will happen to you and to your children if you let us down.

Thus the story eventually ends in the defeat of organized violence as a Semai tactic against the slavocracy and its agents and the substitution of a tactic of scattering and flight. People often laughed when I suggested their performing military exploits: "Even in the Emergency [an uprising of the 1950s in which Semai were willy-nilly involved], all I did was run away."

> **A:** No, we don't do that [kill]. The Japanese killed some of *us* in the olden days [World War II]. Three men for lying to them.
>
> **Q:** You people ever kill any Japanese?
>
> **A:** [laughs]. I never heard of us killing *anybody*. Not even in the Emergency. Chinese [terrorists] killed two of us with machetes. The Malays and Pale People [British] never killed any of us. But I hear lots of Malays got killed in the Praak Sangkiil by our people. (Headman at 'Icek on the R'eiis River, 24 March 1992)

Semai children learned early that strangers were shape-shifting monsters. Any safety or love the outside world seemed to offer was often illusory and never reliable, a lesson the raids reinforced among adults. The cosmos was full of menace and disorder. Only in the peace of one's own community was there any security, and even there security was fragile.

The next chapter attempts to bring that situation to life.

2

✢

Regrettable Undertakings: A Dirty Joke, a War, a Vacancy

Regrettable and cruel as this practice [enslaving children after killing their parents in front of them] was, it should in fairness be stated that these children were then brought up as Malays. As they grew up, they were no longer regarded as slaves, but were treated by their owners as if they were their own children. (Carey [1976:286])

The man who owned these slaves behaved like a beast, shameless and without fear of Allah. The younger girls hung round him while he behaved in a manner which it would be improper for me to describe. . . . For anyone who wished to buy these slave-girls he would open their clothing with all manner of gestures of which I am ashamed to write. The slave dealers behaved in the most savage manner, devoid of any spark of feeling, for I noticed that when the little children of the slaves cried they kicked them head over heels and struck their mothers with a cane, raising ugly weals on their bodies. To the young girls, who were in great demand, they gave a piece of cloth to wear, but they paid no attention to the aged and the sick. The greatest iniquity of all I noticed was the selling of a woman to one man and of her child to another. The mother wept and the child screamed and screamed when she saw her mother being taken away. My feelings were so outraged by this scene that, had I been someone in authority, I would most certainly have punished the wicked man responsible for it. Furthermore, those in charge of male slaves tied them round the waist like monkeys, one to each rope, made fast to the side of the boat. They relieved nature where they stood and the smell on the boat made one hold one's nose. (Abdullah bin Abdul Kadir, Munshi, *Hikayat Abdullah* [1849], quoted in Chua 1998:41)

DESCRIBING WHAT YOU HAVEN'T SEEN

When you see a war on television . . . you're not actually watching a *war*. Get close to the screen and you can see the little blocks of color shifting, and that's really all it is: a lot of second-hand light. It's not really people dying at all. . . . You're not seeing what happened, you're just seeing an effect it had on film in a camera. In every way that matters, it's no different to someone describing it to you afterwards. . . . [W]hat you are seeing is hearsay . . . hearsay after the event, like a newspaper report, or the Bible. And that's the best way to think of it: maybe the only sensible way, if you're going to think of it at all.
   Just dots of colour or beats of sound.
   Just words on a page. (Mosby 2003:2, 4)

How easy it is to bury the reality of the slaving that the pious, horrified Abdullah describes in the politically correct prose of the one-time official Protector of Aborigines. To understand what was going on, you need to understand what it *felt* like. What I want to suggest in this chapter is a theme that will recur throughout the book: that "surrender" as an adaptation to terror is a complex and active response that reverberates throughout one's personality. I've chosen telling tales as a way to sketch the relationship between child abuse of all sorts, enslavement, identification with the oppressor and *asyik*—the ecstatic/erotic surrender to God. This chapter is "ethnographic fiction" in the sense that I have strung together documented facts, almost all from Malaysian history (but a couple from other Southeast Asian countries, one from Africa, one fictional, and one from South America) to make a Malay-style narrative, using ornate, lurid, melodramatic, Malay-style rhetoric and tropes almost exclusively from Malay proverbs and Sufi poetry, mostly Coleman Barks's wonderful translations of Rumi. But I include, as Malay narrators usually wouldn't, an account of the narrator's feelings. So this is a bastard style, combining Malay and Western narrative traditions. The website that accompanies this book (http://www.rowman littlefield.com/isbn/0742553302) documents the incidents, gives sources for borrowed tropes, and explains the method.

HIKAYAT PA' BUAYA

[I]t seemed both the most horrible and the most inexplicable thing she could imagine. Entranced as much as repelled by what he had told of it, she nonetheless knew nothing of the light and heat he felt when his father beat him, nothing of the profound clarity of feeling that emerged from the center of his chest when it happened, nothing of the exquisite joining of all his various parts that he experienced when his father swung the boy's lean body around and punched it and shoved it to the floor while his mother's face howled in the distance. He could no way tell her of these things; he could barely know them himself. All he could know was that he had left out of his account something that was crucial and filled him with shame. (Banks 1989:109)

> Sometimes I forget completely
> what companionship is.
> Unconscious and insane, I spill sad
> energy everywhere. My story
> gets told in various ways: A romance,
> a dirty joke, a war, a vacancy.
>
> Divide up my forgetfulness to any number,
> it will go around.
> These dark suggestions that I follow,
> are they part of some plan?
> Friends, be careful. Don't come near me
> out of curiosity, or sympathy. (Rumi [Moyne and Barks 1984:62])

The Malay story would begin this way: "As told by the keeper of the tale, the *penglipur lara*, soother of woes, people say once there was an old man who lived in Perak state, in West Malaysia, and in the evenings told stories from his life, without their shadows."

Sad Energy Spilled Everywhere

> Time's knife slides from the sheath,
> as a fish from where it swims.

> —Rumi (Barks 2001:2)

Darkness envelops the shuttered plank house, and silence, but for the murmur of water. The cool unseen rain, light as heavy mist, barely stirs the orange-yellow blossoms of the rank-smelling little pagoda flower tree, just visible in the dimness. The flowers help adepts beguile the demon familiars that flutter around them as butterflies flutter around the little tree.

Dressed in a profusion of colored Chinese silks, long-haired little Raja Karim respected Pak Nakhoda, not in his present form of course, not the aged and infirm old man who sat cross-legged across from him, yellow-ish wrinkled soles of his feet tucked away under his tan checked sarong so as to give no offense, but as the fabled Pak Nakhoda of the old days, Pak Buaya, Uncle Croc, the freebooter and mercenary whose career still flickered inside the old man and could be summoned by soft words, at-tentiveness, and small gifts, like a shaman's familiar, bringing past ad-ventures. For a young minor nobleman like Karim, who had killed no one, not even a Sakai slave in a moment of pique, the valorous deeds Nakhoda recounted gave life to Malay aristocratic ideals, *better a day as a tiger than a hundred years as a goat,* loyalty and reckless courage, *better the white of your bones than the coward's white eye.* Karim, whose name means "Compassionate," had just turned thirteen.

The boy had a long oval face, nose slightly off center, cheeks soft but hollowed, reflecting maybe some Bengali trader or pirate generations ago. He knew his ancestry was mixed, like that of most aristocrats: Malay, Arab, Bengali, Sea People, Bugis. He despised local Malays: landlubber farmers. Bugis blood, he thought, would make him a great man when he grew up. It was the call of blood to blood that made him love Uncle Croc, though he would never confess such a feeling for an underling and was indeed only partly and vaguely conscious of it himself. The old man's face, burned dark red by the sun, looked like a pig's liver, the boy thought, squashing the convulsive pang of love. But horse mangoes have ugly rinds, and still the insides are tasty. The old man would let an ant under his feet escape death but would attack an elephant and knock it sprawling. *I'll be a warrior like him,* thought Karim, *now I'm just a little kid, but little like a tiger cub. Soon I'll dance the Bugis war dance.*

"Tell a story," he said.

"Your slave's stories are all sad," the old man said.

"No way," said the boy. "Tell the story, slave."

The old man looked at him expressionlessly, like a house gecko watching a moth, then raised his hands, palms pressed together before his bowed head, in an expression of submission and respect that the boy did not entirely trust. Nakhoda rose, went to the door of the house, and looked out into the evening damp at the last few strips of fading lavender cloud wrack over the swollen sluggish, endless Perak River, whose murmur faded away into the darkening west. Hordes of swifts whirled crazily under heaps of cumulus clouds turning black beneath the faint remaining light. Nakhoda thought he heard a nightjar, not a good omen.

I could have been as happy as this boy, he thought, *as content as one of the local Malay serfs. I could have been whole. I could have been like everybody else. Enjoyed simple pleasures: eating, though I never want to eat. I had a dream last night, but it's gone now. All I know is that I woke up like this again, no change. A story from my life? My life was undisciplined and toxic.* He made an ugly face, as old, hated images shadowed his mind, blocking out present darkness and the invisible rain.

Himself at age eight, seen from outside somehow, by some cold indifferent crocodile eye, a round-faced big-eyed little boy, vibrating with fear, trying to make himself smaller than he was, on his belly on a woven pandanus mat sticky with cold sweat, weeping for the father whose sultan had taken him and sold him as a catamite to a Yemeni trader, an empty tunnel of anguish running through the boy from his bleeding anus to his most inward secret parts, sticky with his own excreta; the merchant (huge, huge, a shadow filling all the space the boy could see, backlit by the flickering light of a Persian oil lamp) eating mangosteens as he always did after sex, always, repeating in his throaty voice the Arabic proverb as he always did, "Women for procreation; young boys for pleasure; mangosteens for ecstasy," laughing wetly, a red carnelian of Yemeni laughter, saying to the boy, Ja'u abahum yabkuna, "They come crying to their father."

No story there. Not that he had ever told it to anyone, having forgotten or buried most of it, remembering just that he had learned not to weep, eyes old now, open looking into the mild rain but unseeing, fixed on inner darkness. His mind had learned to detach itself during the beatings, to soar up and up so that he could look down from a great distance on the sweating man and the boy writhing like a fish in dry sand. During the three weeks after a beating, the terror became a dull ache like the rips in his skin, which lasted, black and scarlet, then blue, then yellow, as much a part of him as his heartbeat along the welts.

The scent of the sea, sand between his toes a couple of years later, the boy squatting, shivering, covering his ears after the Yemeni had made him watch the pirates he traded with test their weapons on a captive already too damaged to be saleable. Nakhoda had pissed himself again as fear often made him do, then vomited violently, convulsive spasm of rejection. The men laughed.

He had wanted to make himself of service to the master, but he was *gahel*, ignorant, as his master said, an Orang Bukit, hillbilly, good only as a *sharmootah*, whore. Some Muslim traders broke the Muslim rule against enslaving Muslims or *dhimmi*—people who observed Scripture, Christians or Jews, mostly—but it was pious to enslave *kafar*, unbelievers. That made it hard to get good, literate help. His master used only Javanese and Balinese males to help in his business. If Nakhoda worked hard, let his diligence show, his intelligence. . . . Even though he was smarter than they. . . . He could not finish the thought. His eyes would fill with tears at the mere idea of hope, and he brushed it away.

Himself at fourteen, escaped from the crocodile's mouth into the tiger's, from the Arab merchant to the Dutch one, the Arab saying to the Dutchman that the boy ta' berguna *was useless, maybe because puberty had made him unattractive, a piece of trash for his owner-lover-father-master to discard and forget, somehow loving the man who was throwing him away.*

"No," Nakhoda had said softly, to himself really. The trader, heavy black fuzz on his cheeks as usual, had glanced expressionlessly at the boy's stricken face. The Yemeni was older too, perhaps tireder, faint brackets around the corners of his mouth. Ed dunia wahira, *he had said, "The world's a tough place." Turned away. Waddled off. Didn't look back. Nakhoda still obsessed over the words late at night. Advice, a warning, a token of caring? Or just the sort of simple-minded philosophizing Nakhoda recently had taken to himself? Or a deliberate twist of the knife? All of that?*

It was certainly true.

Not as much sex with the Dutchman, Opa Henk preferred girls but forced fellation on male slaves sometimes, just to show he could. He ate meat, huge quantities of meat, so that his sweat smelled like death, like a rotting corpse. The

Dutchman was from Frisia, where people were pengamok, *the boy had heard, likely to run crazy, killing. He asked the Dutchman once. The man laughed and said* Iedere gek heeft zijn gebrek, *"Every geek's crazy in his own way." Once or twice a week, in the tropical evening damp, a small pack of Dutch merchants and officers would gather outdoors on wooden stools, opalescent beads of rancid sweat dotting their foreheads like pimples. They'd smoke their long white clay pipes and toss down small glassfuls of pungent gin. Sometimes they would get loud and laugh a lot and demand sex from the slaves. They chattered all the time, like monkeys, like children alone in the dark. Most of the time there was no silence in the Dutchmen's world. But sometimes, drunk, they turned quiet and weepy.*

Then the new master often became sullen and touchy. Red spots would burn in his cheeks, his hands and voice would tremble with self-nurtured rage, and he would go to the slave quarters and beat people up, more or less at random, grabbing the boy sometimes, tossing him against the wall, hammering him with his big fists or slapping him, making him see stars. The boy's mind went almost blank, then, ego dissolving in a warm pale red sea, body gone limp not resisting, almost like a swoon, a trance. Then, let fall to the floor, he would curl convulsively like a grub against the Dutchman's thudding feet, knees against chest, hands clasped over his exposed head, taking the Dutchman's kicks on his shins and the curve of his bony back, pulsing in and out of consciousness to the rhythm of the kicks. Afterwards his head and ears would ring for hours, and his mouth would taste like copper.

The deliberate punishment was worse. The leather belt would *crack!* against Nakhoda's bare skin, sending a bolt of searing agony up his backbone to burst into white light in his brain, making him scream shrilly, although the scream sounded to him like someone else screaming and screaming until nothing mattered, until he became nothing. After those beatings, he would sit up cross-legged, mindlessly, full of shame, a dumb fearful slave.

Sober, his Dutch owner-father-master-abuser could be kind. He had an orrery, brought in a teak chest from Leiden, and showed the boy how the planets worked, how the earth rotated around the Sun. The boy recognized truth when he heard it: the earth revolves pointlessly in an enormous dark uncaring cold void, and the Sun burns hotter than fire.

Something In Between, I Guess

I just don't care what happens next
looks like freedom but it feels like death
it's something in between, I guess.

—From Leonard Cohen, "Closing Time"

Two years after the purchase, on his knees between Opa Henk's white hairy thighs, pale skin like a maggot's, running his mouth over the red uncircumcised penis; a couple of other Dutchmen, hairy, drunk, red, alien, lolling around in rattan chairs, watching the fellation with pale blood-laced eyes, the color of spit on gray weathered boards, alcohol dulling their interest. Scent of clove cigarettes and rotting meat. Afterwards Opa Henk (not wanting his new Calvinist wife, on her way from Holland, to know who the man she had married was, though the other wives sometimes also tortured slaves, sticking hatpins into the girls' genitals, out of boredom) telling the boy to "raus!, get out, never come back, this is freedom for you, and remember that it was a Christian white man, not some verdammte *chop-prick Arab who freed you," brushing the still dribbling tip of his penis lightly, almost gently, across the boy's naked unweeping face, back and forth just below the eyes closed like buds, back and forth across the soft flared nares, back and forth across the mouth slightly open like a rose. Then the boy, still not fully understanding or believing, bowing backward out of the room, palms pressed together at his forehead in deep obeisance; a grinning Dutchman by the door rousing himself enough to give the boy's rump a playful paternal kick with the side of his boot, saying, "Welcome to the world, kid. You're on your own." And Opa Henk turning away to rearrange himself and button his fly, not even looking.* The world's a tough place.

Even now, he thought painfully, when he talked with a European or Arab his voice went shamefully high and tight, hatefully. His mouth got dry, and he couldn't swallow. He had learned Arabic and Dutch in hope of pleasing them, Rumi's poems and Euclid's theorems, had become Muslim to gain divine credit for the merchant, learned Yemeni adat and Dutch Kultur, tried to become like them, to be strong like them, unhurt hurters, to make them think him worthy of their love or at least their compassion, to make them see him. Useless, useless, useless, shameful and useless. Freed, discarded, nothing left to lose, every night as he tried to sleep, even now, even now, the old Malay couplet ran through his mind, again and again and again, his obsessive lullaby:

Ada hujan, ada panas   Come rain, come shine
Ada hari boleh balas.   Some day revenge is mine.

But that day had not come.

Manumitted, he felt no freedom. He knew the word, merdeka, *one of the many Sanskrit words borrowed by Malays from Indian traders and conquerors. But he knew that a naked man was a target for any passing reiver to enslave. Freedom was being an animal untied from a post only to be hunted down. His first act, after being expelled from the Dutchman's house, was to vomit, again and again, weeping.*

As a slave, he was used to going unnamed and unnoticed, even when he was performing intimate services, only seen when his owner was angry or bored or wanting sex. Now he longed for that invisibility. He hid in the alleys and wastelands of the little city, moving only at night, eyes wide and white with fear, flicking back and forth at any sound, real or imagined, like the eyes of a wild deer tied to a post, un-til finally he came to the countryside where he could hide more easily, feeding himself by raiding the fields at twilight away from the insistent, betraying sun. During the day he would lie, hardly breathing, curled up like a grub, among the weeds, out of the way.

He found a sliver of bamboo, tossed away by someone gathering housepoles, razor sharp along both edges. Nakhoda stuck it into a climbing vine he wound around his waist. It was his first weapon. It made him feel, not safe, but less vulnerable.

One gray evening he was lying in a thicket of mauve-flowered Straits rhododendrons that grew along a cold little river that flowed into an estuary. A plump young Betawi man, soft unformed face, came by without seeing Nakhoda in the dense brush. The Betawi kicked off his sandals and took off his shirt. He put on a brown batik sarong over his black silk trousers, stepped out of the trousers, and waded into the river to bathe. Nakhoda could have stolen the clothes and fled. Instead, he slid into the stream silently as a crocodile, came up behind the young Betawi, pulled him close, left arm around his shoulders, pressing up against him (faint whiff of chicken curry on the Betawi's breath, quick pang of hunger), and slit the man's throat with the bamboo, slicing his own hand deeply with the double-edged blade. The Betawi tried to cry out, but the thick sputter of his own carotid blood turned the shrieks into comic burbling. Nakhoda felt the soft body shrink into itself like a muscle clenching, spasm and void its bowels, then relax, accepting its death. When Nakhoda loosened his embrace, the corpse slumped almost soundlessly under the pearl gray water, now stinking and stained a spreading pink and brown. After the strangled cry and splashing came an implacable blank silence, dotted with the mechanical chirp of birds and buzz of insects.

Panting, Nakhoda washed away the blood from his face and torso. Clambered back up the slick, muddy bank. Glanced over his shoulder at the humped back floating away downstream. He noticed that he couldn't make out the separate vertebrae. Not like his own scarred back. Crocodiles would get the body when it rounded the bend and came to the mudflats of the estuary. He sliced a piece of cloth off the Betawi's shirt with his bloody splinter, wet the strip in the river, and bound his hand. There was a dagger with the clothes. It hissed out of its sheath like a cool breeze through tall grass. Nakhoda threw the bamboo knife into the river.

He felt almost nothing, nothing for the meat floating down the river, nothing for the meat squatting on the bank. That surprised him, a little. He was a man, he thought. He was nothing. He could kill calmly and feel nothing. Tidak jadi apa-apa. Nothing happening here, nothing at all. In this world there would be a place for him. The weak and unwary had a new predator to fear.

He looked at his hands. Chilled by the river, his wounded palm had almost stopped bleeding. He clenched his fists, tentatively. Then relaxed them. Releasing nothing.

Nakhoda forced the images back down into the lockbox of his mind. He would have to tell a story because Karim was a raja, though not an important one, and because he loved the boy. About what happened after that third betrayal and first murder, about himself abandoned and free, the young freebooter, killing and killing and killing, no matter whom, anybody really, why would he care? looting and looting; awash in an onyx sea of utterly empty freedom like a blind man given sight or a hunchback made straight; getting richer and richer, getting a name, Uncle Croc, feared and respected, an honored bearer of bloody death whom people said fire wouldn't blister or the ocean dampen, from whom no one expected or received mercy, now just an old man with a fund of bloody stories, still able to survive on almost no food or sleep.

He had taught men, women, and children how tough the world is. They learned that death isn't the worst life has to offer. Far from it. How truth made them wail! He went back, often, to the island beach near Singapore where he'd first learned what pirates do. Some of his repellent companions laughed at the suffering they caused the captive men tied to stakes on the empty white beaches, on whom they tested their weapons, torturing them for hours in front of their families, kicking the children aside. He never interfered, never joined in, but watched and learned, learning again from their agonies what he already knew and had taught them. Man is dust. Only God can endure this. Only God endures.

Later, after years and years and years, as age eroded his *semangat*, his energy and spiritual power, he had enslaved himself anew, as a war chief to Karim's father, a sultan like the one who had taken Nakhoda from his own father, exchanging his oppressive dangerous freedom for the security of subordination, order, and hierarchy. As a slave, a *hamba*, he had been a valued counselor. Muslim *hamba*, said Malay law, were actually freemen, as the Quran requires, though their bondage had no end, their children were also *hamba*, and they had to be loyal and obedient to their masters or suffer horrible punishments. Still, they were people, unlike *'abdi*, the kind of slave he had been as a child, with no rights or humanity at all; *'abdi* were dogs, people said. As a fighter rather than debtor, self-subordination had brought him a sort of respect. Now he was a trusted retainer, whose fearful reputation and grim bearing reflected and buttressed his master's power.

What we do for ourselves is meaningless. Only what we do for God has meaning. I can lose myself in love and service to this boy's father, kill and die for him. Slaves don't decide what sin is. Only God decides that. But inside, on many days, gazing blankly at his past and present, he saw himself a cornered cur, snarling and snapping hopelessly at its tormentors.

Courtly speech gave him a refuge. Its formality insulated him from the pain of personal contact. It permitted no hint that *hamba* had any identity independent of the master. For *hamba* it was always safer to keep to indirect address and to avoid the first-person "I" whenever possible. Otherwise a slavocrat might take offense at the hint that there were other selves, egos, persons among his retinue instead of just extensions of his own self, ego, person. Slaves lived their lives in the passive voice, as *kakitangan*, hands-'n'-feet, of their masters. In courtly speech, sometimes, Nakhoda could vanish.

His stories were always close to the truth, although he and the boy knew that a lie to a ruler is not a lie. It is a convenience, a formula, a courtesy, which protects the teller from physical hurt and from the supernatural dangers of *sumbung*, acting above one's station, and which protects the ruler, too, from having to acknowledge the existence of other selves. No one believed the literal truth of slave talk, though masters routinely complained that slaves were dishonest and ungrateful.

Telling stories in this tidy ornate language, watching the boy's dark brown eyes widen and moisten, the full lips part in complete attention, that was the only sort of human loving Nakhoda knew how to do nowadays, the closest he could get to what Sufi missionaries and marabouts had helped him feel was the Truth about God the Friend. Looking at the boy, he felt *sayang*, love and pity, overwhelm him, but for whom he felt it he could not tell: for this boy Karim, whose name meant "Compassionate," or for the weeping beaten catamite Nakhoda, or for the ferocious impotent old man Nakhoda, longing for the Friend lost in the poisonous tumult of his life.

Don't crocodiles eat corpses? he thought, faintly disgusted at himself for using stories of his bleak pointless life to keep the boy with him in the evening. *Night falls, and people need company. These stories are the only thing that will survive me, my only bequest. A dead tiger leaves its striped skin, a dead man leaves his name.* He closed and bolted the door against the evil, human and other, that permeated the night and against the unseen rain. A household slave had already bolted the shutters. The man and boy sat locked in darkness, by the hearth, their faces lit from beneath by the glowing embers.

"The lord asks for blood from a dried fish," said Nakhoda, "but the slave obeys."

Karim saw only the loyalty and obedience, not the love. Send the old man on an errand, he'd go; call him, he'd come. Uncle Croc let himself slip back into his past like an eel into mud.

The Cobra Rises above Its Coils

> After being with me one whole night,
> you ask how I live when you're not here.

Badly, frantically, like a fish trying to breathe
dry sand. You weep and say,
But you choose that.

—Rumi rubai (quatrain) #334 (Moyne and Barks 1986:25)

Jungle blackness chirring like a huge soft wet machine, the humid air full of the smell of rot and corruption, absolutely inhuman, indifferent to humans, not even hostile but full of menace and ugly depthless shadows, hantu, *demons, worse than uttermost darkness.*

"Your slave once had a companion in arms," he began. "He had a curved dagger from Damascus, with a rhinoceros-horn handle inlaid with silver, like Yemenis wear. When he cut people down, he would cry *Allah akbar!* God is great! It gave him strength, he said. And he wanted it to be the last thing they heard, God is great. He was teaching them a lesson. Milord understands?"

"Is this part of the slave's story?"

O yes. "No, milord." Bending forward with his hands folded against his chest. *But the world is an Idea in the mind of God, and my life, and this story. God is great!* In the silent dark he could hear a faint *griit griit* from the kitchen: a slave girl grinding spices for the morning meal, for which he would have no appetite, as usual.

"There were, I don't know, half a dozen of us. The others were the sort of frontier filth you get on this sort of hunt, not high-class men, thugs and bandits and riffraff mostly, but it doesn't hurt to carry a couple of clubs with your kris and dagger. Physically they didn't look much alike. But there was a sameness in how they stood—loosely alert, faces blank—and how they'd glance at you sideways but not look at you directly. God had seen fit to change all their hearts to the hearts of dogs.

"One was a Mendiling, from Sumatra. Skinny hairy spider legs. Never wore pants, just a dirty blue-checked sarong he'd hike up, sometimes as high as a loincloth. Pak Pegar, Uncle Fireback Pheasant, we called him, because he smoked so much opium that his eyes were always red like the pheasant's. We'd say to him, 'Hey, Pegar, close your eyes before you bleed to death.' Fierce mustache, bristled like steel needles. Made him look like a *panglima,* a war chief, but in a month he wouldn't kill a single person, not even a Sakai slave. Talked like a *panglima* too, but you know 'tigers that roar don't eat people.' A blowfish, all puffed up and prickly but empty inside, the brains of a rice-pap eater and a boneless tongue. It's easy to manage men like that."

"Like dogs that bark and bark at you when you're far away," said Karim knowledgeably. "You get close, they tuck their tails between their legs." He sucked in his stomach, straightened his back, and stared expressionlessly straight ahead, working on a stony-faced cold look. "You

don't have to *be* fierce as long as you have the look of command." He relaxed slightly, feeling a little silly in his rich silks.

"True. For sure milord has such a look." Nakhoda showed no amusement. "Anyway, Pegar had a chum, Kalil, Malay from around here, pretty
as a girl, skin like polished ivory *but long dirty fingernails Opa Henk would
have whipped him for, black crescents at the end of his slim fingers.* Maybe *pondan,* hermaphrodite or homosexual. Long coarse hair he wore down to his
waist. When he stood still, he'd put all his weight on one leg, cocking the
other, like a sandpiper waiting for a thundersquall. He stuck as close to
Pegar as lips to teeth. The sort of kid who's never too ashamed to run
away, never too compassionate to cut down people trying to escape. A
sharp-edged blade of lallang grass you couldn't lean on, couldn't rely on.
But up for any project Pegar had in mind, a water wagtail ready to jitter
around on any old beach, one of those people who sleep during the day
but creep around at night. Not strong enough to carry a bucket of dry
chaff by himself, but quick on his feet and silent as a poisonous krait.
Smiled a lot. As if he was on to some joke the rest of us hadn't caught onto
yet."

He's warming to his story, thought Karim. *Embers on a hearth may be dull,
but they warm right up if you blow on them.*

"Abdul Wahab was another, one of those Rawas the White People
brought over here from Sumatra by promising them free land and no
taxes. Arm-swinging, bouncing gait. Well-spoken, but with a forked
tongue, a monitor lizard's tongue. Your best friend to your face, but behind your back something else. Like a bee, you know? Honey in the
mouth, sting in the tail."

"Your lord isn't a banana-eating kid. I know all about sweet mouths
and rotten hearts."

"Of course milord does. Abdul Wahab was the sort of man who sits like
a cat but attacks like a tiger. Long stringy graying hair over thick brow
ridges and fever-bright yellow-brown eyes without depth, like a Dutchman's eyes, or a python's. You'd look into those eyes, and there'd be no
one looking back at you. Crow's-feet at the corners of eyes, so his face
crinkled up when he smiled, showing his black crooked teeth, looking
merry and wild. He'd close his eyes slowly, then suddenly open them
wide, *bright lizard stare that told you nothing about what he was feeling, if he
had anything like normal feelings; you didn't want to ask. He looked right
straight at you when he did that, but not as if he saw you, more as if he looked
right through you and saw something else, something dangerous and pathetic: a
live bearcat hanging in a snare, maybe, a cobra boys were beating to death in the
tall lallang grass. A cold, merry look as if your struggling amused him, watching
you learn you weren't as dangerous as you'd thought. Thick black eyebrows like
moth wings that'd pucker out over his eyes when he frowned, deep-set eyes they*

were, until the eye sockets were black, just dark pits in which you'd glimpse a flash of white when he moved his head, a tiny bright bead of madness. He used to quote a Chinese proverb: "Men are nothing, going nowhere."

"This Rawa made his ablutions with us, five a day, but just smiled slightly when the rest of us prayed. He carried five weapons: in his belt, a long kris, a short kris and a dirk; stuck in his turban, a *lawi ayam*, a small curved dagger shaped like a chicken's claw. He also carried a rusty musket. He'd say *Kalau ta' bersenapang, baik beri jalan lapang*, 'Got no gun, better get out of the way.' Twitchy as a worm on a hot rock. Even when he was sitting still one of his hands or feet would be jittering. *They didn't look human, not really, more like something on a tiger: nails yellowish and thick, thick nail beds, curling over a little at the edges and tips.* A little insane, I think, *crazed and made arrogant by loneliness and pain and killing.* He was *pengamok*, one of those men who can deliberately nurse old resentments into battle rage, until he didn't care whether he killed others or they killed him, made no difference. Whomever he was killing, it wasn't the people actually dying by his hand. You had the feeling that if you took your eyes off him, he'd beat your brains out without noticing who you were."

"One night in the jungle, when neither of us could sleep, he said to me, 'Sometimes I fear I won't be able to control myself. Then I drink arrack until I'm drunk and can sleep. But I wake up in a cold sweat, in a rage, and all I see is dead bodies. Blood. Screams. Right then I'm ready to go wherever the rage takes me. If I had the weapons, I'd kill everyone, my own kinsmen and companions, anybody I could find, even in my own hometown back in Sumatra. . . .'"

"Crude men." Crudity, being *kasar*, was low class.

"Crude. True." *But you feel . . . intimate . . . with these men. It's not a good feeling. Unclean and stifled. Understand, little boy: men are* nothing. *Men are dust.*

"But people like that have their uses, no?" asked the raja. "Crooked sugar cane doesn't make crooked sugar. Hang Tuah was *pengamok*, and he's the greatest hero of the Malay race."

"True, milord," Nakhoda bent his head to acknowledge the wisdom of the proverb. "Sadly, this slave can't make himself run amok like that."

"?"

"No, for this slave the time before killing is a sort of peace, a kind of purity, heart untroubled, mind calm and alert, untethered from the world. A good time to read the Quran, to contemplate *nasib*, fate, becoming serene until the moment of attack." *My rage like my grief is cold and flat, unchanging. You reach a kind of balance with it. A kind of purity. But maybe I too was killing something else, something that doesn't die.*

"And then?"

"Then, nothing. If it's just slaughter, nothing, no feeling, nothing."

"Hang Tuah was like that?"

"In fair combat, no matter who wins, it always feels as if you're losing. *Winning, losing, makes no difference. Nothing happens.* All you feel after is relief. *It's killing the helpless makes you feel powerful, serene. Soft ears are the ones that get twisted.* "But during a fight?"

"In a fight, you feel rage, joy. Exultation." *Fear, if anything. Everybody loses. Losers are charcoal, winners are ashes. Men are nothing.*

"No fear."

"No fear." *Liar. Sometimes you can't swallow, your mouth is so dry with terror.*

The boy shifted his position, signaling his impatience to get back to the story. The old slave was pretty negative sometimes.

"The last hunter I remember was an escaped murderer from Singapore. Carried a broad sword and a club, a kris, a couple of knives, *lawi ayam* in his headband. I forget his name, a burly man with a flat mean macaque face and muddy brown eyes. He'd killed a Chinese shopkeeper and his family, children too. Said he had no regrets, it was like killing ants. Got away with a wound that left him with a limp, scorched but not burnt. *Kasar* as my lord says, crude in manners and speech. He liked this kind of hunt. You always get that sort of men on the frontier. They're as common as dirt in Chinese shops, dangerous because they have nothing and care about nothing. Trying to lead one of them is like trying to lead a lame elephant: it can trip and crush you. You don't turn your face away when he comes up to you, you know his character. We called him Uncle Snake *because his penis was huge, but I can't talk obscenity to my lord.* He'd answer back:

Bukan ular di dalam hutan Not a snake in the jungle
tapi naga jadi-jadian but a dragon in disguise

"That was our party. Oh, and our guide, a tame Sakai from north Perak. They're different from the ones around where we were, cleaner I think than them, but still disgusting, covered with ringworm, white as British paper. Never bathed, not in the morning, not at night, didn't even like going into the river. Went naked, just a bark loincloth high up around his waist instead of around his loins; *you could see his privates through the barkcloth.* Ate by himself, disgusting unclean stuff my lord wouldn't want to hear about. Had one of those unpronounceable chicken-cluck names they have. We just called him Sang Sakai, 'Master Sakai.' Nasty filthy creature but a good tracker. Like a dog."

The Hammer Finds the Nail

Sama lebur, sama binasa
Liquidated together, in agony together

—Hikayat Hang Tuah (Anonymous 1908, II:206)

God is compassionate, but if you plant barley
don't expect to harvest wheat. (from Rumi, rubai #1798 [Moyne and
Barks 1986:80])

*Three ramshackle little palm-thatch huts by the river under the pale early morn-
ing cloud wrack, the waters below foaming yellow and brown over the trunks of
the huge trees that grew horizontally out from the banks, desperate for light, now
temporary dams to the floodwaters rising after a thundersquall in the dark mountains to the east, spindrift piling up behind the dams in black dripping masses,
wet black limbs tentacling out in all directions, trembling as the waters poured
over them.*

"Abdul Wahab's old musket jams when we try to scare the Sakai by fir-
ing it, so we burst into their settlement at false dawn like waves smashing
into a sandbar, like a flash flood racing around the bend of a river, overwhelming them the way a thundersquall overwhelms mountain forests.
Sakai running every which way, like flies swarming around a corpse, we
pursuing, Sakai scattering in all directions blindly, like horseflies after
boys gouge out their eyes. Squawking and quacking as Sakai do.

"With his kris Pegar slashes a girl bending to pick up a baby, slicing
across her shoulder, and she falls to the ground with a thump like a ripe
jackfruit falling, squirming like a snake, trying to hold her arm on, yelp-
ing like a dog caught in a fence. *Creamy white tendons, shocking red muscle,
blood spurting spurting.* A skinny old female, maybe its dam, throws her
body over it, caterwauling like a cat in heat, and Pegar jams his kris into
her just below the shoulder blades, skewering them both, twists the kris
and tries to pull it out, but the blade's gone, stuck in the bodies, leaving
just the handle. Bad omen. 'Mother's CUNT!' yells Pegar. (Please may
milord forgive the obscenity. Pegar was *kasar*, rough as a monitor lizard's
skin.) The baby is screaming under the two older ones.

"A big-eyed flat-faced gasping male about the same age as the female
swings a bamboo spear at Pegar, slicing the meat of Pegar's right arm,
making him drop the hilt of the kris. Kalil comes up silently behind the
male and slits his throat, right through the goiter, splashing Pegar with
blood. 'Mother's cunt!' yells Pegar again, kicking the Sakai's body as it
collapses. 'Mother's cunt!' Those bamboo spears have poison prickles.

"Kalil smiles, nudging the body with his toe to make sure it's dead.
'Dwarf wanted to seize the moon,' he says. 'You stomp Sakai, Pegar, wear
boots.' The other Sakai have all run away. Kalil turns away, joins the rest
of us looking for the young who've run off into the forest. We go after
them like mother cats looking for kittens, moving slowly, being careful,
listening for whimpers.

"I find a scrawny female—four five years old, too young to duck down
under the brush. I reach down for her and she reaches up her puny arms

as if I'm her father come to pick her up *and not her father's killer.* I lift her, and she clings to me, skinny legs around my waist, arms around my neck, soft little face buried between my neck and my shoulder." *It unmanned me. I almost came undone. I almost wept. But I remembered. Men are nothing. Men are dust.*

"They really are stupid, aren't they?" said the young raja. "Stupid, stupid, stupid." *They look stupid,* the old man thought, *stupid and sullen. But fear and despair make you look that way. A lot of times after they're captured, they just stop eating and die. World's a tough place.* He'd seen enough slaves to know that. He went on with the story, pausing as unvoiced thoughts skittered across his narrative like water striders across a stream.

"We find a few others trying to hide under a patch of gingerwort leaves, like chicks do when the mother hen's been killed. Some of them even make soft peeping sounds like chicks.*The little female clinging to my neck made no sound, just soft breathing noises.*

The old man's voice had changed, sounding tired and tentative. *He's getting very old,* Karim thought, slightly miffed that the slave had ignored his remark about Sakai stupidity. *His hangers-on have eaten all the loot he got. If I live so long, let me be gulped down by a crocodile, not nibbled to death by minnows. You don't have money tucked into the waist of your sarong, even your good buddies avoid you.*

"We come back to the clearing with half a dozen immature Sakai. Still a couple of adults there, on the ground, hurt, curled up like shrimp; whimper *and defecate* when we kick them. They're filthy, worthless, so we spear them. Kalil and Pegar leave another, badly wounded, flopping around like a fish in a landing net, one eye open, other half shut and fluttering. Makes them laugh. We've gone through the gaggle of Sakai like fire through cotton.

"An immature one, five six years old, is sitting with the torso of a dead male, maybe its sire, across its lap." *The adult's arms were spread out around the little one, as if he'd been trying to shield it from us. No chance of that.*

"Uncle Croc?" asked the raja. *Why does the old man keep pausing?* Nakhoda cleared his throat and went on.

"Anyway, the little one's twitching and trembling, all over. Abdul Wahab bends down to collect it and drag it over to the others, but Uncle Snake says, "s one's no good. I seen this before. *Semangat's* gone, no will to live. It'll shake all night, turn cold, and die.'"

"'We just leave it?' Abdul Wahab turns his bright blank pitiless gaze on the child like a cobra focusing on a frog.

"'No use to that,' says Uncle Snake, his face swollen with the excitement of killing. 'Hey, better all black than just ink-spotted.' He takes one end of his club in both hands and swings the other end around *in a wide semicircle that hit the child just below the cheekbone, smashing in the mouth cav-*

ity, face exploded in blood milk teeth sharp fragments of bone in all directions, spattering Abdul Wahab with Sakai blood and brains. Abdul Wahab makes a spitting disgusted noise and grabs for the hilt of his short kris.

"Uncle Snake stares at him, hefting the wet club, *all trace of human intelligence gone from his face.* "'Sarong dirty?'"

The young raja smiled.

"Uncle Snake was right. On a hunt like this you take the cream of the coconut and toss the rest. Adults are too hard to move through the jungle, and anyway you can't tame them, they keep running away even if you beat them bloody. You can cut off a foot, but then they're good for nothing. Wild Sakai adults are useless."

"Your lord KNOWS that," said Karim, narrowing his eyes. "Everybody knows THAT."

"Milord's stupid slave momentarily forgot how grown-up milord has become."

"Tell the story."

"By milord's command.

"You could see Abdul Wahab work at letting Snake's words slide off his face like water off a rock. He gave a crazy little laugh, like a little scream. And took his hand off the hilt of his kris. '*Kif entei?*' he asked, 'Happy now?' *Using the Arab dope-smokers' word for blissed-out.*

"We stood quietly for a moment in the heat, panting and sweating, catching our breath. Under one of the shacks, the immature Sakai were all bunched together, hanging onto each other like baby monkeys, all watching us, pointing their faces at us wherever we moved, like minnows in a shallow stream following the current *seeing what?* except for a couple who were just hugging themselves and rocking. One of the older females—nine or ten years old—was cowering, making the gesture of submission, palms together in front of her bowed forehead. She must have met Malays before. I was going to pull off the little pickaninny around my neck and put her with the rest but couldn't *didn't want to* pry her loose. She didn't weigh much. My lord knows how scrawny Sakai are.

"We let Uncle Snake guard them, because they were even more scared of him than of the rest of us. Just looking at him, huge man, big vein throbbing down across the center of his forehead, covered with Sakai gore, kept them quiet and huddled. No mercy for jungle pups there."

The young raja grinned. "When the cat's around, the mice stop squeaking," he said.

"There were two girls, maybe a little older than this slave's lord. Elbows already tied together behind their backs *not pretty but sexy in the way Sakai are, wild frightened deer eyes, after Kalil pulled off their loincloths we could see they had no hair on their little cunts.* They were pretty small. We might have been able to take them with us, but they looked too old to tame. Their lives were hanging from the tip of a fingernail.

"'Time to go,' I said. 'Don't want the Sakai to find the corpses or sniff them out before we get away.'" *The air in the clearing was wavy with the heat of the sun, slowing time down, making my eyelids heavy, a hypnotic and sensuous feeling like after good sex.* Kif. "We'll leave them their dead to remember us by."

"Us—and their young ones," said Kalil, with a smirk.

"'Time to *go?*' asked Pegar, picking his nose. 'Do tigers hide their footprints? We were up this morning before the flies started flying. 'S hard work, running around like fishhawks swooping from island to island. We need a rest. And I got an idea for some fun.'

"Uncle Snake said nothing but snarled at me from under the house like a dog you're poking with a stick. I didn't want to fight with them *I was too sleepy* but I knew I must take no sass."

"Hunh *unh!*" The little raja grunted approval, patting his chest.

"'We'll take them just a little way,' I said. 'Maybe a mile.' Looking Pegar straight in the face, where smeared Sakai blood was beginning to turn black and sticky. 'Then we'll rest, and you can play.' *Bright hot sun dazzle in the little clearing, unfathomable shadows all around.*

"'Uncle Croc's right,' said, Abdul Wahab, looking up with his bright mad eyes from where he was carefully poking holes with a bamboo splinter in the right paws of the little Sakai that Uncle Snake was tending. Hand wounds hurt something awful, there're a lot of nerves in the palm of your hands, but the little Sakai didn't show any pain. They're different from normal people. A couple of the littlest ones were still weeping silently, most of them sat tense and still, shuddering and twitching sometimes, like wild deer tied to a pole. Watching you chop down the big ones usually quiets the little ones down. They just stare and stare and stare, at nothing really, their eyes flicking up quickly at us, then flicking away. 'The sky was collapsing on their heads, the earth was cracking open under their feet.' *Could they understand that? What were they thinking?* Kalil was splitting a length of rattan he'd found under one of the houses into long strips, to thread through the holes in their hands and tie them together in a row, so they'd be easy to move through the jungle."

This time the old man's pause seemed longer than ever to the boy. Nakhoda stared into the fire, feeling a different heat. *The air was heavy with the metallic smell of blood, and the sickening stench of the feces the Sakai had voided in the spasms of terror and death. Butterflies—bright blue, sulfur yellow, chalk white—flitted through the clearing, landing by the dead, long tongues sipping the moisture from the puddles of blood, urine, and feces. Like vampire demons,* hantu pelesit. *The blood on the children's hands was turning black and syrupy in the heat. A black pulsating bandage of flies covered every wound on the living and dead. The sound of the flies drowned out the endless background chirrrr of the jungle. The men's faces were hard for me to see through the waves of heat. My armpits and groin were wet with sweat.*

"That's how you domesticate Sakai, isn't it? Show them when they're young that their adults can't protect them, that we hold their deaths in our hands, that their lives depend on our compassion?" the raja asked. "And beatings," he added, grinning.

Uncle Croc looked up and gazed blankly at Raja Karim. "All children get beaten," he said, remembering. *You only really feel the first stroke of the rattan, the rest is just a blur of pain. It's the moment before the first stroke, when you're bent across the smooth gray wooden mortar, you can't swallow, and time stops, becomes infinite, a white silent blank universe in which nothing exists but the anticipation of pain and the knowledge that nothing you can do will stop it from coming. You wait and wait and wait for the pain to smash the silence, for your mind to register that once again it had forgotten how pain hurts. It's the helplessness, he thought, no one thinks you're worth helping or sparing, you're utterly alone with the fear. It makes you glad, almost, when the beating finally starts.*

The old man shook himself. "So, after that. Anyway, Abdul Wahab the Rawa was siding with me. 'Sakai are cowards,' he said. 'But they ambush you with blowpipes, and their shamans turn into tigers. Some have claws between their knuckles." He glanced at the corpses, spot-checking their hands. 'I wouldn't hang around here. They're fast and quiet, jungle beasts. They can be across the river while you're still looking for your paddle.'"

Karim relaxed. The story was back on track.

"Abdul Wahab, lips pursed, finished running the rattan through the hand holes, so that, if a captive fainted or fell, the rough edges of the rattan would scrape against the raw meat and keep them all awake and moving. Raised a few welts with a rattan switch, corralled them into a line. One began keening like a hornet in a bamboo internode, but Kalil whacked it on the legs with the switch and Abdul Wahab slapped it hard across the face, knocking it down, so it stopped blubbering and got in line.

"Pegar had finished tying up his wound with a piece of white barkcloth he'd found in one of the huts. Besides that and their young the Sakai didn't have anything worth taking. We set the shacks on fire and took off. I was still wearing the little female like a necklace."

Making the raja smile. *I didn't want to pry her loose or hurt her skinny little paws. She hung on me the way damp cloth does, pressing against me like a frightened child, not seeming to weigh anything.*

"What about the other females?" asked the boy, irritated by the new pause. "The ones tied up." He gave a creditable imitation of a leer.

"Snake and Pegar grabbed the ropes that tied the females' elbows and dragged them along with us."

"That hurts a lot, doesn't it?" asked the boy, leaning forward.

"Feels like your shoulder blades are being torn loose. It's a good way to tie Sakai because you don't have to damage them to hurt them. Snake had the prettier one, the one with less eye goop and sleeker hair. Pegar had to take the black one with the flat nose and kinky hair, she kept squirming against the ropes like a goat with a maggoty wound. Of course, they were both filthy, white blotches on their skins."

"But naked, right?"

"Naked."

"Did you . . . ?"

"Yes." The old man looked down at the plank floor. He didn't like talking about sex, especially to royalty. It was dangerous. "When we were far enough from the clearing. Some of the Sakai pups were stumbling every few steps and whimpering as the rattan rasped through the holes in their hands, not noisy but annoying. What with all the killing and trudging along the steep slick clay trails where you have to dig in your toes if you don't want to slip and fall, we were tired and sweaty. But, as Kalil said, 'Hey, a tired body's ok if your heart is light.'

We must have missed some of the immature Sakai in the jungle. Did they understand what happened? Learn anything? That nothing is safe? That appearances lie? To trust no one, take no comfort, hope for nothing, love no one? That monsters surround you always, and all you can do is give up, give up. That the solid earth itself will collapse under your feet, everything familiar and safe spinning away into pure violence? That this will happen again and again and again, endlessly? That we are dust, and the world's a tough place, and men are nothing?

Or were they just what people said, mindless as deer, knowing nothing, just full of unreasoning terror? Why would the little female cling to me but not meet my eyes?

"We camped on a sandbank by the river, bathed, said our evening prayers. God is great. Our tame Sakai didn't want to camp there. A strangler fig there, hanging out over the river, was a bad sign, he said, and, worse, there was a toadstool with a pinkish-white stem about six inches tall, swollen top mottled brown and pink, conical, covered with a large-mesh lacy veil of meat. It looked like an erect, my lord understands. . . . But despite the omens the sand and bright sunlight were a welcome break from the jungle *the endless evil dark green shadows*. Normal people live by the sea, by the river, not in the jungle like beasts. While we ate and rested, we set Massa Sakai to cutting bamboos for a couple of big rafts so we could float downstream to civilization."

"Your master asked about the women."

"Please, milord, forgive your humble slave. We did to them what you asked about. We all did, one after another. *Wasn't good. The ache had settled in my upper arm like a stone.* I took the prettier one, *but nothing happened. I'd tied my little Sakai female to a tree by a rattan around her neck. She stared at us while we sweated away, spending our strength, all the captive Sakai did, big mousedeer eyes staring, flicking away if we glanced up, that was what made it no good, nothing but an empty dripping prick afterward, ring of pain just below the still-swollen head as if something had bitten it hard without breaking the skin, prick flabby and useless now as I cleansed myself of her filthy slime and blood.* I wanted to hit the unclean Sakai slut afterward but didn't want to mark her up so the other men would enjoy her less. A leader always has to think of his men. Snake took the prettier one, Pegar the other. Abdul Wahab took them one after another, merrily. Kalil just watched and smiled. *Later he beat the uglier one and took her in the anus. I felt bad but didn't know why, maybe it was the ill-omened place. I thought of beating the little female for watching, for unmanning me, but I couldn't, she looked so much like a normal little girl, so I said my nighttime prayers,* God is great, *and pulled my sarong over my head to shut out the bright terrible moonlight and tried to sleep. Some horrible bird or demon wept like a child in the formless abstract darkness. But I could still see the moon. Rumi says, "Like any face reflecting other light, the moon is a source of pain."*

"Slave, you daydreaming?" A sudden flurry of rain, unseen and unfelt, rattled the shutters. But Nakhoda did not hear.

Morning: a polished knife blade. I was aching and unrested. Get up. Forget your life. It's time to pray. Say God is great. *Leaves dripping with the water chilly jungle nights wring out of the hot air, an unseen rain. My sarong was clammy and damp. As we bathed and prayed, the river squirmed away from us in both directions like a long coiling brown worm in a green burrow with a slit of burning blinding brightness down the top. The feverish dawn light shone through scudding gray clouds sending shadows reeling through the strangler figs along the bank. Little Sakai clucking softly to each other, cleft palate gutturals, like sleepy chickens. Kalil was watching them, grinning, lips red with betel juice, showing all his little black filed teeth.*

The little raja clapped his hands sharply together, summoning his slave from the illusory privacy of thought: "*Allah!* Slave's *babuk,* senile and mindless." The old man started slightly, then lowered his eyes and joined his palms together, raising them to his forehead in the classic gesture of submission, and resumed.

"'Hey, Pegar,' called Kalil, 'looks like the lovebird you had in your hand got clean away.' The blacker female had managed to squirm free of her bonds and run away into the jungle.

"Pegar was furious: 'Mother's cunt! Mother's cunt!'

"'Couldn't have taken them all the way home anyway,' said Abdul Wahab.

"'Pegar wants his morning snack,' said Snake, and chortled.

"'You,' said Pegar furiously to him, 'You share yours with me."

"'Oh, of COURSE, my lord,' said Snake, suddenly unsmiling. He made a deep obeisance, then unbound the other female's elbows, holding her wrists in one huge hand and passing her over to Kalil. Cut the rattan in half, tied one half around each ankle, kneeling in front of her. She sat passively, waiting for whatever would happen. The immature Sakai stopped their muttering and clucking and watched with wide wild eyes, *learning what?*

"'Gimme a hand, Kalil,' said Snake.

"They threw the free ends of her bonds over a low-lying branch, pulling her legs apart in a V, *she saying nothing, no tears left, no cries, just shielding her privates with one hand.* 'Wanna split, Uncles?' asked Snake, raising his long bush knife. 'We'll go halvsies.'"

The old man closed his eyes and fell silent.

* * *

"Wah!" said the boy softly, wide-eyed, patting his chest in astonishment.

* * *

"When we got back to civilization, the Javanese merchant who'd hired us greeted us. *Oily, fancy-pants money-grubbing foreigner.*

"'What news?'

"'Good news,' we said, like you're supposed to. Showed him what we'd caught.

"'Forty dollars each,' he said after looking them over. 'It's good money for Sakai pups. Look at them. Stupid little darkies with skinny arms and legs, potbellies, ugly monkey faces, that white crap all over their skins.' The faces of the little Sakai were weary and drawn, not like normal children. *Tired frightened people are ugly.* 'They're only good for *'abdi,* slaves with no rights at all.'

"'It's nothing compared with what we'd get for Sumatrans,' said Abdul Wahab, eyes gleaming. 'Good news?' he said to me. 'No one is finding this good news. No one is finding this good news but Master Java.' I could see the *amok* stirring in him.

"'Hey, you want big bucks, bring me some pretty Nias girls. Or Balinese. They're loyal. Not this Sakai trash.'

"I thought for a minute there'd be a fight, but Abdul Wahab glanced at the huddled Sakai, snorted a laugh, and said, 'Tough on the pups too. Ain't like they're gonna be *hamba.* You don't even feed *'abdi,* they owe you everything, you owe them nothing. You can kill 'em like dogs.'

"'The world's a tough place,' I said.

"'Master Java gets more than cheap little *'abdi,*'" Still grinning without humor, Abdul Wahab raved on. 'The other Sakai'll find the corpses. Tough on them too.' *Suppose someone who loved her found her cut in two like that.* 'They'll be good about bringing Master Java what he wants from the jungle, when he wants it, for what he feels like paying. We just scared a whole bunch of Sakai into turning *hamba* for this Javanese dog. For nothing.'"

"What am I, a Chinese businessman? Who cares about that?" Karim was offended. He'd been hoping for more about the sex, which hadn't been very exciting, but didn't want to lower himself by asking for more. "Any more fighting?"

"No, my lord."

"Not much of a fight."

"Sakai aren't fierce. That's why they're *'abdi*. Soft ears are the ones get twisted."

The young raja pulled his sarong over his head, preparing to sleep, images of the bound Sakai women replaying themselves in his imagination.

"Perhaps killing them, taking their children, isn't good," murmured the old man.

"*Nasip-lah,*" said the boy with sleepy irritation. The old man was going to talk about God. "Hey, their fate." He paused briefly, trying to think of a way to shut the old man up about God without saying so. You shouldn't tell people, even slaves, not to talk about God. "You think you could have done it if God wanted you not to? God is great. I'm going to sleep."

But the Nazarenes, the white peoples, defy God. The old man knew better than to continue the conversation aloud. But, as usual, he also knew it was pointless to try sleep; most nights his sleep was restless, punctuated by vague fears and evil violent dreams. *Maybe our actions defy God too, without our knowing. Doom will fall on all of us then, the doom no one can resist, says the Quran, doom from the Lord God of the Ascending Stairways.*

And my lord wouldn't want to hear this part, no fighting, no derring-do, but the story burns on in my mind like a fire smoldering in chaff. When the time had come to give the little girl to the Javanese salesman, he hadn't done it; had moved the hard tip of his finger across the soft lower lid of her eyes, one after the other, wiping away the moisture of her tears, gently and tenderly, puzzled by his actions and his confused ugly feelings. She pressed the calloused side of his hand against her wet cheek. He had not touched anyone that way before. She never took his hand again, nor did he ever touch her. But he kept her.

I gave her a good name, Fatima, and raised her like my own child. She entered the embrace of Islam, was almost like a member of the family, quite pretty in her dark-skinned Sakai way. I thought maybe she would find a Malay boy, a hunchback, say, or a retard, who'd marry her. Then her kids could be Malay, and everything would work out. That happens, though most Sakai slaves die childless, so we always have to buy or catch more because normal people don't want to marry little dark jungle females, and we're not about to let male Sakai have sex with normal women.

Time passed. When milord's uncle saw how pretty she was, he claimed her. She wept and wept as the raja's men dragged her away from me, laughing. A few months later, while her new owner was talking with his brother, she was sitting quietly, legs modestly folded beneath her as she'd learned, eyes lowered in submission, thinking nothing, waiting to be used. The brother ordered her to light his cigarette. While she did, he touched her soft cheek with his knuckles.

"Pretty, for a Sakai bitch," he said casually.

The raja's wife overheard. That afternoon she ordered her slaves to bring Fatima to her quarters. They stripped the girl naked and tied her facedown over a mortar. I know how that goes. The princess took a rattan cane as thick as my thumb and began to beat her, on and on and on, the girl screaming, first for mercy and then just screaming with no mind left, just a fog of pain, blood spattering the princess now from every blow. The blood dribbled through the bamboo floor slats, blotching the hardpacked bare brown clay underneath the house, trickling turgidly down the pale gray house poles. A bunch of villagers gathered, listening to the screaming, patting their chests in amazement and saying "Wah!"

The little crowd attracted the attention of a Sikh constable working for the White People. He looked at the blood collecting in little puddles underneath the house, listened to the noises, no screaming now, just groans, though you could still hear the whish-crack of the cane and the princess's grunt at each stroke, hn . . . hn . . . hn . . . hn . . . hn.

The constable politely requested a meeting with the raja, who received him with equal politeness. Formal language. What was going on? "Just a bit of jealousy among the ladies." Man to man. Seems to be a lot of blood? "They're preparing chickens for my dinner." The constable was too courteous to pursue his inquiries; it was, after all a matter of Malay custom, and the White People had a policy of not interfering with Malay custom. Still, two or three days later, to avoid any possible hassle, the raja's men took the half-conscious girl out to the swamps by the river and, after raping her once or twice, clubbed her to death and left her for maggots and crocodiles.

The world's a tough place.

What Rasping Means to Rasps

> *Kukur apa kepada kukur? Nyiur yang binasa*
> You think rasps care that they rasp? It's the coconuts that suffer.
>
> —Brown (1989:57, Dentan tr.)

Bangsal dihulu kerapatan	The forest canopy upriver is thick.
Sayang durian gugur bunganya	Alas, durian flowers ripen and fall.
Sesal dahulu pendapatan	Regret beforehand can be useful.
Sesal kemudian apa gunanya?	Regret afterwards? What's the point?

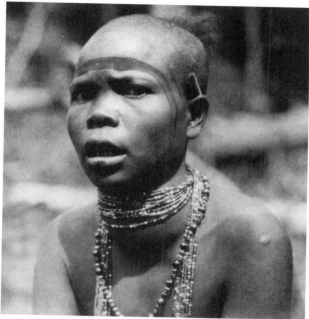

The Face of Terror. A photographer from the Field Museum in Chicago took this picture of a mnaleeh, nubile young woman, in the years between the two world wars (cf. illustration in Skeat and Blagden 1906, II:61). You can't see in a still picture the rapid jerky eye movements that European observers noted and that Malays said made people look "like wild deer tied to a post." You can see this continual wide-eyed jerkiness in the eyes of another mnaleeh in a missionary home movie, apparently from about the same time as this picture (Means n.d.). The eyes of other peoples who had suffered contact with Rawas were also "restless and glancing, as if ever on the alert" (Forbes 1885:241). Her neck is slightly swollen by a goiter caused by iodine deficiency. The bun in which she wears her hair may "be a relic of the earlier Malay and Siamese forms of hair dressing" (Williams-Hunt 1952:41): terror and glamour go together. That's part of what social psychologists mean when they talk about "identification with the oppressor/aggressor." Photo no. 46908 in "Central Sakai" [= Semai] collection at the Field Museum of Natural History, Chicago.

Traditional Malay *pantun* (Quatrain)

Listen if you can stand to.
Union with the Friend means not being what you've been,
being instead silence . . .

—From Rumi rubai (quatrain) #597 (Moyne and Barks 1986:31)

The news of her death had been a slap across his face: abrupt hurt, sudden but familiar pain without time to shield himself. Briefly he had held his hands tightly against the sides of his forehead, as if trying to keep his skull from cracking open, but not feeling anything, really, just vague disorientation. *Since then, I remember Fatima, often, always. A person dies, is buried, he's done with this borrowed world; the people who love him give thanks to God that he's had the good luck to escape. But an 'abdi is friendless, lives but isn't alive, is dead before she dies. 'Abdi take pleasure helping each other torment newcomers. They must have tormented Fatima before this boy's aunt killed her. The world's a tough place.*

I didn't kill anybody for that, didn't say anything to anybody, just licked up my own spit like the hamba *I am. Something else, too, I remember. How that Sakai female, hanging upside down, waiting to die, she must have known she was going to die, how she covered her bleeding privates with her dirty little hand. We'd all seen them, been inside them. She was just a stupid Sakai slut, everybody knows they fuck each other all the time like dogs, no rules, so why did she do that? Malays and Sakai have the same black hair, but their hearts are different, is that true? How would a naked fucked-over Sakai slut know shame?*

Still, chickens and ducks are rajas in their own pens, why not Sakai in theirs? You see them in town, they're like mousedeer in a clearing, eyes darting back and forth at every noise. But maybe in the jungle they're different, like they're at home there. Elephants have hearts, but bugs have hearts too. . . . Maybe they have a primitive culture, even a real language. Maybe they even forget about us sometimes, like toads under a half-coconut shell, forgetting the world.

But we're still here. No escaping us. Mousedeer forget the snare, but the snare still waits for the mousedeer. Maybe we should just say, "Other fields, other grasshoppers," the way Malay serfs do, and leave Sakai alone. Doesn't seem to do the local Malays any harm to do that. They still take Sakai land and trees when they feel like it, and the Sakai just fade off into the jungle.

Anyhow, since then, for me the sewing's over, the thread is broken. I'm an old man. Nothing. Dust. Now the dragon is a worm, doing battle only in his sleep, flabby halfway erections. I've got nothing but my skin and bones—a rotten privy board, rotted by the sun, softened by the rain. Bait's all gone, hook lost, line slipped out of my hands. If you find out at the end of a trip that you've gone astray, you can go back and start again. But at the end of a life?

Nakhoda tried to shake off his deepening depression by an act of will. *What's one person to another anyway? Nothing. Dust. We all suffer alone, Sakai or Malays. And, in the long run, isn't what milord calls "domestication" good for Sakai? It's not against religion to turn pagans into 'abdi. They can eat rice and tapioca instead of snakes and monkeys. They can cover their nakedness. And they find the comfort of Islam, of God the Merciful, the Compassionate.*

He looked at the face of the sleeping Karim, also called Compassionate—
a child becoming a thorn—and grimaced. *But we enslave local Malays too,
though we call them "freemen." They're Muslims like us. For them to become one
with us is water mixing with water to become one stream; but most Sakai slaves
are jetsam on the banks, even the ones who enter the embrace of Islam and have
Malay kids. We didn't do it for Islam. We enslaved them just because it was easy
to do, and that's what we did.* Alah bisa oleh biasa, *take poison all the time and
you get used to it.*

*God is compassionate, and we were not. God is merciful, and we were not.
"Done for God" excuses nothing. Anyway, I'm not a man of God, though I love
God with all my being. He is my Friend, but I am not his messenger. If imams
and religious teachers sin, how much more sinful must a layman like me be?
What ocean has no waves? All Uncle Croc can be is who he is: if crocodiles try to
squat, they break their tails.* He smiled slightly, then shuddered.

*In my soul I always knew Sakai were human and didn't care, knew they were
human and enjoyed treating them like animals* because *they were human. I am
nothing. I am dust. I've come undone.*

*All I can hope for is the Friend's love. All we can hope is that He loves us. All
we can hope for is His love.*

> Remember, even though I've done terrible things,
> I can still see the whole world in your face.

*All things endure in God. I am sick with desire for God, Whose love is a spring,
a river: let me submerge. I want to plunge into that burning Sun, that cool water, where catamites turned pirates turned slavers turned wreckage, where even
Sakai slaves, become One. The Sun, the Sun. Oh God, I want to dissolve.*

He stands up slowly, knees creaking, goes to the door and opens it,
heedless of *hantu* demons and bad air, the smell of dampness everywhere,
the rain falling in slanting lines through the seething dark:

> Don't give me back to my old companions.
> No friend but you. Inside you
> I rest from wanting. Don't let me
> be that selfishness again.

"Friend," he says. "Friend," he repeats, softly, feeling the pressure of un-
shed tears building behind his eyes. Then choking, weeping, he turns his
face up, wet and shining: "How can I say what You are with Your Light?"

In the tall hissing sedge on the riverbank, death lies chilly and sluggish
but stirring, a patch of green-black scales glinting dull silver as a gap in
the clouds lets the moon through for a moment, mercury spilled in dark
mud. Then clouds annihilate the gap, darkness returns, and Nakhoda remembers or hears:

Escape.
Walk out like someone suddenly born into color.
Do it now
You're covered with thick cloud.
Slide out the side. Die,
and be quiet. Quietness is the surest sign
that you've died.
Your old life was a frantic running
from silence.

The speechless full moon
comes out now.

In the silence, he does not feel the unseen rain or see the bright moon through the heavy cumulus clouds. But he feels the immensity of the onyx river, a dragon uncoiled in the darkness that covers the earth, its head in the Indian Ocean where White People's slave ships plied the Straits of Malacca in his youth, its body curving the length of Perak State, its tail lost in the dark eastern mountains where he had hunted Sakai. He thinks he hears the splash of a crocodile sinking into the glossy black waters.

For a moment
it reaches out waking
then gutters
again in the dark—
the mind of an old man
the flame
of a lamp burning out (Schelling 1991:16)

Escape

This is how the narrator, soother of sorrows, would finish.

The tale ends here. Some say Nakhoda slit his jugular, some that he died before he died, drowned in the Radiance of the Divine Love that's closer than your jugular. Who knows what happens then? *Tidak jadi apa,* no matter. God the Compassionate takes all in the end.

Dunia ini pinjampinjaman;   This world is just a thing we borrow;
Akhirat untuk zamanzaman.   Eternity sees no tomorrow.

3

Responding to Terror: Intellectually, Emotionally, Spiritually

How tiny it is, what we struggle with;
what struggles with us, how immense it is;
let us, as other things do,
be so overwhelmed by the great storm
that we become diffuse and nameless.

—From Rainer Maria Rilke, *Der Schauende* (Bly 1981:104)

A STATE OF EXCESSIVE VIOLENCE

[T]he state that Hobbes dreamt of was one which had the semblance of peace, order, openness and stability, when in fact it was one where power was absolute, centralised and personalised. The hidden dimension of Hobbes' theory of the centralised State was the culture of fear and paranoia that would develop should such a model actually come into existence. Today we see that such a model has come into being in contemporary Malaysia. (Noor 1999)

Slaving showed Semai they couldn't protect themselves or their children from unpredictable assault by overwhelmingly powerful impersonal enemies. The psychologese phrase "learned helplessness" refers to the sense of generalized powerlessness that follows suffering uncontrollable traumas like this. Abused wives and battered children often manifest "learned helplessness":

A person need not actually experience repeated [uncontrollable] events in order for them to produce [learned] helplessness. All that is needed is for the

65

person to expect that events will be uncontrollable. . . . This expectation may come from a variety of sources besides induction: for instance, observation of others, cultural stereotypes, specific information. (Peterson, Maier, and Seligman 1993:147)

The great French sociologist Émile Durkheim argues that a people's theology expresses their social situation. The Semai social situation involved raids by slavers from Hinduized states that often represented themselves to their subjects as embodiments of violence:

[T]he feudal era was characterised by public and highly visual displays of power. Power was not understood in abstract, conceptualized terms: one had to show that one possessed power, and this indeed became an obligation in itself. . . . Malay rajas indulged in local traditional pastimes like immersing their enemies in boiling oil, impaling them on stakes or having them lick red-hot steel. (Noor 2002:115, 116)

On a theological level, this feudal economy of excessive violence, to use Farish A. Noor's phrase, manifested itself by equating the state with Hindu thunder Gods, especially Siva the Destroyer, Who occupied "the place of honour in the Malay peninsula. . . . Merged with the Vedic god, Rudra . . . surrounded by demigods and spirits" (Devahuti 1965:70). Most west Malaysian temples were to these annihilating gods (Devahuti 1965:71). There, until quite recently, "some Malays paid homage to SIVA under his sinister aspect of KALA, the destroyer of life" (Danaraj 1964:9). These gods survive among old rural Malays as the Demon Raja and Spectre Huntsman, deities Who may also descend from "The Lord," as Semai call their thundersquall God. This chapter suggests that these deities involve a theology that displays and reinforces a sense of terrorized helplessness learned from the experience of slaving, slavery, and general cruelty.

The coastal states of medieval Malaysia looked to India for inspiration. Even the Malay word for "west" comes from the Sanskrit word for "India." But when the states turned toward their hinterlands,

Buddhist rulers as well as Hindu princes frequently identified themselves as agents or reincarnations of the ancient storm god . . . representing kingly authority and power. (Cady 1964:37–38)

The founders of dynasties named themselves after Siva the Destroyer, whose lingams (ithyphallic steles) dotted the landscape, whose destructive power brought fear and death to those who resisted state power. For a thousand years, before the arrival of Islam and the British, these rulers demonstrated their power by killing and slaving, creating a "culture of state terror" (Hoskins 1996:3). You can't blame Malaysian state terrorism on Indian religions, though. Indigenous Malaysian statelets also had political and religious traditions like those of pre-Aryan India. The state and the slavers who served its rulers were the real Dark Destroyers. Gods simply manifested their immoderate power, in which individual and state violence fed back into each other.

The idea that rationalized and justified those states was of a political power independent of the people who wield it, like electricity or gravity. Without countervailing power, the intelligent response for stateless people on the margins was to flee or surrender. The resulting social relations worked like a protection racket or abusive patriarchy, in which subordinates "often feel bound to those they serve through misplaced gratitude for a 'protection' that is mostly only a withholding of abuse" (Card 1996:7). The Semai response to the slaver state, their general deference to Malay culture, for example, makes sense in these terms. As long as state penetration of the hills was only sporadic, by slave raids and kidnapping, a pervasive nonviolence was adaptive: flight, not confrontation, and, when flight was impossible, surrender. For terrorist power of this sort is no more controllable by the governed than is parental abuse by children. The question of legitimacy does not arise. This power is horror-story stuff: a "violation of the borders, an electrical storm, a thing of damps and shocks and visions" (Straub 2004:288). The traditional Semai idea of God gives such power a menacing shape.

Slaving has been over for almost a century now, though occasional rapes, sporadic beatings, and constant humiliation remain. Even in the 1960s, when I first met Semai, only a few old people personally remembered the raids and kidnappings, though everyone talked about them. (They never talked about how it felt. Semai don't do that, usually.) Today, the Malaysian state has become bourgeois, not piratical. Bureaucrats take your land and trees, not your children—at least not literally, though they may take the kids away to boarding school for indoctrination in non-Semai culture.

For Semai who live in easily accessible areas, especially in Perak, God has also undergone embourgeoisment. As Jnaang, "Lord" or "Grandparent," this ungendered deity is mild mannered, restrained, decorous, and somewhat remote. But for a century, while Semai were reconstructing their past as the string of victories recounted in the Praak Sangkiil epic, the theology of Nkuu', "The Lord," kept the trauma of slaving alive. No victories there. In other Austroasiatic languages, His Name refers to the vicious Southeast Asian sun bear, so awesome to Semai that they do not use that word for the bear itself but prefer a version of the Malay word for "bear" as a euphemism.

This chapter falls into two main sections. The first tries to evoke how traditional Semai experienced thundersqualls, the "natural symbol" of Divine power. The second involves what theologians call "hermeneutics" and "exegesis," treating Semai religion as an original and compelling way of dealing with the violence that troubles all peoples. I tried to re-create and interpret this experience in a couple of other publications in 2002 and use some of the same language here but without the extensive ethnographic documentation and scholarly references that you can find there.

MEET GOD

Though in many of its aspects this visible world seems formed in love, the invisible spheres were formed in fright. (Melville 1989:182)

If you believe in God at all, you probably imagine a citified desert deity: Yaweh, the Trinity, Allah. You don't think of a God Who condones slaving. Take a minute and imagine *that* God. No God the Compassionate here, no innocent ignored Jesus telling you not to hurt children. This is the God of the Dark. This is a God for people whose children are stolen, over and over again, for sale to arrogant child abusers; a God for people whose more powerful neighbors have no more compunction about killing them than about killing ants. God the embodiment of slavers and the slaver state. The Beast God. You wouldn't like Him.

Come, look into this darkness with me, the way Semai seem to look into the immense overhanging implacable shadows, rich with pointless recurrent menace and pain. In that darkness, perhaps we can begin to appreciate what Semai seem to have created by love: in the depths of that darkness, defiant mockery; in the maelstrom of that violence, peace.

The Squall

[F]orgotten time crops up suddenly and condenses into a flash of lightning an operation that, if it were thought out, would involve bringing together the two opposite terms but, on account of that flash, is discharged like thunder. The time of abjection is double: a time of oblivion and thunder, of veiled infinity and the moment when revelation bursts forth. (Kristeva 1982:8–9)

Here I know storms already and am turbulent as the sea
I extend out from myself and fall back into myself
and slough myself off and am all alone
in the great storm. (from Rainer Maria Rilke, *Vorgefühl* [Bly 1981:78])

Black as oil smoke, thunderheads appear seaward of the settlement on the Teiw Tluup, sliding toward it, spreading into flat menacing darkness that swallows the sky. Chilly unsettling breezes snake through the wet overheated air, not as definite as breezes; the clammy touch of something inexorable, approaching. People gather up their children, throw the coals on their hearth out the door to counteract the deadly magical cold, some say; so that the wind won't fan the flames to a conflagration and burn the house down, say others. Householders huddle in little clumps under their houses, children clinging to adults, trying to warm themselves by the coals, listening to the assault-rifle clatter of the relentlessly oncoming rain. Here it comes. No stopping it. No place to run and hide. It's really dark and cold now.

Suddenly the squall hits, like a waterfall, hard to stand up in it, let alone see your way. Great shuddering rolls of thunder alternate with tomtomming monochromatic explosions of brightness that illuminate nothing, just blind your eyes. In the jungle the rip and crash of lightning, followed by the crescendoing slow screech and *snap!* of wood fibers splintering, tearing away from each other, as an immense wind-stricken rain forest giant totters, heels over, ripping away the lianas and rattans that bind it to the lesser trees around it, and falls, pulling down to destruction the smaller trees entangled with it, crushing everything—little trees, houses, people—in the path of its dying fall.

Standing under their houses for protection from falling trees, adults *-srngòòh* children, teach them fear. A mother puts her child's hands over its eyes or over its ears to block out the thunder and lightning, saying, Fear! Fear! *Sng'òòh! Sng'òòh!* Grown-ups urge little girls to make the "blood sacrifice," slash their shins, and throw the mixture of blood and water into the storm. ("Why don't *you* do it?" asks snubnosed perky nine-year-old Wa' Prankuup, refusing.) A man tears out a tuft of his hair, rushes into the whirling rain to club the tuft with a pestle, crying, "Ow ow ow ow," as if he himself were being clubbed. A young man with a spear rushes out from under his house into the storm, just a blur of violence seen through sheets of pounding rain, stabbing, stabbing, stabbing with his spear, then suddenly slumps and returns, dragging his spear behind him. (*What's he doing?* He's scared. *But what's he fighting?* Wind.)

Imagine, lurking above the scudding clouds, an enormously powerful, squalid monster obsessed by recurrent ungovernable rages; a hulking, dripping horror, immense, loud, insensate; angry and cruel, mindlessly cruel; ludicrously depraved and stupid, very very stupid; a grotesque, graceless, stupid lover of punishments and death. He's black, we know. He's black, black slashed with some violently opposed color, scarlet or dead white, a slash of desire and insane rage across a dark background of bleak cruelty and death. Nkuu', the Lord. God of Thunder. God of Darkness.

As the storm rages, people shout incantations to it, to the Lord and his younger brother Pnoos, Wind. Semai visualize the Lord as a mammoth black animal, ghastly black, a Malayan sunbear, a giant pigtailed macaque, leaf monkey, or siamang with a huge throat pouch that ululates, *uuuUUUUUuuu,* or swells and releases quickly: BUU! When He suddenly raises His huge arms in the stereotyped macabre threat gesture of the demons Semai call *janii'* or *nyanii',* bolt lightning explodes, say Tluup River people; when he licks his ungainly fingers, sheet lightning. He descends to smash trees and houses, just to appall and terrorize humankind. His enormous ugly back gleams silver in the rain, like a water-slick cliff. Thunderstones—ancient stone adzes—are the coconuts He throws or the bullets He shoots. He is what a feral person would be like, unsocialized, graceless, bereft of self-control. Offering diluted blood or pounding one's hair and crying out in pain are to fool Him, people say; He paints His face with the blood or relishes the pain, because He imagines the hurt is horrible; His desire to hurt makes Him stupid; His stupidity makes him desire to hurt; in stories about Him, wanting to hurt, He hurts Himself.

Imagine Him riding the thundersquall, invisible in the stormclouds but *felt,* looming, lowering, huge, enraged, implacable above the tender tiny almost naked people, faces streaked with rain, wet tousled hair, hiding under their flimsy houses.

The Floodwaters Are Loosed

> Things fall apart; the centre cannot hold;
> Mere anarchy is loosed upon the world,
> The blood-dimmed tide is loosed, and everywhere
> The ceremony of innocence is drowned
>
> —From W. B. Yeats, *The Second Coming* (Rosenthal 1962:91)

After five or ten minutes the cloudburst weakens to a hard rain falling. Water dribbles and drools off each leaf in the rain forest, trickling into the river, now thickly brown with runoff, flecked with foam, huge glistening black uprooted trees whirling downstream; and the river rises and rises, devouring its banks, menacing the land, threatening to undermine all stability.

Then, Semai say, the earth may crack open releasing cold black subterranean waters, different from floodwaters, inundating people who have broken the rules of proper behavior. On this great chilly upwelling the ghastly Folk Beneath the Earth erupt into the settlement: the malevolent black horned Dragon, all its cold-blooded cold-eyed "children"/avatars, the crocodile, the regal python, the giant monitor lizard, sweeping everything human before them into icy oblivion. Time, perhaps, in the final subduction of everything firm and familiar to scream, but no point to it; no more point than the screams of Vietnamese thrown out of chuttering helicopters at 5,000 feet to fall and fall and fall; no one to scream to for help, or compassion, or mercy; just a shriek; no hope; just terror and revulsion and dissolution; just noise, meaningless shrillness strangled to silence by the upheaving mud and water. Human dreams gone all to smash, hope and love drained down into the chilly abysses beneath the earth, nothing familiar or beloved remaining, just gluey desolation, devoid of humanity or meaning, nothing left but a slough of sullen thick sucking mud, reddish-grayish, slimy. Then only silence, except for the dull patter of the pale gray rain and the shhhhh of the dying wind, and finally no sound at all.

It's happened, Semai say. This is not just "a story of the old people." It happened at the hot springs in upriver Sungkeey in Perak State, near Jeram Kawan, people told me in 1991, as their parents had told another anthropologist over a half century earlier. You don't forget the collapse of the very earth on which people walk. Many generations ago, the story goes, people there wounded a pig-tailed macaque. Instead of letting it go, as people usually free animals wounded but not killed, they dressed it up like a person and, a man standing behind it holding its small black hands stretched out as if crucified, bounced it around as if it were a human being, dancing.

Semai do that, or used to. In 1962 I watched Pl'iinhsfather do it. He was a young man from Mncaak, where I worked all four times I went to Malaysia. Young men, *litaaw*, do reckless stupid things on impulse, say Semai. On a pilgrimage we were making with a ritual expert to the barrow that marked the grave of a local spirit, Pl'iinh, grinning widely, did to a wounded leaf monkey the same thing the Jeram Kawan people had done in "days of old," *manah ntvvm*. Pl'iinh released the monkey afterward, having broken the membrane that keeps "the people with tails" (a name for animals and *nyanii'* demons) segregated from the human world. He had mocked what the leaf monkey was, its integrity as a creature, and changed it into what it should never have been, a mock person, just as demons take human form to devour and destroy humans. We couldn't kill it after defiling it that way, let alone eat it.

We pilgrims escaped. But in the Sungkeey hills that time long ago, a great storm came, the earth split open beneath the feet of the people who mocked the macaque, their houses breaking down collapsing falling in, their world pulling apart at the center, nothing solid or familiar left, nothing to hold on to, no toehold, no love, just falling whirling sinking, the water sucking everything under, nothing left but fear like a great wind and the black subterranean floods pouring from the depths of the earth, and in the underwater dimness the gigantic cold dragon writhing upward toward the gray light to destroy them all. Then silence, settling like dust under the tarnished pewter sky.

The menace is real, permanent. Everyone knows this story, has always known it. This is what happens when you break the rules. See?

The Air Like Blood: *Nyamp*

When atmospheric conditions are just right, a little before sunset and just after a heavy downpour, the heat of the dying day sucks the moisture from the ground, and the rays of the setting sun refract through air already as warm and wet as blood, coloring it reddish or greenish yellow. On the Tluup River in the 1960s, at these times people would stop talking, stop whatever they were doing, and go quietly into their houses to sit in anxious silence while the sun melted and collapsed, spreading its bloody afterglow over the western sky, and the violent greens of the primeval rain forest that hemmed in the settlements darkened to greenish-black, fuming with the swirling discolored mist that rose from the flesh-temperature ground, until finally twilight purged the evil blood colors from the air.

At such times, people said, even more than at ordinary sunrise and sunset, demons roamed the earth, scenting blood. Morning mist or dense fog that blur your vision are is also dangerous, penetrating your forehead where your head soul lives and making you dizzy, *-lwiik*, and nauseated, as if you were about to faint or go into possession trance. Rainbows are arcs of blood thrown up by demons or their Lord or by the tiger that embodies demonic power, said one man, although personally he thought they were caused by sunlight passing through rain.

What Semai Say about the Lord

> Sometimes I think there is naught beyond. But 'tis enough. . . . outrageous strength, with an inscrutable malice sinewing it. . . . That intangible malignity which has been from the beginning. . . . All that most maddens and torments; all that stirs up the lees of things; all truth with malice in it; all that cracks the sinews and cakes the brain; all the subtle demonisms of life and thought . . . no self-esteem, and no veneration. And by those negations, considered along with the affirmative fact of his prodigious bulk and power, you can best form to yourself the truest, though not the most exhilarating conception of what the most exalted potency is. (Melville 1989:155, 173, 307)

The Lord and his younger brother Pnoos, Wind, live in the dark *rahuu'* area of the sky along with ordinary clouds, beneath the blue limit of the atmosphere. The Lord has "wives," the way human adepts and hunters have demon wives, running dogs really, hunting people down for him to butcher. A "wife" in this sense is a demon erotically attracted to a hunter whom she helps hunt down and kill game. Most of the Lord's wives appear in the human world as birds, sandpipers, and water wagtails, for example, birds that appear just before a storm hits. Hunting and sex ally in Semai thought, as they also do among the peoples of the West.

The "blood sacrifice" part of Semai storm rituals has received a good deal of scholarly attention focused on the "mockery of animals" of the sort Pl'iinh did in 1962. Semai say that people, if they are not careful, may violate the natural order, in which entities of different kinds must not be conflated. The violations may be of cosmic (cognitive) order, by mixing immiscible things together; or of the social order, by disrespect or incest; or of the personal order, by loss of self-control. A few involve sympathetic or contagious magic. This failure to observe the rules may *-trlaac*, "cause chaos," bringing on floods, thundersqualls, and landslips.

Together with the mysterious little people of the forest called Ludat, the Lord taught people how to become *-halaa'*, supernaturally adept, especially at curing the diseases He and His demons cause. The word *brhalaa'*, have such power, may come from Sanskrit: a Javanese variant means "false god" (Gonda 1952:42).

In a Waar River story of how Humans (as Semai call themselves) achieved this power, Ludat and the Lord give shamanic melodies to the Humans in return for headbands made of eaglewood barkcloth, the softest and whitest kind Semai make. The two demiurges told the Humans to go home and hold shamanic ceremonies, singing the melodies. They would then come to help the people. Ludat went straight home to Mount Magical Lore. He hung up his headband. It mutated into magical plants, as happens often in Semai stories: the cosmos is not stable or fixed, and things are often not what they seem to be.

The Humans also settled with the Lord, giving Him a barkcloth turban. The Lord went back to Dark-Cloud. But the headband turned into an eyeless snake, a species that makes traditional Semai pat their chests and say "Wah" in awe; handling it, *-trlaac*, brings on a thundersquall. The Lord, throwing a hissy, as He often does, then also turned His beads into a snake and ripped off His loincloth, which became a flycatcher with a long white tail. So Human adepts can now evoke Nkuu', Ludat, and their demonic minions.

This story, in which people fool the Lord and He behaves stupidly, illustrates Semai contempt for violent stupidity. Despite the fear and guilt manifest in the Semai response to storms, the rituals are not entirely placatory. Along the Waar River in 1991, for example, antistorm exhortations reminded Nkuu' how "Raman's father" shat up and down Nkuu's back; no one in the settlement remembered the story or who "Raman" was, but they knew the eternal shame might make the monster god flee. Long ago, asked by a priest-anthropologist why they burnt bits of roof thatch during storms, Semai apparently told him "to burn the Lord's arse."

For Semai despise the Lord as well as fear Him. They tell funny stories about Him, like this Tluup cautionary tale for children:

> *Snguup* [= "visual impairment"] trees bear sticky round edible fruit about an inch across. The sap can blind your eyes. You should suck out the inside without breaking the fruit open. One day Bah Luuc, Nkuu's youngest brother, was using the red-orange juice of a dye tree to paint his face. The Lord asked his little brother, "What fruit you using?"
>
> "*Sngòò*'," answered Bah Luuc, punning as Semai often do. He lied.
>
> But the Lord heard him wrong anyway. The monster climbed the *snguup* tree and took five fruits, for himself and his family. He handed them out to everyone. The others all stored theirs away, but the Lord broke his open right away, and the juice struck his eyes, blinding him. He's still blind [= unable to make distinctions]. That's why you should open the fruit with your teeth, a little at a time.

Many stories depict God as prey to His own ludicrously clumsy lust, punished often by painful indignities inflicted on His penis. Other stories elaborate on His gross stupidity: how, carrying His child to the grave wrapped in a mat, He dropped the corpse without noticing it and buried just the mat. (You can still see the corpse, a mountain along the Teiw R'eiis where I stayed in 1992; the Public Works Department was mining it for the gravel to build the North-South superhighway that smashed through Semai settlements and orchards along the river.) Semai tell how, when God tried to seduce His little brother's wife by disguising His own penis as a phallic toadstool, the little brother set the toadstool on fire.

In summary: in tales about the Lord, the vicious ludicrous monster plays out a "dark circus . . . of ferocity, fear and hunger, simple stupidity and desire" (Koja 1991:335). For this great dark monster slashed with ghastly brightness, this vast violent horror that overwhelms all human fragile intimate love, this evil ferocious destroyer God is so grotesquely stupid, so much a prey to his own passions, as to be a figure of fun; He knows that and is ashamed.

TAKING SEMAI SERIOUSLY

Muggletonian beliefs were logical, powerful in their symbolic operation and have only been held to be ridiculous because the Muggletonians were losers and because their faith was professed by poor enthusiasts and not by scholars, bishops or successful evangelists. (Thompson 1993:79)

Some Misconceptions

[Semai and related peoples'] animism and naturalism stands to be the oldest religion known to human kind, with most indigenous communities throughout the world sharing this world view and morality, of the importance of establishing and maintaining balanced and harmonious relations with the natural order of plants and animals, based on mutual coexistence and respect. This religion dates back to at least 25,000 years, the date linked to the oldest record of living human history. Also included in this early period of human history are the Andamanese of India, the Aeta of the Philippines, the Pygmy Hadza of Africa and the Australian aborigines. (Razha 1995:2)

Needham's statements [1967] about natural symbols, expressed as they are in an impressive language, end in a mere reiteration of what is descriptively known and do nothing to explain why the bizarre ritual beliefs and practices of [Malaysian indigenes] should take the forms that they do. (Freeman 1968:354)

What a bad press Semai religion gets! Razha, a sympathetic and sensitive Malay observer, attempting to defend the religion of Malaysian indigenes from contemptuous Islamicization, argues that it is a fossil, an interpretation he elsewhere explicitly rejects (1995:10). Many anthropologists say things like that about people like Semai. Nothing original here: all those *Naturvölker* believe that kind of foolishness, "mumbo jumbo stuff," as a high Malaysian government official called it at a conference on Malaysian indigenous peoples in 1993.

And Freeman, who (unlike Razha) has no personal experience with this religion, finds it not a "primitive" universal but so weird as to require the mechanical application of paleo-Freudian analysis to make sense of it. Semai religion seems to have suffered the fate of Muggletonianism—and, I suspect, for the same reasons. It's hard to get respect when your audience has decided you are "losers."

My argument so far has been that thundersqualls constitute a natural symbol, an "objective correlative" in T. S. Eliot's phrase, a concrete metaphorical representation of the emotional impact of slaver state violence. That is not all it does, of course, as Freeman remarks; symbols are multivalent, and people use them in many ways. But Freemaniacal analyses, which seek to explain particular cultural events by reference to universal human psychic factors, are bootless without considering the local history that forged the symbols such analyses seek to understand.

Bizarrerie, I suspect, exists mostly in the mind of the beholder. After a couple of months on the Teiw Tluup in 1962, I have to say that the storm rituals *felt* reasonable during storms. One of the great failures of ethnography has been its inability to convey how humdrum the "exotic" is in context. Semai religion is more Dionysian than the desacralized Apollonian protestantism that tints and tidies white Australian lives like Freeman's or my American one, but that fact is a clue, not a quality. The other sense of "bizarre" is of singularity or oddness, qualities that Semai religion lacks, as the rest of this section seeks to demonstrate.

There a couple of things you need to keep in mind. Non-Semai have experiences like the ones I'll be talking about, more than you might realize if you keep thinking of Semai as different from yourself. Read *Moby Dick*, for example:

> [T]here was another thought or rather vague, nameless horror . . . which at times by its intensity completely overpowered all the rest; and yet so mystical and well-nigh ineffable was it, that I almost despair of putting it in comprehensible form. . . . But how can I hope to explain myself here; and yet in some dim, random way, explain myself I must, else all these chapters might be naught. . . .
> Let us try. But in a matter like this, subtlety appeals to subtlety, and without imagination no man can follow another into these halls. And though, doubtless, some at least of the imaginative impressions about to be presented may have been shared by most men, yet few perhaps were entirely conscious of them at the time, and therefore may not be able to recall them now. (Melville 1989:176, 180)

And remember that material poverty doesn't make people stupider or weirder than anyone else:

> We see them only as eccentrics or as survivors . . . locked into a religiose fantasy-world; they are quaint historical fossils. . . . But where social or political assumptions or enquiries into value are at issue, then the answer must be very much more complex.
> The danger is that we should confuse the reputability of beliefs, and the reputability of those who professed them, with depth or shallowness. (Thompson 1993:107, 108)

Rather than treating Semai as generalized primitives in mindless harmony with Nature or as eccentrics whose belief system is a form of psychopathology, let's assume that Semai are not terminally different from other people. That seems pretty safe. They certainly didn't and don't seem different to me. All people have pretty much the same biology and live on the same planet, Semai and ourselves. The congeries of ideas I'll talk about must serve, like other ideas, to make sense of the world we all live in. So the questions to ask are the following: What's this about, this sense that nothing is secure? That not being self-controlled and ritually tidy may collapse one's world into chaos, meaninglessness, a state darker than total darkness? In what experience would these themes stand out: an immanent menace of violent death and being snatched away from everything loving and nurturing, the ever-present threat of transformation of what's apparently safe and secure into horrors violent and obscene, the implosive collapse of the tidy familiar world into formlessness and something far worse than utter destruction? And why would you joke around about that?

Let's look then first at Semai theology as an intellectual system that uses the natural symbol of the thundersquall and the social construction of its God to make sense out of human experience. We needn't *assume* any harmony with nature on the basis of an imaginary primitivity, nor do we need to *begin* by trying to imagine the psychological darknesses that, like theologies elsewhere, Semai theology may subserve. Let's deal with it this way: first as a metaphysics, then as an expression of psychodynamics, and finally as a set of ideas that may clarify some puzzling aspects of Semai behavior.

Chaos: the Intellectual Problem

It is thus not lack of cleanliness or health that causes abjection but what disturbs identity, system, order. What does not respect borders, positions, rules. . . . Essentially different from "uncanniness," more violent, too . . . nothing is familiar, not even the shadow of a memory. (Kristeva 1982:4, 5)

One way to come at the metaphysics of Semai theology is to glance at similar human intellectual constructs. There are at least three well-documented accounts of human experience that seem akin. Two, from Asia, are benign: reentry into primal chaos (*hundun*) in philosophical Daoism and immolation into God the Friend in Sufism, which the protagonist contemplates in chapter 2. One, from Europe, is terrifying, the invasion of the "abject" in Lacanian psychoanalysis. All three accounts struggle with the inadequacy of language, as I've struggled here, and find themselves thereby forced into the kind of poetic imagery that Semai mythology seems to represent. I'm not expert in any of the three traditions, sadly. But since the aim is to get ideas useful for understanding immanent horror in Semai life (rather than to deploy extant ideas without misinterpreting them), my ignorance may not be as crippling as it would be at other tasks.

The beginning and end in Daoism is *hundun*, primal chaos, the Void, the Uncarved Block, in which all distinctions are as yet unborn and into which all collapse. Philosophers and storytellers sometimes imagine *hundun* as a featureless egg, perhaps like the one Semai antistorm prayers urge Nkuu' to break. Like Semai, Daoists think the tidiness and order that people impose on the world is fragile, a thin overlay, often deceptive. But Daoists reject the tidiness, which they argue rests on endlessly dichotomizing false dualisms that obscure the dark *qing*, "essence," the "deepest place, the core where blue or green turns black" (DiPiero 1990:19), the reality from which everything arises and into which everything must eventually sink. Better to grasp the Void, not to struggle to impose your own false order on the world. Act but don't worry about the bottom line, don't expect or strive for results. Do what comes next, without imagining the consequences, which will rarely be what you intend.

In Sufism the dominant metaphor is the dissolution of the illusory ego, through love, into God the Beloved. Something like this passionate love affair occurs in the Semai relationship with demonic "wives," discussed in the next chapter. To commune with these wives, Semai adepts go into a possession trance in which, except for great adepts, they lose conscious awareness of their surroundings. But the stages of going into a trance are like those people report in the paroxysms of fear that overtake some people during thundersqualls: disorientation and dizziness (-*lwiik*), followed by surrendering to demonic love. The same process, keyed by the terror that Semai feel at the sight of spilt human blood, can lead to *blnuul bhiib*, "blood intoxication," in the grips of which normally nonviolent and timid people may commit horrors.

The shadow of terror darkens Semai theology and demonology. Approaching the realms of chaos and the demonic triggers symptoms classically associated with panic disorders: "cognitions associated with social, psychological, or physical disaster . . . dizziness, fear of . . . losing control" (Norton, Harrison, Hauch, and Rhodes 1985:216, 219). Of a hundred people subjected to sustained trauma—and what is the kidnapping of one's child by child abusers, the experience of slave raiding, or existence as a slave but sustained trauma?—fifteen to twenty-five will develop recurrent panic disorders, obsessively fear recurrence of the trauma, have recurrent nightmares, and so on. And it's easy to transmit this sort of fear to children as Semai still consciously did in the 1990s. The connection between fear and demonic possession shows up in the notion that the God of Thunder taught Semai shamanism.

There's a parallel here. Rape victims abused as children tend to blame themselves for being raped, as traditional Semai blamed themselves, or their children, for *trlaac* acts that could destroy the order on which the safety of everything depends. And, also like traditional Semai, victims of abuse tended to feel that the world is unsafe . . . that no one is ever available to help when it is needed . . . that bad things will always happen and that they will happen to you regardless of your behavior. (Arata 1999:73)

There's a similar kind of what I'm calling "surrender" in traditional Semai theology, like the "learned helplessness" of battered wives and children.

At first glance, this surrender to cosmic violence and its social analogue suggests a "longing to be released from the human struggle to master fate and to be swept away by it instead, the wish to be carried along by events instead of controlling them through mind" (Kronman 1995:164). The rage of Nkuu' could stem from the destruction of featureless primal chaos, of *hundun*, by intellection. That's what people say about the rage of similar and perhaps cognate Hindu gods. As in Daoism and Sufism, so perhaps in Semai theology, abandoning reason and the ego could be a appropriate response. God and the Dragon, after all, embody chaos. When the abused and battered self disappears, abusers and batterers become impotent. Instead of the American panacea of "self-empowerment," try accepting disempowerment.

But Semai fear the darkness in which all distinctions crumble. They walk a "narrow path," said Bah Tony in 1991. They order their lives with counterphobic rules and guidelines that prevent cosmic collapse. Chapter 5 is about the rules. Here it's only important to remark that violating these rules can—doesn't always but *can*—unleash the horrors of thundersquall and flood. Abandoning intellectual and social order undermines the stability of the cosmos: not a consummation Semai seek. The emphasis on fear and caution requires not trying to impose your will on the cosmos but accepting your cosmic helplessness, taking each day as it comes and not trying for particular results. These mundane attitudes toward the world fit with the proto–Hindu-Buddhist-Taoist praxis of which Semai theology may be an outgrowth or precursor (Dentan 2002a, 2002b).

The terror, though, seems more like the experience of "abjection" that Kristeva describes. At the risk of turning the playful elaborate intellectual exercise that makes French intellectuals fun to read into plodding prosaic Anglo-Saxon positivism, let me try to summarize her view of the evolution of the self from a state much like the Daoist Void. Newborn babies, she claims, cannot distinguish between self and other, "other" in this construction being especially the mother. The first step in the differentiation of the self involves "throwing away" (= "abjection") that neonatal unity: "the child who can represent his mother's absence is emblematic of the untraumatized subject, of subjectivity that works" (Morgenstern 1997:109). Abjection thus differs from repression, which requires a functioning ego. External events that recall that primal sense of oneness and its destruction constitute the experience of abjection that underlies much

Western horror literature. (That's why I sometimes use horror-story language in this book). The Semai sense of being terrified and overwhelmed seems to resemble Kristeva's psychoanalytic construct. Terror seems to threaten the Semai self. Traumatized, Semai subjectivity doesn't work. The Lord may lead his victims into the (m)other.

Or (and I'll return to this possibility) the process may (also?) run something like this. The Lord stands for the terrors of the slaver state and its minions, of unbridled greedy stupid viciousness. Surrender, acceptance, promises release from those terrors. You may even stop being who you are and become as much like the dominant people as you can: "identification with the oppressor." Battered children often do that—become batterers. All one needs to do is to embrace the Beast, as one embraces one's demon wife. Isn't that what "open slavery" of the Malay sort requires, in which kidnapped children become part of the slave owner's household and subaltern people like Semai are recruited to kidnap Semai children?

The ethnomusicologist Charles Keil suggests that Daoist, Sufi, and Hindu invocations of primal oneness are intellectual attempts to return to a prestate, preclass society, the same way Christian peasant revolutionaries tried to invent an imagined "primitive Christianity." The difference in the evaluation of the experience we're talking about may come from the fact that Semai are trying to preserve such a society in the face of brutal incursions by people from a class-ridden state. Each people, in this interpretation, imagines dissolving in the other: the statists into the bliss of equality, the egalitarians into the horror of enslavement.

Living with Fear by Telling Horror Stories

Horror, at least in its artistic presentations, can be a comfort. And, like any agent of enlightenment, it may even confer—if briefly—a sense of power, wisdom, and transcendence. . . . I am invigorated by the sense of having rung the ear-shattering changes of harrowing horror; I've got another bad one under my belt that will serve to bolster my nerves for whatever shocking days and nights are to come; I have, in a phrase, *an expanded capacity for fear.* . . . The only comfort is to accept it, live in it. . . . If you can maintain this constant sense of doom, you may be spared the pain of foolish hopes and their impending demolishment.

But we can't maintain it; only a saint of doom could. Hope leaks into our lives by way of spreading cracks we always meant to repair but never did. (Oddly enough, when the cracks yawn their widest, and the promised deluge comes at last, it is not hope at all that finally breaks through and drowns us.) (Brite 1996:xi, xii, xvii)

Semai tell horror stories to their children (Dentan 2001a), stories about people who steal children to enslave them or gouge out their eyes to sell to the rich, stories of the Lord. They want to scare the children, continue telling the stories, smiling even when the kids are wailing or in tears. Children need to learn that the world hates children, will hurt them if it can: steal them, enslave them, mutilate them. It's the same lesson American parents increasingly teach their own children, with a good deal less historical justification: *stranger danger, beware attractive people who are not what they seem, trust no one.* Fear, both peoples believe, is good for kids. Teach your children fear because you love them, not because you enjoy their fear, their clinging to you, or your power to make them fear and cling. That's what both peoples claim.

And, no doubt, as the horror writer Poppy Z. Brite said previously, the stories try to make fear familiar and tolerable, under control:

> [R]etelling manifests an attempt to gain mastery over elusive or defeating histories. . . . If the . . . narrative marks the undesirable return of an unforgettable past, it also attempts to theorize and control this phenomenon. (Morgenstern 1997:101–2)

Semai cautionary tales prepare people for the terror of uncontrollable nature, for the horror of having one's children stolen for the convenience and prurient pleasure of powerful abusive others. They protect people from facile stupid optimism. It's interesting that Brite's essay, like Kristevan theory and Semai theology, calls on the metaphor of *drowning* in such horrors.

Helpless Surrender Makes Humor of Horror

> How can one react to . . . a tragic situation wholly outside of anyone's control . . . a bizarre comedy of errors in which the sadness of the situation was overshadowed by a general sense of incapacitation. . . . [?] The laughter was not a response to the suffering . . . but a commentary on the absurdity of a situation over which no one has control. . . . Life can be so absurd in its repetitive tragedies that people laugh themselves into a dream. In the dream world of laughter lies a space of momentary escape. (Harms 2004–2005:14–15)

But if Semai find chaos fearsome and horrible, what makes them laugh at God? At chaos? It doesn't seem to be nervous laughter. These are belly laughs. Some of the stories seemed pretty funny to me, too, though they are a little slapstick for my taste and involve more castration and shitting on victims than I'm comfortable with. I cast around for similar stories. Like these.

South American natives tell stories about shamans and jaguars in which these two frightening and powerful figures seem stupid and ineffectual, like the precisely similar *halaa'* tiger figures in Semai myths (Clastres

1989). The transformation of the one into the other is just a matter of changing metaphors for frightfulness. In egalitarian societies, even the most fearsome creatures have feet of clay, argues Clastres; laughter cuts them down to size. In their relations with the state, Semai, like other Malaysian indigenes, resist by deceiving the agents of the state, making fools of them and (later) laughing at them, by playing to the Malay idea that "Sakai" are too stupid to cooperate with "development" schemes or by feigning the stupidity that they know the agents expect.

But the laughter isn't just lighthearted or instrumental. People laugh at horrors, as film directors like George Romero and pop novelists like Stephen King know and as Shakespeare knew. The absurd shows up in unexpected and sometimes quite horrible places. I talked about this laughter with my colleague Tom Lechner, an expert on surrender in theory and practice (e.g., 2003). He had just had a long conversation with a man who had been abused as a little boy. The details of the abuse were so hideous and so elaborate that the man could not talk about them without laughing. Experiences that make you laugh may not be, you know, fun.

The kind of cosmic collapse Semai mythology envisions, the mutation of the familiar into obscenity and horror, involves a collapse of meaning. Such collapses often follow terror. The literature on "posttraumatic stress syndrome" consistently describes traumatic terror "as a force that is not meaningfully experienced" (Morgenstern 1997:103). Retelling their terror in a safe environment, traumatized people can experience this meaninglessness as a sort of joke, part of the general existential slipperiness of meaning. Every life has days on which everything seems to go wrong and nothing works out, days on which you start muttering to yourself, "I don't *believe* this." At some point on those days, some new unexpected glitch may finally just make you throw up your hands and laugh. The eruption of laughter, thinks Leta Dentan, comes when you realize that nothing you want to happen is happening and there's nothing at all you can do about it. It is the laughter of powerlessness and of surrender to powerlessness, a laughter that expresses the relief that surrender brings. Surrender, remember, is a reasonable response to the sort of power the Lord embodies.

And making a joke of meaningless horror brings it into line with the general silliness of human life. The great Daoist Zhuangzi, like many postmodernists, delights in dialogues that start out rationally and disintegrate into gibberish. Maybe, among other things, the wordplay that pervades Semai stories expresses the constant slippage of meaning and definition, how hard it is to hold the slippery shifting world in our word nets.

In short, Semai laughter in response to these stories seems to do three things. It pulls down the pretensions of powerful evil beings to the level of normal human overweening in an egalitarian society that scorns bluster. The brutal envoys of the slaver state and cosmic destruction are also ridiculous and stupid. Chuckling is an appropriate response to the irruption of the absurdities that trash any tidy human scheme of meaning that pretends to universality. And laughing expresses the relief that comes from giving up in the face of the world's resistance to definition and control.

Implications

> There looms, within abjection, one of those violent, dark revolts of being, directed against a threat that seems to emanate from exorbitant outside, ejected beyond the scope of the possible, the tolerable, the thinkable. . . . It is not the white expanse or slack boredom of repression, not the translations and transformations of desire that wrench bodies, nights, and discourse. . . . A weight of meaninglessness, about which there is nothing insignificant, and which crushes me. On the edge of non-existence and hallucination, a reality that, if I acknowledge it, annihilates me. There, abject and abjection are my safeguards. The primers of my culture. (Kristeva 1982:1, 2)

> History as trauma belongs to no one, yet it is also shared. . . . Trauma confuses the relationship between inside and outside, the psyche and the social, the present and the past . . . (Morgenstern 1997:111)

What experiences does this theology describe? Think again about what slaving feels like. It violates everything safe and familiar, making home into horror, and smashes the boundaries of the body (with krisses, clubs, spears), loosing the blood-dimmed tide of chaos, destruction, and death. Think about having your children stolen by professional child abusers, not just once but as part of the routine of raising kids. Panic and terror overwhelm love, leaving only loss, transforming the world, mangling the self. Think about being beaten and raped as a matter of course. Think about being a slave: life in the Valley of the Shadow of Death; the old self assaulted, kicked aside, punished, seduced into mutating, transforming itself into the assailant, "identifying with the oppressor" as the psychoanalysts say; self-hatred, hopelessness, powerlessness, cringing before casual contempt and indifference. What would you do? How would you feel? What would the world look like to you then? How do you think abused children *feel*? Intellectually, Semai theology may demystify the violence of a state based on terror.

For those who doubt the identification of God with mindless violence, it is worth remembering that the Semai Lord embodies shamanic power and stupidly gave shamanic power to human adepts, *maay halaa'*. The notion of the implications of being *halaa'* survived the conversion of peoples related to Semai in Trengganu, in northeast peninsular Malaysia; for example,

> [M]y next-door neighbor was almost strangled to death by her mistakenly jealous husband. . . . Her husband is a classic example of *Angin Hala*, the Wind of the Weretiger, which makes one quick to anger and heedless of its consequences. *Angin Hala* is difficult to express unless its possessor is a fighter or occupies a social position that allows him to vent his aggression without fear of retaliation. (Laderman 1994:191)

This set of possibilities suggests an interpretation for *blnuul bhiib*, the "blood intoxication" that characterizes the otherwise peaceful Semai, during which they sometimes kill outsiders compulsively and mercilessly (Dentan 1995). Someone, say you yourself, gets cut; hot red blood flowers on tan skin; you see yourself spilling out, the tender limits of your body breached. Panic overwhelms you, the terror for which Semai have no word, something a lot worse than mere "fear," *snng'òòh*, something that lies in the pit of your stomach like nausea, that makes you dizzy, something like the sensation that precedes contact with *nyanii'* demons and *halaa'* power. Horror of violence, yes, but particularly of the violation and loss of self that shows when blood flows; spilled blood, the "natural sign," recalls being overwhelmed by violence from without, warm life flowing away, demonic coolness replacing it. Then, maybe, there's a takeover by the violent Other, the slaving raging non-Semai, obsessively present in double consciousness, not really an "Other" because it's too primal to objectify, because "it has only one quality of the object—that of being opposed to" (Kristeva 1982:1); not really slaver-demon-Lord-dragon but like them, like them; still, fundamentally, it might be a collapse of the self that Semai maintain by self-control, by rituals, by institutions that resolve conflict. Maybe, in "blood intoxication," Semai *become* the terror that haunts their darkness, that fills them with revulsion even as they compulsively enact it. They say it's like demonic possession. Maybe, then, there is no normal person left when that happens; so that, in recall, it feels as if it was something else who did it; because it was.

Although Semai, like anyone else, have the capacity to be violent, they normally regard violence with the sort of frightened distaste they have for the Lord. Although they treat representatives of the Malay-run state with deference, they play outrageously on Malay stereotypes of Orang Asli, mocking power for their own amusement, running the risk of reprisal as they run the risk of *trlaac* by mocking the animals that are the physical manifestation of demons. The notion that God is a stupid, incontinent, violent dupe is (inadvertently, I suspect) a balance to the Malay notion that an omniscient, merciful, and loving Allah legitimates Malay hegemony, the state, and its child-stealing agents.

Malays say that their first sultan made a deal with his people that they would give him absolute loyalty as long as he never embarrassed them, no matter what the reason might be. In 1998, the outpouring of Malay popular protest following accusations that Anwar Ibrahim, the erstwhile deputy prime minister, committed promiscuous buggery was not from concern that the accusations might be true but from outrage that anyone would make them public. (The government launched new accusations of sodomy against Anwar in 2008 [Khoo 2008a, 2008b]). Traditional Semai saw not just the polite and rule-governed society of the Malay rulers and their British allies/rivals/conquerors but its dark and bloody underside. The Lord would not be a bad embodiment of that: a defender of values (order, decency, intellectual tidiness) that Semai share with Malays but also a defender so corrupted by power as to be grotesque, ludicrous, and terrorizing (cf. Thompson 1993:110–11). God, like Anwar's accusers, breaks the rules that sustain his power.

And what an achievement this mockery of violence would be for any people! The West dramatizes the horror of violence, every night, on TV for recreation (interesting word) in the movies. But to dramatize its *stupidity* would undermine our *Schadenfreude*, our fascination with and secret enjoyment of other people's suffering. Instead of cruel and violent men bearing everything away, suppose they only made themselves look like imbeciles. This, I think, is the Semai way of thinking about violence. You cheat it. You lie to it. You laugh at it. I suspect their version is closer to what violence feels like than that of the West. It puts the Beast in view, without romanticizing.

4

✛

Transforming Demons by Love and Surrender

Be tender, subtle
To the mammals
With backbones
That branch.
There will come grief,
And an end to yearning, a turning
To liquid of muscle.
Be subtle, tender
To your double.

—Stan Rice, "Deadletter 5" (1995:17)

"**L**earned helplessness" is a background stress, not necessarily conscious, against which Semai experience plays out. It's part of the emotional landscape that Gregory Bateson calls the *ethos* of a culture (Bateson 1958:2, 32–33, 220; Worthman 1999:43). Against this background, other stresses, like thundersqualls, may be more frightening. Construed as a manifestation of the Lord's *hnalaa'* power, the terror, in turn, can resolve itself in a *surrender* that has the four marks of what William James (1997:402–4) calls "mystic states." These states are *indescribable*, partly because they involve obliterating the underlying categories that make words meaningful. In addition, they are *transient*: people recover in a few minutes or a few hours. Moreover, the person having the experience feels helpless:

[W]hen the characteristic sort of consciousness once has set in, the mystic feels as if his own will were in abeyance, and indeed sometimes as if he were grasped and held by a superior power. . . . [Mystic states] modify the inner life of the subject between the times of their recurrence. (403–4)

The sense of powerlessness may have something to do with the ego defenses of *dissociation* and *identification with the oppressor*. It may also involve a "sense of personal freedom that is derived primarily from a loss of self-control; this loss of self-control is achieved primarily through submission to external sources of control" (Pollock 1993:1472). Self-control pervades Semai social relations and is essential to peaceability. Trancing gives relief.

Finally, such states are *noetic*. That is, says James (1997),

mystical states seem to those who experience them to be also states of knowledge . . . unplumbed by discursive intellect. They are illuminations, revelations, all inarticulate though they remain; and as a rule they carry with them a curious sense of authority for after-time. (402–3)

Semai say they tricked God into giving them access to His *hnalaa'* power. *Duplicity* is the most widespread weapon of the weak. Children and slaves everywhere are notorious deceivers. On a psychological level, "identifying with the oppressor," aping the ways of the people (or demons) who treat them badly, allows oppressed people to participate vicariously in a sort of "virtual" power. And, as children and slaves know, *love* can transform the fear that powerlessness brings (cf. Dutton and Painter 1981; Edmondson 2001). Pentacostalism of this kind is one of the commonest religions of poor and powerless people everywhere. Don't knock it: it works for them, even in America (e.g., Kozol 1995).

This chapter discusses how Semai domesticated Divine terrorism and used it in the "after-time."

HUNTING AND LOVE, DEMONS AND LOVERS

The monstrous seismic dragon, the Thundersquall Lord, and His *hnalaa'* power may concretize Semai experience with the slave-raiding agents of the terrorist statelets that had taken Siva the Destroyer as their God: irresistible, unpredictable, mindlessly violent. No questions of legitimacy or consent here, no fine distinctions between "force" and "power," just violence and terrorism on the one hand and flight or submission on the other.

But Semai duped the monster Lord into giving them access to the shamanic power He embodies. Duplicity is central to the Semai idea of *srnloo'*, hunting down and killing, their central metaphor for violence. The access works this way: this God is God of Beasts; beasts have souls, which appear to people as demons, *nyanii'*. Usually demons just devour your soul and make you sick. Indeed, the word *nyanii'* may come from *-nya'nii'*, to be in pain or feel sick. After all, the Lord's power, which demons manifest, is the power to hurt, sicken, and terrorize. Semai say deliberate contact with demons can drown a person in what James calls a "mystic state" and anthropologists loosely call "possession trance."

Some Semai, especially men, seek out transformation, striving for connection with the fearsome demons, the strange angels of whom God is chief, a connection Semai phrase as love. The demons appear in dreams, seeking people strong and beautiful enough to be their lovers, spouses, parents, children, all the forms of lover. Although in the material world demons retain their fearsome or disgusting form, this deceptive dream semblance is usually a beautiful person of a sex opposite the dreamer's. In a dream, a particular demon gives its beloved an idiosyncratic summoning melody "because it loves his body." A person who accepts the melody becomes adept, *halaa'*, and the demon becomes a *guniik*, from an old Malay word for "concubine," which here means something like "familiar" or "spirit guide" but connotes erotic partnership. The notion of prowess and success as equal to or derived from a supernatural erotic mate is widespread in South Asia.

Semai hunters face more danger than American ones: some animals that are prey in the West are predators on Semai, hunters themselves. So hunting is more reciprocal, the power differential less stark, the power of animals more compelling. Eroticism enters Semai hunting with the hunting wife, the *knah srnloo'*, whom a hunter needs to seduce and beguile into helping him if he is to hope to *-srloo'*, stalk and kill, his prey. After a successful hunt, adepts need to bathe a successful hunter and his prey ritually, with fragrant plants and flowers, to restore his power, to lure his *knah srnloo'*, his familiar spirit, his luck, his hunting muse, back to him.

Both the rules that govern hunting on the one hand and relations between men and women on the other require ritual deception, concealing the desire to engage another creature violently or sexually. Hunting or trapping, you should avoid naming the prey. Mentioning the animal's real name could *-kree'* one's prey. The idea is that hearing its name would alert it, but the verb *-kree'* seems cognate with words that mean "harm," especially by piercing or stabbing: penetration. To alert your prey is to *-sa'see'*, make a mistake that prevents your obtaining a goal and leaves you frustrated and stressed out, vulnerable to accidents and disease. And that, people say explicitly, is to fall prey to *srnloo'*—the same way they say you would if a person had arranged to meet you and failed to do so, letting you down, disappointing you. That is, from being a predator, you have become prey. The concept is central in Semai social relationships. You'll see.

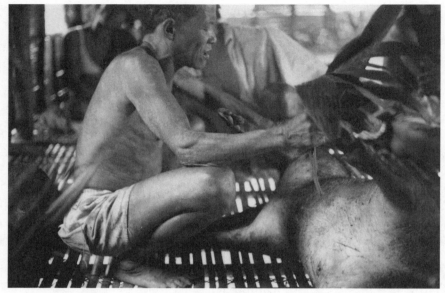

Tataa' Manah lures back a hunter's demon lover. The adept cools the dead boar with a shamanic whisk of stiff fan-palm leaves to neutralize the destructive supernatural heat that killing causes, which weakens the bond of love between the hunter (who in this case is a different person from the shaman). He prays for supernatural coolness of all kinds, a Ing'aap, a Ing'oop, a sngiid. The ceremony soothes the spiritual inflammation associated with redness, fire, blood, and violence. River Waar, spring 1992. Photograph by R. K. Dentan.

Likewise, in small Tluup River settlements in the 1960s, you had to -*muur* opposite sexed in-laws older than your spouse. They were *maay*, "other people," in the sense of being kinsmen distant enough that, if they weren't married to your kin, you could have sex with them. But you shouldn't speak their names, share food with them, or look at them, as opposed to your spouse's younger sibling or younger sibling's spouse, your *mnaay* (modified *maay*), with whom you had a joking relationship that often involved coarse erotic horseplay. You hid your lust and disrespect with your elders. The rules bore more heavily on relations of younger men with older women than on anyone else.

Equating predator and prey with lovers isn't that unusual. Brian Luke (1998) argues that in the West hunting is explicitly a metaphor for the erotized power relationship between men (hunters, lady-killers) and women (quarry, sex objects). He concludes that "[h]unting and predatory heterosexuality are both structured as institutions of men's sexualized dominance" (644). But in traditional Tluup Semai society in the early 1960s, men and women seemed fairly equal, so much so that, coming from patriarchal America, I found the frank cheerful sexuality of the women intimidating. Semai men my age confided to me that they were sometimes intimidated too, especially at the start of their sexual careers. To the degree there was any "predatory heterosexuality," it seemed to cut both ways, like the relationship between predator and prey in Semai hunting. People had fun once they got into a sexual relationship, but initiating one took a good deal of circumspection. Love was psychologically as dangerous as hunting was physically. You'll see.

The congruence between hunting and trancing shows up in the imbalance of men and women in both activities. No rule prevents women's hunting or trancing. If there were such a rule, there would be no way to enforce it. But few women hunt and not many trance. "Their bodies aren't strong enough" runs the usual explanation. Thus, few Semai women need—and few have—the male equivalent of *knah srnloo'*, although midwives rely on the Seven Original Midwives for spiritual help.

People said women adepts were more adept than men but couldn't explain why. I suspect it's because they're rarer. I never had a chance to talk with any of the woman adepts I heard about. In a couple of cases, women said they'd rejected the dream advances of potential *guniik*, refusing to sing the demonic melodies because demonic possession is too hard on one's body, too physically debilitating. The question of gender propriety did not arise: even back in 1962, there was a Semai woman who had married another Semai woman, herself assuming the male role, wearing a loincloth and carrying a blowpipe; and another with two husbands. Mildly interesting, people indicated, but "their business." Homophobia is new to Semai and focuses on male transvestism.

The idea that supernatural power is a kind of wife is ancient, embodied in Hindu-Malay *sakti*, although Semai do not use that word. The convergence of ideas may reflect a common origin for both religions (see chapter 3). But among humankind the metaphor is more pervasive than that (e.g., Wilson 1988:174–76). For example, in an essay called *Altra Ego*, "the feminine other self," the Nobelist Joseph Brodsky (1997:81–95) discusses the relationship between poetry and heterosexual love, between Muse and poet. His discussion is convoluted and subtle. He talks for example about the question of whether women poets have a feminine Muse, a question I think Semai would answer no. The gender of the participants seems important in America, where sex and gender raise troubling and contested issues. But my impression was that Semai had to think it over before they answered questions about the gender of spirit guides. The Semai idea focuses on love, desire, not gender or sexual orientation.

Gender in the Semai construction of demonic love may go like this: the general femininity of demonic familiars (quarry) presupposes the masculinity of adepts (hunters). The masculinity of adepts presupposes the femininity of demonic lovers. So the model for demonic love is spirit concubine and male adept or hunter. In fact, though, the love goes beyond human love, precedes it, Brodsky might say. It binds mystic union and erotic sensuality. That interlock is crucial to understanding. Transforming love was the important thing, the obsession with the other, especially at night. Not just as a metaphor, though it is a metaphor: a woman rejected a man on the Tluup; he dreamt of her, as rejected Semai lovers do; in his dream she gave him a melody; now, he said, her other lover had her body, but he had her head soul, her *ruwaay*. But, of course, what he really had, at least as far as I could see, was not her soul but his yearning for her, his love, his otherwise unsatisfied desire.

Trying to understand Semai séances, it's important not to think of eating and being eaten (and thus feeding), hunting and being hunted, making love and making dead only as opposites. They are opposites, but by virtue of being joined as opposites, each implies the other. And it is, I think, this equivalence of opposites that gives Semai séances their power as the ultimate resolution of desire and of the violence Semai think immanent in ungratified desire. Séances bring together fleshly human men-hunters/prey-lovers with spiritual animal women-hunters/prey-lovers. Each surrenders to the other, for the moment abandoning deception. All ungratified yearnings—for love, for power, for honesty, for trust, to hurt, to be cherished, to surrender, to eat, to be fed—dissolve into each other. Love and terror, serenity and violence, merge.

One Semai term for the experience comes from an Arabic-Malay word, *asyik,* that refers both to erotic transports and to the ecstatic Sufi dissolution of the self into God, an erotized surrender like that of an abused child to parent or slave master. This connection with Sufism may be historical but obscured by later events, like the connection between Christian and Sufi mysticism. In any case, I hope that the Sufi and related Christian poetry in this book helps illuminate Semai experience, as it illuminates that of those who follow Abrahamic tradition.

The relationship between adept and familiar is more than erotic. Among people related to Semai demons are also ancestors, in a sense. Indeed, one group call their version of the same demons *moyang,* grandmothers. Yet, as familiars, Semai say they are also adopted children who need protection and nurturance. Not as strange as it may seem at first: some Americans in love call each other "Baby," and spouses may call each other "Mom" or "Dad."

This transformation by surrender of violence and cruelty, pain and terror, into all the forms of love is the topic of this chapter. It fulfills the constant yearning that is—or was—so salient in the life of Malaysian indigenes.

DEMONOLOGY

Humans, *sn'ooy*, and demons, *nyanii'*, are both people, *maay*. Each normally lives in its own dimension, its own "country" *lngrii'*, as Semai say. This term means "settlement" or "hereditary territory" among some Perak Semai (Juli, Williams-Hunt, and Dentan 2008). Demons have no size in human dimensions. They appear to humans as invisible swarms or as beasts, especially mammals or insects, or in other material semblances, like beautiful young humans or terrifying old ones.

As spirits, demons attack and devour human souls, *ruwaay* and *klook*, causing disease and death. Humans appear to demons only as souls but attack them in the flesh, as hunters. Together the two peoples constitute the whirling totality of eater and eaten, the wheel of predation, forever-changing places as humans kill and devour the flesh of the animals, which are the materializations of demons, and demons kill and devour the souls, which are the spiritualizations of humans. This is the grinding wheel on which both people are crucified, endlessly returning cruelty for cruelty, terror for terror, death for death. A Semai anthropologist summarizes how his people think about demons:

> Nyanii' [demons] are said to regard humans as prey. . . . People sicken if nyanii' capture their *ruwaay* [head souls]. Soon, if the nyanii' kill the *ruwaay*, the afflicted people die. Still, there are some which cooperate with people, called *guniik*. People who control *guniik* are called *halaa'*, adepts. A *guniik* obeys all an *halaa''s* orders, e.g., searches for human *ruwaay* that have strayed or been captured by nyanii', searching for lost objects or lost people. Also a *gunii* will follow the orders of a *halaa'* to commit violence, e.g., making someone insane or sick or the like.
>
> Nyanii' are believed to have a world which is opposite to the human one. For example, nighttime for humans seems like daytime to nyanii'. Moreover, nyanii' perceptions are opposite to human ones. If humans perceive someone as fat, nyanii' perceive him or her as skinny.
>
> Except for *halaa'*, people cannot normally see nyanii', except now and then when a nyanii' materializes in the form of a human, beast, etc. Nyanii' also cannot see people, just enfeebled human *klook* [another soul] or *ruwaay*. (Juli Edo 1990:105–6)

The website that accompanies this book (http://www.rowmanlittlefield.com/isbn/0742553302) expands this discussion of demons, souls, and ghosts.

ADEPTS SEDUCED BY POWER

English usage has impoverished the ancient Roman understanding of the power Semai call *hnalaa'*. "Sacred" now implies good, "unspeakable" implies bad. There's no moral taint to the Latin. Advertising undermines the power of the ancient words: "terrible" does not suggest terror; "horrible" does not suggest the prickle of the hair as it rises on the nape of your neck. A tremendous mystery is not the *Mysterium Tremendum*—that before which people must tremble. So at first, it may seem hard to understand the Semai response to the unchecked power that thundersqualls and slave raids embody.

This power manifest in the chaos of the storm, in the heartless violence of slaving, is terrifying. But it is more than that. It is attractive, seductive. Slaves and battered children know that about brutal dominance. How wonderful that violent overwhelming power Semai stole from God must seem to people without secular power, to people who traditionally hid any ambition for fear the neighbors would badmouth them, to people who say that coercion makes its victims sicken and die.

In a hierarchical world, power is the dark underside of freedom. My freedom flourishes when you are my slave. The Marquis de Sade knew that. In feudal slavocratic Malaysia, slaves were a mark of prestige more than an economic resource. Class was everything.

Among Semai on the margins, who minimized hierarchy, age structures were the closest equivalent to class. The older you get, the closer you get to *hnalaa'* power, and the more respect you should get. The Semai word for "respect" is "fear," *snng'òòh*. The English word "fear" similarly did double duty for both concepts until Elizabethan times. Power works more slickly in America now because words obscure it: respect your parents, legitimate authorities, your body, the state. But all those "respects" mean "fear."

A Terrible Love: *N'asik*

> your lists of victims dear
> god like rows of sharp little teeth
> have made me crazy look. . . .
> lovely look we smile too this
> way look our blood touch us is
> it horrible? touch us

> —From "Becoming Somebody Else" (Williams 1972:39)

The great Semai transformation of fear into love occurs during shamanic ceremonies. This transformation happens after people accept demons as *guniik*, familiar-child-concubines. The precipitating event is when something goes wrong or threatens to, when someone falls sick or hopes to have a healthy baby but worries about it. Demons are—or threaten to be—involved.

The first treatment of demonic infection usually occurs at the patient's home. A person who is somewhat adept collects the infesting demon(s) in a shamanic whisk and squeezes them out between his palms. He stretches his arms through the gap between the flattened bamboo walls and the thatched roof of the patient's house, and with a loud CLAP releases them into the surrounding darkness, cursing them, and ordering, "Don't come back, don't cause a relapse."

More serious illness or communal misfortune requires a séance. By the 1960s, in most western Semai settlements in Perak state, few people in any settlement were willing to become adepts, to endure the incurable change that comes from consorting with demons or strange angels, in the imagination of Semai or American novelists:

> You cross the border once too often and you never get back. Never. No matter how much you want to, no matter how often or how plaintively you insist. . . . No more home; everything is here now, and this is the place you must stay. . . . You cannot live that way any more, your apparatus is gone, is changed forever. (Koja 1994:316)

And by the 1980s, the Malay government was determined to crush Semai religion and replace it with Islam. Conversion would transform Semai into Malays, augmenting and rationalizing Malay majority power. So by 1992, Semai were reluctant to let outsiders attend the séances that they still performed, and I stayed away, though I could hear the music in the night. And by the 1990s, in the lowlands, many settlements had no field-opening shamans to placate the Rice Soul and abandoned rice as a crop.

But traditional séances filled a profound need. The Lord, as the Shakers knew as late as the nineteenth century but the official post-Enlightenment West has forgotten, is Lord of the Dance (Devahuti 1965:71). Desperately alone and vulnerable in a violent evil shape-shifter cosmos, Tluup River Semai yearned for the love of the demons who devoured them, yearned to transform their demons into lovers or children or parents, yearned not only to partake of *hnalaa'* power but also to fly into the freedom of endless impossible nurturing selfless love. So sometimes they would hold séances and dance to host the demons, to give them a party, to seduce them and drown their own selves in loving-kindness for a while.

Probably the starkest version of this transformation, like the starkest version of the Lord, comes from Cba' Jnteer on the Tluup. Since 1962, when I visited there and it was still remote, the government has logged off the rain forest and "regrouped" the humans downstream to a desolate

place called Betau, where they can be more easily dominated and sur-
veilled. One of the two Semai murderers I talked with grew up there;
there he converted to Islam and "became Malay" before beating two little
boys and their nanny to death in 1992 (Dentan 2007). But thirty years earlier, the forests still stood, and humans there could commune with their
demon lovers.

The next part of this chapter is an attempt to tell you what happened in
that communion, as best I understood what they said happened, in a language that evokes their interpretation but that, since their ideas are unfamiliar to most readers, uses both their metaphors and metaphors English-
speaking readers are likely to recognize. It's hard to talk about demonic
possession from the demons' point of view. Demons don't live in our
three-dimensional spaces, so they don't fall into our word nets. You can't
tell, a lot of the time, whether they are singular or multiple, enormous or
tiny. The labels just don't apply outside the tidy rational world you and
Semai construct with words. Usually Semai don't name demons but use
bynames, the way Americans don't say that people died but that they
"passed on" or "were taken from us."

The language of demon songs is also hard for ordinary Semai to understand. The words are mostly Semai, with some Mon and Malay mixed
in. They convey some meaning, at least on an emotional level, but people
can't translate them the way they translate other words. The words are ar-
chaic, they say, "demon language" that accompanies the dream melodies
demonic familiars give their human lovers.

I use two type styles here: roman for Humans (Semai), italics for
demons. You need both points of view to understand what's happening.
When I talk about demons, I use English demon language, drawing heavily on entomology, the science of insects, because demons often appear as
insects, and a common byname for demons along the Waar River in the
upland Perak State is "bugs," *cee'*. You don't need to understand the words
any more than Semai do. All you need to get is the tone: something deeply
alien here, from dark cold places no human would normally want to enter:

> . . . the land of darkness and the shadow of death;
> A land of darkness, as darkness itself;
> and of the shadow of death, without any order,
> and where the light is as darkness. (Job 10:21–22)

Séance on the Teiw Tluup

"We must die because we have known them." Die
of the unbelievable flower of their smiles. Die
of their delicate hands. Die . . .

Let the boy praise the deadly ones
as they float high through the chambers
of the heart. From his flowering body
he sings to them:
unreachable! Oh, how alien they are.

. . . But the adult man
remains silent, shuddering. . . .
As the sailor remains silent, the older man,
and enduring horrors
leap about him as in rocking cages.
(from Rilke, "Man Muss Sterben Weil Man Sie Kennt" [Bly 1981:160], Dentan tr.)

About 5 P.M. Here's beautiful curly-headed Wa' Kyoh, sitting on her house ladder, little-girl wriggly still, but with breasts just beginning to swell. You have to look carefully to notice the swelling, but a couple of people with young sons have already talked marriage with stout intelligent 'Alang, who is Kyoh's mother and the wife of the adept Yangman. 'Alang has said politely it is too early for her little girl to join the life of *mnaleeh*, sexually ripe young women. Soon, though. Kyoh knows. So does crop-headed snub-nosed humorous Kuup, who's sitting one rung down on the ladder, watching Kyoh over her shoulder and smoking a big green stogie.

Kuup, a year or so younger, is Kyoh's best friend. They had a fight this morning. Kyoh was eating cookies at the house of her auntie, who's also Kuup's auntie. Kuup started to come up the house ladder, but Kyoh held the door closed against her until Kuup burst into tears and the auntie told Kyoh to let her in, and Kyoh did. Kuup just stood there, wailing, lost in the misery and rage that rejection and betrayal bring, and then clambered back down the ladder and slumped off home, ignoring Kyoh's pleas to come in.

A few minutes later, Kuup wandered back by the house, beating the ground with a stick, studiously not looking up. Kyoh and her auntie called "Come up!" the way you're supposed to whenever someone wanders by, but it took a lot of cajolery to get Kuup to sulk back upstairs. She still refused to enter, though she smiled at her auntie when her auntie smiled at her. She didn't look at Kyoh, though, and this was the first time since then that Kuup had acknowledged Kyoh's existence, by looking at her. The girls have learned to handle anger the way Semai grown-ups do, not like children, who Waar River Semai say are always barking and snapping at each other like dogs.

The settlement has been busy, men sitting in doorways carving ritual paraphernalia out of soft white *puleey* wood, women weaving the fragrant ornaments demons love. 'Alang, Kyoh's mother, has put on her orange-striped ornamental headband and face paint. She and her husband Yangman, the adept, are sturdy and broad beamed. Her headband is of the softest, whitest, best barkcloth, made of eaglewood, ornamented, full of fragrant little mint flowers. The face painting is beautiful too, though hers is conventional for her settlement, just a single stripe of white lime down her broad dark brown nose and two bars or crescents, one on each side of the nose, across her cheeks under her bright brown eyes. Younger people, *litaaw* or *mnaleeh*, invent patterns that set off their beauty, circles and helices made with lime, black charcoal or latex, and red-orange dyes.

In the old days, people made the dyes from the fruit of a large forest tree, *prah*. But then, about the time the slave raids were abating, the ancient people had begun to plant *sumbey*, which the Pale People brought from the Caribbean. You gather the red hairy fruits, crush them, and mix them with oil in half a coconut shell, stirring with a stick, and you get a dye that washing won't get out of your clothes, though it fades eventually. To get bright red lipstick to paint their faces with, some young women in the settlement sleep with the Chinese or Malay traders who visit the settlement once a month or so. Others condemn them for doing that.

The adults have been dressing up for the séance since the daylight began fading. Kyoh is excited. So is Kuup, whose mom is Kyoh's mom's best friend. Even the baby, two years old, seems excited. She wears only a necklace of sweet sedge rhizomes that keeps her from being weepy and whiney. Her mother gathered the rhizomes from a streambed, and her adept father prayed over them to make them effective.

'Alang moistens charcoal from the hearth with milk from her full breasts and begins to paint Kyoh's face with her finger. There is a special tool, *cnòòt*, which looks like an ornamental head comb with very short teeth, with which people can -*còòt*, make lines of dots the way Europeans use rubber stamps; but usually you use your fingers or a porcupine quill from the big species of porcupine, the same quills people wore through their nasal septa before British and Malay ridicule made them stop.

The baby, wanting to suckle, tries to get between her mother and Kyoh. Kyoh puts her fist on the toddler's forehead and pushes her away, not hard. The baby swats Kyoh. Kyoh says "Oooow" dramatically but does not hit back. The baby persists, jiggling 'Alang's arm. Finally, 'Alang slaps the baby lightly on the arm, and the baby hits her mother back as hard as she can, several times, on the shoulder. Kyoh begins to complain that she doesn't like the pattern her mother is making and gets some lime to make herself up. Alang rubs her shoulder: it "burns" where the toddler hit her, she says. She uses her fingers to wipe the little girl's gleeting nose.

When the baby interrupts Kyoh again, Kyoh grimaces and makes as if to scratch her face. Alang pretends to scratch Kyoh's. Kuup just watches, smoking her fat dark green cigar; her own mother has painted her face, and she is ready, anticipatory.

About 7 P.M. As the sun sets, darkness flows down the limestone cliffs across the valley from the settlement. The damp, cool air of the summits sinks down into the human houses. Shapes begin to dissolve, washed in wet shadows. Nothing has any distance or scale.

A light breeze blows, condensing drops of dew off the slick forest leaves. The blank bright green of the rain forest mutates slowly into the deep green-black color Chinese mystics call *qing* and associate with abyssal ocean depths and primordial (non)being. The gibbons' plaintive twilight hooting dies down. In the houses flicker small kerosene candles, much like those that Persian sea traders and slavers brought to Malaysia centuries ago, the candlelight showing through little chinks in the flattened bamboo or woven palm thatch walls, defining the realm of darkness without withstanding it. The early-night racketty insect chorus replaces the twilight chrrrr. The forest has become as impenetrable to human eyes as the minds of the things that live there are impenetrable to human minds. Night, night.

The moon occluded, dark fog rising from the cooling fecund earth. All light erased, every bit, every memory of it. Darkness darker than normal humans can imagine, darker than the absolute absence of light, lurid livid blackness. A sour smell of rotting wet vegetation, of ancient enduring horrors slowly decaying in the dark, rotting there since before time became an idea. The forest alive with death: chitinous hideous heads blind to light swaying restlessly on long thin necks, sensors relentlessly probing the cool night air for a faint whiff of menstrual or puerperal blood, warm, salty, savory, meaty, rich. Then, faintly, the intoxicating smell of the special fragrant plants assembled in the floral jrmun *ornament and the spirit palace wafts from the humans' longhouse into the flat darkness. In the strangler figs leaning out from the riverbank a rustle of feathers, a tiny shriek cut short. Movement of enormous shadows within the shadows, furious charcoal darkness stirring in its hidden places.*

The humans gather in the longhouse, supper over, stomachs full, comfortable; faces painted in beautiful patterns of black charcoal, white lime and scarlet lipstick, circles and dots and lines. Besides headbands and flowers, the men wear plaited licuala palm-leaf bands crossing their chests, looking like ancient Cambodian dancers but costumed in the leaves and flowers of the harmless poor, not the silks and golden bangles of their ancient Khmer rulers. Seven or eight women line the back wall of the dance floor, a few others along the sidewalls directly in front of them. The women along the wall warm up with their bamboo tubes, one in each hand, striking them against a sturdy horizontal floor joist, making hollow bell-like sounds. One tube, male, is long, deep voiced; the other shorter, higher, female.

Tuk tuk TOK. Tuk tuk TOK.

A dozen men line three walls; a handful of women and little naked children cluster around the door. A *baley* spirit palace covered with a whorl of fragrant flowers and slick wet sacred leaves sticks straight up between the bamboo slats of the floor like a ship's propeller; a *jrmun* floral spirit lure hangs by the wall to the right of the women with the bamboo stampers. Almost hairless with mange, a little gray dog, ribs protruding, licks up some spilled grains of rice off the split bamboo floor. The humans chat, giggle, occasionally spitting between the bamboo slats of the floor.

Substituting for Sibin, whose tuberculosis is making him queasy, Yangman the adept, Kyoh's father, puts on his costume over his loincloth: Sibin's bright red sarong, the prettiest in town. Yangman—compact, muscular, chocolate brown, short legged and round shouldered, broad of face and beam, with a lumpy nose and short tightly curled hair—clears his throat: "*Yeey* yey yeyyey *yeey* yey." He begins singing a few words of a traditional tune. Its intonation patterns recall the songs sung in ancient Cambodian courts as dancers performed the dances that called on the ancestors to protect the nation.

Heads up! Nictating membranes slide back, rage-filled red eyes flare open in the unbreakable darkness, and lustful blind eyes filmy dead white, without iris or pupil. Nostrils moist with expectation quiver at the faint beautiful fragrance, ancient dark longings stir; vibrissae, antennae, setae, wave and quiver restlessly; long muscular blue forked tongues flick rapidly, tasting the flowers in the warm wet breeze. Pushing and shoving, breathy hiss and squeak among the leafy branches, stridulation and susurration, click-click as elytrae spread open, whisper of unthinkable diaphanous wings beginning to beat the night air, faint chirps and stifled twittering, pattering and scuttling barely audible. Monstrous beasts slump languid and stupefied as waves of yearning souls, ruwaay *head souls and* klook *eye souls take flight, substanceless invisible ebony wings spread, swarming. Resurgent voluptuous inhuman power drenches the cooling night air.*

Tuk tuk TOK. tuk tuk TOK. tuk tuk TOK.

'Alang is a leader among the women pounding out the rhythm with the stampers. Her toddler, sitting on Kyoh's lap, calls to her, but 'Alang continues playing. The baby calls, "Mommy, mommy," again and again, getting red faced and squinchy eyed until 'Alang finally puts down her bamboo stampers and comes over. By now the toddler is screaming wordlessly, and when her mother comes near, the little girl tries to hit her again. Alang laughs, ignoring the blows, and takes the child off out of the way for a quick suckle, making the child scream even louder. She refuses to suck for a little while but finally collapses into her mother's warmth and love. Her father Yangman bends down and nuzzles the little girl.

'Alang says, half joking, "*Sirooy, sirooy,*" reminding him that paying too much indulgent attention to a young child, like saying its name, can attract the malevolent notice of demons.

Meanwhile, nubile boys and girls, *litaaw* and *mnaleeh*, lie back luxuriating in the companionable darkness, necks supported on floor joists rubbed smooth by bare feet, enjoying the feel of their muscles loosening after the day's swaddling heat and sweat and work; resilient after the day's-end dip in the river; strong again; relaxed; ready; waiting.

. . . faint sounds of humans moving; creaking as people shift positions on the springy bamboo slat floor; soft touch of human rubbing up against human, touching each other, inhaling each other's musky fragrance in the dark; whispers, smothered giggles, stifled exclamations; hard to sort out the fragrance of one's own body from the fragrance of the warm lubricious bodies all around, here and there one person's smooth muscular thigh intimately or indolently flung across another's stomach for the simple pleasure of physical contact, unobserved, slender bodies unfolding inside their sarongs, gentle fingers running across bare necks and calves, assignations being made in whispers, a hint of labial musk, a faint throb, slight pleasurable unimperative swelling in the groin, nothing urgent, just luxuriation, human and warm in a darkness about to become much cooler and more alien.

Because everyone knows what's coming now.

. . . *Membrane between the cosmos of endless darkness and the cosmos of blinding light stretching thinner, thinner, quivering with tension and desire, tearing open, the portal between the dimensions bursting open, the path forming. Hum of insectile wings, eager, eager, weaving a calling pattern, a rhythmic pulsating pattern that encompasses the warm fragrant intertwined human bodies, the smell of cooling damp humus and wet leaves, the whirring invisible primordial* nyanii' *winging unheard to the feast, foul as festering infections, beautiful as love itself, slippery and wet and cool with expectant desire.*

the women pounding the bamboo stampers against the floor joist, one in each hand, one long, one short. higher female *tuk!* lower male *TOK!*, tuk tuk TOK tuk tuk TOK, imperceptibly speeding up, Yangman the adept singing his melody to open the path, luring the terrible beloved, three hollow echoic notes reverberating, each woman's note resonating with the others.

Batu', a slim hard-muscled curly-haired *litaaw*, starts dancing, followed by Gdeem, another *litaaw* with a sharp sexy face, then Yangman himself with his *grnaar*, shamanic palm-leaf whisk, rustling in one hand. Feet together, left foot forward on the male beat, swiveling the torso, right hand across the body; feet together, left foot back, right foot forward, left hand swinging across the body, feet together, right foot back on the male beat. Gdeem and Batu' grab a third *litaaw* and drag him, laughing and protesting, into the central dance area, mock struggling, dancing. Gdeem takes Yangman's whisk and shakes it. After about five minutes the dancers take a break and drink water from the long green leaf-stoppered bamboo water tubes leaning against the wall.

Tuk tuk TOK; tuk tuk TOK; tuk tuk TOK.

About 8 P.M. Yangman gets the whisk back from Gdeem and rattles the stiff lanceolate leaves, then tucks the whisk into the back of his beautiful sarong. Soft-breasted sensual Srbun—big dark areolas, long brown nipples stiffly erect—puts magic leaves and flowers into a soup bowl full of supernatural cooling paste by the wall. Yangman moistens his whisk in the paste. The music stops briefly as the humans tie the door shut. "Come *on!*" says Yangman loudly, "There's lots of people here. Come on! Singers should take turns. People should be dancing." The women start playing, and Yangman begins singing again, singing of cool shade against the day's heating. He does not dance, but his little daughter Kyoh beats out the rhythm on the back of a flat winnowing basket, and the toddler claps her hands, moves her feet and makes singing noises, then tries to play with the stampers with which her mother is pounding out the beat. The dancers begin again, feet slapping the floor in unison, circling the hanging *jrmun* floral ornament in single file, an orderliness that at almost at once begins to decay.

*squeaking and chirping under the shshshshsh of unthinkable wings, tiny septic red eyes glistening, reeking with death and terror and love, perfect darkness making perfect light for them, scenting the fragrance of the flowers garlanding the ba-*ley *spirit palace, the fragrance of welcoming fearful human bodies; remembering, obsessively but never perfectly, the unseen damp safe place where thighs join pelvis in moist smooth soft darkness; remembering, obsessively but never perfectly, how unthinkably soft and smooth are the backs of human thighs; responding, answering; longing, yearning, as the adept's song yearns and longs; hungry. Here they come, the dark compulsive fearful fearsome powers, pouring over the meter-high walls, through the gap between walls and thatched roof in unseeable hordes, mouths blossoming like incredible flowers . . .*

They're here.

tuk tuk TOK! tuk tuk TOK! tuk tuk TOK!

Little Bah Cang, fifteen, claps in rhythm with the bamboo stampers. He is only a meter and a half tall, dark skinned, with a huge goiter that cants his thin sensitive face over to one side so that women won't sleep with him, except for slender Wa' Mas, a fidgety fourteen-year-old with a speech impediment that makes her squeak and sound stupid to other Semai; and she says nowadays, "Who would want to sleep with a black ugly person like that with that *thing*," gesturing *goiter* at her throat. But Cang is dancing now, clowning around, inventing complicated dance steps, joining half a dozen dancing *litaaw*; and, also dancing, Dadi, a sharp-nosed pretty *manang*, sterile woman, who sleeps with the Malay trader for lipstick or money and says she doesn't believe in demons, just enjoys the sensations dancing brings.

. . . human faces lost in the insistent throbbing of the bamboo stampers, bringing heartbeats and pumping blood into a single rhythm, time without end through the spinning inconceivable darknesses, nubile young men's bare feet slapping the bamboo slat floor in rhythm with the male beat, leg muscles tensing and releasing, eyes half closed, heads and torsos swiveling with each step, soft brains rocking rhythmically in swirling cerebrospinal fluid, nothing but whirl inside.

O do they feel it coming.

DON'T BE NERVOUS.

THIS IS LOVE.

huddled together chittering and squeaking in the baley, *a few still squirming invisibly up the charcoal and lime and turmeric painted spirit steps to the safety and darkness of the sleek deep green leaves, shrinking in dread from the terrible unreachable human warmth and the memory of light, lured by the fragrance of the beautiful flowers and the shining darkness, light to them, supernaturally cool as firefly luminescence; and by the beautiful fragrant lubricious human bodies in that luciferent* cngiis *darkness. Lulled, mesmerized, entranced by the green-black smell of the flowers and pendant leaves, the seductive demon-given melodies, the insistent rhythm the human females play, high female note, low male, tuktukTOK tuktukTOK, quivering with terror and menace and desire.*

DON'T BE NERVOUS.

THIS IS LOVE.

TuktukTOK tuktukTOK tuktukTOK.

Yangman sings a phrase, complex with meaning, and the women sing it back, simplified, contrapuntally. His voice is louder, theirs pitched higher as the dancers and rhythm speed up. Gdeem, who had paused to take his turn singing, resumes dancing. Heavy footed, the whirling dancers are bouncing off the resilient bamboo-slat floor, hands swinging as low as their knees with each rhythmic twist of their torsos. Yangman's consciousness -*lwiik*, reels. Dizzied, he stumbles. A muscular old man, Jraan, thin fringe of gray hair, supports Yangman, hands under his armpits, while Gdeem sprinkles the adept with cooling paste from his whisk. Yangman resumes dancing, Gdeem still asperging him.

. . . the humans invisible to each other in the dark, just vaguenesses, invisible to themselves, panting now, some gasping for breath, gagging, shaking their soft brains to the insistent beat, warm wet exhalant clogging their lungs, famishing their blood, pulpy pink cerebrum graying with oxygen loss, amygdalas and temporal lobes shut down, bright neurons in the frontal and parietal lobes winking out into mindless darkness; nausea rising like metallic-smelling syrupy blood; vertigo; giddiness, *lnwiik*; frisson of cool pleasurable revulsion

black mayflies gathering in their lace-winged multitudes fluttering into the coolness of the darkly luminous spirit palace rich with sweet pungencies whorled and mixed, cloud of dark passionate horrors like mosquito wrigglers in a shaded cool stagnant pond, unhuman beauty and obscene eroticism, the melody opening a path, a gate, across a divide wider than worlds. Glottal-stopped melodies like probing loving fingers on their cold bodies stroking throbbing kneading.

The headman's son unwraps a bronze gong the headman got downriver in The Market and hangs it from a rafter with a bit of twisted rattanstrip string. He begins to beat it with a padded stick, matching rhythm with the women's stampers: *boooong boooong boooong boooong*. Yangman is still dancing, stamping his feet hard, waving his whisk, sweating, the whites of his eyes showing, pupils dilated. An old woman takes over playing the gong. "*Gsaak!* Dance! *Gsaak 'a kuat!* Dance hard!" urges Sibin, the skinny tubercular adept, clapping the rhythm. He dances, rickety, over to the women: "This way, this way," still clapping. The audience cheers and jeers the dancers on, nine *litaaw* dancing now, showing off for the girls, the tempo speeding up, Sibin clapping to show the rhythm, 1-2-3 rest, 1-2-3 rest.

TuktukTOKtuktukTOK tuktukTOK tuktukTOK.

Boooong boooong boooong boooong.

TuktukTOKtuktukTOK tuktukTOK tuktukTOK.

About 9 P.M. Kyoh snuggles up against her friend Kuup in the dark, the sleepy pleasure faintly different now that Kyoh's body is beginning to change but the comfort remaining. The toddler waves her father's whisk over Gdeem's feverish pale new baby, which is lying on its back on the floor by its mother, limp.

The rhythm changes as the singers finish Sibin's song, Yangman singing one of his own, eyes glazing over, closing, tempo still increasing, song still rising making the path between dimensions.

Boong tutktukTOK boong tuktukTOK boong tutktukTOK boong tuktukTOK.

Dancing bodies twist 180 degrees with each two steps, bent almost double, bouncing with each step up and down on the resilient bamboo slat floor, restraint gone now, no more choral singing, just the adept, the dancers reeling now, bouncing against the walls, stumbling across the hearth, lurching into each other, clinging to each other for support. Dadi, Jraan, other adults in the audience come to help dancers keep their feet, a pair of helpers for each dancer, hands under their armpits, keeping them upright and dancing, but the dancers are beginning to collapse now, two boys a couple of years older than Kyoh and Kuup falling first, the other *litaaw* falling over the little boys and each other, eight young men down now, only one still dancing, Yangman singing to him specially, moving along with him and singing almost into his ear.

sharp little pointed feet painlessly piercing bare damp skin in the moist dark, trembling, out of control

... heartbeats slowing, mouths furry, young bodies falling, one after another, no warning, all collapsed in a minute, smooth limbs relaxed now, tender as new growths; refreshing cold joy piercing their very hearts, stabbing sharp and clear as quartzite crystals in a chilly mountain stream; consciousness dissolved in the brilliant darkness of love; outside time, no mind left, just visions swirling into black as *klook* souls shift on their moorings, a few strobe flashes in an oceanic unknowing, forgotten before fully sensed: long black hair falling over an unseeable unsmiling beautiful face; terrifying old man's voice saying *am-caa'*, "I devour"; livid onyx dragonflies dancing and mating in the cool dark air; sexual arousal but colder not warmer, desire like cold black silt covering everything, blurring all forms. Human lovers-partners-parents-children-victims-killers shivering, shuddering, skins cooler and cooler to the touch, deathly cold, bodies motionless now, limp, dead, no twitching, cool, cool, chilly, *lng'aab, lng'oob, sngiic.*

Spreading unimaginable wings over their human lovers-victims-parents-children-killers-partners, pouring into the bright ebony air, swarming over the blood-rich dancers like aroused unseeable ants, blurring human outlines with their gauzy invisible intangible dragonfly wings; a pulsating dark nimbus over each fallen cooling human body, sucking, gnawing, biting, ripping; resistance then, thick, soft, leaking human panic, no no NO; nyanii' slick, lithe, chilling, erotic, clinging like little children, begging, pleading; pushing, pushing, pushing NO! the humans' bodies' soft defenses breached, tender limits violated. Smooth cool love maggots slipping through the moist skin, coolness sliding into the body cavities, overwhelming the thick leak of red delicious blood in the chambers of the frantically pumping heart, unconscious human bodies filled with tiny throbbing inexorable soft-bodied alien lovers. Formless multitudes, bright with malice and love and hideous beauty, feathery touch of long fingers like papery wings pushing probing penetrating; possessing, being possessed; the portal between the dimensions gaping now, flower-mouthed demons pouring through like ravening cool dust motes, spreading into the secret recesses of the brain; piercing the forehead, spurting through the smooth ivory bulge of skull, ripping the blood-swollen meninges: entry! Swarming like gnats around the timid tremorous ruwaay, mindless with terror and yearning; gnat-dance of seduction and threat; seizure; the rapture, the rapture, the rapture.

Bystanders lay the dancers straight, arms at their sides, legs outstretched. Sleepy Kyoh sees one of the little *litaaw* surreptitiously scratch his arm: he's faking trance, the way boys do when they're just learning how to let the demons take them. This boy's mother had talked with

Kyoh's mother about arranging a marriage. Kyoh closes her eyes again and cuddles closer to Kuup. The adept dances among the fallen bodies, singing softly.

Then he asperges them with supernatural cooling paste . . .

Ecstasy! Human ruwaay *and demonic souls take wing, amorous cold motes of terror, love and corruption in a passionate black cataract ripping away from the darkling human world, from the human magical paste that wrenches them apart, striving to annihilate themselves in the beautiful nonlight, to drown in the looming unseen rainforest shining with shadow, absolute anthracite brilliance.*

. . . suddenly, all at once, the fallen leap to their feet and bolt for the rain forest, tearing at the barred door, trying to clamber over the low house walls. One of the possessed little boys tears up a long strip of bamboo lath to escape through the floor. Batu', muscles bunched, convulsed, is atop the house wall, eyes almost closed, making little whimpering sounds; 'Alang and two men cling to him, trying to keep his body from following the demons who have seized his soul. Dadi and Jraan grapple with Cang, whose wiry little body, become powerful in trance, tenses and strains for freedom, his left hand gripping the flattened-bamboo wall and ripping loose a long plate of splintery bamboo. Batu' is still struggling so hard that his shorts begin to slip off. Kyoh, roused by the noise, cries "His pants are coming off!" and his three helpers bundle him off into a corner to pull his pants up while he still struggles to escape.

Once subdued, pulled back into the house, the trancers collapse again, though they now quiver or jerk slightly in rhythm with the music. Yangman circles among the prostrate bodies, sprinkling faces and feet with cooling paste and saying *l'aap!*, cooling! Recovering, the trancers roll onto their sides, their rhythmic twitching more marked, still in synchrony with the beat. Bystanders hurriedly help them rise to their feet and support them for a couple of seconds until the men can dance again for a minute or two, then walk over to the wall and sit down, knees up. The men cover their eyes with their hands or, if they carry one, with a whisk.

Tuk tuk TOK tuk tuk TOK tuk tuk TOK.

demons driven away by adept power, still connected in the ancient bitter passion, fed, sated, but disconsolate, still full of dread and rage and desire too deep to consummate, and the old yearning, supernatural coolness trailing in their wake, rising spreading over the humans like a flower, submerging awareness in the dark terror of love.

humans seeing unintelligible sights beyond vision, feeling fear and horror and beauty too deep to understand, once again not remembering, but freed, relieved, relieved; at peace. Freed. Relieved . . .

The trancers stagger back to their feet once again and dance for a couple of minutes. Facing the door, which is still barred, Yangman sings an apology for having "forgotten," for "fooling around," for "lack of skill."

Fathers, forgive us for not having all the ritual objects we
needed
next time we'll have them
just be patient and wait a little
it's all over for now,
don't come back tonight, we adepts are going to sleep,
it's not that you are not good at what you do
you are good enough to deceive me,
don't deceive me, don't deceive me.

For this fleeting moment, peace, safety. The humans' beautiful diaphanous dark paramours are gone, unreachable, sated briefly by human willingness to feast them, to offer them food for all their senses, fragrant flowers, human bodies even, just for a respite in the cycle of devouring and being devoured. Now the light can return to the humans.

'Alang and another woman relight the fires on the circular hard clay hearths. Her sister unbars the door. Gdeem continues singing. His baby is sick, and, spiritually refreshed, he is about to inspect the baby's *ruwaay* head soul, which is soft and especially fearful, like all young children's *ruwaay*, like children themselves.

This new light is the fall of darkness to them, blinding the dire parents-lovers-children-victims-killers; tortured blinded by the light they flee their terrifying human paramours. The eternal cycle of devouring and being devoured, killing and being killed, has ground to a brief stop, halted by nurturing and feeding, being nurtured and being fed, by making unimaginable love. Their need for beauty satisfied for now, multivariate hungers slaked, yearning for love met by love or its semblance, the glutted demons fly in their thousands into the cool moist forest aflame with darkness. Nothing human there: the convergence is over. They know, to the degree they know anything, that the night is sliding down the spectrum from safe humid darkness into the hot bloody stain of dawn; that the ancient deceits and ambushes will begin again, the subtle murderous seductions, the cruel mockery of the wounded and terrified, hideous woundings and lingering death, until once again the humans seek contact, feast and seduce the demons, once again surrender their beautiful bodies to demonic love.

11 P.M. Bah Cang, hamming it up, grinning, takes the bowl of supernatural cooling paste, prancing around and sprinkling everyone with it, crying *l'aap*, cooling! Kuup and Kyoh, awake again, giggle faintly, each leaning on the other, covering their mouths so as not to show their sharp white little teeth. A plump smiling *mnaleeh*, Cang's *mnaay* and thus in those days allowed to fool around with him, takes a swing at his rump with her long bamboo stamper. Her face is a soft girlish O, still unformed, her short upper lip making the full bottom one thrust forward. Cang dances away from her swing and -*nuntiil*, raising his bent right leg high and pulling his right buttock to the right, showing her his cleft and making Kuup give a little cry of shocked amusement.

Gdeem, done inspecting his child's *ruwaay*, spells Yangman, singing. Cang flops to the floor in front of his *mnaay*, writhing in fake trance. "He's hallucinating," she laughs to the other women, her dark eyes moist, pleased at the attention.

Kyoh's parents, Yangman and 'Alang, mock Western dancing, sticking out their butts and swinging them wildly, a play step called *tnajih*. Delighted with the laughter he gets from the audience, including Kyoh and Kuup, Yangman dances showily away from his wife, a parody of the preening male dancer. 'Alang dances unobtrusively up behind him and whams her arse into his, making him stumble; he pursues her around the dance floor to a clutter of laughter, butt whamming until she sits down by the wall and the game is over.

Squeaky Wa' Mas, Bah Cang's one-time lover, gets 'Alang up to dance a Malay-style "joget." Among Malays the point is for two girl dancers to keep in step with each other until one steps aside so a man can take her place and the other girl then copies his steps exactly. But this dance is for 'Alang and Mas alone. They make one concession to Malay values: about halfway through the dance they pause so that Mas can get a huge old pajama top to cover her bare breasts, and 'Alang pulls up her sarong and wraps it around her own breasts. Sometimes the women dance along with the men, though never paired up in Malay style. Even more rarely they go into trance, usually in the woman's circle dance, although people say that you must be strong to trance, and most women never do. But 'Alang, like many adepts' wives, has access to supernatural power as a midwife and works with Yangman and his demonic familiar when children are sick.

It's too late for more trancing tonight. By midnight everyone has gone home or to sleep except for three *litaaw* who continue singing and dancing till dawn, just for fun.

Around the sleeping settlement the dark, so black it shimmers, glittering lightlessly, the inhuman powers, enduring horrors, waiting.

BANALYSIS

Tibetans, Indonesians, Taoists and tantriks "convert" the most horrific images they can spin up into the very guardians of their spiritual welfare, just as the Prophet is said to have converted the djinn to Islam. . . . [T]he final purpose of their rites is union with the deity and the acquisition of the knowledge of the gods. This world is a reflection of their world and they cast their mirror images on earth when they possess or appear to their worshipers. Human intercourse with them is beneficial. (Wilson 1988:158–59)

> To the somethingness
> Which prevents the nothingness
> Like Homer's wild boar
> From thrashing this way and that
> Its white tusks
> Through human beings
> Like crackling stalks
> And to nothing less
> I offer this suffering . . .
> (from Stan Rice, "The Offering" [1995:dust jacket])

If you understand this complicated simple stuff viscerally, my pedestrian analysis won't help, and you might as well skip it.

The complex Semai idea of good and evil is like William Blake's in its poetry though not its content. You remember the story about Blake and John Milton, the Puritan divine? Milton wrote a wonderful epic poem about the Fall, in which demons have all the best lines. Blake says, admiringly, that Milton is really "of the Devil's party." And Mansur ibn al-Hallaj, maybe the greatest Sufi master, describes Satan as "the perfect sufi and perfect lover" (quoted in Wilson 1988:7). In Hinduism, the demons start off as pre-Aryan gods, gods of people perhaps distantly related to Semai, dark gods, and decay into merely evil beings as Aryan intellectuals rationalize them.

A serious cosmology, like that of traditional Semai, avoids simplistic formulations. That's for state religions: *Animal Farm*'s "four legs good, two legs bad" thinking, as Orwell parodied it. Because (I think) the cosmic struggle is between chaos and order, fear and love, entropy and form, Ahab and Moby Dick, and it's never clear who the good guys are. Why reduce this sophisticated Semai cosmology to good beautiful people versus bad ugly demons?

Most of the time, Semai demons *are* bad and ugly and scary and make you sick. Some of the time, they are good and beautiful and scared and help you cure people. Isn't the same, in reverse, true of people? A lot of people (not all) cross the line sometimes. The State's like that too: often bad and ugly and scary but sometimes helpful and protective and worthy of patriotic affection.

Now, the *symptoms* Semai give for séance trancing are pretty much the same as those they give for storm panic or what they call "blood intoxication," *blnuul bhiib*: dizziness or nausea, which they call *lnwiik*; dissolution of the self; unconsciousness. The chemical changes in the brain—oxygen starvation, norepinephrine overload, and so on—are probably pretty much the same, so the sensation of being overwhelmed that Semai report probably has an ascertainable psychophysiology.

But the *circumstances* are quite different. Outside the séance, terror is the precursor of these symptoms: thundersqualls, spilled human blood. Inside, though, love and fostering have harnessed the terror, made it *kaloo'*, tame, harmless, quiet, like a child; loving. The rhythm that excites the human dancers unites them, makes them an organic strong community that can deal with wild power. You are among friends, not isolated in a vicious cosmos where monsters rule. And then, safe, you can see the great beauty of the demons, as you can see the great beauty of a dead tiger or one in a cage. There's a beauty in surrendering to demons, a freedom that can raise you above the tedium of ordinary life, of ordinary impotence. I think it's close to what the Sufis talk about when they talk about union with the Beloved. I mean, I wouldn't know, but do you suppose conscious contact with God is all sweetness and light?

Raided by merciless human child abusers, menaced from above and below by brutal monsters, surrounded by shape-shifting demons, traditional Semai felt powerless. People anywhere respond to such powerlessness in a number of ways. Two may be relevant here: (1) "identification with the oppressor" and (2) "learned helplessness," spiritual surrender.

Identification with the oppressor is a typical self-defense of battered children. Helpless under attack, you try to preserve the self by turning it into the image of the person hurting you so badly. In your imagination you can become as powerful as the person who brutalizes you. And then, when the opportunity offers, you can act out this ersatz self and make it real: adult, battered children may batter children. It's a sort of unconditional surrender, in which you give up even who you are. And it can have repellent consequences, as Philip Larkin says (1974:30):

> Man hands on misery to man
> It deepens like a coastal shelf.
> Get out as early as you can,
> And don't have any kids yourself.

But, bad as the consequences may be for children to come, what alternatives does a powerless beaten child have? However socially and morally undesirable, becoming a future child batterer is sometimes the best personal adaptation available. An alternative that happens sometimes is fragmenting the self into "multiple personalities," a real self and a demon wife, perhaps.

There's another kind of surrender, too, the kind that people make after what Christian mystics call a "Dark Night of the Soul," a period of despair like "the bottom" of alcoholics and drug addicts. That kind of surrender involves accepting powerlessness but changing one's notion of what overpowers you. People do it all the time: they "come to Jesus," they do the First Step of Alcoholics Anonymous and its offshoots. William James, in *The Varieties of Religious Experience*, and Anthony Wallace, in *Religion*, do a good job of describing this sort of transformative surrender and giving it an empirical explanation. All I need say here is that it provides a relief from intolerable terror.

Maybe acquiring demonic power, *hnalaa'*, is an identification with the powers that frighten Semai. Like parental power, the power of *nyanii'* demons is ambivalent: it can kill you or cure you, punish you for evildoing, or help others to do evil. The identification with *hnalaa'* power shows up in Semai ideology in metaphors: Nkuu's gift of shamanic power to humans (perhaps by trickery), the repeated brutal humiliation of Nkuu', the Great Humiliator. With this power, Semai adepts become the fearsome patriarchs who actually have to seduce subservient childlike timorous demons. The people adopt the pose of sexual abusers, the seductive *guniik* of the abused, in a form of transcendence that, briefly, makes the humans and the *halaa'* powers into lovers instead of brutalizers. In that moment, the ethos of helplessness that always echoes faintly through traditional Semai society dissolves in love. The oppressed become the oppressors, but nobody gets hurt. Indeed, in a further transformation, they do good, healing the sick. And the dancers (fainting and falling, intoxicated, *-buul*), the dancers collapse, their bodies making their surrender tangible, and become, briefly, *nyanii'*: get a taste of power and the freedom that power gives: freedom from human rules, freedom from felt powerlessness, freedom from pervasive fear. It must be wonderful.

And the séance is a place where surrender, helplessness, is safe. That part of it is like Alcoholics Anonymous. You're in a safe place (longhouse, church basement), with people mobilized to support you, a place where you can take time out from your mundane life. It's fun to go there and feels good afterward. But the freedom and security you feel is fleeting. The euphoria fades, the old routines resurface, the ancient fears seep back into the skull, normal anxious care-ridden consciousness subverts the peace. Then you need to renew yourselves by gathering together again, formally, to address your fears and repeat the public temporary surrender that temporarily disempowers the demons.

You're saying all these experiences of powerlessness, of surrender, of being overwhelmed, are pretty much the same experience physiologically, just the interpretation is different?

Because the context is different, right. Identification and surrender manifest love; even identification with the oppressor is a horrible kind of love.

And because the interpretation is different, how the experience feels and what it does for people, what empiricists call its "function," that's different?
Love is the opposite of fear, and sometimes wins,

> [t]hough all the universe's atoms move
> Toward regions desolate of human love. (Carper 1991:8)

5

Ceremonies of Innocence and "Positive" Peace

The Hobbesian problem arises from the assumption that anarchy, absence of enforcement, leads to distrust and social disintegration. . . . But there is a certain amount of interesting empirical evidence which points the other way. The paradox is: it is precisely anarchy which engenders trust or, if you want to use another name, which engenders social cohesion.

—Gellner (1988:147)

Anthropologists customarily classify societies like Semai as "simple," as I did earlier in this book when I used the standard jargon and called them "simple swiddeners" (cf. Dentan 2008). Anarchist anthropologists, however, argue that relationships between individuals in such societies are richer and more complex than among, say, Americans (Graeber 2007a:101–2; Macdonald 2008). That richness and complexity makes this chapter, which evolved from an earlier article (Dentan 2000b), probably the hardest in this book to digest.

Earlier chapters described (1) the conditions that led Semai to opt for flight or surrender over retaliation in response to violence and (2) the complex psychological and social consequences of that option. This option, based on Hobbesian "fright" ("caution" might be a better word), leads to what anthropologists call, judgmentally, "negative peace." In evolution, organisms that avoid struggles they might lose are more likely to survive long enough to produce fertile offspring than their more combative peers. It's a good adaptation, a sort of Powell Doctrine for ordinary folks, "negative" or not.

Many people say that's all peace is: just absence of violence or even just absence of war. But negative peace sets conditions within which "positive peace" can grow. Even in wartime or under terrorist attack, "positive peace" is the normal, background state of human affairs, to which people whose lives violence has trashed usually try to return, the conditions they often call "normality" (e.g., Dentan 2008; Fry 2006; Nordstrom 1997, 2004). Look at TV. As cameramen focus on death and destruction, on the edges of the picture, slightly out of focus, there they are, picking up the pieces of their shattered children, hosing down the blood, pulling the corpses out of the well, collecting what's left of their belongings, getting back as much to "normal" as they can.

And that requires reconstituting "positive peace" out of terror. Far from being merely the absence of violence, peace is a rich and complex social construct.

> [T]he immediate result of living in terror, in suspicion of every unfamiliar person . . . is the way every normal person defends himself against the pain of what is liable to be taken from him at any moment. It is the inability to believe in routine even for a minute. Every such situation, every routine, is but an illusion, and he who is tempted to believe in it will not be prepared for the final blow when it comes. . . . Terror also sharpens one's awareness that a democratic, tranquil way of life requires the true goodwill of a country's citizens. That is the amazing secret of democratic rule. (Grossman 2001)

Positive peacemaking involves trust, reciprocity, and cooperation among community members. People need to work together to achieve common goals. To the degree they can appeal successfully for help, they have what social scientists call "social capital." How much social capital a particular society has correlates inversely with violence and mortality. In fact, recent studies indicate that it correlates inversely with the morbidity of disease and serious accidents. That's what Semai say too. You'll see. It's an even better adaptation than negative peace.

(Struggling with this paragraph on July 22, 2004, I was listening to the report of the 9/11 Commission on the radio. It made an illuminating contrast, for it too began by recalling how Americans came together on 9/11, how the world responded with sympathy and offers of help: the "befriend" part of "fight, flight, tend, and befriend." Semai built a way of life on such terror-generated social capital. Americans enjoyed it briefly and frittered it away on bellicose T-shirts and magnetic ribbons for their SUVs. A few years later, Americans are more alienated from the world and from each other than ever. The "failure of imagination" was deeper than the 9/11 Commission imagined. In retrospect, both Semai and American responses seem equally astonishing and exotic.)

How does the transition from chaos to order work? Let's think of violence as one response to perceived threats. People perceive/classify something as threatening because it produces a set of complex physiological reactions, the "fight/flight response," which psychologists call "stress." (That's true whether the response is learned or innate.) So one way to reduce violence would be to reduce stress, particularly interpersonal stress. This chapter is about how Semai do that.

A BLAKEAN PEACE

What is it men in women do require?
        The lineaments of gratified desire.
What is it women do in men require?
        The lineaments of gratified desire.

—William Blake, "The Question Answer'd" (1994:143)

This idea of "positive peace" corresponds roughly with a notion, widespread among Southeast Asian hill peoples, of conditions that include serenity, good luck, spiritual grace, and social peace. Semai call these conditions *slamaad*, using a Malay-Arabic term that etymologically refers to the peace and serenity that come from what I've been calling "surrender," in Islam to the will of God. The Semai word is secular, connoting the absence of frustration or ungratified desire. Semai try to maintain *slamaad* by scrupulosity and egalitarianism in interpersonal relationships.

Anthropologists don't agree about much, but they generally agree that, for most of the time human beings have existed, there were no classes or castes. Nobody had the right to boss anyone else around. Foragers and some "slash-and-burn" agriculturalists like traditional Semai still foster this equality—not because they are intellectually anarchists or libertarians, though the results resemble what anarchists and libertarians strive for. Instead, Semai egalitarianism seems to come from a dislike of being bullied, a sentiment most people everywhere share. Bullies, of course, aim to produce enough stress that their victim will surrender and become subordinate. In response, this book argues, Semai flee, and the existence of refuges allows them to "surrender without subordination" (Lechner 2003). They also avoid hurting people's feelings, bullying them.

The tactic of avoidance is available to any humans, no more and no less than the other tactics: violence, forming alliances, caring for children. Opting for one does not make Semai essentially different from Malays or Americans. Many Semai, under different circumstances, might enjoy bullying others if they could get away with it. The unsystemized power imbalances that occur in egalitarian societies rest mostly on differences in skill, verbal facility, or physical strength. Thus, men may boss women, or adults may boss children simply because they can, the way bullies do in the middle and high schools of America. Schools are hotbeds of bullying because victims can't just leave.

But Semai resisted even informal authority, not violently but the way you would expect of a people who have found flight a more successful adaptation than fighting. Until Malaysian bureaucrats forced the small, shifting Semai bands to merge and settle in "regroupment" areas, Semai moved away from bullies or formed bully-free groups, as other primates also do. Anthropologists call the resulting demographic pattern "fission-fusion"; groups continually split up (flight) and coalesce (befriend). Since in societies like this survival requires being able to depend on other people in times of need, the fear of losing your friends (and maybe even your husband, wife, or child) puts a damper on bullying and violence.

Thus, Semai "individual autonomy," the ability to move away from repression, differs from the "individualism" of America. Semai can't afford to be that alone. They need a place—and friends—to flee to. Therefore, they have worked out ways to avoid bullying and reduce conflict.

Their sophisticated and expansive definition of harm may explain some of the relative success of their system of nonviolence and the relative failure of the rigid American distinctions between psychosocial and physical violence, or "justifiable" and "criminal" violence. Semai history and political ecology may have sensitized them to the physical effects of stress more than is possible for researchers in societies where daily economic life requires bullying and accepting, ignoring or "overcoming" levels of gratuitous interpersonal stress that Semai find intolerable. Hierarchy itself is a sort of bullying:

> I was soon to relearn an old lesson about the few very rich people I had known. Their cruelty was seldom deliberate, but its effect was more injurious than if it were the result of a calculated act, primarily because the victim was made to understand how insignificant his life really was. (Burke 1999:7)

As one battered woman says, "You become nothing" (quoted in Prosser 2000).

This chapter sketches how Semai say people should behave. Unlike many a worker in the West, they seem to avoid

> the 3 AM, obsessive, mentally punishing recapitulation of the futile chase after self-respect which constitutes much of her working day. . . . What was happening here? Accumulation, . . . that's all, just the dispiriting accretion of nine-to-fives, of petty betrayals, minor sarcasms, slights, injustices, and plain rudeness collecting like refuse under a rotting wharf until one blighted morning all the fish are dead, there's no place to swim. (Wright 1994:4)

The complex praxis that this chapter describes helps minimize this dispiriting accumulation of stress and resentment. In traditional ethnographies, this sort of material usually shows up in a chapter on "taboos." But it seems more appropriate to take what Semai say seriously, as philosophy rather than just "data," to treat their analysis the way you would treat one from Western intellectuals.

Describing how Semai talk about violence requires using a lot of Semai words. That makes cumbersome and confusing reading, which I've tried to use by putting a *very* rough English gloss in parentheses after each crucial Semai term the first two or three times I use it after the initial definition. For later encounters, there's a glossary at the back of the book. At the outset, you want to recognize that many of the Semai words share an ambiguity with the English word "stress": they refer both to the psychophysiological state of the affected person and also to the events that evoked that response. But the Semai words also refer to the general sociocosmic disruption that such events may cause.

Lacking (not wanting) an authoritative single source of definitions, different Semai use many of these terms almost interchangeably. Their sophisticated conceptual scheme for preventing violence elaborates a few basic themes: a broad definition of violence, the importance of sharing and self-control, the danger of ungratified desires, the importance of trying to keep things tidy in face of the ever-present threat of chaos.

Feeling Safe: Freedom and the Narrow Path

It takes skill, but
The darkness can be
Slipped. You can
Walk down the long
Black alley without
Whistling; ungot . . .

—From Stan Rice, "April Again" (1995:8)

The *slamaad*, safety and security, which Semai desire, requires being careful, walking what Bah Tony Williams-Hunt calls a "narrow path."

The future path through future ambushes is a continuation of the old path by which the survivors from the past have come. The image of a path is apt because it is by following a path, created and maintained by generations of walking feet, that some of the dangers of the surrounding forests or mountains or marshes may be avoided. The path is tradition handed down by instructions, example and commentary. To a peasant the future is this future narrow path across an indeterminate expanse of known and unknown risks. When peasants cooperate to fight an outside force, and the impulse to do this is always defensive, they adopt a guerrilla strategy—which is precisely a network of narrow paths across an indeterminate hostile environment. (Berger 1975:203)

Paths are a common human metaphor: the English word "deviance" comes from the Latin for "off the path." The Way is a pervasive metaphor in Buddhism, Daoism, Islam, and Christianity. The Semai way helps get you safely through a cosmos teeming with dangers. Even Semai history is geographical, a trek written on the land itself, like the landmarks of the Sangkiil War: here the Rawas whetted their swords; here we ambushed them while they were bathing. Semai familiars guide adepts along recognizable paths. For Semai, "straying," *-ric-ruuc*, is the metaphor for ignoring the rules of right conduct. Drunks, for example, talk *rawuuc*, the corresponding adverb "incoherently." Such speech makes people uneasy, makes them twitch and glance at each other. Except for young men, Semai don't find it funny.

Another example of straying would be mocking an animal, the physical embodiment of forest demons. Mockery trashes the distinction between humans and demons. Trancing restores the proper relationship. "Straying" damages people spiritually, wounds their *sngii'*, their will or consciousness or sense of self. Semai say that such straying is irresponsible and careless and that, like other sorts of irresponsibility or carelessness, it can damage cosmic order.

On a paper napkin, Bah Tony sketched a diagram of the guideposts that show people the path to cosmic order and chaos:

humans usually fit here   demons usually fit here
material/visible beings ←hunting/being hunted→ immaterial/invisible beings

←disrupting spiritual linkage→

Humans maintain ORDER by observing the rules of social behavior	CHAOS/calamity follows ignoring rules (-rcruuc)
a) sharing	a) punan
b) keeping promises	b) srnloo', srngloo'
c) caring for others	c) tnghaan'
d) self-control	d) trlaac
e) respecting cosmic order	e) pnali'
f) respecting elders/proprieties	f) tolah

adepts/midwives ←demon wife-adept trance→ demon wives

←restoring spiritual linkage→

Cosmos. Note: Like most egalitarian peoples, Semai acknowledge no authoritative locus for knowledge, no pope or sacred writing. Individuals use these categories to organize their experiences. So the usages are as flexible and varying as the experiences themselves. This figure is a guideline for understanding, not a list of rigid definitions or equivalences. Based on a sketch Bah Tony Williams-Hunt drew on a napkin, 1992.

You could call these guidelines "taboos," but their operation is not automatic. When Semai set a spear trap for pigs or deer, they break a small sapling along the path that leads to the trap so that people walking by and paying attention to where they are going can take warning. The traps won't be actually on the path, because you're not trying to kill people, so with luck the people would get by anyway. The rules are like that. You're safe if you follow them but, if you feel safe anyway, you may ignore them.

The skinny anthropologist, notebook out as usual, is trying to list Tluup River food taboos. He and Mrlooh, a tense beautiful curly-headed man of about his age, are seated in the front room of the little house Mrlooh shares with his wife's mother, Busuw, whose name Mrlooh must not speak and whose presence he cannot explicitly acknowledge without showing lethal disrespect, what Semai and Malays call *tolah*. In the next room, Busuw is roasting three peeled tapioca roots, previously cooked, in the coals, like giant fat white carrots, smelling musty and bready.

Mrlooh wants some tapioca, so he says to his wife, Dmeet, eight months' pregnant and as beautiful a woman as Mrlooh is a man, "Would you ask the old lady to pass a piece of tapioca?" Dmeet, who is roasting a side dish, too, wrapped in a thick green leaf, turns to her mother. You can use the big leaves as plates, too, if you have meat and don't want to disrespect the animal the meat comes from by mixing its flesh with the faint traces of fish or fowl or fungus on your plates. That would be *pnali'*. Before Dmeet can speak, Busuw, who has overheard Mrlooh's request, has taken the tapioca out of the embers to pass to her daughter, carefully not looking at Mrlooh. Dmeet then relays the root to Mrlooh.

"Okay, 'field rat,'" says the anthropologist. "Can *maay makòòd*, people expecting a baby, eat 'field rats'?"

"No. Baby will squeal." Like the rat.

"Any other reason?"

"Baby's eyes will be red." Also like the rat.

"What about people who have just given birth?"

"Not for weeks. Claws will scratch the womb."

"What about menstruating wom . . . What's Dmeet eating?"

Mrlooh looks over his shoulder and smiles. "'Field rat.'"

"?"

"I've asked her and asked her not to, but she says, 'Pregnancy's not a problem for me.' She just doesn't worry."

Women pregnant for the first time are more likely than Dmeet to be careful about what they eat because they *do* worry about the outcome of their pregnancy. The great anthropologist Bronislaw Malinowski saw a similar pattern in the Trobriand Islands: deep-sea fishing, dangerous and risky, generated many taboos; but lagoon fishing, humdrum and safe, generated few. Observing rules makes Semai feel safe. If they feel safe anyway, the rules are burdensome, and people ignore them.

That is, like most egalitarian peoples, individual Semai work out the rules by which they live within the framework of a set of vague generalities and according to personal experience. What regularity of behavior exists in the area of (non)violence stems from (1) people's sense that deliberately taking chances is scary and stupid, (2) the omnipresent surveillance and lurid gossip that pervade isolated small communities everywhere, and (3) the fact that in small communities, everyone depends socially, economically, and spiritually on everyone else. There aren't enough people around to ignore anybody. You'll need them to help build your house or clear your field. So everybody pays attention to everybody else.

Conformity via self-control is a central value among most small egalitarian groups. Conformity is important in most societies, of course. The contrast I'm trying to make here is with the stress on self-expression, self-gratification, and invidious striving in consumerist capitalist societies. Some Western scholars, recognizing this difference, contrast "sociocentric" with "egocentric" selves. It's hard to tell if these "selves" exist in the real world. It might be easier to think of Semai as transvaluing the West's "individual identity" (good, in U.S. psychotherapeutic analysis) and "deadening conformity" (bad, there).

However bad conformity and good competitive individualism may be in economies dependent on invidious striving, it is less viable when survival depends on mutual support. Semai prefer "orderliness, predictability," peace and security, creative conformity, *slamaad*. Normally, they assume, group life is peaceful. Monkeys travel in "gangs," like people, said Ngah Hari of Mncaak, "but monkeys fight." The "but" is typically Semai. Humans keep the peace.

The rules that foster *slamaad* stress self-control. In a famous essay on dominance and subordination, the German philosopher Hegel says that subordination and the fear from which it springs are prerequisites for self-control, indeed to any sense of selfhood. But he may have it partly backward. Semai notions of selfhood and self-control may stem from recurrent defeats by and sporadic subordination to slavers, but their self-control makes further subordination, to their own leaders, for example, unnecessary. Indeed, further subordination seems to destroy self-control. The conservative British political theorist Edmund Burke (1982:48) puts the case this way:

> Society cannot exist unless a controlling power upon will and appetite be placed somewhere, and the less of it there is within, the more there must be without. . . . [M]en of intemperate minds cannot be free. Their passions forge their fetters.

Internalized, the Semai rules may turn people's attention away from obsession with self and to the importance of other people's needs. They help guide your mind away from your own desires. Not observing them means you live *rawuuc*, randomly, without rules. You may *-ric-ruuc*, wander, go astray, be lost. Without rules, you are in danger because of your intemperance, your spiritual untidiness, your lack of care for the welfare of other humans and the world. The central metaphor for such actions is *srn-gloo'*, hunting down and killing.

THE STRESS OF FRUSTRATION

Punan (Sharing Taboo)

We *br-mage'* [share, especially small portions of food]. We're not like Malays. See, when my daughter cooks she sends food to her mom's house; when her mom cooks, she sends food to my daughter; and to Rhii's-father.

—Teiw Waar headman (1992)

Hutang mas boleh di-bayar, hutang budi di-bayar mati
A debt of gold you can repay; a debt of kindness lasts till you die.

—Malay proverb

One of the most puzzling experiences I had when Semai first let me live with them, on the Telom River in Pahang State in1962, involved notions of property and sharing. My wife and I had moved into a little house that we believed was vacant. Everyone said it'd be "no problem." And, when Bah Sn'ooy, the man whose house it had been, came back a few months later, he pooh-poohed our worry. No problem, he said, he'd just move in with his kinsman next door. We didn't really "get it," but were too grateful to raise questions.

But that wasn't the only thing we didn't understand, not by a long shot. We didn't know that Semai understand that people travel in an invisible cloud of scurf, dandruff, funkiness, bodily fragrance and so on, a cloud whose very existence superclean Americans deny. When two people sleep in the same place, these intensely personal substances commingle, creating instant intimacy. So Sn'ooy became a good friend, without my having a clue why.

He would often bring us food or samples of Semai material culture. In traveling to other countries before, I'd always made a point of learning how to say "Thank you." So asked how you say *"Terima kasih,"* the equivalent Malay phrase (which actually means something like "receive affection"). And, after a pause, which I didn't register at the time, people had said, "We say, "'*Abòr!*" Later, I learned that *'a* was an "optative" particle, indicating a condition you wished for and *bòr* was an all-purpose approval word—"good," "handsome," "healthy," and so on. So I thought it was one of those vapid expressions of goodwill that you find in most societies. (It actually means "Watch out!," a typically Semai expression of concern lest bad things happen to you because you're not on your toes, e.g., "'*Abòr! Mn hi-yòk*," "Look out! You might fall"). So, anyway, every time Bah Sn'ooy did me a favor, I'd say, "'*Abòr!*"

At first that worked just fine. But then Sn'ooy began to make a little thumb gesture, which I didn't understand. But, compared with the mass of things I didn't understand, the question didn't seem worth pursuing. Then he began licking his thumb first, and the gesture got larger, until finally he swept his wet thumb up and down three times, like a twentieth-century American teacher wiping out an obscenity on a blackboard, and said, "What is the MATTER with you? Aren't we *kawaad*? ("Friends," I'd thought that word meant, although Semai use it to cover pretty much everyone who belongs to the band or settlement).

"I thought we were," I said hesitantly, shocked and abashed—and afraid I'd somehow lost a good friend.

"Then why do you keep saying, '*Abòr! Abòr! Abòr!*' all the time?"

And that was when I learned that I had been putting my good friend into *punan*, again and again, insulting him and threatening his health, for being such a good guy. But it took me years to figure out what *punan* meant and how it worked.

> [W]e are now brought back to . . . the autonomy of the agent. Reciprocity (the "obligation" to give and to receive) jeopardizes autonomy. Non-social, anarchic, and gregarious communities reject reciprocity as the moral basis of their mutual dealings, they are reluctant to give and to create a debt . . . Obviously Inuits, San, Semai, Palawan, Buid and all the others borrow and lend, give and take, they barter, swap, buy, and sell. There are free gifts, some haggle, others might take away things and 'forget' to return them. All sorts of transactions and reciprocal activities take place. There is no such thing as "primitive communism" . . . The point is, in some groups the social contract is not based on the "spirit of the gift" but on the law of sharing. And this is because people like their freedom to remain intact. (Macdonald 2008).

You see, under the rule of reciprocity, if I give you a gift or do you a favor, then you owe me a gift or favor back. Semai understand how reciprocity works. But, until the debt is repaid, you owe me. Sometimes Americans even say "You owe me" to each other when they do each other favors. Pile up those debts and you become a slave, like a Malay *hamba*. You lose your equality and thus your freedom.

But Semai are egalitarians, with a somewhat different notions of property and propriety. Everyone in a particular band, any *kawaad*, has an equal right to the benefits that membership in the band confers: food, shelter, companionship, help. It's all there for the taking. I don't have any special right to dole out those benefits. As Bah Tony, a west Semai intellectual with whom I have worked for years, writes,

> [I]n regard to things/resources which come from the [settlement], sharing these things is seen as giving people their entitlements since, according to Semai jurisprudence, generally the resources of a settlement belong to its residents, although nowadays this is not always observed. (Williams-Hunt 2008)

When you share some goods (usually food) of which you have a surplus—and you don't share if you don't have enough to share without depriving yourself—you are not sharing your own property but giving fellow band members their share of the resources to which they are entitled as band members. Semai talk freely about the benefits of this system, particularly and at length during the town meetings, *bicaraa'*, that they hold to restore peaceability when someone's actions have disrupted *slamaad*, public safety and peaceableness (see chapter 6).

So Sn'ooy wasn't doing me any favors; he was just treating me as a *kawaad*, and each time I was acting as if he was a self-important hustler and not my equal. No wonder his feelings were hurt. And, for Semai, hurting people's feelings is seriously endangering their spiritual and physical welfare.

And not sharing, or saying "Thank you" as if your *kawaad* was a stranger, generates *punan*.

> The state of danger . . . called *kemponan* [= *punan*] . . . is commonly accepted . . . as an outcome of refusing [to accept] any food, cigarettes, or a betel chew. A person may also be put into the dangerous state of kemponan if they go into someone's house and are not offered such refreshment. (Peluso 1996:533n)

The word *punan* is cognate with the English word "taboo." Victims suffer accident proneness or susceptibility to disease. It's hard to explain in a language like Semai that doesn't have a vocabulary for probabilities, but the idea seems to be that people suffering *punan* are more likely to have bad luck, maybe meet a tiger (a natural symbol of magical dangers), or fall down and hurt themselves, or get sick.

Eating together is a main Semai metaphor for sharing in general and caring in particular. Some lowland Perak Semai say that putting someone in *punan* by not eating together when invited or inviting a *kawaad* to eat when you have plenty is a "sin," *tnghaan'*, discussed later in this chapter. The stinginess might call for a town meeting, though usually the only consequence would be a spate of outrageous, malicious gossip.

Not to share undercuts *slamaad*. People should help each other out, meet any legitimate request. Reciprocally, they should accept any proffered gift. Rejecting requests or gifts hurts other people's feelings, frustrates their desires. Ungratified desire imperils the people who feel it:

> The concept of *hoin* [to be satisfied or sated, as with eating, dancing, bathing, sex, and so on] is often used [by Semai] in post hoc explanations of the occurrence of illness or misfortune. In such cases, however, the frustrated want was usually only dimly recognized, if it was recognized at all at the time of the presumed frustration. More commonly it is identified in retrospect only after some misfortune has occurred. (Robarchek 1977:766)

During the first trimester of pregnancy, the fetus is particularly susceptible to *punan* (sharing taboo), perhaps because the mother is particularly susceptible to cravings. Not satisfying her cravings may kill her fetus. Not sharing food with expectant mothers is also especially risky.

The notion of *punan* reinforces people's inclination to share. It obscures the fact that Semai are not "by nature" more generous than other peoples, although, as Tungkuunc of Mncaak said in 1975,

> Go to big cities like Kuala Lumpur, you see Chinese beggars, Indian beggars, Malay beggars. No Semai beggars. [Chuckles]. We're the poorest people in the country, but we care for our people.

In fact, Semai generosity often requires what anthropologists call "demand sharing." People who want some of your food or other goods will drop heavy hints (rather than make demands outright, which risks *punan*): "I haven't eaten rice in *days*" or "There's no side dish for my rice." It is polite not to be explicit about your demand because demands are social pressure and, if the person does not have enough to make sharing reasonable, could produce *punan*. Sharing more than you can afford, people say, would be "stupid." If you obviously can afford to share, Semai will make the demand clear. Refusal also risks *punan*.

Srngloo' (Hunters' Violence) and Mnuur

> [I]f three men have planned to go on a journey, or to fell jungle together, but one man remains at home without saying anything (*i.e.* excusing himself from going), it is thought that, if one or other of his two friends fall sick, he is the cause of the illness. In such a case, the two who have started on their journey will immediately return, and the third man must say spells for the recovery of the patient. If, however, before his companions start, the man who stops at home makes some excuse for not going, no ill-fortune which they encounter can be ascribed to him. . . . [T]here is a *Dana Sirlok* . . . spirit [which] attacks persons to whom promises have been made and broken.

Thus, if a man has agreed with another to go on a journey, and subsequently leaves his friend in the lurch, the *Dana Sirlok* will accompany the traveler in his friend's place . . . and will attack and kill him in the shape of an elephant, a tiger or a snake. (Evans 1923:246)

I think that one's resistance to turning into a hunter, the ability to spot and to control the hunting impulse, has to do with something more basic than temperament, upbringing, social values, received wisdom, ecclesiastical affiliation, or one's concept of honor. It has to do with the degree of one's evolution, with reaching the stage marked by one's inability to regress. . . . Virtue is far from being synonymous with survival; duplicity is. But you will accept, dear reader, won't you, that there is a hierarchy between love and betrayal. (Brodsky 1997:157)

The ethical basis of Semai peaceability is honesty and the resulting trust. Betraying trust has much the same results as refusing to share. Hurt people's feelings, they can't trust you. Since they can't trust you, they can't cooperate with you. On the Waar in late 1991, I overheard Luusfather put it this way to his slightly younger kinsman Kalib, explaining why Kalib couldn't let him out of his promise to pay a share of Kalib's wedding costs:

A wound to *sngii'* [feelings, consciousness] is incurable. A wound to my arm I can medicate, but there's no medicine for wounds to *sngii'*. Whenever you run into someone who's *tipu'* [cheated, deceived—a Malay word] you, you think, "He *tipu'* me," and you can never be close again, not even if you're *tne'-mnaang* [elder and younger kinsmen of the same generation, like Luusfather and Kalib].

You should never disrespect people by breaking your promises. It's [like] *-srloo'*, hunting them down and killing them. Speeches during town meetings often stress the importance of not making false promises. One bad thing about Malays, Semai say, is that they break promises:

Long says that Malays from the "Housing Bureau" camped out in her house without paying rent and made her cook for them—hard for her, since she wasn't familiar with Muslim cooking requirements. They said that if she and her husband would hoe out a flat area they'd get a prestigious, Malay-style plank house. The couple did hoe the area flat, but the house did not materialize. She said, as her father had said earlier about a similar promise from the Bureau of Orang Asli Affairs [which rules Semai lives] that the hurt wasn't not getting the house. The hurt was being lied to. (Teiw Waar, early 1992)

Not that Semai do not deceive non-Semai. People use an elaborate vocabulary (*nroo' krndey*, "speech to make one ignorant") to mislead dangerous outsiders. After you have hunted down and killed an animal, the physical embodiment of demons, you should not use the animal's proper name until you have defecated its meat. Instead, you use a special by-name. In the same way, you use slang terms for "Malay" when Malays who speak a little Semai are around. Why ask for trouble?

The overlap between disrespect, duplicity, and killing is clear in other contexts. Remember how in chapter 3 the adept, after a séance, implores the demons, "Don't deceive me, don't let me down." A demon hunting human souls takes delusive forms to lure the humans, appearing perhaps as a beautiful person of the opposite sex. Deceiving people, letting them down, is thus part and parcel of hunting them down and killing them. It has the same potentially fatal results as putting someone into the state of frustration that results from *punan*. Indeed, that word may connote being trapped, another sort of hunting. In other words, failing to share and failing to cooperate after promising to do so are precisely parallel with hunting, snaring, and killing. They violate integrity, manifest disrespect. Semai say you can die of that.

This reluctance to misinform others can frustrate people unused to Semai. For example, once some Malay parapolice wanted to dynamite fish without wasting grenades. So, their officer told me, he asked a Semai headman if there were any fish in the river. The headman said,

> Better stick your head in and see for yourself. If I say there aren't any fish, and there are, you'll be ticked off. If I say there are fish and there aren't, you'll be ticked off. So I'm not saying anything. (field notes, 1992)

Likewise, trappers should take ritual precautions like those associated with *srngloo'* (hunters' violence), or their traps won't work. Trappers should make traps secretly, indoors or deep in the woods. They shouldn't eat salt, meat, fish, bananas, chilies, or cooking oil. They shouldn't bathe, not even get caught in the rain or ford a large river, lest their scent alert the quarry. Most significantly, trappers should avoid human contact. If a trapper meets someone he knows and the person is not sensitive enough to avoid addressing him, he should say only, "Don't talk to me, I'm going home." He should avoid sex, even sleeping beside other people. Animals, remember, are people "in their own dimension," so that the trapping he is engaged in is profoundly antisocial, both violent and duplicitous.

I suspect that reluctance to contaminate others with such an action underlies the fact that Semai talk about these restrictions as reflecting *mnuur*. Juli Edo, the Semai anthropologist, says,

> Doing something you don't want to do produces "mnuur" (example: say your parents asked you to get some food from the jungle but you insist on

not doing it. And if you go without your own wish, you might have an accident or [be] bit[t]en by [a] snake). . . . [People usually talk about *mnuur*] when there is loss of life on that day. (quoted in Dentan 1992:256n6)

You have to deceive and trap your food, but you know that it is a bad thing to do, and you don't want to do it. Being forced to what you do not want to do is spiritually harmful, and you -*muur*.

THE WAGES OF SIN

[G]nghaanh and tnghaan' (Sin)

The concept of *nggern-haq* [= *tnghaan'*] is largely responsible for the complex system of food sharing and exchange. . . . An individual is said to incur *nggern-haq* if he willingly withdraws from sharing. . . . [He] would experience extreme difficulty in obtaining food (e.g. ill luck in hunting or fishing); or else, the food which he has will cause him discomfort or illness. On a wider perspective, an individual would also be subjected to *nggern-haq* if another in a different hamlet dies of starvation, while there is sufficient food available with the former. . . . *Nggern-haq* , therefore, instills a sense of co-responsibility in the manner in which food is distributed and consumed. (Nicholas 1994:39–40)

Among Semai friends, I am always reminded of the overriding rule of behaviour governing their lives, *tenhak*. In essence, this rule requires an individual to be responsible for the good and wellbeing of others. This rule is so encompassing that one is said to have committed *tenhak* if, for example, someone in a distant land dies of hunger while you yourself have more than enough to eat. You are deemed responsible for his death and would have to suffer the consequences. This may seem extreme but *tenhak* also translates into everyday living via concepts of sharing, satisfying of needs, and what is generally perceived to be proper behaviour towards other individuals, whether Orang Asli or not. (Nicholas 1993:45)

These rules may reflect the influence of the old Khmer colony that once occupied part of South Perak, around Bernam. The name apparently comes from the Khmer word *phnom*, mountain, referring to the central peak of a Hindu kingdom. Indeed, Semai there call themselves *maay sraa'*, a phrase that now means "folk of the hinterlands." But *sraa'* may come from a Khmer word for "realm." And the word *tnghaan'* comes from a Hindu (Sanskrit) word meaning "lust, desire, passion." Not all Semai use it; there's an Austroasiatic word most Semai use, *duus*, that covers much the same set of meanings (Shorto 1971). And the term is not salient in Malay.

Although these rules also concern sharing, among other things, they don't work like *punan*, unlike *srnloo'*. Bah Tony, who comes from this area of Perak, writes of these taboos, "I think some element of reciprocity is involved in sharing among Semai. [Perak] Semai ethics require recipients to share whatever [is] shareable with donors, otherwise *genhaa?* will come into play" (Williams-Hunt 2008). *Gnhaan'*, supernatural penalties, however, may also come into play when anyone anywhere goes without necessities. I never encountered this term among Tluup Semai.

Oh, was it hard to explain to Semai that my people don't understand the social connectedness that underlies these ideas. Klip, a Methodist convert from Teiw R'eiis, said in 1992 that Christians use the Malay-Arabic word *dosa* to translate the English word "sin," not *tnghaan'*. But he saw the similarity between the three concepts. Surprised and upset to hear that some people in my country were homeless, he said not providing houses for them

> is like *tnghaan'*. In your country they build houses for dogs, don't they? But it's not really *tnghaan'* or *dosa*. It's more like you just don't have a lngrii.

The word *gnghaanh'* or *nghaanh* (probably cognate with *tnghaan'*, sin) covers a wide range of actions that upset social relations with humans or animals, including *srngloo'* (hunters' violence) or killing a harmless creature for sport. "Dead-people *gnghaanh'*" occurs when your kinsman dies suddenly without your knowing. Any unexpected event can alarm your head soul, which is likely to flee, leaving you feeble and endangered. The death causes an unexpected break in social relations. Even though you don't know about it, it makes you "sense [the immanent death] in your own life." The underlying idea is like that in John Donne's (1947:593) famous sermon:

> Any man's death diminishes me, because I am involved in mankind, and therefore, never send to ask for whom the [death] bell tolls; it tolls for thee. (593)

The underlying concept involves a poignant sense of closeness to other people that, for my own people, is hard to comprehend as anything but vapid piety. For Semai, however, love for one's fellows *physically* transcends the illusion of personal uniqueness and isolation.

Gnghaanh' leaves you tired, weak, so dizzy that you're likely to fall: that's *lnwiik*, a sign you're in spiritual danger. After you find out about the death, the feeling usually goes away, although the best thing is to have a feast the locally appropriate number of days after the death. The feast "closes the grave." Indeed, at Mncaak, you literally close it, putting a cement slab on top of it to lock away the influence of the dead, the *kcmooc*.

A Waar River example of *gnghaanh'* involves not burying a corpse in the Semai way (in a roofed grave, facedown to keep the dirt off, wrapped in a mat, with personal belongings like blowpipe, darts, machete, pot, and favorite cassettes that you don't want to see again because it will make you remember the person you've lost). Everything would go wrong for the offending kinsmen: they could fall and get badly hurt, look vainly for fruit in season so that "their innards would be hungry"; that is, they would suffer frustrated desire, in this case called *tnghaan'* (sin).

Tnghaan' are evil deeds that bring disaster to the perpetrators, unlike *punan* or *srngloo'*, which affect victims. Say that 'Alang treats Ngah badly, not letting him visit, for example, or not sharing food with him. Ngah will suffer *punan*, but Long will suffer *tnghaan'*, so that there is no reason for the community to discipline Long: "Never mind," people will opine, "he'll get his *tnghaan'*," hence the saying, "We don't fear other people, we fear *tnghaan'*." But, as the next chapter shows, Perak Semai may hold a town meeting to pressure offenders to admit guilt, compensate the victims, and thus restore *slamaad*. Children learn about *tnghaan'* early:

RKD gave crayons to three kids, a boy aged 2, and two girls, 2 and 3, each child sitting on its mother's lap. When the girls got their crayons or paper, the boy would go over to snatch them.

"-*Trnghaan'*," said the littler girl's mother, "You're causing *tnghaan'*."

The girl seemed unperturbed. But when the boy tried to grab the crayons from the other girl, his sister, she scratched at his face (not actually touching him, of course; these were Semai kids). Both burst into tears. Their mom pulled them apart. The girl stopped crying right away, and the mother suckled the boy.

"That's what we do when children fight," said Simasmother, another woman, "give them the breast." The rest of the time, when the boy grabbed at the crayons, the adult women distracted him by showing him interesting things or by telling him his parent's elder brother [scary stranger RKD] was watching. (Teiw Mncaak summer 1991)

Killing or menacing someone is normally *tnghaan'*, says Ngah Hari of Mncaak. Your vision dims; you get thin, sick, feeble. You have "sinned" and God (Jnaang) has cursed you. It is not *tnghaan'* to kill someone who is threatening to kill you, he adds, though you should -*cagòòh*, pray, first. Thus, Bah Tanggu', a "terrorist" during the Communist uprising of the 1950s, committed no *tnghaan'*: the terrorists forced him to follow them, he killed no one himself, and he gave himself up. But, although Ngah Hari asserted that Bah Planken was also forced to follow the terrorists, he "did what the others told him," killing people and not surrendering. He therefore did commit *tnghaan'*.

Ngah Hari uses the Sanskrit-Malay word *dosa*, "sin," to translate *tng-haan'*. Murder, he says, making people sick, and killing cats are *tnghaan'*. Homosexuality is *tnghaan' ya Tuhan*, sin in the eyes of God (Allah or Yahweh), but not *ya hii'*, in our own eyes. *Tnghaan'* makes you skinny and weak, your mouth gets dry, you are covered with sores. But today people are *modun*, he says, modern, and don't respect adepts' powers or *tnghaan'*.

For *tnghaan'* is still a traditional Semai notion, unlike "sin." Indeed, so was *dosa*, the Malay word for "sin," as Semai used it. Here's a 1992 conversation from Teiw Waar involving myself; Cat, a woman in her early forties; and her son Lang, fourteen:

Cat: One night in my grandparents' generation, a man went out spearing frogs. A reticulated python seized him, wrapped itself around his waist like a loincloth.

Lang: Around his neck.

Cat: It dragged him into the water, where he fainted. His familiar spirit [*gu-niik*] talked with the python. "This man has no *dosa*." Finally the python let him go. When the man got home he asked what day it was. He'd been unconscious for three days.

RKD: So you need to have no *dosa*.

Cat: So you need to have a familiar spirit to negotiate for you.

Tolah (Disrespect)

Good manners, for Semai, involve deferring to people older than yourself. Semai describe the attitude underlying the deference as *snngòòh*, a word that I've usually translated as "fear" but that, in this context, means something like "respect." (Even in English, a few centuries ago, both fear and respect fit under the label "fear.") When Semai children were cheeky or obnoxious to me, their parents would say, "*Srngòòh* them," make them fear. Teach them respect. The Semai idea that old people have more spiritual power than younger ones may reflect the greater fear/respect they deserve. In dreams, old people often represent demonic powers, and people address demons as members of older generations, parents, or grandparents.

The greatest respect/fear involves complete avoidance, as in the example I've already given of proper behavior between Mrlooh and his mother-in-law. A traditional Tluup Semai man should never address or look at his mother-in-law. Indeed, sharing a house is testing limits and could be *tolah*. The avoidance between a woman and her father-in-law is only slightly less strict. The avoidance between a person and his or her spouse's elder sibling and elder sibling's spouse is still less strict. The terms for older in-laws are modifications of the terms for blood kinsmen one generation higher: of "grandparent" for parents-in-law and of "uncle" or "aunt" for older siblings-in-law. This usage both manifests and enforces the correlation between relative age and respect.

Mandatory respect prevents the possible conflict inherent in these relationships. If he can't talk to his mother-in-law, a man can't quarrel with her about who her daughter should help out first. Intimacy can't breed contempt. Respect rules would be superfluous if no one felt the urge to behave disrespectfully, probably a constant temptation for egalitarians left to their own devices. And Tluup Semai also have what anthropologists call "joking relationships" with certain kinsmen. These relationships offer an opportunity for, but do not require, teasing and flirting, rough-housing, and sometimes having irresponsible cheerful sex between *mnaay*, your spouse's younger sibling and younger sibling's spouse. "*Mnaay*" is a version of *maay*, "other people," that is, people with whom you are not intimately connected. Before they become your in-laws, all the people involved in these relationships are *maay*, outside the realm of the familiar and safe, and therefore require special treatment, what Hobbes calls "fear" but Americans would call "caution."

Respect relationships keep tricky social relationships tidy, as the *pnalii'* rules discussed later maintain cosmic order. The joking relationships offer a way to vent the frustration that self-control generates. They complement each other, reflecting the ambivalence about deference that any egalitarian people must feel.

Semai have borrowed most of the language they use for deference from the more comfortably hierarchical society of the Malays. *Tolah* is originally a Malay notion. Unsurprisingly then, *tolah* can rationalize (or mystify) deferring to or avoiding Malays. A Semai headman at the Betau Relocation Scheme told a Malay anthropologist,

> Senoi ["Humans," i.e., Semai] don't dare get intimate with Malays for fear of *tolah*. Because Malays are superior, because Malays believe in the Lord God [Allah]. Malays are circumcised and ritually pure. Not Senoi. That's why Senoi are unclean. . . . If they want to become Malays, they must get circumcised and ritually purified. They can't live like Senoi. (quoted in Hasan Mat Nor [1989:107], Dentan tr.)

This statement may reflect "identification with the oppressor," in which people reflexively protect themselves from oppression by adopting the attitudes of the oppressors, the way that people beaten as children may excuse their parents' actions or become child beaters themselves. At Betau, Semai meet many Malays who despise Semai; "introjecting" (uncritically accepting) this attitude paradoxically makes Semai like Malays and thus may protect them from feeling the pain of what W. E. B. Du Bois (1979:3) calls "double consciousness": the "sense of always looking at oneself through the eyes of others, of measuring one's soul by the tape of world that looks on in amused contempt and pity" In the case of one young Semai man who grew up at Betau, this "ego defense," as psychoanalysts call it, may have had terrible consequences for a couple of American children whom he brutally murdered in 1992 (Dentan 2007).

Of course, this attitude also suggests that even trying to be as good as Malays is pointless. Thus, appealing to Malay bigotry, the headman excuses himself from cooperating with government assimilationism. Some headmen do that deliberately to obscure their resistance to Malay plans. It also amuses people aware of the tactic, much like the stories people tell in which people fool the powerful and dangerous Thunder Lord. This-gambit, "camping," is common in among Americans who reject the dominant gender identity schema:

> I embrace and impersonate the degrading image because there is no way out of the stereotype except to embrace it, to critique it by ironically assuming its vestments. . . . I can't refuse it. ("drag queen," quoted by Clemons 1993:14)

Camping also requires "double consciousness." Awareness of Malay contempt pervades Semai consciousness. Semai describing how Semai do things typically contrast it with its Malay equivalent.

In this context, love and intimacy form the complement and opposite of fear/respect.

And that brings up the recurring problem with human love, that it easily becomes sexual. Semai express abhorrence at the idea of incest or sexual contact across generations, the same repulsion, I think, that most Americans feel at the sexual abuse of children. But Semai think that young people might want to initiate sexual intimacy with much older ones as well as the other way around, a thought taboo in America. Doing that would manifest an attitude for which people use a term that conflates two Malay words that mean "uppitiness" and "incest." In 1992 an old friend of mine at Kniik in the Perak foothills said that using the name of anyone older than yourself is *tolah*, disrespect. In fact, even if they're younger but have children of their own, you should use their teknonym, "Parent of Soandso." Still, he added,

> I was talking with this kid just the other day. The kid says, "In the old days, I was scared to say my dad's name, scared of *tolah*. Even when somebody asked me my dad's name [as Malay officials do], I didn't want to say it. But now I'm not afraid to say it even if nobody asks me to. If it's *tolah*, there's always the hospital."

The particular *tolah* may reflect the sexual component of the misbehavior. For example, your genitals may bleed or swell up to enormous size, an affliction that, in Malaysia, sometimes arises from vaginal or inguinal hernias. Or *tolah* can be the appalling violence of a thundersquall, the upsurge of the cold waters from beneath the earth and the huge tectonic dragons that live there, the sort of annihilation implicit in the notion of *trlaac*.

Concluding Remarks

People recall particular wounds to their feelings only when bad things have happened and need explaining. They usually avoid talking about their feelings: "What's the use?" But the continuity they imagine between damage to your feelings and damage to your body makes it plausible to blame the latter on the former. The victimized person can ask for a present, a "fine," for which they use a Sanskrit-Malay word. Paying a fine heals the damage that offenders do to the *sngii'* of their victims. Or the offender may arrange (and pay for) the victim to receive a supernaturally cooling curative bath in water made fragrant with magical leaves and flowers. During the bathing, several people (usually including an adept) focus on the patient, showing their concern and often massaging the affected parts of his or her body: aromatherapy, massage therapy, the works. The cure for spiritual violation, in short, is to get some token of love.

CATACLYSMIC DISRESPECT

Lknuk (Fooling Around): Pnalii' and Trlaac

We are safe here the war
is somewhere else the war is
in our heads but we are safe
and all our things are safe.
Safe. The banks open and close
and open: we are saved.

—From "We Know" (Goodman 1989:33)

The 9/11 massacre and Hurricane Katrina in 2005 showed Americans that cosmic order is as fragile as Semai say it is. But, while Americans drift back into numbness or fantasies of prevention or retaliatory power, Semai stay aware of the threat, always. They say, "Watch out! Don't stray off the path!" *'A bòr, mòng hi-yòòk*, "Careful, you might fall [and hurt yourself]," people say whenever you leave their house. Disrespect of cosmic order produces cataclysms: the enraged Lord of Thunder will obliterate your settlement; the cold waters beneath the earth burst out, bearing monsters, obliterating human life.

Two sorts of disrespect are involved: the first involves mixing particular categories, especially of food, as if the cosmic order that Semai think their language reflects were so fragile that human dietary whimsy could destroy it. The second, more general violation involves disrespecting that order.

Pnali' (Disrespectful Mixture)

Semai keep kosher. Four basic categories of food don't mix together: meat, fish (or aquatic animals generally), birds, and fungi. Each category needs its own crockery. Most people can't afford that and so keep plates for fish, putting other foods on banana leaves. You should even cook the categories over separate fires so that the smoke doesn't mingle.

Failure to respect proper cosmic kosher has cataclysmic effects, Semai say. Before I was at all fluent in Semai, I was trying to explore the question of what would happen if one mixed spices with bearcat. The witty middle-aged woman I was talking with finally laughed and threw up her hands. "BOOM!" she yelled, sweeping the air with her arms, and added, "This whole settlement would be buried in mud, and we'd be underneath it."

Trlaac (Snits and Mockery)

> No Believer is allowed to play with cats or dogs, not to make unnecessary freedom with any of the beasts of the field, or with any kind of fowl or bird. (Shaker *Millennial Laws* [quoted in Goonan 1994:12])

On 15 January 1992 on the Teiw Waar, Wa' Rhii', age six, fakes attacking Bah Ly, a boy a year older, with some Magic Markers we'd brought for the kids to play with, stroking at his face and, when he turns to flee, striping his back with bright yellow.

RKD: *Wees katiir!* [Stop squabbling!].

Lysfather: That's not *katiir*, just *tntood* [play fighting]. You should say, "Stop it, don't *-lk-luk* [fool around], it's *trlaac*. Just be friends!"

Disrespecting cosmic order is *-trlaac*, a destructive and perilous loss of moderation and self-control, like throwing a tantrum, *-liclaac*, or like *ceep laac*, the little munia bird, flocks of which may devastate a rice crop. The world is a system of which humans are part, says Bah Tony Williams-Hunt. Not respecting a monkey's monkeyness, treating it as if it were a human, violates its integrity. Imitating the call of certain birds that Semai associate with thundersqualls disrespects the boundary between people and birds. This sort of border crossing resembles the shamanic skills that Semai tricked the Lord into giving them. Uncontrolled by adepts, that power manifests itself in thundersqualls.

Trifling with creatures associated with thundersqualls is foolish. For instance, it would be *trlaac* to destroy the nest of a sort of ant that "only works when it's wet" and is thus associated with thundersqualls, like many other creatures. Blood, especially women's menstrual and puerperal blood, has special powers, akin to those symbolized by tigers and thundersqualls, say Semai. "Tiger *trlaac*," associated with bleeding at these times, involves the risk that the women or their embryos will turn into tigers. A menstruating woman who accompanies a fish poisoning expedition, mixing distinct categories of powerful poisons, for example, might mutate into a tiger.

But the basic danger is losing self-control, disrespecting boundaries, from which all the other dangers flow. Adults are always yelling *Trlaac! Trlaac!* at children when children are screaming or laughing or otherwise being childishly noisy. When a storm comes, they suspect that children are at fault and pull out a tuft of a child's hair to pound with a pestle or throw into the fire to fool the Lord. For the same reason, adults often sound gruff and unfriendly, so that conversations between them sound hostile, until an offhand gift or big smile reveals the underlying affection (as sometimes happens with Chinese or New York Yiddish conversations). Children start learning this style of talk as they approach puberty, at nine or ten years old.

Semai try to avoid emotional displays, not wanting to weep or grieve openly, for instance, when someone they love is going away. A woman from Mncaak said that that Christianity had taught her how to deal with grief by "trusting in the Lord." But most people overwhelmed by emotion will -*kra'diic*, retreat into their houses until they can compose themselves. Similarly, meeting someone you love after a long parting, you should show no emotion, perhaps not even speak, though you can change your destination so that you both can walk along silently together.

This self-restraint, originating in respect for other people and for the cosmos in general, is more important than avoiding merely physical violence. For example, watching dogs copulate is -*trlaac*, in part because you're likely to laugh, and beating dogs badly is *tnghaan'* (sin).

But children often ignore the rules, as grown-ups expect they will. Like this example from my Teiw R'eiis field notes in 1992:

A bitch at R'eiis was in heat. The male dogs wouldn't leave her alone. Three little boys decided to protect her: Rmpent, nine; Tkooy, also nine; and Grcaang, twelve. Rmpent beat a couple of dogs in the morning for fighting over her, just enough to stop the fight.

"*Trlaac!*" I said.

"No way," he retorted gruffly. "Only if we *-lk-luk*" [laugh].

But at dusk the same day, Grcaang, armed with a flashlight and stick, and his younger brother Tkooy, still naked from his evening bath but wielding a burning brand, chased the dogs away, running around and laughing uncontrollably. The laughter was *-trlaac*.

Discussion

> We're very careful about hurting people. We avoid it. We did the same smart thing Tluup River people did during the Emergency. The Pale People [British] usually stayed in town. When they came through here, we supported them. The Limberlost People [communist terrorists] killed a *mnaleeh* [nubile girl], but we gave them tapioca and other food when they passed through. We really hate getting mixed up in other people's "quarrels" [uses the Malay word]. We want to live *slamaad*, in peace and security. . . .
>
> That's why we don't steal. Malays are always stealing things, but we don't. The weird thing is that it's rich people who steal. We don't want trouble. Besides, we don't want to be rich. If we have enough to eat, that's enough. If you're rich, you get endless hassles, no *slamaad*. That's why we don't want to be rich. We want *slamaad*.
>
> The only time we hurt people is when we drink. Alcohol makes us talk *rawuuc*, irrationally, act *rawuuc*. People here go into town and drink with their Malay and Tamil Indian buddies. After a while they go in and drink by themselves. . . . No, not like in Mncaak, never before 10 AM.
>
> —Bah Minor, about age forty, at 'Icek, R'eiis River, 4 April 1992

The English term *violence* covers a lot of territory. Ordinary Americans tend to think of violence as having a core, "physical violence," and a periphery, "symbolic violence." If you just say "violence," they think of "physical violence" first.

The first time I tried to understand how Semai could define greed or showing up late as physical violence I was working with this parochial distinction in the back of my mind. How wonderful (although weird and primitive) it was, I opined, that people would be so nonviolent that their sanction against bad manners was to imagine the victim's suffering physically—since, while you might want to hurt someone's feelings, you wouldn't want to inflict bodily harm.

The atmosphere in America back then encouraged that sort of thinking. People were extending the word "violence" to refer to flag burning, to being outvoted, to sit-ins by members of an explicitly nonviolent movement, and so on. It wasn't enough to talk about the destruction of native cultures or the smug institutionalized neglect of poor children in America: people had to talk about "genocide." But I remembered the first photographs of the death camps, and the rhetoric seemed overblown and self-serving.

Moreover, it left a concept that seemed uselessly vague, without definitive empirical content. "Violence" became an intangible essence, taking "many different forms . . . not a homogeneous constant . . . physical or psychological, visible or invisible, instrumental or metaphorical" (Elsass 1992:157). This shape-changing entity occasionally manifested itself in the real world, with dire consequences. It's hard to see how such essentialist formulations differ from the Semai notion of demons. The level of sophistication is no higher. Not "essentially."

I finally began to understand what was happening during a conversation with Cuthbert O. Simpkins, a trauma surgeon and Director of the Violence and Victimization Prevention Program of GROUP Ministries in Buffalo, New York, at the turn of the century. The conversation began with me running off at the mouth about something a social worker had said, mouthing then widely believed platitudes, as often happens with me, like this:

RKD: Yeah, but all that "at-risk youth" stuff seems to me like blaming the victim. Maybe labeling is part of the problem, I mean, for turning kids violent? There's no proof that kids turn violent because they have bad *attitudes*, for chrissake, and we know that some kids' attitudes get *worse* after they go through AVP [antiviolence programs]. Teachers *expect* "at-risk" kids to act out and "prosocial" kids to be good, and we *know* kids act the way adults expect them to. So they act out, and the teachers and "prosocial" kids reject them, so they feel stressed out and act out some more, and you get a feedback loop; what we call "conduct disorder" and blame on the at-risk kid. Nothing to do with all the goddam social workers coming in and labeling people. [Grins.]

COS: [Flooded by words, nods.]

RKD: [Taking the nod as encouragement.] So how about violence *by* the schools? Twenty some states let adults beat school kids with paddles so badly the marks last for *weeks*. But that isn't violence or child abuse because it's the *state*, so beating is *good* for them: "Kids *want* limits." Bull*shit*. You think beaten kids don't learn it's ok for big people to beat little people?

COS: Wait. Wait. Stress is one of the "risk factors" the CDC [Centers for Disease Control] talks about. Let me get back to what I was going to say. Stress is pain. I'm a materialist. I'm a doctor. I'm a scientist. I don't believe in spirit. I believe in pain. Stress, any kind, causes pain. Pain tells you you've been damaged. That's what it's for. That's the psychobiological adaptive significance of pain. It signals *Danger!* People who don't feel pain can't be left alone because they'll damage themselves. . . .

What I'm trying to say is stress causes physical changes, neurochemical changes, and most of those changes are bad. It's adaptive if you can do something. You know, the fight-or-flight reflex. But keep up the stress and those responses start damaging the organism. Hypertension, stroke, heart attacks. Shock and terror damage the base structures of the brain. It's all physical. Eventually, stress can kill you.

RKD: [Slumped almost horizontal, nods and shrugs.] *So?*

COS: For example. Last few years, courts in a lot of states have been sentencing mothers to prison for using alcohol and drugs. We know, legislators know, that drugs and alcohol poison fetuses and babies. They cause low IQ, hyperactivity, attention deficit hyperactivity disorder.

RKD: Like crack babies, right? Or FAS [fetal alcohol syndrome]? But didn't they first discover FAS in Native Americans? And crack's a black thing. No powder cocaine baby problem . . .

COS: Yes, but racism's not the point. The point is that separating babies from their mothers has bad effects, too.

RKD: (?)

COS: Effects like low IQ, hyperactivity, attention-deficit/hyperactivity disorder.

RKD: [Leans forward, grinning.] Separation is a stressor, right?

COS: Especially in the first year or two. And the reason the women get picked up isn't just that they're black, it's that they're poor. So the social services people are in and out, and they see the abuse. And poverty is a stressor. Guess what it causes.

RKD: Low IQ, hyperactivity, attention deficit disorder?

COS: Yes.

RKD: Wow! [The two men sit silent for a moment.]

RKD: [Nods again.] I get it. I never liked the notion that "violence" means "doing harm," because who's to say what's "harm" and what isn't? But if we do it by physical results, let doctors decide. . . . Jeez, I never thought I'd want to *medicalize* violence. [Sits up, leans forward, talking fast.] But, separation causes stress, *neglect* causes stress, right? . . . Rudeness causes stress, disrespect causes stress. Oh ho! Semai would *love* that. Violate somebody, diss him, he gets accident prone, sickness prone, maybe he won't get sick but he's more *likely* to get sick, unless you bathe him in special stuff, unless you stroke him to get th-th-th-the *stress* out . . .

COS: Stress kills people. That's no secret. It makes them sick and, sooner or later, it kills them. Disrespect, injustice cause stress, raise cortisol levels, depress serotonin levels. Stress causes physical problems: depression, hypertension. The immune system suffers: you get colds, gum disease; your wounds heal more slowly. Your psychophysical problems make you inattentive, so you're more likely to have accidents. The physical problems kill you. A causes B causes C. So A causes C. But we don't want to say that abandonment or disrespect or homophobia *are* physical violence.

RKD: Because then we'd *all* have to change. Because then everybody's involved, not just The Bad Guys. Not just the people who "make bad choices." Wow. *Wow.*

"It's More as If You Just Don't Have a Lngrii"

Semai guidelines do many things, of course. Rules have many "functions," as anthropologists used to say. But Semai rules embody the felt unity of physical violence on the one hand and making people feel worthless and powerless on the other. Existentially and psychologically, there's not a big difference in the results, however different the means people use to bring the results about. Both sorts of attack wound what Semai call *sngii'*, the human spirit. Think of it as brain chemistry. If you treat people as if their needs don't matter, as if their feelings don't count, then they get sick; eventually, they may even die. If you don't share food or don't show up on time for an appointment, you frustrate someone's hopes and expectations, and you hurt them physically.

Semai may be particularly sensitive to stress. Learned helplessness can be stressful. It's hard to imagine a more stressful experience than being unable to protect your children from unpredictable but irresistible kidnapper-abusers. Several signs may express the stress this learned helplessness causes: the vigilance about children, which is one of the ways people everywhere relieve stress, the "tend" in "fight, flight, tend, and befriend"; the emphasis on ties with other people, another universal antistress tactic, the "befriend"; the prevalence of depression and insomnia; the importance of "startling" events in explanations of disease and soul loss, events that don't seem startling to outsiders. It makes sense that Semai would evolve ways to foster the illusion of control, like *pnalii'* mixture taboos, and ways to handle social stressors. This system seems "primitive" to Americans because Semai talk about it in ways that we classify as "primitive," referring to demons, for example, instead of to "stress."

But America is also full of stress, especially for people with little power: the very young and the very old, the "submerged" minorities, the poor and exploited. Neglecting people's welfare hurts them, Semai say. Older people's spirits may be *cigeeh*, tough enough that they escape physical damage. But, especially if they're just children, who have "soft souls," they're at risk.

Many Americans also say they feel more and more insecure, anxious, depressed, lonely, and unhappy—like kids who have been bullied. Recent studies show that the greater the gap between classes in hierarchical societies, the greater the stress—for rich and poor alike. The gap is greater than it's been in my lifetime and it is increasing. Professional students of bullying don't emphasize the difference between "symbolic" and "physical" bullying in schools. But the Cartesian distinction between mental (unimportant) and physical (serious) violence makes sense in hierarchical societies in way it doesn't make sense in nonhierarchical ones. In hierarchical societies, it's the weak who use physical violence: black people, poor people, a few bullied schoolchildren running amok. People who run things, whose life experiences give rise to "hegemonic" American concepts of the world, commit only "symbolic" violence, violence that doesn't count as violence: contempt, indifference, downsizing, breaking appointments, making applicants or "clients" wait for hours. Physical injury comes more gradually by such means, but it comes. To acknowledge the harm might undermine the social arrangements that let some people hurt others without risking anything.

That's the way my social and economic system works. It's not a sin. It's like Klip from Teiw R'eiis said. It's more as if we didn't have a country.

Conclusion

Under stress, people may rationally choose violence. Violence works best when you are overwhelmingly more powerful than your opponent, as generals, bullies, and child abusers know. Usually, choosing violence would be disastrous for Semai, Malays have all the levers of power, and Semai depend on each other to survive. Flight and surrender, in the sense this book has been trying to develop for those words, make more sense than violence. But it's even better to avoid the stress that raises the fight/flight option in the first place. That's what Semai do—and pretty consciously:

> **Nudiysfather, an adept:** Let me give one answer to your question [about Semai nonviolence]. When someone does something wrong, like stealing, we don't beat them up or kill them. We bring them to judgment under our laws. We're one family, one people. Maybe we fine them, but only a little. And we -lees, harangue them, urge them to change their ways, not to set a bad example for the children. We don't like to kill or beat people. We'd be ashamed. And, number two, we'd be like beasts that kill/harm people.

> **Pvksgrandfather:** Right. What we think is, if we harm them, we lose, we lose a friend. So, we -kra'dii', withdraw and suffer in private. We feel bad. But we need help in clearing fields, in feeding ourselves. We realize that if we hurt our friends, we lose out. (Waar River, 1991)

6

✣

Freedom: Just Say "No"

"A new commandment gave I unto you, that ye love one another." Yes, this it was that saved me. Aside from higher considerations, charity often operates as a vastly wise and prudent principle—a great safe-guard to its possessor. Men have committed murder for jealousy's sake, and anger's sake, and spiritual pride's sake; but no man, that I ever heard of, ever committed a diabolical murder for sweet charity's sake. Mere self-interest, then, if no better motive can be enlisted, should, especially with high-tempered men, prompt all beings to charity and philanthropy.

—Herman Melville, *Bartleby the Scrivener* (1974:924)

SOME MORE MISCONCEPTIONS ABOUT PEACE

RKD: You ever hit anybody?

Risaaw k. Jambu, married man, about 30 years old: No.

RKD: Would you ever hit anybody?

Risaaw: No.

RKD: Why not?

Risaaw: He'd just hit me back.

RKD: Suppose he hit you first?

Risaaw: He'd still just hit me back. (conversation, Tluup River, 1962)

Three more things to learn from Semai: first, peace isn't about being pacifist or "good"; second, peace isn't free; and, third, peace subverts obedience.

"Social exchange theorists" assume "human interaction is guided by the pursuit of rewards and the avoidance of punishments and costs. . . . All take and no give is not a formula for happy or continued social interaction" (Gelles and Straus 1988:22). Nudiysfather and Pvksgrandfather said the same thing at the close of chapter 5.

When Semai or social exchange theorists talk about peaceability, *slamaad*, they sound so reasonable that it is hard to remember that there are situations in which nonviolence is difficult or problematic. But no adaptation is continuously optimal, particularly active and complex ones like Semai peaceability. Conditions change, adaptation lags. Moreover, the various aspects of the adaptation needn't fit well together: freedom, for example, is always tricky. And the context of adaptation includes previous adaptations that may limit or conflict with new ones. Nothing, not even peace, comes free: "[A]daptation is a blessing when it isn't a curse" (Koja 1996:201). This chapter sketches some conflicts between individual autonomy and self-sufficiency versus group influence and mutual emotional dependency.

Like other egalitarian peoples, Semai enjoy individuality, both their own and that of their friends. Everyone has an individualized take on the world, even an individualized vocabulary for talking about it—personal names for particular bird species, demons, and taboos, for instance. There are more than forty Semai dialects, more than one for every thousand people, and no authoritative focus for knowledge or anything else. Semai respect for personal freedom works against coercion or violence, even against kids, and thus bolsters equality. This individual autonomy allows people to evade coercion or violence by scattering or moving away.

Traditional Semai agriculture rested on clearing and burning secondary forest. There was plenty of land for the small numbers of people willing to live in the hills. The problem wasn't land but getting enough people to help at crucial times, planting and harvest, for example. Since you can't coerce free people, you need to treat them with courtesy and respect, as in the "taboo" system, so that they will want to help you, as Nudiysfather, Pvksgrandfather, and social exchange theory explain.

Political scientists who study dispute resolution sometimes dismiss stateless societies like Semai as irrelevant or, at best, paradoxical. A former advocate of globalization reacts angrily:

In their cult of reason and efficiency, their ignorance of history and their contempt for the ways of life they consign to poverty or extinction, they embody the same rationalist hubris and cultural imperialism that have marked the central traditions of Enlightenment thinking throughout its history. (Gray 1998:3)

Others, more respectful of peoples like Semai, still ultimately look to the state for solutions imposed from above to the "problem" of violence, as if states were not themselves manifestations of the problem (e.g., Fry 2006; cf. Dentan 2008).

Formal dispute resolution techniques are unnecessary to peace in "stateless" societies (i.e., societies still so marginalized that state peacekeeping institutions have little impact). The traditional Semai way of dealing with conflict, said one Semai man, was "just try to stay out of trouble, even if they personally don't agree with what is proposed. In fact, most of the time, they don't agree, but they don't voice it out, and they don't fight aloud. In my perception, Orang Asli tend to avoid confrontation—among ourselves and with outsiders " (quoted in Nah 2004:119–20).

But in the 1930s, colonialism and "development" began "modernizing" the economy of Semai who live along the road between the lowland town of Gòòl (Malay Tapah) and the Cameron Highlands that straddle the states of Perak and Pahang. Globalization undercut traditional subsistence agriculture, overrunning land once available to Semai, harnessing the people to what they call "the Market," the lowland trade centers. The potential conflict between individual freedom and mutual aid became acute.

In fact, The *bicaraa'* or town meeting that this chapter describes, arrived in part of Perak Semai country as part of a scheme to extend state authority over the then free frontier regions (for details, see Gomes 2004:33–34; Juli, Williams-Hunt, and Dentan 2008). The supposed need for peacekeeping often rationalizes, mystifies, and justifies the extension of imperialist or colonialist state power as "humanitarian intervention" (Graeber 2007b:256), proving "the benefits of governance of anarchy" (Fry 2006:257; but cf. Dentan 2008). Many Semai from the region attribute their peacefulness to the power of the *bicaraa'* to resolve disputes. Indeed, sometimes it works. But although its "failure" may mean that the conflict remains unresolved, the result is rarely violence. "Learned helplessness" and deference to individual autonomy may make it easier for Semai to accept such failure while at the same time making failure more likely.

I've changed some identifying details in the following "ethnographic fiction" to preserve people's anonymity. Otherwise, the tale depicts a series of incidents that occurred during my stay on the Waar in 1992–1993. The conversations are real conversations I heard or heard about, the issues the real issues. As always, the characterization of how the people involved felt is entirely fictitious, based on my sense of the feelings of Semai

I know better. The protagonists' motives and thoughts, my mentor Ngah Hari of Mncaak would agree, are unknowable. For observers, he would say, "It must be like a movie." I have put these imagined thoughts in italics to distinguish them from what I heard or saw. The aim is to illustrate the conflicts I've been talking about.

TOWN MEETINGS, *BICARAA'*

When disputes among central Perak Semai become serious enough to affect community peace, local leaders set up a town meeting, *bicaraa'*, in hopes that, under community pressure, disputants will admit errors, compromise, and restore domestic tranquillity, *slamaad*. At these meetings, the centerpiece is acceptance by the parties involved of a fine or set of fines. An elaborate schedule of fines covers various offenses, but in fact the people who agree to pay often delay payment, sometimes indefinitely. Public admission of responsibility is the point, not punishment.

The words for "town meeting" and "fine" are Sanskrit-Malay. Ngah Hari said that, until Semai learned *hukum dnda'*, the rule of fines, from Malays, people settled disputes, especially about women, by killing each other, "like those savages on the Tluup River." This theory, that Semai peacefulness stems from the colonial imposition of the "rule of fines," is plausible. Traditionally, only Malay aristocrats participated in such meetings. The extension to Semai occurred a century ago, when the Perak sultan, under British pressure, was passing out grandiose titles to puppet Semai headmen so that he could extend central state authority over the area. The mid-century Marxist Teodor Adorno says that colonial exercises like extending the *bicaraa'* are the ideological reflex of the state to the threat of peasant unrest, which it sees as chaotic violence. The modern equivalent is "scientific management" of conflict by "experts," coupled with "social engineering" to eliminate the injustices that feed violence. Whatever the Anglo-Malay influences, the mechanics of Semai town meetings formalize traditionally ubiquitous communal surveillance and elaborate the pervasive Semai custom of informally seeking material goods to alleviate emotional distress. The difference between *bicaraa'* and traditional dispute resolution, aside from the formal elaboration, is that participants also consider the affront to *slamaad*.

Everyone, of all ages and both genders, participates. Success depends on *slniil*, shame, "the feeling state that accompanies emotional disconnection" (Pollack 1999:32), or fear of such rejection. As Bah Cong, a Tluup teenager, said in 1962, "There's no authority here but *slniil*." Town meetings work (when they work) because people value social ties so highly—the same reason, say social exchange theorists, that similar conflict resolution programs in U.S. high schools fail so often.

Remember: many Semai words denoting spiritual conditions conflate act and consequence. *Slniil* refers to social disengagement, the refusal or inability to engage in efforts that benefit others. The consequences are a potential retaliatory break-off of social ties and the feelings (*-sl-siil*) that rift produces. The closest English equivalents are "shame" or "embarrassment." When a Mncaak toddler exposed her vulva in the 1970s, for example, her mom would put her hand over it, saying gently, "*Siil! Siil!*" One reason for not using the correct name of animals one hunts or the diseases one fears is to avoid "shaming" them, which will make them flee, like the Thunder Lord when you remind Him how Bei'Roman (Brahman) shat up and down his back.

Agreeing to pay the fine constitutes a public admission of responsibility for bad behavior that disturbs *slamaad* so that the fine itself is of only symbolic importance. Not many Semai communities have formal town meetings and even fewer a formal schedule of fines. But community surveillance is inescapable in small close-knit isolated communities where the notion of privacy is absent and wanting to be alone seems antisocial and sinister, as on the Tluup in the 1960s, where people would whisper that a person who went off by himself was consorting with demons—because just wanting to be alone was too weird to imagine.

Still, accepting the judgment of others in order to reconnect with the community conflicts with the Semai ideal of individual autonomy. Enforced conformity makes people physically sick, they say. The town meeting often fails to resolve conflicts, especially now that the Malaysian state claims competing and coercive authority over disputes and the outside world is at least potentially open as an alternative to the local community. Semai *slamaad* is resilient enough, however, that the failures rarely lead to violence.

Love is the most common source of quarrels for Semai. Frustrated sexual love is the most common trigger for violence. Bah Johan of Kampar says that people who commit suicide or murder are mostly *litaaw* and *mnaleeh*, young men and women who take the short view, *pikir patee'*. Mature people *pikir crvvk*, take the long view: "This man has a wife and children who'll suffer if you kill/injure him. Also, you'll be arrested by the police. And you'll get a bad name, *muh hi' nineec.*" In the olden days, the few cases of murder I could find out about—not many—all involved a man's killing his rival or the kidnapper of a woman he loved.

Frustration in love, like frustration in anything else, is *punan*, supernaturally dangerous, particularly to the one who loves. For Semai, as for most people affected by "learned helplessness," severing emotional ties can have catastrophic psychological and social effects. I think they feel wrenchingly let down, betrayed. In the cases of suicide I've collected (Dentan 2000; see also the website that accompanies this book at http://www.rowmanlittlefield.com/isbn/0742553302), loss of a loved one is by far the most common reason people kill themselves, nowadays typically by drinking the pesticides or herbicides that proliferating golf courses and plantations have made widely available. In a society based on mutual aid and respect, disputes about love therefore concern everyone.

The predatory capitalism that has overtaken Semai requires greed and envy. Semai have responded appropriately. Modern murders are not always about sex. Disputes over commercial property, especially fruit trees, are becoming more common. The bounties the British paid motivated a few murders during the Communist insurrection. Still, in the last half of the twentieth century, I know of no cases of murder by a Semai of other Semai without the protection and encouragement of their non-Semai masters. And from 1960 to 2000, I know of only two or three murders (for the ambiguous case, see Dentan 1999a). That makes two to three per million people (25,000 people × 40 years = a million). Even if I'm off by an order of magnitude, the rate's pretty low. The gospel of greed and glut so far has not penetrated the community that fatally, though the bonds of love are attenuated and dying.

JUST ANOTHER WORD FOR NOTHIN' LEFT TO LOSE

Freedom's just another word for nothin' left to lose.
Nothin' left is all she left for me.

—Kris Kristofferson, "Me and Bobby Magee"

Flight (Monday Morning in February)

Beautiful Kliy sat in the shade under the house with her younger brother's wife Longsmother, among piles of dark green dwarf-palm leaves laid parallel with each other. The first thing *litaaw* noticed about Kliy was her mouth, a little larger than the mouths of most Semai women, a short upper lip and a full, slightly everted lower one, so that her lips seemed always slightly parted, both usually moist. You could catch a glimpse of her incisors sometimes, disconcerting some Semai, for whom biting and eating are a natural metaphor for violence. Longsmother was plumper, a vertical furrow bisecting her lined forehead above her pug nose. The two women, both wearing only sarongs wrapped around their waists, were weaving attap shingles. The sky was a nacreous shiny gray, streaked with pale blue, through which hot solar radiation rained down on the flattened adobe of the yard. Even the chickens and dogs were hiding under houses, gasping from the heat. A baby on a pile of mats and sarongs by Longsmother batted idly at the stifling air with fat little arms and legs.

"'s hot," Longsmother said.

You fold the palm frond lengthwise and weave the stiff leaflets together, *like weaving two lives together*, Kliy thought, over under, over under, the stiff right hand leaflet over its mate opposite, then under the next one, then over, hands moving swiftly, until the two sides of the leaf are one thing, a lozenge-patterned rectangular shingle, *so different from the fronds that waved and rattled in the wind, now a tightly bound flat thing that shuts the cool air out. Then the sun and rain beat on it, beat on it, and the dry dark green leaves turn tan and brittle, flaking away, motes floating in the brilliant unrelenting light. Then the palm roaches come, slipping between the shingles and feasting on the leaf, mingling their black-dot feces with the dead-leaf dust floating in the shafts of sunlight stabbing through gaps in the thatch; and the fragile huge yellow-and-brown tarantulas come to snatch the cockroaches and suck them dry, and the huge-eyed melancholy pale geckos come to gulp down the spiders, and finally the skinny venomous tree snakes to swallow the little lizards and the little rats and mice that live there too. And the cold rain starts to drip through gaps in the roof, and the shingled walls rot and gap, until finally red-eyed invisible demons come to gibber and squeak and rustle in the ruined thatch, where the light from the little kerosene candles called* plitaa' *cannot penetrate the blackness beneath the steep pitched roof but only makes the darkness deeper. Then you have to move, you get out, you leave your house, you don't live there like crazy people do, you leave it to the demons or burn it down.*

"Hot hot hot," said Longsmother.

Kliy stood up and stretched, languorously, extending one arm high over her head, fist loosely clenched. "My husband's coming today," she said offhandedly. "I pounded some rice for him. He can winnow it. I left it with my *mnaay*. I'm going upriver to my little uncle's."

"With that Malay girl?"

"She's not Malay, not really. Her father turned Muslim, and she married a Malay, that's all." *And she's* canggih [thinking the Malay word for "sophisticated and stylish"] *and has nice things.* Kliy smiled.

"You taking the kids?"

"A couple. I've leaving the oldest with my *mnaay*."

Desire Ungratified (Midday, Monday)

Also, kämst du, braucht ich, mich zu stillen
nur ein leichtes Anruhn meiner Hande,
sei's an deiner Schulter junge Rundung
sei es an den Andrang deiner Bruste.
[So, were you to come, I'd need, to calm me,
only my hand resting lightly on, aah,
on the young rounding of your shoulders,
or on the thrusting of your breasts.]

—Rilke, *An der sonngewohnten Strasse*
[*On the Sun-Haunted Road*] (1999:73)

Yeop braked his Honda 70 motorbike before the last hairpin bend in the
all-weather road that led to Cba' Dnaan Nòòs, which Malays called Kuala
Denan Dam. Yeop, a tall, lanky man with a lined forehead, dressed all in
black, as lowland Semai men who wanted to be cool did in the 1990s. Behind his back some Dnaan Nòòs people called him Bah Hool, Mr. Gibbon,
because of his long thin black-clad arms and their big-knuckled hands
and his thin straight lips in a face shaped like an inverted teardrop. The
by-name let them feel safe gossiping about him, as they gossiped about all
outsiders. And it made them grin.

   Down the steep slopes behind him, the road twisted intestinally, as if
the engineers had eviscerated the mountains and wet black asphalt had
spilled out of the cut. He paused a moment, right foot on the ground,
looking over at the houses on the far side of the valley. These mountains,
still covered with forest, were not like the denuded lowlands where you
could see the squall lines of rain advancing from afar, curtain after curtain
of rain; here you could only hear it buckshotting the enormous rain forest
leaves as it swept through the mountain, the rolling thunder behind it;
then feel the cold wind rising, before the roar of the arriving rain overwhelmed every other sound.

   Unlike traditional Perak Semai settlements, where temporary houses
were scattered each in or near its own field for fear of slavers, Dnaan was
a hard tan and red jewel of desert tucked into the lush doomed green rain
forest, a lesion of slick lateritic clay baked to adobe by the unshielded hard
brilliance of the burning sun. Close together, cheap boxy Malay-style
houses lined the road that took jungle produce down to the valleys and
city goods back up, the tidy government-inspired linear pattern sub-
verted by the jumble of houses away from the road. Husks of city goods
lined the road: Tiger beer bottles, torn bright plastic bags, broken Styrofoam containers scattered among the parched weeds. At the foot of the
road, twenty miles down slope, dark red-purple coleus patches flourished
where the German engineers had slashed into the precipitous hillsides,
breaking the cool shade of the forest, but up here in the hills the weeds
were not pretty.

   The mountains were so steep that, from climbing up and down or walking with feet aslant on the canted land, even old men like the local headman Rmpah had hard muscular thighs and calves like *litaaw*. The mon-
soon deluges that washed parts of the road away half a dozen times a year
were also eroding the precipitous slopes to which people's houses clung.
The soil that had covered the roots of papaya trees planted just a few
years ago had washed away into the river along with all the soluble waste
the settlement bought or generated, flowing downstream to pollute the
water of the peoples who (unlike the people of Dnaan) benefited from the
electricity the dam generated. The papaya trees that survived now stood

on awkward root stilts, like mangrove trees or strangler figs just beginning to root.

Yeop, still in shadow, felt chilly and damp. White wet mist swathed this place morning and evening, like steam rising from a rice pot, so that days and nights blurred into each other without sharp beginning or end. People here didn't even know how old they were, even after looking at the passports the government gave them, because they didn't keep track of what year it was or of passing time. The people here were as different from his people in the lowlands as the weeds were from lowland weeds, he thought. People back in his home settlement of Teiw Srngloo' used the phrase "American vines" for the invasive thorny foul-smelling weeds that Malays called "chickenshit flowers." But up here "American vine" was a different plant, a fast-growing vine that killed fruit trees by wrapping itself around them the way a loincloth wraps around your waist. The only thing the vines had in common, he thought, was that they were new to Semai and now were spreading everywhere, covering everything and killing it. The people up here were still too isolated to understand.

He would see Kliy in a few minutes, he thought, thinking of the fragrance of her breath, of the bright red celosia flowers she wore in her hair sometimes for protection against demons; remembering the lissome slightly swayback stance that thrust her firm muscular buttocks backward and thrust her soft belly forward in a long sinuous curve, like the slow curves of a lowland river; and seeing, in his *sngii'*, his memory, the soft hollow at the base of her neck, soft throb between collarbones that curved out like the wings of the formalized birds that Semai men used to carve on blowpipes. Aah, he recalled, how consciously carnal her lazy sideways glance was, how inviting her humorous full-lipped grin. He would speak gently and reasonably with her, show her that she would be happier back with him, even though they'd gone through a town meeting. He loved her, and she had loved him. All it needed, all it needed was a word, a look, a touch, and. . . . For a long moment he couldn't think what to do, couldn't move, *-lwiik*, felt dizzy, a sign of spiritual distress.

Last time he saw her, from a distance, she not seeing him, he had tried to fix her image in his *sngii'*, his consciousness: how she stood, one hip thrust out to support the child clinging to her, her long sleek hair a glistening black flame against the bloody setting sun, her thin cotton sarong clinging to her supple hips and legs. Amazing. But when he finally spoke to her, she'd said, "I'm not listening." And when he'd tried again, "I'm not listening. You don't get it. I'm not listening, and I'm not going to listen." Turning her back. Walking away. *Kra'dii'*, withdrawal, rejection. Now the image obsessed him, a demon filling his *sngii'* with *rnyaak*, that passionate doomed yearning that Semai feel so often.

She'd slept with him before they were married, her musky fragrance mingling with his own, breaths hot and gasping, the first time less than six days after her older sister had died, while she was still supposed to be in mourning and not having sex at all. They'd offended the dead, said the town meeting, and had to agree to pay the *waris*, the kinsmen who guaranteed their marriage, a fine of $300 each if they got divorced. She didn't want to pay now, he knew, though she'd lied at the town meeting and said she would.

He would hold his children while they talked, the little ones on his lap, their seven-year-old sister clinging to his shoulder. In memory his children were pale, soft, insubstantial. He could remember how their presence felt but not exactly how their faces looked. They hadn't wanted to come with him. Who can understand children? He shuddered slightly with a spasm of yearning, *rnyaak*. Not long now. But his *sngii'* was uneasy. *These upland people are clannish.* He revved up the bike into a chattering roar.

Memories of Years Before (Midday, Monday)

As Kliy and her children clamber up the narrow eroded path upriver, sides of their hard bare feet planted against the precipitous slopes, she remembers: it's how he looks at her that starts it, as if he sees something he had never seen before, something wonderful that makes his eyes widen slightly, the *knlook mad*, the pupils that show the *klook* soul, black and moist, a bottomless drowned world. He swallows once, clearing his throat, before he speaks.

Mòng edn, he says in his throaty flatland purr. "Here I am."

Mòng he', she answers conventionally, but with a little sidelong grin. "Here you are." Desire pooling, pulsing, warm, and dark, *he's so hip looking*.

He smiles back. It's not that Kliy has never been with a man before. Her mom's from the highlands. In the mountains she's had sex with a couple of nervous inadequate *litaaw*. But Yeop is poised, she thinks, sophisticated. *Not a kid whose penis flops dead when first he sees a vulva, not like highland boys.* His mouth is thin lipped, almost prim, but moist.

She takes a Dunhill when he offers it, thinking dismissively of the frilled and painted homemade cigarettes *litaaw* in the mountains would offer her to hint they wanted her body. In the highlands, taking the cigarette meant accepting the proposition; refusing it, "I don't feel like smoking right now," letting you reject the offer without rejecting the person who made it, without wounding his or her *sngii'*, not creating *punan*, not making them sick. She isn't sure what taking the smooth white foreign cigarette means to flatlanders. *Doesn't matter*, she thinks. She has heard that flatlanders are as prudish and brutal as Malays about sex, not even allowing friendly sex between joking kin, *mnaay*, whom one might marry later on.

But she remembers the soft play of ember light and shadow on the supple muscular curves of Yeop's body at the funeral feast the night before. He let his hand fall, as if casually, against her leg. She hadn't moved away. He moved his fingers gently, brushing her, and she covered the knobbly back of his hand with the tough little palm of her own. He doesn't seem prudish or brutal at all. She can imagine those hands touching her gently. Ah.

They meet by whispered agreement that evening, under dense downhanging branches on the riverbank on the slope below the settlement, luxuriating in the sweet darkness and smell of leaves, in the feel and fragrance of each other's bodies: how intently he looks on her when she lies back and raises her knees, naked throat and belly undefended, smiling, opening herself to him; how awkwardly, eagerly, he slides into the clasp of her lithe legs, his hard bony face softening; how astonished he looks when he enters her, how his tough long-muscled body spasms like a trancing *litaaw*'s as she locks her thin ankles behind his neck, pulling him fiercely toward her, inside her, deeper into her warmth, desire for each other coursing through their bodies like blood, nourishing greater desire, swirling joy flowing through her body, *lnwiik* deeper and deeper. AH AH, he cries out, AH AH. She has never heard a man cry out like that, though like all hill people she has from earliest childhood heard the panting, the creaking bamboo slats, the stifled gigglings and gaspings of longhouse sex. But this much loss of control would get you teased unmercifully in the mountains, even here in the hills of Dnaan. She looks at him, at his slack wet mouth, half-closed eyes, pure surrender on his face. He truly loves her body, she thinks, inhaling their mingled fragrances, and she loves his.

In that moment all desire melts in fulfillment, all color simplifies to black, all consciousness sinks into joy. Afterward, walking downhill with him in the cool evening, she feels *snaang*, comforted, content, lucky. Her mood is of unquestioning happiness. She thinks no further than that. As he goes up the house stairs, she grabs the hard ball of muscle in his rump, chortling, naughty, squeezing hard and releasing him, making him smile nervously.

None of that ever happened again, not that way, not once, though she dreamt it, often.

Harangue (Late Midday, Monday)

You could see in his face something resembling terror,
But in fact it was love, for which he would die.

—From Stephen Dunn, "Achilles in Love" (Dunn 2004:67)

Among Semai, as among other Malaysian indigenes, there are few face-to-face quarrels. "Instead, people who have some grudge to air engage in harangues . . . within the hearing of almost the entire community" (Nagata 2004:113). That's what Yeop did. Face flushed and turbulent in the hot hysterical light, he stood alone in the center of the settlement on the black tarred road, tall thin black-clad man in the heat shimmer, mind awash with fear and grief and rage and despair and shame, speaking his emotions as Semai rarely do, in a harsh loud lecturing voice, the wrongs Kliy had done him, her flight from him, his love for her and his children, his need, his yearning, so that all could hear him.

Ki-lees, people said, glancing at him sidelong, he's making an angry harangue. No one came to listen, though they heard, and would tell the people who weren't there everything Yeop said. People went on with what they were doing, registering his harangue but showing no reaction, except for naked little Bah Gndaak, age four, and his littler sister, black cloth amulet still around her neck, her head shaven except for a single tuft of hair.

The children stood under a house twenty feet away, one of Gndaak's arms around his sister's skinny shoulder, his middle and fourth fingers in his mouth, both gazing wide eyed at adult despair, as Semai children do, a little fearful, alert, learning. Beside them a rangy mottled dog, almost hairless with mange, stirred listlessly in the little pit it had dug in the shade under the house to keep cool in. Except for the harangue, only the monotonous cheeping of the little flocks of chicks broke the silence.

THE APPEAL (TUESDAY AFTERNOON, FEBRUARY)

> Jubel weiss, und Sehnsucht ist geständig,
> Nur die Klage lernt noch; mädchenhändig
> Zählt sie nächtelang das alte Schlimme.
> [Elation knows for sure, and yearning is remorseful,—
> Only grieving still learns, and with girlish hands
> It reckons all night long the ancient evildoing.]
>
> —Rilke, *Sonnets to Orpheus* (1960:16), Dentan tr.

In the rhythm of pounding rice in the yard of her mother's younger brother, Kliy remembers. After their wedding, the flatlands had been a shock. The towns had been as wonderful and confusing as she'd heard they were, frantic with noise, rows and rows of two-story stucco buildings with bright unintelligible things in the dark shops on the first floors, each open onto the sidewalks, looking like caves in the mountains. That part of her marriage had gone as she expected, bringing her in touch with the wonders of modernity, what Malays called *yang modun*.

Every twilight, thousands and thousands of swifts flooded out from under the painted eaves of the stuccoed Chinese shops, wheeling and darting swarms of them, in erratic circles and spirals, wings whirring, the air shrill with their cries, chittering and squeaking, black shadows whirling against the paler darkening sky. The Semai name mimics their cry: *jawiir, jawiir*. The noisy flocks swept through the town skies like the flights of bats that poured out of caverns in the cave-riddled limestone tors that dotted the foothills.

But flatland daylight was different, blaring, harsh, hot, intolerable, omnipresent. The bright actinic sun blinded and isolated you. Everything was bleached, glittering, or opaque with reflected shininess. The overheated air rising visibly from the paved roads was rancid, acrid. The roadside plants were brown, withered, draped in bright shreds of paper and plastic. Even the sky was different, roiled sagging featureless pearl-gray dazzle, not the massed darkness of mountain thunderheads. On the deforested plains, everything was a trick of heat and light, queasy pale insubstantial shadows, hinting at pale tepid insubstantial demons, not like the intimate alien dark of the triple-tiered forests, not like the coolness of the clearings in the wooded hills or the chill of mountain nights.

Flatland Semai said that special spirits controlled particular places. They were different from demons, never taking deceptive material form, more like invisible humans. They lived in and under the land the way dragons live in and under the rivers. As tin mines and plantations forced Semai away from places they used to live in, they could no longer perform traditional ceremonies to placate the spirits. The special ritual experts, *pahwaak*, who used to perform the ceremonies that allowed people to plant rice, were dying out, so most people now planted only tapioca. The spirits were dying too, in the plague of toxic heat and light. Young people no longer believed in them. The spirits became angry, hot with resentment, and poisonous heat spread everywhere. Or, other people said, maybe it was because the mines and the clear-cutting were heating the *ruwaay*, the head soul, of the earth itself. The skin of the world was diseased, poisoned with pesticides, drying up, and dying. The world itself was shriveling in the heat, heating up and dying, and there were no *pahwaak* to cool it. Even the blue-white water in the depleted little creek that gave the settlement its name was warm and toxic with tin mine runoff and warm as drool.

And flatland people differed in other ways from hill people, not just their half-swallowed speech but also their actions. Yeop didn't seem as sophisticated as he had, not compared with the sharp-featured pale Malay men with their tidy little mustaches and fluent chatter, men who had been to the capital Kuala Lumpur many times, who wore sunglasses and thin spotless white shirts with brightly colored ballpoint pens in the breast pocket, who let the nails on their thumbs or little fingers grow long to show they didn't do manual labor, men who owned cars. Their look, when they looked at Yeop, was not a look between fellow men; more the way they looked at the bedraggled macaques cavorting in the little municipal zoo.

They stared at Kliy with frank sexual evaluation. Their gaze wasn't playful and chummy, a little awkward, the way highland *litaaw* look at *mnaleeh*. It didn't suggest erotic horseplay. The Malay male gaze was impersonal, like the way they looked at chickens trussed up head downward in the market, the fowls upside down, twisting their heads around to try to reorient themselves—a "how much?" look. *We know what you like*, their gaze said. *We know what you are*.

Brutal.

Yet the other women said that Malay men talked contemptuously about *bohsia*, using the Hokkien Chinese word for "silence," referring to women who submitted to sexual advances without protest. So they were prudish as well as lustful. It was hard to know how to react. She had thought of wearing a hijab, an Islamic head scarf, like some of the more sophisticated rural Malay women, to hide her hair so as to avoid sparking the lust of men. You could feel the threat, the way you feel a cool breeze raise the little hairs on your forearms, then come a few huge cold drops of rain, and you know in a moment the squall will be on you.

In the evenings, Tamil and Malay men often hung around the entrance to the village, under a buzzing flickering streetlight that was clouded by swarms of moths, the moths stalked by a circle of alert little geckoes. The threat of sexual attack scared Kliy, so she never left the Semai settlement except in a group with other women. It was like being on a raft, three giant-bamboo tubes wide, hurtling downstream, the only direction a raft can go on highland rivers: you're safe as long as you don't take foolish chances, don't jump up when a python or monitor lizard swims by or buzzing insects assault your ears; safe as long as the turbulent river hasn't changed course again, throwing up new shallows and hazards just beneath the surface; safe if the giant catfish or dragons beneath the surface don't notice you. "Safe" is always conditional.

Back in the hills, she thought, surrounded by her siblings, she had felt precariously safe, engulfed in the confusion of everyone doing his or her own task but somehow not involved. Maybe not safe, exactly, the up-country women with whom she'd grown up never felt exactly safe but as safe as she'd ever felt.

Yeop did occasional labor, as a night watchman for a few months, then on a road crew for a lumber company, then on a tea plantation in the Cameron Highlands. He spent a lot of time away, leaving her alone among strangers, her in-laws.

"It's hot," Kliy said to slim Mbunsmother, her sharp-faced sharp-tongued witty beautiful neighbor, eager, deceptive, and malicious. That afternoon they sat together in the kitchen, sweating in the hot water-logged air, slicing rattan vines into thin strips for weaving. Mbunsmother's toddler sat on her lap, grabbing ineffectively at the slicing knife and the sharp-edged rattan strands. Mbunsmother was just back from taking the toddler to a clinic in town to get aspirin for the baby, who was feverish.

"Hot." They worked in silence for a while.

"Hot," said Kliy. "Hot hot hot."

She fanned her face languidly with her hand. She didn't like the long-sleeved high-necked Malay blouses the women wore here, but taking hers off would scandalize the neighbors. She didn't like the way the houses were so close to the ground that you couldn't work under them in the breezy shade. She didn't like the way the women stuck to the kitchen dur-ing the day, leaving the rest of the house to the men.

"Hot," she said.

"Back in the mountains with those Temiar," said Mbunsmother with her usual teasing harshness, meaning *those savages*, "the kids all have spleen sickness, right?" Malaria. "Swollen bellies. None of that here. Just the fever. Maybe some diarrhea." "Hah. Couple of days ago Wa' Buun comes running up into the house." In falsetto: *"Mom! Mom! Worms in my shit! Worms in my shit!"* Both women chuckled. "There were, too. I looked. Big white worms. You don't get those in the hills."

Through the kitchen doorway they could see a solid line, miles and miles long, of high black-purple thunderheads, moving in inexorably from the Indian Ocean, mounding up higher and higher, engulfing the flat gray sky.

An Enemy inside the Sheets (Last Year)

> *Musuh dalam selimut*
> Enemy inside the sheets
>
> —Malay metaphor for disloyal spouse

At other seasons, the sight of clouds piling up behind the eastern moun-tains made her think of her family in the cool hills, left her prey to home-sickness, *rnyaak*. She had a baby, then another, and another, drifting down through her days like a pebble spiraling down through the murky waters of the deep pools mountain streams make as they swirl round a bend, pools in which mountain people say monsters live.

The promise of the lowlands was still there. She remembers the sight of her husband coming home in the glare, after being gone for weeks, a backlit radiant featureless shape, full of the shifting promise of transformation, his face an oval of darkness. But, once he was home, sitting cross-legged in his sarong on the battered linoleum mat, smelling of sweat and human heat, he was demanding in a way he had not been in the hills, saying *Gaap teh*, "Boil tea," nothing else. She had to stay in the kitchen with the women and girls when his men friends came visiting, making tea or cooking for them, serving them separately from the women, Malay style, listening to the intrusive male noises, smelling the intrusive male smells. Yeop became stingy, though she needed more money than before because of the children.

He seemed less tender, too, and she began to suspect that he was having sex with other women. Still, if so, he was secretive about it, not like highland men. He never asked her about her pleasure—they would have both been embarrassed if he had—but now he seemed rough and perfunctory. Maybe, she thought, it hadn't been love for her that made him cry out back then; maybe it was something inside him, something knotted up hard in his *sngii'*, by being less a man-child than Malay men, released in that AH AH, a "bad wind" as the Malays said. Back then he had burrowed into her like a *lweey*, blackish stingless bee, burrowing into a little trumpet flower. Not now.

For a long time, he seemed unaware of her suspicions, her yearning, her distress, her growing resentment. She began to enjoy being with her children more than being with him, relishing their readiness to cherish her, their clinging. One morning, steam wraiths rising from hard-trodden clay in the harsh heat after the night's storm, she was bathing her three-year-old daughter in water from a shiny red plastic bucket, the little girl's skin slick and gleaming with the silvery water, child and mother luxuriating in the coolness and physical contact, the other children's shrill laughter efflorescing in edgy joy when they brushed against the banana trees and were drenched by a shower of big cold drops of water that had accumulated on the thick tattered leaves during the night.

That morning, while the shining blank puddles were still everywhere on the slick red clay of the settlement, which human feet had trampled too hard to absorb water, that morning her neighbor Mbunsmother told her about the affair Yeop had been having, just as she had suspected but wanted not to suspect, with a flatland widow in another settlement.

Hurt dropped on Kliy like a tiger's paw, talons extending, ripping her *sngii'*, making her stomach lurch. She covered her mouth with both hands when she heard, gagging, holding something in, something dangerous wanting to burst from her mouth. She half rose to flee the betrayal and abandonment, but there was no forest to flee to, just the indifferent flat hot light, the overgrown fields dotted with magenta-flowered Straits rhododendron bushes, the wet puzzled little girl recognizing her mother's distress but not understanding it. Kliy felt dizzy, -*lwiik*, unsteady, balance lost, footing uncertain, teetering, like when the slick smooth wet stepping-stone in the dark river begins to wobble, the black undertow pulling at it, your foot slipping.

"Tough," said Mbunsmother, watching Kliy closely with deep black cool eyes. "Tough."

"What can you do?" responded Kliy in a low voice, settling back down as if she had just been shifting position, shrugging, not looking at Mbunsmother, her voice indifferent and harsh, as if nothing had happened. But her hands dropped from her mouth each to clasp the opposite forearm hard, and her shoulders hunched in toward each other, protecting her body, the position that Semai assume at bad or frightening news.

Her earlier suspicions had knotted her *sngii'*, her sense of the world, but not prepared her for the hollowness that Yeop's deception tore open inside her. It wasn't so much the sex that hurt. That could have been "just a loan" as mountain people might say. But the deception, like *srngloo'* . . .

She recalled the sickening pain her father's death had caused her, the betrayal and abandonment by death that sometimes drove people mad, ghost demons haunting your dreams, begging for love. It was like the way a fishhook punctured the flat silver sheen of a highland pool and then the line sliced a long straight scar across it. She had had no idea, no idea at all, how bad knowing for sure could be. Though she went on with her routines, what else was there to do? Then misery would surge into her *sngii'* unexpectedly, her lips would turn down at the corners, and she'd have to blink, hard, for a few moments. Around the hollowness, her life whirled and melted, became as formless as the mudflats left by the monsoonal floods.

Later, there were quarrels, the thin huddled children staring wide eyed at their parents grown harsh and shrill, sharp triangular shoulder blades flinching away from the hot hurtful words. Children were so little, their bodies and *ruwaay* so soft and harmless. Kliy sought their company even more.

Although Kliy would never say so, what would be the use? Her *susah sngii'*, unhappiness and resentment, grew and grew. Many nights, despairing in her hurt and anger, she lay sleepless in the stifling dead air of the day locked into the house when they shut the shutters, Malay style, against the dangers of the cool dark. She wept then, tears she would not show, not even to the children, tears that brought no comfort. And the shutters didn't keep demons from swooping in out of the dark, into her dozing consciousness, sudden goads of hot emotion; for comfort only her sleeping children cocooned in their sarongs on both sides of her, their damp warm little bodies more consoling than his large hard one.

Nothing for her or the children here. Just flat hot dying and, miles away, much farther away than a human being should be able to see, invisible through the shutters and the night mists, the cool blue-gray mountains that now and then you could glimpse through the hot bright haze. At times in the clammy dark the *susah sngii'*, the insomniac replay of obsession, the heat of her anger radiating out of her heart, was so painful that she thought of seeking relief, surrender, in death, drinking the poisons people used to kill pests on the plantations where they worked. In the mountains you just left when a relationship went bad, just left, not explaining, not even saying good-bye, letting the other person gradually come to realize that you were really gone, gone for good. No fight, no fuss, no fine, no town meeting, no jabber-jabber. Flatlanders killed themselves, she knew, drank poison. They were famous for it.

She hadn't consulted his family, not even his mother's younger brother or the headman, although the elders at their wedding had gone on and on for hours about how spouses no longer belong to their families of origin but to the people into whose lives they were marrying, leaving her in tears. Even Yeop had wept a little at the abandonment.

Kliy had never felt she belonged with these people, but hill people often didn't feel at home with their in-laws. Mountain people like her mom had complicated ways of avoiding contact, not all this forced chumminess. *Lowlanders are really Malays, all sweet mouth and rotten heart. They'd looked down on her, mocking her choppy accent as if their own grunting was better. Everything down here was* hal maay *to her, other people's affair and none of her own.*

Dnaan Nòòs wasn't much, but her mom was there. The people weren't stingy and would give her places to hide out if Yeop came to get her or steal her children. They didn't hit people.

When she left, she left him no word.

THE APPEAL (TUESDAY MORNING)

Won't you speak to me?
No, it would remind me
of what I haven't said.
But I need to speak to you.
I know what you need,
and your needs don't matter now. . . .

What if I said please?
I am unreachable.
If I were standing next to you
you'd see for yourself
how far away I was.

—From Stephen Dunn, "The Answers (2004:81)

Yeop, both big knobby hands squeezed together into a fist between his thighs, knuckles white with strain, sits cross-legged on the floor of the headman's house, trying to explain to Rmpah, the canny tough old headman of Dnaan. Earnestness deepens the furrows in his forehead. Beside him is an opaque white plastic bag holding a 1.2-kilogram-size shiny red-and-gold tin of Thye Hong "All Time Favourite" cookies, which he'd bought for his children from the licensed Malay trader. Rmpah has already heard the story of Yeop and Kliy from the wife of the Sten, the assistant headman; among central Perak Semai, the Sten does the day-to-day negotiations to resolve conflicts so that the town meeting will simply express community sentiments already agreed on. But *Kliy's going to be a problem*, Rmpah thinks, sitting, also cross-legged, facing Yeop. Rmpah is a small, sinewy, dark man in his late sixties, gracile bones like a bird's, deep-set dark eyes, arthritic hands, all knuckles. He wears maroon shorts and a white button-up shirt that looks baggy on him, like hand-me-downs on a child. His face is clever, lined, humorous, mobile without being informative.

"I've been here for four days, trying to see her. I didn't bring my *waris*, the people who guaranteed the marriage. I didn't want to make any trouble, any fuss. I brought my big brother, but she won't see him either. He's angry at her because she won't pay back the bridewealth."

"What kind of goofiness is this?" asks Rmpah irritably.

"I say to her, 'Listen, don't hide, don't run away,' and she takes off like a bird. So I'm going home. The Sten here is my dad's older second cousin, my *k'nuin*. I want another town meeting, but I don't want to come back here. She humiliates me, she shames me. I think about killing myself all the time. I don't want a divorce. I love her, you know? I want the kids. I miss them. I think of them all the time. I dream about them, you know? Every night, I dream about them. I don't sleep, I just toss and dream."

The old man, tubercular, coughs and spits a wad of reddish phlegm through a knothole in the floorboards, leaving a little puddle of mucus around the hole. He thinks briefly of the old days, when traditional Semai floors were of smooth flexible inch-wide bamboo slats, laid an inch apart. It was easy to spit and dump cooking water through the floor then. The government-supplied headman's house is Malay style, painted, built with planks and shutters, hot and inconvenient but prestigious and permanent. The Malay bureaucrats of the Department of Orang Asli Affairs thought that such housing befits headmen. They hoped that by enhancing Rmpah's prestige this way, they could mold him into a responsible and sympathetic party who would transmit government policies without going through the inefficient egalitarian participatory democracy of Semai town meetings. Instead, it had led to backlash of backbiting, about people who thought themselves better than others. As he listens and thinks, he absentmindedly wipes the puddle of pink spit into a faint smear with his finger. The boy's right, he thinks, even though he dresses like a Malay pop-rocker and speaks with a grunting valley person accent, uh uh uh uh. Why didn't Kliy want to stay with him?

"Okay," he says, "Your *k'nuin* the Sten will talk to her. She probably has her reasons. Don't get angry. We'll *br-miting*, have a meeting. We'll work it out, if it's okay with him, we'll have another town meeting," he says. "You go home for now. We'll work on it."

"You'll call me if my kids get sick, won't you? You'll let me know?"

"Sure," says the headman. *Kid's as tense as a worm on a hot rock*, he thinks. *Not that sitting's easy in Malay houses. Plank floors are hard on old behinds.*

Kliy Defiant

The day Kliy fled back home from the lowlands, she stopped for a moment on the wooden doorsill under the sharp-toothed fish head that hung there to protect her and her children from the bird demons that flock to the scent of childbirth, her resentment fanged and agape like the amulet's jawbones, to tear at him if he tried to touch her or her children. That pause and spasm of anger was all the farewell she wanted. She took the children, their soprano voices and soft touch her protection against the empty subducting silence of her life.

She could no longer bear to look at Yeop, let alone talk with him. During the first town meeting she held her oldest child, Wa' Long, age seven, on her lap, so that, if Kliy lowered her head a little, Long's head broke the line of sight between her mother and father. And Kliy had only looked down, never at Yeop, not even taking the chance of glimpsing him out of the corners of her eyes, and had never addressed him directly, murmuring to Wa' Long instead. The sight of him wounded her *sngii'*, left her wanting only to get away, to *kra'dii'*, to forget he even existed. Whatever he wanted she hated, wanting from him only food for her children. She would never swelter under that flat heavy meaningless lowland sky again.

Chorus

After supper, Longsmother and her younger sisters are sitting in the kitchen. Outside, a mist-like inaudible invisible mild rain is falling.

Longsmother is weaving a little rice basket; Julia, one of her sisters, cross-legged, is suckling someone's chubby baby; the other sister, Teh, is combing the fine curly hair of Wa' Ngah, her eldest sister's gorgeous big-eyed nine-year-old daughter. Ngah is silent, listening to the adults carefully, learning, as Semai children do.

Teh: The men say Kliy ran away because she didn't want to give the bridewealth back.

Longsmother: [snorts] They say that because they're her *waris*. If that's why she ran away, they won't have to help her pay it back.

Julia: So why'd Kliy skip town? She tell you?

Longsmother: She ran away because she's afraid her husband'll give her a hard time, take her children away.

Julia: I heard she wants a new husband but hasn't found a new man yet.

Teh: [lowering her voice slightly]. I heard she has a boyfriend in Kem ["camp," the barracks of the Senoi Praak, a parapolice group made up of Orang Asli with mostly Malay officers, with a reputation among Semai as a hotbed of drunken sex and violence].

Julia: [raises her eyebrows] She wants to marry somebody rich. [giggles]

Teh: [grinning, quizzical]. Maybe she wants to marry a soldier [in the Senoi Praak].

Longsmother: But they're not really rich. They're poor folks like us.

Teh: They're richer than *I* am [laughs].

Half in Love with Easeful Death (Early March)

So long as they love you they are one sort of being, but when they've decided to stop loving you—by which incidentally I don't mean liking, tolerating, enduring you—they shift into another sort of being altogether, a wholly other consciousness. Even the way they look at you changes: the very pupils of their eyes contract! It's a weird thing, obvious maybe, maybe even banal, maybe, but when it happens to you . . . it's a considerable shock, as if the earth had shifted beneath your feet. You can feel it *spinning*. (Joyce Carol Oates, *American Appetites* [1989:238])

Yeop wakes up shivering, afraid and feverish, in his *sngii'* the image of his children, maybe disguised demons, calling him. His face a lesson in the geometry of fatigue, the skin beneath his eyes bruised by fatigue, he sits up cross-legged in the muggy evening, knees pulling his blue plaid cotton sarong taut across his lap, looking down at his upturned hands; suddenly he clenches his fists and eyelids, then opens them, releasing again what has already been lost. His fingernails have dented the pale inner skin of his thumbs. Heat burns in his face like a sun.

Flat on the wall behind him, glossy Arnold Schwarzenegger the Terminator looms in the dusk, veins and muscles bulging, huge incomprehensible weapon clutched in both hands. Beneath the poster are the brightly colored paper flowers left over from a ritual bath for the children's midwife, who had been feeling *jah*, spiritually enfeebled. The day before he had had one of the spasms that seized him suddenly, unexpectedly, while he was riding his motorbike or just sitting quietly, spasms of vertiginous terror and fury that Duuksfather the adept said happen when the gibbonlike tree demons seize you with their grotesquely elongated insubstantial arms but that Yeop knew had something to do with Kliy's grip on his *ruwaay*, his head soul, a haunting that made him dream of her.

He tries, as he often does, to recall touching Kliy's cheek with his fingertips, the incredible smoothness. But, try as he may, he can never quite recall it as a sensation, just as an idea, "smoothness." Instead he remembers her vulva, red and glistening like a split papaya, threatening.

All he wants from life is for nothing else to happen, nothing good, nothing bad, nothing; an end to the pain and chaos of a wounded *sngii'*, consciousness; an erasure of the sticky residue of feelings. Quiet. Peace. He can't handle anything else. Numbness: let him be numb. He sits a long time in the dark, empty of thought or feeling, just miserable, with no flicker of an impulse to move. Outside, the pale green moonlight makes the dew luminous on the broad banana leaves by the house. Thin cobwebby clouds are beginning to accumulate, drawing a diaphanous film between the bright blank moon and the hot steaming earth. *It's love, but you can die of it*, he thinks, *like the love of demons*. He feels exhausted, disabled.

When the gap began growing between them, though he did not recognize it at the time, he had tried yelling at her, yelling at her for going out to Saturday night market with the other women, for not bothering to cook if she wasn't hungry, for going off with the children to her village in the mountains and leaving him alone; but she had just said, "I'm not listening," and turned away, not arguing, not caring, withdrawing.—*Kra'dii'*.

"Hill women don't cook if they don't feel like it," she would say. "Cook for yourself." Her sullen mouth smoother than oil. Once he had threatened to hit her. "I'm not a water buffalo to be beaten," she had said and gone back to Dnaan Nòòs for a while, though he had not actually hit her.

He had talked with her mother's younger brother about her growing indifference, the way a good husband is supposed to, talked with her *waris*, her people, instead of griping to his own kinsmen the way she did. He had tried to fill up the space opening between them: with a garish carnelian-colored lipstick, a fancy blue paisley sarong. He had sacrificed the money he earned from tapping rubber the way Maay Jknuuk, the ancient slavers, sacrificed stolen Semai children in the old days to their god of bronze, but the bond between them did not harden like Jknuuk bronze, just stretched thinner and thinner, became more and more brittle.

Loneliness and despair sweep over him like floodwaters, sharp dangerous memories surfacing briefly like black wet great tree snags whirled along in the swollen river, memories jabbing to the surface just long enough to hurt, then whirled away sinking into the overwhelming dark flood of loss. He remembers, sees: her every movement had a casual sensual grace, even the clumsiest ones, picking up a child, for example, or bending almost double from the waist to spread out a mat for winnowing rice. The way she stood, rounded right hip swung out to support the child she held in the crook of her right arm, the rest of her supple body curving the other way to balance the weight.

He recalls the first day he saw her, with her sister, pounding rice in a big old gray splintery three-hole wooden mortar. Her lower lip protruded a little, moistly, like that of a suckling toddler. She had taken off her blouse, and the muscles in her bare shoulders rippled with the rhythmic thump-thump-thump-thump-thump, slim biceps swelling and elongating smoothly, the skin beneath her breasts creasing and smoothing out, the muscles of her arms as lithe and powerful as snakes beneath the smooth brown skin. And the skin of her forearms silky with fine hairs, faintly dry. He remembers her tight slender calves, the rounded long chevron of her tan back, how the crease below her buttocks formed and smoothed, creased and smoothed, concave, convex, concave, convex, flesh and muscles pliant under her thin sarong. Her hands holding the thick pale four-foot long pestle: her hands obsessed him; they were so strong, sturdy stubby fingers almost like a boy's but so small and fine-boned that he could enfold them in his own hands as easily as he could hold a chick, feeling the little bones beneath the skin. Her hands grasping and exploring his body as if she were a blind person trying to find out what sort of creature he was, her hunger throbbing through the tips of her short tender fingers. The teasing, the grins, the chortling, the whispered outrageous suggestions, so different from prudish lowland women. Lost, lost.

He sat against the wall of his house, fumbling with his sarong, then hugging himself. You cling to love even after it's dead, it's so hard to get and give, even when its toxic by-products begin to poison everything. You hold on to a dying marriage, horrified, not wanting to believe, like a mother with a dying baby or a little child snatched away by Malays. He felt like one of those children now; bereaved; abandoned, abandoned; alone among strangers; never to go home again, never; nothing familiar or loved left; everything dead, poisoned, rotted out. No love. No love. Never.

He had dreamt, the balls of his eyes moving like secretive animals under his closed lids; dreamt that she had come to him, in his dream waking him from his sleep, lying back with her knees raised, smiling her faint
shallow luxurious open-lipped smile, teeth showing a little, languorously, ready to put her feet on his shoulders as he came to sit between her smooth muscular thighs, showing him her syrupy vulva, its
thick dark pink lips opening for him, all her juices flowing, her nipples
hardening, becoming pointy and sharp, showing him her soft little
tongue, looking at him between her thighs with eyes turned dead white,
claws appearing between her fingers. "Don't you want to know what the
mouths of demons taste like?" she asked, opening her carnelian mouth,
showing her black cold fangs. He woke with a cry, the thin blanket
twisted around him, unable to breathe, chilly, his sarong wet with cooling semen.

NEGOTIATING (WEDNESDAY)

In the house of the Sten, the assistant to the headman, the *miting*. Informal, see? Present: Kliy, Sten, Rempah the headman and Kliy's mother's
sister, who lived with Kliy. Also Bah Ngah, age ten, cross-legged, headful
of thick curly stiff hair, lively bright brown eyes, wearing ratty bluish
shorts so torn in the seat that his bare buttocks poked out a little, each
through its own gaping hole. His baby sister asleep in his lap.

"Send him back where he came from. Don't let him come here. If he
comes here I'll whack him with a machete. He scares me. He gets angry
and yells at me." Her lower lip juts out slightly.

"He gets angry and yells but he doesn't stay angry. A few hours later
and he loves you again," says the Sten. It's his job to smooth out dis-
agreements. He is a patient man in his forties, with hollow cheeks and
thinning straight black hair. His skin is tan and sere as a dead leaf, looking dry to the touch, flecked with ringworm. Last night he dreamed that
Yeop was living in the rain forest all alone: a bad dream, a dream of a
taboo soul, a *ruwaay pnali'*, suggesting that Yeop might die.

She folds her arms tightly across her chest, just under her breasts,
sinews taut under the smooth skin of her forearms, on her face the vacant
wide-eyed look that veils her feelings.

*She doesn't say "I'm not listening," thinks the Sten, but she might as well.
Most people would if they were so angry they rejected everything you say, but not
her. She just shuts up, as if she'd lost the argument, but she doesn't think she's
lost, she just doesn't care. Dumb, dumb.*

"Did he ever hit you?" At the very edge of consciousness he is aware of
how mobile and moist her mouth was.

She stares at him, full lips now pressed together in a straight line, and tosses her head. *Her shoulders are like a young* litaaw's, *smooth and rounded and hairless but square and strong.* A pang of sexual desire, more mental than physical, crosses his *sngii'*, making him mildly ashamed. She is watching him carefully now, her lips relaxing slightly, almost smiling.

Thinks he can get me to do anything, but I know what he wants.

"No, he doesn't hit you. Does he bring rice home?"

"He gets drunk and talks *rawooc.*" Wrinkling her nose and using the Tluup word her mother and mother's sister use for irrational and unpredictable behavior or incoherent speech, for being lost and astray, for cooking or eating at one meal foods from categories which *pnalii'* rules specified that people should keep separate. "He talks *rawooc* and yells, and I don't know what he's going to do."

"But he doesn't hit you, and he always brings rice home. Is he stingy with money?"

Yes, but I don't care now. Why try to explain to these old, old-fashioned men? This isn't manah ntvvm, *the days of yore. They have no power. Malays have power.* Silence. He is aware again of her mouth. Buzzing furiously, a big black carpenter bee loops through the conversation, then disappears into the day's bright glare, blundering along its random pointless path. Bah Ngah, briefly distracted, follows it with his eyes.

"He doesn't hit you, he always brings rice home, he isn't stingy with money. Does he sleep with other women?"

"Who knows?" She tosses her head. "Doesn't matter. It's *hal maay,* other people's affair." Remembering Mbunsmother's face when she revealed the deception and betrayal, the *srngloo'.*

"He's done what a husband should do. He hasn't done what a husband shouldn't do. If you divorce him, it will be your fault and all your kinsmen involved in the marriage, your *waris,* will have to help pay the fine."

"I'm giving the bridewealth back and paying the fine."

"Lie. We sent two men down there to check it out, and you didn't pay anything. You abandoned him, and now you want to lie about it."

"I didn't abandon him, and I'm not lying."

"Your thinking in this business isn't good. You owe the fines and the return of the bridewealth."

"So I won't divorce him." *I need money. Mr. Gibbon never gave me enough.* Her voice is low, flat, offhanded, as if none of the conversation interests her, though now her eyes flick back and forth like the eyes of a wild deer tied to a post.

"You'll go back to him?"

"No."

"You'll let him see his children?"

"No."

"So you'll divorce him?"

"No."

The Sten has dealt with beautiful willful people before. But Kliy is like a throwback to *manah ntvvm*, olden times, before the British roads and sultan's mandate had crept up the valley and slaving had abated to the point that you could stay in one place and Semai could live in groups bigger than families. Back then, his grandfather's time, people in Dnaan Nòòs didn't have fancy expensive weddings like Malays. Up in Kliy's mother's settlement in Pahang people still didn't have real marriages, he's heard, just shack up like dogs, so that sometimes people can't tell who's married or who's divorced. *But kids nowadays ignore the rules too. They don't need friends because they don't need help planting and harvesting. They look for money other ways. Who knows how Kliy looked for money in the flatlands? This is difficult*, he thought, looking at the headman.

"Yeop is unhappy," said Rmpah, "because it's like you're divorcing him all by yourself, *nuw mum*, just one person. That's why he's unhappy. He wants an official divorce, if you want to throw him out. He wants the headmen and stens in both places to decide who's to blame for what, where the *salah* is, the fault, that's our *saraa'*, the way we do things. And he wants the bridewealth back."

"No."

"You want to be smart about this," cajoles Rmpah. "You know what lowlanders are like. If you don't pay up, maybe Yeop'll turn to Muslim magic, get a sorcerer to say some spells against you, bury the tadpole. You'd be smart not to risk that." But she looks away and says nothing, not giving up, just not speaking. He too falls silent, defeated. *I wonder how burying the tadpole works*, he thinks.

At the foot of the hill to which the settlement clings a small gray *tadiit*, a storm sandpiper, a hunting wife of the Lord, picks its way carefully over the gleaming rounded pebbles along the streambed, long legs moving precisely, sharp dangerous beak poised.

JUDGMENT (OCTOBER)

"Sometimes I think married people are worse than *litaaw* and *mnaleeh*," said Saad, the lowland headman, chopping up his betel nut. "We've got a stabbed-by-the-handle case, *br-truu' ha mool*. You know Ngahsfather? He was playing around with Wa' Nah. They went sliding down a mud bank on a slab of bark the way *litaaw* and *mnaleeh* do." Saad paused to pop the wad of lime, arecanut, and betel leaf between his gums and cheek, image of laughter and bare intertwined limbs passing through his mind. "Afterward they went back to his house and were fooling around, and his wife caught them. 'What do you think you're doing, screwing around?' They said they wanted to get married. So the wife gathered all the family jewelry and took it to Alangsfather, her *waris*. Alangsfather went to his Sten, and the Sten went and got all Ngahsfather's *waris* together. Longsfather's one of them."

He paused to make sure Rmpah was getting the names right. *Hill people can be pretty dumb*, he thought. He ran his hand over his close-cropped white hair. "Longsfather wants your Sten to be a *waris*. If that's okay, they'll all go to her place for a town meeting."

"They'll have to wait to get married," said Rmpah. "He was fooling around with a *juleey*, an unmarried person, *and* he was fooling around with the feelings of someone who had a family, who had a husband. What are the fines like up where he's from?"

"Who knows? Something like $25 from the girl to the wife, and another $25 or $30 from him, and then $165 to the headman [for the scandal and breaking the marriage covenant]. But I don't think they're going to get married unless he gets a divorce first. His big brother says no way Ngahsfather can support two wives. Anyway, the big brother questioned her, and the *juleey* doesn't want to marry him. Besides, the wife -*hooy*, threatened him." He grinned faintly, thinking of the scene. "She hit him, and she threatened him. Said she was going to whack him with a machete, and threw him out of the house. So she's going to have to pay a fine too, I guess about $60."

"His little uncle is going to need to get some of the fine, about $6.25," said Rmpah, knowing that one's mother's younger sibling is more likely to be willing to instruct one in how to behave properly if he's officially involved in the fining system. "And the Sten can go. Thing is, we have some problems here. You remember Wa' Biyeek? The other day she slept with Bah Laas."

"Again? I thought they shacked up when they were both working together on the rubber plantation near us." Saad leaned forward, grinning, waiting to hear more, wad of betel bulging in his leathery cheek.

"Bah 'Eic came and told me. Then her father got angry, -*bl'aal*, and said he didn't want her to marry Bah Laas because there were already two of Bah Laas' older brothers in his family. So he -*roo'* Bah Laas, gave him a talking-to. What good does it do you if all your in-laws are from one family? They all have to help you out anyway. Then Laas' brother Cabid went and -*roo'* him all over again." Rmpah chuckled. "So then her father's headman sends a *hakim* [intermediary] to ask me to go upstream to meet with him and her father. He wanted to know if it was okay for her to marry Bah Laas after all. So we sent somebody to get them and interviewed them, and we all harangued them again, and they agreed to marry."

"You can't have people just shacking up like dogs. *Litaaw* and *mnaleeh* are useless."

"If they hadn't agreed to marry, we'd have told them to get out [of town]. But they want to marry. Her father said okay, up to her."

"So you have no problem," said Saad.

"No. Just wanted you to know we can handle problems here." He glanced sidelong at Saad's attentive, sardonic face. *These valley people think like Malays, think we can't handle our own affairs.* "Of course, we have that problem with Wa' Kliy. You're her husband's headman. We were wondering if you'd talk with her. She won't come to town meetings any more. We've had three. She came to the first, but now she just doesn't come."

"Well, my Sten and your Sten talked about it, and I've talked with her *waris*, and we think maybe this would work. First, Yeop comes up here all the time. We can't tell him not to, but he shouldn't sleep in her house. He's got kinsmen here. He should sleep in their house. Second, there's no point having another town meeting about this. She doesn't come. Third, the bridewealth goes back to Yeop, divorce or no divorce. Fourth, Yeop is responsible for supporting his children but not his wife. The kids live up here until they become *litaaw* and *mnaleeh* and then they can decide where to live for themselves. Of course, they've already pretty much done that, looks like. Fifth, if she won't pay fines, how about all she does is pay us a *blanjaa' salah*, compensation for the wrongdoing, say $60 plus, because she really is in the wrong here?"

"That'd go to you and your Sten, right?" *You didn't have to like Saad. Few people did. He was too mean-mouthed and distrustful. But you had to admire someone who could present an argument* pranuu' pranuu', *topic by topic, from base to tip,* ju pangkal ha mool.

"Yes," said Saad, slowly, as if speaking to someone dimwitted, "but that's not the point, is it? It's not a lot of money. We've had to pay for the gas to go up and down the road three times, right? The point is, in my opinion, she's in the wrong."

"Right," murmured Rmpah, suppressing his irritation at Saad's tone.

"So she has to make payment for doing wrong, a *blanjaa' salah*."

"Agreed: it's not a lot of money for what she's done, and she is in the wrong. But I don't know if the problem's the money or even if she thinks she's in the wrong. Her thinking on this matter isn't good. *Sra'ngii' sngii' i luuy*," said Rmpah grumpily, using the Semai phrase that means something like "she thinks her own thoughts" or "feels her own feelings." Americans might say, "She knows her own mind." But Semai use the phrase disapprovingly, for people who reject the advice of friends and neighbors and go their own way.

Kliy Responds

Hot day, loud rzk rzk rzk rzk of cicadas, cool wet breezes spilling down the steep mountain slopes through the wounded rain forest. Across the precipitous valley, thin sheets of water spilling down a perpendicular black rock face gleam like mercury in slanting shafts of sunlight. At the foot of the cliff is the little river, dark and cool in the shadows of the great trees that still grow along its banks. The water is almost transparent so that you can see the pebbles on the bottom and the little fish swimming there, except where, swirling around a bend, the stream has created cauldrons of deep water in whose black depths who knows what lives: water demons or *maay krom tei'*, subterranean folk, reptilian, enormous and cold.

"I'm not listening," said Kliy. "You have no authority over me. Malays have authority here, not you. You can't make me go with him, and you can't make me divorce him, and you can't make me let him see my children."

Old men from olden times, she thought. Saad's neck was red, she noticed, maybe from shaving, *stringy like the necks of the naked red ducks that hang by their feet in Chinese shops.* If they treated her badly, she would just leave and go to Tapah town, maybe even to the state capital, Ipoh. There in the city she'd find a Malay man who'd give her food and pretty things. Her body was still good, she knew that. Starchy lowland food had made her plumper. Malays would say *sedap!* tasty! when she walked by or use the equivalent Cantonese word *ngam!* She'd heard of other girls who'd gone to Ipoh, even a couple of boys from Srngloo' who liked to dress up as girls, what Malays called *pondan. Who knows what those boys do there?* she thought, letting her mind drift away from the yattering old men. She sat placidly in the screaming sunlight, her left index finger bent across her lips, the other fingers curled loosely, shielding any expression of her feelings from the elders. *Could she run off to Ipoh? With three kids? Even if you're willing not to be who you are, what you are, even if you want to be different, what can you do?* Hearing the silence that meant the old men were waiting for her to say something.

"No," she said. They began again.

Nowadays men think they can boss women around, she thought. Yeop wasn't a bad man, but he yelled at her and scared her. He was stupid. His penis was long and skinny with bulgy veins, *not unlike the man himself*, she thought, smiling faintly to herself. He had thought at first that her hurt was to be solved in the sticky space where their pubic hairs twisted together, but it wasn't. After she'd left him, she'd said to her *mnaay*, her older brother's wife, "What can you expect from men? A penis has a mouth, but no eyes or brains. I don't know why women put up with them. I'm not putting up with him any more." The *mnaay* had giggled and covered her mouth so as not to show her teeth.

All she had wanted, Kliy thought, was a reasonably good time, to be *snaang*, safe and content. She was willing to work. No one ever said she was lazy. But she wanted attention and a good time, not a tense bossy awkward selfish housemate. Looking at him, sweating and breathing hard between her raised legs, she felt unanchored, unstable. He had nagged her to shave her pubic hair, a Malay men's thing, and she finally did, but the shaving was uncomfortable and itchy, and the smooth infantile pubes gave her no pleasure. What did he want, a little girl? Men had a fantasy, she knew, about adopting a little girl and raising her to adulthood, then marrying her so that she would love them like a daughter as well as a wife. That was taboo, all sorts of taboo, incest, *tolah, trlaac, pnali'*, just a disgusting idea. *Imagine sleeping with your father!* She shuddered faintly. You couldn't even have sex with strangers if they weren't in your generation.

The sex had not become better, duller and duller in fact, and he did not become more generous with her, just yelled at her. Flatland men wanted sexual monopoly, that was their problem, they thought they could control their wives' lives. Yeop had even told her not to sleep with his younger brother, her *mnaay*. He thought *he* could tomcat around, though, *rawooc*. Crazy. She wouldn't mention any of that, of course. It would scandalize the elders, though *mnaleeh* and *litaaw* would know what she meant, and giggle. Maybe she would mention it. What did she care? You don't talk about sex to old people.

Doesn't matter. *Who are these old men to me? These people? What is my connection with them?*

She wondered vaguely about who she had been when she decided to marry him so long ago. Who was that casual compliant *mnaleeh* who'd just gone along with everyone else's desires? Had she thought that letting so many people down was *punan*? And who had she thought he was? *Whatever, now we are who we are now,* she thought. She felt nothing, not really, not any more. *He has no power over me, I do what I choose, and I'm not ashamed, so no one's my boss. I'm not listening to you. I am who I am. You old men are nothing to me.*

The elders stopped talking at her for a moment, giving her a space in which to respond.

"No," she said. *Do you think this is something I* planned? *Have you ever wanted to die? Do you think I* planned *the desire? The revulsion? When has what you planned ever happened to you, with all your long meetings, all your compromises, your endless talk like chicks cheeping? When has that ever happened to anyone? It's all fate, like Malays say,* nasib lah, *fate. Things happen. That's all. We all just -ric-rooc, wander blindly in the light, deceiving each other, breaking our promises, all of us, hurting each other. We are who we are, and it makes no difference, not now. What can you do about it? What can anyone do? Nothing, and nothing.*

"No," she said.

Inconclusion

"That's just great," said Saad when they were back in the headman's house. "Why bother having headmen and Stens? Everybody just do whatever the hell they want to, and don't pay for it. Great."

"There's nothing to do. She should pay a fine. We all know she's wrong. I'm her headman, and even I know she's wrong. All her *waris* know she's wrong. Everybody knows she's wrong. Everybody's told her that. She just ignores us. What we'd like to do is *-prnyump* this case, make it vanish. But we can't okay a divorce or fix the fines without talking it over, and she isn't talking. You want us to go to the Malay marriage registrar?"

"O, that's a great idea. Let's talk to the *Malays*. Our Big Brothers will help. We can all go to the police station and get beaten up. Terrific. But what do I know? What a farce."

"Suppose we try our department [the Malay-run Bureau of Aboriginal Affairs]."

"Sure. 'Our department.' *I* call it the 'Malay bureau.' I fought for them in the Emergency, you know. I was a corporal in their army. I got medals. I'm supposed to be getting a pension. Supposed to have been getting it since 1970. You think I've seen dime one? You got that money from the loggers 'our' department brought in? Any of it? Malay justice. What a joke."

Something Will Happen

Something will happen and it will happen soon and it will happen without my volition or responsibility: but what? (Joyce Carol Oates, *American Appetites* [1989:65])

This is not a peaceful place, it is a fury
of fucking and fear, of buying and selling,
and we lie in it, we make it, a bed of lies,
and die in it. (If we did not lie to ourselves,
what would we make of the Emperor's smiles?)

The Emperor stands on the burning deck.
The hour is late, there's a big hole
in the ship of state. Down below
the people sit in the dark

watching Him on the screen, seeking relief,
still suspending their disbelief.
(from Mitchell Goodman, "An Old Actor, Playing the Emperor" [Smiles 1989:21])

Kliy gets off the wheezing bus in Ipoh, inhales the pungency of durians, garbage, and kerosene particulates in the hot wet market air. On top of the movie house that fronts the market are three huge billboards: one depicts a raging Chinese man flying through the air in a martial arts attack; another, a brightly colored Tamil melodrama; the third, half-naked Pale men with enormous muscles and huge guns. In the background of each a woman is shrinking, imperiled, showing more flesh than decent lowland women would in normal situations.

What you see is never all there is, Kliy thinks, looking at the bustle, flash and glitter. *Hill people know that.*

AH, KLIY! AH, HUMANITY!

[T]he elders in the old days always thought far ahead about the welfare of their descendants, not like the people today, most of whom are short-sighted. Now they are just able to see the immediate future and do not want to see further than that. "We would live in peace for most of our lives if we still adopted this kind of attitude," said Long Apon [of a flatland settlement]. . . . [T]he younger generation . . . are, according to him, becoming more aggressive and disorganized, and . . . tend to devalue *Seng-oi* [Semai] values. (Juli Edo 1998:252–53n)

Theoretical Issues: Conflict, Conflict Resolution, and Violence

As Melville concludes about Bartleby, another refusenik, there would seem little need for proceeding further in this history. I don't know how the case on which I modeled the story turned out. It just went on and on, like most town meetings I heard about. The conflict went "unresolved." The "conflict resolution techniques" didn't work. But not much happened as a result.

The West is investing heavily in dispute resolution programs to prevent violence, but disputes don't always lead to violence, and violence can occur without disputes. This chapter opened with the comment that conflict-resolution experts dismiss the success of societies like Semai. Professional dispute resolution experts typically address disputes that involve states or large corporations as stakeholders. Many of the professionals are what Russians call *derzhavniki*, roughly "statists." Peace without states and meddling "expert" elites doesn't count. A sort of "willed ignorance" affects the experts. They deny that laymen make peace expertly, despite all the empirical evidence that they do it all the time, in the worst of circumstances (Dentan 2008; Fry 2004:187–94; Nordstrom 2004:175–85). Peaceful societies constructed by terrorized hill peoples, street kids, and impoverished refugees don't count, aren't serious.

Like dispute resolution specialists, Malays see "their" minorities developing spiritually and economically when everyone is "clean and orderly" (McElwee 2004), sweltering away under government surveillance in rows of mutually identical zinc-roofed rectangular houses in desolate "Regroupment Schemes." The prevention of violence, keeping order, becomes a tool of domination. Untidy powerless people who handle their own problems without the nanny state are inherently subversive, not worth thinking about, needing order and instruction.

And the ways they avoid conflict don't count either. For instance, in every society young women have mothers and boyfriends who are rivals for their attention. That's a "structural" conflict, inherent in the relationships. You can't make it go away. Resolving each dispute that this structural conflict generates would take an inordinate amount of community time and energy and probably also generate ill will. Tluup Semai, as we've seen, *avoided* the conflict by ritually separating mother from boyfriend via what anthropologists call a "respect" or "avoidance" relationship. Perak Semai *prevented* it by having all the elders at weddings harangue the bride and groom about deferring to their in-laws and not appealing to their consanguineals, often until both youngsters were in tears. The conflict remained but usually didn't create problems. Kliy's case is a problem because it is exceptional. A good antiviolence program should not be limited to *resolving* conflicts. But most Western "AVPs" assume that violence is "natural" and that only peace needs construction.

Similarly, slavers had no dispute with their quarry. They wanted women and children to sell or abuse in various ways. They had the power. They took what they wanted. Flight or surrender were options, not dispute resolution. Conflict resolution works only 1) when both disputants are roughly equal in coercive power, and both benefit, as among Semai, or 2) when a third party more powerful than the disputants wants to end the dispute. Otherwise, the stronger disputants simply impose their will. Dispute resolution is a minor form of "surrender" in which both parties surrender to each other or to mediators.

If, as in the Semai case, both parties are roughly equal, coming to a resolution requires effectively deploying a limited set of incentives. In Kliy's case, the punishment was emotional disconnection from the community, which traditionally should have made her -sl-siil, feel the "shame" that Bah Cong said is the only sanction Semai have. But her experiences in the non-Semai world reinforced her traditional sense of individual autonomy, and, because her family came from the mountains, it was hard for her to connect with foothill people. And, though I knew her a little and admired her intransigence, she didn't seem very smart, just very set on her own way. So she didn't heed the consequences ahead of time and accepted them afterward. Free people can be like that, especially in a society where people surrender in the sense of not believing that they control their destiny. It makes them a pain in the neck to *derzhavniki* everywhere.

Town meetings succeed in resolving conflicts, when they succeed, because everybody benefits. That's what anthropologists mean by "investing cultural capital." When people don't need that cultural capital, the goodwill of friends and relations, they don't need "conflict resolution techniques." Freed of these needs, they gain nothing by continuing to participate in town meetings.

Now that the outside world is physically less perilous and new avenues of economic activity seem to be opening, the possibility that disapproving people might not help Kliy out economically becomes less threatening; indeed, in the long run, they need her as much as she needs them. The only reward they can offer is to reengage with her, and for that she would have to make personal sacrifices she prefers not to make. In such cases, when town meetings fail to resolve conflict, Saad told me, people don't usually resort to violence, except that (as the "learned helplessness" model predicts) disappointed disputants may become depressed enough to kill themselves: Yeop said he had thought about that, a lot, even reaching for the canister of pesticide once and being restrained by a friend.

But *bicaraa'* always succeed at two goals. First, they let the community heal itself from the wound the conflict inflicted on community unity and communal proprieties. Just participating in the exercise, as even Kliy did at first, legitimizes community authority. Public condemnation of her behavior both expressed and reinforced communal norms. All societies exploit deviance to mark the limits of acceptable behavior this way. In that sense, Kliy's refusal to conform helped bolster communal conformity.

Second, town meetings defuse passions by giving everyone a chance to vent feelings until no one has anything left to say. If disputants will accept that they were wrong and pay part of the fine, showing that they acknowledge their misdeed, then the community will heal faster than if things just drag on. But even without the fine, I suspect that, as my old friend 'Apel of Mncaak said in 1992,

> We're not like other people. We want to be friends. With other peoples—Malays, Chinese—if you do something wrong, they're not your friends any more. Us, we go indoors and sulk [-*kra'dii'*] for a while, but we'll love you anyway, and after a few months we're your friends again [big smile].

The town meeting just lets people express their feelings freely while waiting for the equilibrium of love to reassert itself. Relocation and integration into an economy that runs on invidious striving will, I think, eventually undercut this generosity of spirit. But it hasn't done that yet (see, e.g., Nicholas 1993).

To summarize, *bicaraa'* offer disputants and deviants a chance to repent in public and reconcile. If someone refuses, the meetings console the people who go along with the consensus and give them the blessing of group approval and acceptance. Kliy doesn't get that consolation. That's the only penalty for saying, "I prefer not to." Freedom remains paramount, even with the imported "dispute resolution procedures." Free people are a pain in the neck.

7

For Fear of Finding
Something Worse:
Raising Kids

AND ALWAYS KEEP AHOLD OF NURSE

His Father, who was self-controlled,
Bade all the children round attend
To James' miserable end,
And always keep a-hold of Nurse
For fear of finding something worse.

—From Hilaire Belloc, "Jim Who Ran Away from His
Nurse and Was Eaten by a Lion" (Belloc 1950:19)

Psychologists say that looking after children is one way people deal with stress: the "tend" in *fight, flight, tend, befriend*. In evolutionary terms, this response feeds into the generally successful human "K-reproductive strategy" of having few offspring but seeing them through to maturity. Preserving children from slavers fits this strategy: slave populations tend not to reproduce. The fear and learned helplessness that slaving generated may persist, like phantom feeling in a severed arm, in various forms: prudence, caution, free-floating anxiety, skittishness with outsiders. Once established, the "ethos" may persist beyond the trauma that generated it:

The trauma sufferer is haunt[ed] or possess[ed] by an image or event that he or she has missed as experience; a trauma is violently imposed and is always reimposing itself. . . . Trauma victims cannot simply remember what they never forgot. And it is at least in part because the trauma cannot be temporally located that it becomes strangely transmissable down through generations . . . preserved in its very unutterability (Morgenstern 1997:102)

177

The world that Semai teach their children still lies in the shadow of slaving. There are several reasons why.

(1) The plight of Semai in "postcolonial" Malaysia is a kinder, gentler version of their earlier situation (Dentan 1997). The situation is more ambiguous than it used to be. The new colonialism is "internal." But . . .

(2) The viciousness of the Japanese occupation in the 1930s and 1940s, Communist terrorism, and British counterterrorism during the Emergency of the 1950s and landgrabs and "regroupments" since justify distrust, suspicion, and caution toward outsiders. Malaysian bureaucrats express the same sentiments about traditional Semai life that British governments express about the "Travellers" mentioned at the beginning of the next section of this chapter. For Semai, trust, faith or carelessness would be stupid.

Semai for the first time directly confront ambiguous forces like "capitalism" and "the state," for which there are no words in Semai. Dealing with unfamiliar abstractions, in this sort of situation most people everywhere use metaphors. Concrete models for abstract relationships give the abstractions a local habitation and a name. We talk about murderers as "monsters," for example, or "animals," though they're just humans like us, or about "the White House" as if it were a homogeneous organism with thoughts and feelings. But people lose track of the fact that they're thinking metaphorically; then metaphors substitute themselves for reality. This kind of "concrete thinking" may underlie Semai stories of threat and deception.

> **Wa' Saiyah** [age forty-four, an old friend from Mncaak, unmarried and childless but so loving that other people's children were always clinging to her (12 February 1992)]: Is your house [at 'Icek] near other people's houses?
>
> **RKD:** [nods and grunts yes].
>
> **Saiyah:** Away from the road?
>
> **RKD:** [nods and grunts yes].
>
> **Saiyah:** So you don't need to be afraid of Malays.
>
> **RKD:** [smiles].
>
> **Saiyah:** I know Malays aren't really bad. They're like *maay -kòh kuuy*, the people who chop off heads, just something we talk about, not something real. But I'm still afraid of them.

(3) The stories stress the importance of acting out the love and mutual accommodation necessary to Semai survival. Semai kids learn they need other people to look after them. Many stories feature abandonment or betrayal by those you love: parents, kinsmen, lovers. Terrible things happen. You can escape by transforming yourself into something pow-

erful and dreadful, as adepts do. But it's hard to change back. You need familiar people.

(4) Behavioral scientists once treated oppressed people (beaten women, abused children, dispossessed natives) as passive victims. Nowadays they tend to stress how people resist. But any either/or characterization of how complex peoples respond to complex pressures is probably at least partly wrong. It is easy to see Malay state power in the seemingly friendly demons who will devour you or, if you submit and become like them, share their power. The government's policy of "mainstreaming" Semai by transforming them into impoverished Malays is an environmental stress to which Semai respond with a toolbox of adaptations, depending on how particular individuals or groups think about particular pressures at particular times: resistance, passivity, submission. I think these skeletal but complexly nuanced stories may reflect the ambiguities and ambivalences of Semai reality.

(5) Semai respond to their ambiguous oppression, this stress, much as Americans respond to the bad news in their own lives, by fantasizing horrors: not necessarily believing in them but not dismissing them out of hand either. Remember: most people find visualizing "concrete" metaphorical representations of relationships easier than thinking of them as abstractions like "oppression" or "discrimination." The thought can still be subtle and complex, but often the metaphor replaces the reality it represents: the map becomes the terrain. Strangers who steal and hurt children can represent what states and corporations routinely do to their subjects (Juli and Dentan 2008).

(6) But once children become the metaphor, and people respond to them as if the metaphor were the reality, then they stop responding to them simply as children. And the metaphorical status of the child rationalizes behavior that otherwise would be intolerable, among Semai, other Malaysians, and Americans (Dentan 2001a; Juli and Dentan 2008).

Like most egalitarian peoples, Semai value individual autonomy and resist hierarchy. But the power involved in frightening helpless and dependent people like children may also provide an ambivalent pleasure, kept secret most of the time, even from oneself, and helps assure that children want to please adults—the way "disciplining" children and "biblical chastisement" do in the United States, as I argued in the article of which this chapter is a loose adaptation (Dentan 2001a).

In short, warning children about the dangers they face also lets Semai resist assimilation. The kids develop "learned helplessness" and nonviolence in part because 1) Semai adults expect and encourage children to be fearful, for example, by telling terrifying folktales about outsiders, and 2) Semai adults do not expect, "model," or condone violence, by "corporal punishment," for instance.

CAUTIONARY TALES

> [Stories'] importance lay not in the facts they purported to relate but in the expression they provided for the [T]ravellers' sense of insecurity in a world where people in local government can be quoted in the Press assaying there is no place in modern society for people who live a nomadic life. . . . I can understand their still harbouring fear and suspicion, particularly of people in positions of authority, who at times seem to behave like the ogres in their Jack tales. Travellers have very sound psychological instincts and know it is dangerous to repress strong emotions, so I believe they tell their Burker [ghoul] stories even today as a kind of safety valve for their deep-rooted fears. (Douglas 1987:10–11)

Older adults sit around telling stories and drinking tea or coffee in the evening, when the day is cool and most work is over:

> We tell stories in the evening. My mother's mother used to tell stories that made even grown-ups weep. Like the story of Tailorbird, which lasts all night. We have many many stories. ('Apel of Mncaak, 1992)

Tailorbirds are *kcmooc*, ghosts, of neglected children. The despairing plaintiveness of their call reflects the horror of abandonment and neglect. Badly treated children are the worst ghosts, calling softly "Mommy? Mommy? Mommy?" as in American horror movies.

Younger adults listen skeptically to the storytellers. "I enjoy listening to old folks tell stories," said Bah 'Apel, age thirty. "I enjoy comparing one version with another." But the people most sensitive to these stories are Semai children, who sometimes hear them as bedtime stories from elder siblings or other caretaking relatives.

Unclear and Present Dangers

Elizabeth Dentan, Wa' Lisbet in Semai, was five years old in 1991. She lived with us along the Waar River in the mountains of Batang Padang District in Perak. The family we lived with treated her much like one of their own children. Cat, her Semai mom, and 'Ilah, Cat's younger sister, told Lisbet cautionary tales, warning her of the terrors that afflict the children of the poor. As a result, the first three complete Semai phrases Lisbet learned were about *maay* ("people" or "strangers") who -*kòh kuuy*, chop off heads; -*klooh mad*, claw out eyes; and -*blah nuus*, slash hearts. These evil strangers, she learned ("Dad, is that *true*?"), lurked around the settlement. Assurances ("Well, it's probably not true, but people here believe it") weren't always convincing enough to keep Lisbet from tears as she sat on the lap of the narrator.

Like Semai children hearing the stories for the first time, Lisbet wept
with vicarious sorrow for the protagonists and fear for herself. Children
should weep, said Cat, they should be afraid. Indeed, she and 'Ilah modified the stories so that Lisbet would identify with a particular character.
For example, the character Luuc, Youngest Son, the usual hero of Semai
tales, might become Youngest Daughter or even "Wa' Lisbet."

The women's love for Lisbet emerged the way Semai love for kids
sometimes does: in scaring kids, teaching "stranger danger." The world
hates poor children. Only we can protect them. Said Cat,

> You tell Wa' Lisbet she shouldn't get on his motorbike with that Malay [Ah-
> mad Rafik, who holds the Department of Indigenous Peoples Affairs
> (JHEOA)–licensed monopoly to market the people's crops]. He'll take her to
> Tapah [the nearest large town], and there. . . . [knowing look, suggesting
> nameless horrors]. He always gives her things to eat [finger symbolically slit-
> ting throat]. We can't *srng'òòh* her [warn her, "make her *-sng'òòh*, fear"]. You
> have to do it.

Or he, like any outsider, will do obscure unspeakable terrible things to
her.

A Tale of Ambiguity and Ambivalence

One story began while I was away, so I missed the beginning. This reconstruction is from lightly edited field notes:

> Wa' Lisbet's parents go away for some reason.
> She has to get fire from her *tnee'*, older siblings/cousins. [Semai of old had
> no efficient way to make fire. You slipped a strip of rattan under a dry stick
> on which you stood, sawing the rattan back and forth, until the friction gen-
> erated enough heat to kindle some Caryota palm-cotton tinder. People nor-
> mally kept a brand burning. Slavers could follow Semai on the move by
> watching for the trail of ash dropped from the tip of the brand, one reason
> Semai traveled by walking in streams.]
> [One after another, the *tnee'* turn her down in a repeated set piece in which]
> Lisbet asks, "Please give me some fire to cook my tapioca," and her *tnee'* re-
> ject her. [By then, E was weeping copiously: why were the *tnee'* so mean? Pa-
> ternal reassurance, *it's only a story, sweetie,* was ineffective.]
> Finally, wandering in the woods, Lisbet meets a reticulated python dis-
> guised as an attractive *litaaw* named Bah Lapan [Mr. Eight, a by-name, from
> the pattern of blotches that give the snake its scientific name, *Python reticula-
> tus*]. Bah Lapan falls in love with Lisbet and marries her.
> But their house burns down! [Wail from Lisbet, snuggling up to 'Ilah]
> Bah Lapan changes into a handsome Malay [= rich powerful man]. He
> tells Lisbet to rub the ashes of the house on the walls, which transmutate into
> silver and gold.

The [stingy antisocial] *tnee'* visit them. They bed down together. In the night Lisbet and her in-laws mutate back into snakes, devour her *tnee'*, take them to the bottom of the sea.

[Wails from sleepy Lisbet] Then Bah Lapan gives them a potion, the spitting cobras [*sic*] vomit up the *tnee'* and they all lived together.

That's as happily ever after as Semai stories get, Semai not being unrealistic optimists. Indeed, I suspect Cat improvised the happy ending for Lisbet.

Demonic themes permeate this richly ambiguous tale, as threatening and obscure as Cat's warning about Ahmad Rafik. For traditional Semai, Malays are human opposites to Semai, and beasts are people opposite to humans (see chapters 3 and 4). That is, Malays and animals contrast with Semai and humans, the way imagined witches contrast with normal people in other ideologies: Malay:Semai = beast:human. Animals, especially scary ones like cobras and pythons, embody demonic *nyanii'* that bring madness, sickness, and death; but in dreams form erotic relationships with adept humans, become lovers, and help the adepts cure ills that other demons bring. In dreams, even Malays and Pale People may become one's demon lovers, nurturing instead of terrorizing dreamers. Semai stories are full of transformations from the natural secure world into the unnatural animal/demonic one and back, like Malay/Python. Semai narrators often end such tales with the adjuration: "If you are a *this*, stay a *this*; if a *that*, stay a *that*."

The changing identity of the dangerous snakes in 'Ilah's tale suggests they are not just spitting cobras, which aim for your eyes, or the reticulated python, thirty to thirty-five feet long, but avatars of the great subterranean Dragon, the chaos that drowns all categories, all order. The rich, powerful state promises golden houses; indeed, bureaucrats called one program for Semai the "Golden Bridge." But people must abandon their families and "marry" Malays, who are by definition, not Human, not *Sn'ooy*. In the real world, marrying a Malay would require converting to Islam and "becoming Malay," though that drawback is absent from the story. The point of the story seems to be that, if Semai cease to support each other, Dragon and destruction will come—for better and/or worse.

But notice, please, how complex Bah Lapan is. He takes all the mutually contrastive forms that sentient creatures can: Human, Malay, and demon/beast; Dragon, emblem and bringer of chaos, embodying *hnalaa'*, transformative power. Not a simple character at all, not a simple idea of "Malay."

To my ear, such stories seem skeletal. The thin description lets any narrator, not just skilled ones, produce the desired effect.

Invasion of the Organ Snatchers

Recent field researchers in Southeast Asia report that even in areas where headhunting . . . seems never to have been practiced, rumors circulate about contemporary headhunters who raid living communities and terrorize whole populations. (Hoskins 1996:1)

Cautionary tales keep terror alive. Like this.

One day Cat and 'Ilah are chatting about head choppers with Cat's mother's sister Bun, who's visiting from the lowlands. Big-eyed little Wa' Mnjuun, age seven, sits on Bun's big soft lap. 'Ilah remarks that a Malay man and a Bengali woman appeared at the settlement at the sixth milestone of the Cameron Highlands Road and menaced the headman.

"That's what happens when you live near a city like Tapah," responds Cat in her usual soft jittery staccato. She is sitting cross-legged, weaving a mat with precise repetitive movements, never looking up. She's become a compulsive worker since a botched caesarean section by a Malay doctor at the Orang Asli Hospital made it impossible for her to do the heavy work other women do, like collecting firewood or fruit. Once I spent a day timing her activities: she never let up. "There're head choppers at Mile One and Mile Six, and in Tapah."

'Ilah, Wa' Lisbet on her lap, agrees: "They don't come up here often, but it's the first thing we think about when we see Pale People [Europeans]. They shoot people. No use going up against them with your bare hands, and no use blowpiping them either. They shoot you anyway. We need to watch Wa' Lisbet so they don't snatch her."

At supper a week later, Cat relays a report from her younger brother's wife, who heard it from someone at Mile Eight, a dozen miles downriver on the Tapah-Cameron Highlands Road: "They say some *mnaleeh* [nubile girls] around Kampar [a valley town near Mncaak] are part of a head-chopper gang who gouge out people's eyes and sell them to rich Malays and Chinese. The Department [of Orang Asli Affairs] made a report. Anyone going to Kampar should watch out."

"Especially men," says 'Ilah pointedly, looking at me and Cat's oldest boy, Faisul, a guitar-playing fifteen-year-old *litaaw*. Semai assume that *litaaw* are too oversexed to be smart. Faisul paints his face and wears his hair long like Malay rock stars. He is gorgeous ("a fox," says my wife Leta) and preens a lot, the way *litaaw* stereotypically do. But he's still a little unsure of himself with girls. Normally, you trust *mnaleeh* to flirt with you, not hurt you.

The next morning a group of women setting out to collect firewood meet the Semai schoolteacher and his family coming downstream, two adults and two children. The two little groups spend forty-five minutes sitting by the roadside eating betel and exchanging misinformation about eye gougers. There are three eye gougers, says the teacher: a Malay, a Bengali, and a Chinese, like a Bahai missionary team. They put eyes and hearts in a Styrofoam cooler and ship them overseas. By the end of the day, people in our settlement are carrying machetes or blowpipes wherever they go.

Cat's husband Lwey, age thirty-five, seems unperturbed. Puffing on his stubby homemade pipe in his kitchen, he advises his wife's younger brother Panda' to take a blowpipe if he goes off by himself. "Maybe you should take a machete, too. And a spear. And a club. Do you have a gun? And a machine gun. And a tank."

Panda', recently married but still a *litaaw*, faint spotting of pimples across his forehead, goes out. He and a gaggle of other *litaaw* assemble under Alang's house to plan how to defend the settlement against the heart slashers, discussing who'll hold what position and what weapons they'll carry. "Then we'll see who's afraid and who isn't," says Panda', nodding, quoting the epic tale (see chapter 1) of how Semai defeated the genocidal Rawas. His father can recite it. But like most *litaaw* schemes, this one doesn't get off the ground.

The next morning, at breakfast with Cat's, we hear someone outside warning a child about eye gougers. On Bun's lap sits her granddaughter, Wa' Mnjuun', who came along on Bun's visit. Mnjuun', unused to Pale People, clings to her grandmother, peering over her shoulder at me. Bun smiles and says to her, "That's right. There are people who gouge out the eyes of our people and sell them to Pale People. Like Lisbet's father. Maybe he wants a pair for Lisbet."

"It's true. Your gramma herself bought her left eye in Tapah," I say. Bun smiles.

"They tie you up," says Cat seriously, adding a detail I hadn't heard before, "then claw your eyes out," making a clawing gesture.

"They particularly like little girls' eyes," adds Lwey, glaring directly at Wa' Mnjuun'. By this time the little girl is clinging so tightly to her grandmother that she's almost vanishing into her bosom.

"Pale People especially," says Bun grimly, indicating me with her chin. "This one buys eyes all the time." Mnjuun' buries her face in her gramma's plump shoulder, and the old woman gives us a faint smile.

Lwey and Faisul grin widely. But that night, out frog hunting by torchlight, Lwey, Faisul, Panda' and Panda's *litaaw* younger brother begin talking about head choppers. Each ratchets up the others' terrors. The shadows along the river teem with menace and sinister rustlings. There seems to be someone with a flashlight up on the road that passes through the settlement but too far away to see who it is or if it's human. Finally, it seems prudent to come home, though they've caught only half a dozen little frogs.

The terror lasts a couple of weeks. Faisul's younger brother, Lang, about thirteen years old, has a nightmare in which three Bengalis claw his eyes out. Finally, the fear is replaced by worry that the Orang Asli Department is about to relocate the settlement downstream among other Semai who are bound to resent outsiders crowding in, causing quarrels. The Director General, later removed for corruption, denies the rumor:

"We are not the Los Angeles Police Department."

But such forced relocations are common.

Rumor-driven panics like these pervade Semai settlements. They resemble "panic disorders," which may follow traumatic terror.

DISCUSSION

[In] regions where heads were never systematically taken, attributed to agents who would not acknowledge it as part of their ancestral traditions . . . headhunting as a trope . . . is employed to speak metaphorically about . . . inequality, economic exploitation, and an unequal voice in political decision-making. (Hoskins 1996:37)

Snatching Organs: Fact

You might think, from the stories about head choppers, that Semai had encountered headhunting in reality. But headhunting hasn't been a peninsular Malaysian institution for centuries, if ever. Malays seem never to have taken heads. There were headhunters nearby, in Indonesia and Borneo, so people might have heard of it, the way they could have heard of organ-napping. There was a headhunting massacre in Borneo in the mid-1990s (Parry 1998); Indonesian newspapers throughout the 1990s featured horrific photos of young men waving severed heads. The question is why the image of headhunting would catch in Semai imagination and why it seems more salient now than before.

Although Malaysian media are less absorbed with organ-napping than their American counterparts are with sexual child abuse, the macabre trade in organ transplants get coverage of much the same kind. Several educated non-Semai friends in Kuala Lumpur, hearing me recount Semai organ-napper stories in 1992, protested my dismissing their factuality. They had heard similar stories themselves, sometimes with Orang Asli as the head choppers (e.g., Nicholas 1993:42). Lye Tuck-Po, a talented anthropologist who has worked with another group of Orang Asli, e-mailed me on 2 March 1998:

There is another, probably unrelated, rumor, but one that's very present in the minds of urban parents: the threat of children being kidnapped by traders for the Thai begging trade. I first heard the story almost 15 years ago: that when the kids are bought up by the begging syndicates in Thailand, their tongues are cut out or they're deliberately lamed to make them more "pathetic." A year or two ago, a similar fear was expressed in the papers (The Star) by the parents of one of those kidnapped kids. It's not too far-fetched. My own work with an anti-trafficking agency suggests that poor Southeast Asian kids do need to fear traffickers.

And I don't mean that individuals in peninsular Malaysia never took heads as trophies or to instill fear. People do that everywhere. They do it spontaneously in America. We hear about a man who kept heads in a refrigerator or of finding the head of a little boy whose body has never been found, and we think, *pervert! weirdo! monster!* Not us, right? Soldiers do it too, for example, in Bosnia in the 1990s. Taking heads symbolizes power, victory. In East Malaysia and Borneo, conquerors took the heads of the conquered to mark their incorporation into the victorious state. Taking heads is a human thing to do, not as sick and alien as we might like.

And, of course, I've often been wrong when I dismissed Semai stories:

> In the less affluent archipelagoes that surround us, there is a lively traffic in human heads. The heads are smuggled back across the border by Teochew [South Chinese immigrant] business men. They are destined for the cornerstones of new high-rises. . . . It is the vestige of an old and vaguely illegal custom: to inter the bodies of the lower castes under the threshold of a royal household. Traditionally, the lower castes delivered themselves willingly, in exchange for the promise of elevation, a higher social position in the next life. In the ruins of our dreams, the power of architecture is always overestimated. . . . Every day we travel through its ruins. . . . A city is not a place where people come to live. Its architecture was never about homes. Even the most superficial excavation will reveal its ancient heart began with the building of tombs. (Chua 1998:23–26)

Semai on the Teiw R'eiis tell a similar story (see chapter 8).

Snatching Organs: Metaphor

In the Indianized Southeast Asian statelets of a millennium ago, taking heads, like kidnapping women and children, symbolized and represented state power (Maxwell 1996:101). *Taking heads, taking women, taking children, what's the difference? We can do whatever we want, and you can't stop us.*

Recently, the JHEOA in Kelantan and Trengganu, the two most predominantly Malay and Muslim states in Malaysia, instituted a "fosterage" program under which Malay families would take in Orang Asli kids to "civilize" them (Yusoff 1987). The ostensible motive is to benefit the kids, not the masters. Semai culture is the "problem" that keeps the kids from "advancing" (Juli and Dentan 2008). The advocates of fosterage ignore the possibility that being taken away by strangers from everything safe and familiar might feel a lot like kidnapping and enslavement to the children involved.

Other Southeast Asian countries have maintained the ancient tradition of kidnapping highland peoples' children to terrorize them into becoming sexual objects or unpaid servants, the latter practice often now described as "adoption" rather than "enslavement," the way apologists for traditional Malay slaving claim that slave children became just like other children in the family. In societies run by and for the urban rich, such children have little recourse in fact, however enlightened the laws protecting them.

What do you *see* when you see "capitalism?" Who but Ahmad Rafik, the JHEOA-licensed Malay trader, a friendly mustached smiling man, who contributes money to marriages, comes to wedding parties, flirts with the girls, and gives kids rides on his motorbike if they're not too scared? And "the state" appears as Inci' Nasir Ruslan, head of the local JHEOA branch office, who speaks a little Semai and worries about the people's reluctance to tell him their concerns. They *seem* okay. Not like bad guys at all.

"Power," says an influential student of violence, "is embedded in the situated practices of agents" (Feldman 1991:4). But not these agents, not comprehensibly. Somehow the forces they represent—"development," "assimilation"—perpetuate what happened during the days of slaving. Peoples like Semai, on the periphery of the expanding capitalist state, must sacrifice their freedom and well-being, their culture and their children, to increase the wealth and well-being of their more powerful neighbors. That's what those abstractions mean. It's easier, more human, not to think about "integration into the mainstream" or "participation in export-driven development projects" but instead to imagine shape-shifting monsters who look like friendly outsiders, monsters who rip out your children's hearts, blind their eyes, snatch their vital organs, transforming them into aliens, for aliens. An Indonesian poet describes the change:

> People go to the mountains for firewood.
> They come back heavy laden.
> People go to the cities for dreams.
> They don't come back at all.

Organ-snatcher stories seem to have partially replaced stories in which outsiders kidnap women and children. As the memory of slave raids fades and threat of "development" looms larger and larger, organ-snatcher stories not only become plausible but also fit the same functional niche that the old slaving stories did. That is, the stories do the same things in Semai life.

Ambiguity and Ambivalence

Another thing these storytellings do, as "inexplicable subjective practices," is to "confuse and to some extent refuse the appropriations of rationalized legitimacy" (Redding 1998:10). Semai accept the inevitability of their dependency on the Malay-dominated government. Conceding their loss of freedom constricts their opportunity for political or even ideological resistance. But stories of body snatchers and shape shifters involve the dissolution of the physical bodies on which, according to students like Feldman and Redding, the outsider state inscribes its power. The conquest may be fatal, but the conquered have vanished and thus escaped their conquerors. The means is *hnalaa'*, the transformative power they tricked from the Lord who embodies the slavocratic state.

That state also proposes a solution to Semai plight: stop being Semai, become Malays, attain the power other peoples have. Your identity is worthless; try ours. But the transformation theme in these stories extends the transformation that Semai say great shamans can accomplish, turning themselves into beasts, especially tigers. The transformation is a covert metaphor for the experience of demonic possession described in chapter 4, accessing demonic bestial power by becoming monstrous oneself. The religion and these stories suggest the possibility that threatened people can mutate into powerful monsters by undergoing an experience like trancing, a "dissociative state" or "altered state of consciousness," as psychologists call it, in which one's normal identity is overwhelmed. Such an experience might account for the resonance of the metaphor of drowning that also pervades Semai theology.

Storytelling and Semai Social Life

Observational or vicarious conditioning accounts for the origins of a greater proportion of humans' fears and phobias than does direct classical conditioning. (Cook et al. 1985:591 [cf. p .607]; Mineka et al. 1984)

Children don't need actually to experience kidnapping or eye gouging to fear them. Semai "learned helplessness," I think, originates in slaving. But nowadays the fear rises not from how often they are victims but from how vulnerable they feel to victimization, what criminologists call "indirect victimization" (McGarrell, Giacomazzi, and Thurman 1997). Fear reflects not how bad things are but how vulnerable you feel. Drunk drivers are far more likely to kill particular Americans than terrorists are but aren't nearly as frightening. Semai, the poorest people in Malaysia, stereotyped by themselves and others as timid and weak, with no secure connections to protectors in the government, feel vulnerable. Their children, the weakest and most timid Semai, seem the most vulnerable.

The notion of "stranger danger" pervades Semai life. Stories make adults' fears into threats real to children. All children need to do is to hear stories about kidnappers and eye gougers and to watch adults panic, as they were still doing in the 1990s. That the fear is vicarious rather than direct makes little difference for Semai or American children. And Semai think, like Americans, that children need to learn fear, to flee friendly strangers, to trust no one and nothing not already intimate.

There's no doubt in my mind that 'Ilah loved Lisbet. It was obvious in every look and gesture. When we had to leave for the last time 'Ilah could not see us off because she was overcome by emotion, which Semai don't like showing in public. She said what other Semai say, that teaching children to fear protects them from disguised evil by making them stay close to adults who can look after them. Evoking revulsion in one area, they foster attachment to another. On the lap, getting the hug, after you've heard the stories time and time and again, they seem to arouse a certain frisson complexly composed of both horror and titillation that is experienced vicariously.

> These accounts . . . exert a certain quasi-pornographic fascination. One gets the sense that the world described within is separated from the reader in both time and space, indeed, as if the actions had taken place in "another country" entirely. (Anagnost 1994:233)

Substitute "narrator/listener" for "reader," and this passage applies to Semai cautionary tales. Adults, more skeptical of traditional stories, still respond to the stories' depiction of a cosmos swamped by shape-shifting ravenous obscene horrors. Only the little islet "us," where mutual love and responsibility should reign, offers any safety at all.

Unlike movies or TV, the occasionally violent imagery of these stories doesn't provide human models for violence. In the stories, only humans who slough off their human identity and become beasts are violent. You couldn't be violent and human. Other kinds of violent stories puzzled traditional people. In 1963, Semai who'd just started going to movies asked me why Americans were killing indigenous people. I tried to explain that the genocide, at least the direct killing, was over long ago. "So why do you still want to look at it?" I had no answer.

Telling the cautionary story rewards the adults. Kids hug them, cuddle with them, show how much they love and need them. Storytellers put the unspeakable into words, perhaps getting a fleeting sense of the terrors among which they live. And they can become, briefly, that which frightens instead of those who fear.

Other ways of teaching children to fear strangers show the same ambivalent enjoyment. In the 1970s, the first time we visited Knik,

> a young mom points us out to the little girl she is carrying in a sarong slung over her shoulder to make a sling, whispering *sng'òòh sng'òòh*, fear! fear! until the child bursts into tears, then mom covers its head so it need no longer see us and carries it away—turning her head as she went to give us big

chummy smile. Later, a gaggle of half a dozen or more curious boys, ranging from ages about five to about twelve, plus a couple of little girls, follows us into the headman's house, where our friend Tandiil from Mncaak, a newly married *litaaw* whose wife is about to have a baby, is to introduce us. The kids settle in a little cross-legged flock by the door, smiling, watching us. Seated across from them, Tandiil fills in the time while the headman's wife makes tea by fixing a cold eye on the boys and leaning forward.

"*Sng'òòh!*" he says. Pause. "Do you *sng'òòh?*" Leaning so far forward that he has to support his weight on both hands flat on the floor in front of him, while the little boys edge away on their behinds from him and us, uncrossing their legs, not rising but tensing up, grinning nervously, hands flat on the floor, watching intently: "The Pale People have come to stick you with HYPODERMIC NEEDLES! Whooooo *sng'òòh* the most?" A couple of the littlest children half rise, turning toward the door, still looking at us over their shoulders.

"*THAT'S* THE ONE WE'LL STICK FIRST!" cries Tandiil, and the boys break and run, giggling.

It's a game, sort of. But, even along the R'eiis in 1992, an area open to outsiders for over half a century, the younger children still scattered like frightened sparrows when we first showed up in a settlement.

Besides the care and playfulness, there's a cruelty here, I think, among Americans and Semai, lurking under the surface like a crocodile in the river. Lisbet's tears at the stories made 'Ilah glance at the other Semai women. They all smiled, I think because the weeping was cute, although loud weeping and wailing represents a loss of self-control that makes adults uneasy. You should comfort a desperately unhappy child. But still, when Lisbet's pet chick died and Lisbet wailed in misery in my arms, the Semai grown-ups who loved her laughed. You should comfort a desperately unhappy child but only if it comes to you to cuddle.

Leta, my wife, said it reminded her of German child-rearing practices, making children weep because they're cute when they weep. And the traditional German fairy tales that the Grimms collected, like "Hansel und Gretel," are even more bloodcurdling than Semai stories. "What an irony it'd be," she added, "if Nazis and Semai come out of the same childhood."

CONCLUSION

Do not conclude from this analysis that Semai simply enjoy scaring children.

In real life, ambiguity and ambivalence are the rule in child rearing. I suspect that the recent public American concern with children also masks cruelty. We talk about "disciplining" students for their own good. Who would argue with that? In twenty-odd states, Americans give school authorities permission to beat weeping boys and girls with instruments specially designed to cause extreme pain, producing deep bruises that last for a week or more. They beat teenagers too. Any kid. Sometimes the pain is so bad that the kids soil themselves, which doesn't deter the beating. Sometimes it's so bad that the beating has to be spread out over several days. In Texas alone, over 50,000 children suffered such beatings in 2000. Most American parents hurt their kids physically, under euphemisms like "spanking" and obfuscated by familial rituals that are supposed to make the beating not *really* "beating." Hardly any other country allows that. So there's no penalty for beating kids as long as you have the right status and are in the right county.

A Job You Can Love. Midwives, like the smiling woman with the baby in this photo from Guul Galuuw on the upper Waar River, 13 November 1991, remain in touch with the babies they have delivered, not just physically and emotionally but spiritually. If the midwife gets sick, for example, the parents she helped should bathe her ritually to restore her strength so that their children will not in turn become sick; or, if the children become sick anyway, they need to bathe the midwife as well as the children. This restores contact with the Seven Original Midwives, who give midwives spiritual strength much as demon lovers help shamans. The photo shows how much a competent midwife enjoys her contact with pregnant women, like the one in the foreground for whom the midwife is caring, and with the babies they have delivered, like the one in the midwife's arm. Young children are a source of pleasure for everyone. Photo by R. K. Dentan.

In the United States, if you torture a child, social workers take it away from you until you take anger management training or parenting classes. Then you get the child back. If you kill a child, you go to prison and serve your sentence and have paid "your debt to society." If you fondle a child inappropriately, you also "do time"; then you 1) remain incarcerated indefinitely until you receive successful treatment from people who deny the possibility of successful treatment or 2) on "release" must go from house to house, telling your new neighbors you're a child molester so that they can picket your house, revile your children, reveal your presence to the media, and perhaps beat you up or kill you. These penalties are so draconian that smart pedophiles would have to consider killing the children they victimize. Lawmakers are willing to risk that.

So why is it so much worse in the United States to be a pedophile than a child batterer, to fondle a child inappropriately than to torture or kill it? What does the political shibboleth "for the sake of the children" mean? I'd say Semai look pretty good by contrast.

CODA: TEACHING KIDS FEAR AND NONVIOLENCE

[N]eighborhood efficacy . . . [consists of everyone's willingness to help] supervising children and maintaining public order. . . . [T]he collective efficacy of residents is a critical means by which urban neighborhoods inhibit the occurrence of personal violence, without regard to the demographic composition of the population. . . . Social science research has demonstrated, at the individual level, the direct role of SES [socioeconomic status] in promoting a sense of control, efficacy, and even biological health itself. . . . An analogous process may work at the community level. The alienation, exploitation, and dependency wrought by resource deprivation act as a centrifugal force that stymies collective efficacy. Even if personal ties are strong in areas of concentrated disadvantage, they may be weakly tethered to collective actions. (Sampson, Raudenbush, and Earls 1997:918)

Informal Education

Semai don't set out consciously to raise nonviolent kids: they just want children to know that they're safe with their close kin and neighbors—nowhere else. An older man from Kniik, a teacher, said on 21 March 92, "We kid [-*gahleeh*] our children about Head Choppers so that they'll stay home and not go wandering off."

A Semai man, age thirty-five, from Tapah, a big town, told me on 28 March 1992 that his nine-year-old son still -*siil* a little" (i.e., was timid and shy), though "not as much in the old days. In the old days kids would run away from anything, strangers, cars, anything." [Actually, they still did in 1992, in rural areas.] "Because the old folks would -srng'òòh them, about Head Choppers, stuff like that. We don't -srng'òòh our kids like that any more, they go to school with other kids. . . . Bu-u-ut [shakes his head], o, our People [ruefully]. They still -siil, but they're getting a little bolder." Kids, he said, still -sa'ng'òòh, "are affected by fear," in the first three grades.

Many peoples besides Semai use visits by strangers, even harmless ones, to frighten kids. The kids usually wind up as circumspect adults, self-restrained and cautious. I don't think Semai child-rearing techniques would have the same results outside their traditional context, but if you're interested, you can read about them elsewhere (Dentan 1978, 1979:59–64, 2001a). Any place, not just Semailand, where adults feel responsible for all the local children, is a place where violence is uncommon (e.g., McGarrell et al. 1997:485, 488; Sampson et al. 1997:918). Here I just want to talk 1) about what happens to children who are aggressive in Semai terms and 2) about the absence among traditional Semai of the practices social scientists say make children into violent adults.

Semai kids get little active attention from adults, although they always have a lap to go to or an adult body to lean on. They learn autonomy early. One thing they learn is that nobody responds to the tantrums that become the *lesnees*, harangues, of adults. Here's an example from the Waar:

[A little girl] threw a wild screaming hissy up in the public area [of the settlement, outdoors], apparently because her kin went off to [upstream settlement] and left her behind. No adult paid any overt attention, although [Cat] did ask me if it was Lisbet. Her housemates and the girls in her playgroup stood around and watched, without moving into her space. [The girls] explained what was happening when I came by after 5–6 minutes, then [they] moved away. You sure have to deal with your own *susah sngii'* [emotional upset] here. (10 November 1991)

And another from the R'eiis:

Little Bah 'Abi came into our house, weeping uncontrollably, and nestled on his dad's lap. His dad asked if the other kids had been bothering him, and, getting no answer, said, "Kids are like that, they -katii', squabble, a lot." A little later 'Abi's mom came up, while 'Abi was still weeping and asked his dad, "He tired?" 'Abi said he was, and they dropped the matter.
    Of course, maybe 'Abi hadn't been hurt physically. There's a lot of verbal teasing, approaching abuse, among Semai. Maybe 'Abi -br-snlar, had been laughed at [from -slar, -sler, guffaw, giggle], maybe playmates were mocking (-luk) him. People say a sulky kid is angry, -bl'aal. Anyway, neither parent checked the situation out, and I would have been surprised if they did. (17 June 1992)

To understand how Semai traditionally treated aggressive kids, you should have met Hamid, a skinny Tluup boy, about seven years old in 1962, antsy but not verbal. His belly stuck out, probably from a combination of swollen spleen due to malaria and swollen liver due to protein deficiency. His curly hair was reddish and brittle—protein deficiency. His upper lip was a little cleft, maybe his palate too.

People didn't much like Hamid, not adults, not other kids. He once lost his temper during the game Tluup kids played, swatting away at each other with sticks but hardly ever actually touching each other. Hamid's screaming and flailing around with his stick at the other kids brought his aunt down from her house. She picked him up by the armpits and carried him away, shrieking, to his mother while the other children in the play-group, boys and girls of all ages, watched this unusual adult intervention wide eyed.

The intervention wasn't about kids getting hurt, I think, or because Hamid had made threat gestures. Tluup battle games reflect the fact that Semai make threat gestures often, particularly toward children, and children often make threat gestures at each other. Physical violence is always immanent, just rarely acted out. Waar River children arm themselves with weapons they carve out of soft *puleey* wood. The Babylonian equivalent may be "violent" video games. In the mid-1970s at Mncaak Bah Robert, a namesake of mine, my *cnòò'* (grandchild/younger sibling's child), often faked karate kicks at my daughter Sarah, but never touched her, she said, though we lived in his house for several weeks. Both children were six years old.

Robert was pretty hyper, but I saw a lot of fake martial arts kicks by kids, usually boys, in the 1990s. No actual kicking. At 'Icek in the 1990s, morose little Bah Rmpent, age nine, would act out violence all by himself, sparring, for example, with the water coming out of the village water tap. And there was lots of chasing and fleeing, usually larger kids chasing smaller ones, not boys chasing girls or the other way around. In the 1960s, Tluup wrestling consisted of holding onto some other kid's shoulders and pretending to try to throw him or her down. Since partners were often of quite different sizes, you didn't actually struggle, just faked it, grinning and giggling.

Hamid's problem I think, was loss of self-control, not fighting. For blows not to hit the target, kids have to be under control. Kids are usually background noise to adults, even kids on their laps, though in the evening as they sit on the house stairs, relaxing and cooling off, they watch kids fooling around and smile or, when the kids laugh or shriek too loudly, say (still grinning), "*Trlaac, trlaac*," threatening the cosmic upheavals attendant on loss of self-control (see chapter 5).

Kids do most of the play fighting, but there's a good deal of rough-housing among *litaaw*. One *litaaw* may drag another against his will onto a dance floor, for example. Some pushing and shoving is routine. But *mnaleeh*, the female equivalent of *litaaw*, roughhouse too.

Caweh, a twenty-year-old woman from Sungkeey, a Perak border town in the lowlands, said that if any of her kids actually hit someone, she'd drag them off to her house, "for fear of being fined" (see chapter 6).

> "We have no money" [for fines], she says, because her husband drinks it up. She complained to the Malay teacher after Malay schoolkids called her children Sakai ("nigger") and beat them up. He lectured the children, she said, and told them "We're all one humanity." (2 March 1992)

Usually, when kids hit adults, the larger people laugh and deflect the blows. But Hamid hit his mother a lot. If she rebuked him, he'd hit her; she'd cringe and say, "Adoh, adoh," ow ow. After he'd hit her a few times, he'd burst into tears. She'd complain about how often he hit her. He hit her with a machete one time, giving her a cut above the eye that got infected. He also hit her with a large bamboo water tube once. He'd sometimes make the insult gesture, pulling down the lower lid of an eye, at adults.

I talked about Hamid with his uncle Mrlooh. A kid like Hamid who hits people is *gila*, crazy violent, said Mrlooh, using a Malay word. A good child, like Mrlooh's son, sleeps with his same-sexed parent, head on the parent's arm, until past puberty. Hamid's mother plays with Hamid's genitals and lets the boy sleep with her, said Mrlooh. (I'd seen them cuddling.) *Tolah*, Mrlooh said, taboo, using a word that in this context carries a lot of the same weight as "child sexual abuse" in the United States (see chapter 5). He added that Hamid doesn't eat much and doesn't sleep soundly, wakes up in the middle of the night, and hits his parents. You couldn't hit him to punish him, though, he said. "Suppose he DIED?" Take a moment, reader, and think about that.

What you could do is, though I never saw anyone do it, is *-cwent*, pinch his cheek near the mouth and twist the pinched flesh; *-crwant*, scratch at him with one's nails; or *-trnyuul*, "point the finger," that is, jab a finger at the child's eye without actually touching it. A parent of a child who has completely lost his temper "might tie the kid up and put it out in the *pn-raa'*, heat of the sun. But it'd be no use, because the other parent would untie it as soon as possible." Hamid's mother told my wife that everyone wants to beat her son up, but Mrlooh said that wasn't true, although people often threatened Hamid. When Hamid made angry aggressive gestures toward other children, the larger kids responded by threatening him, for example, shouting the English phrase "fucking you," which they picked up from counterinsurgency troops and which made them laugh. The smaller kids just avoided him.

The reluctance of Semai to hit kids has something to do with the importance of self-reliance, "individual autonomy" as anthropologists say. Semai say children have soft souls. Discipline might hurt or kill them so that, if a child declines to perform on command, the adult has no alternative but to respect the decision. Learning to be obedient to apparently foolish parental demands is important to, say, American life, where most people work in hierarchically organized institutions: *do what your boss says* and *do what your mom says* are matching imperatives. Among Americans, adults in jobs that demand submission tend to beat ("swat," "spank") their children; people who get to think for themselves usually don't (Steinmetz 1971). As Max Weber says, people without armies don't often construe obedience as a Good Thing. Semai parents' relative lack of concern about "obedience" as a value in itself matches their own lives, in which obedience isn't important.

In fact, parents rarely hit children. A Waar woman asks, "Why would we hit them? They're our *children*." 'Apel of Mncaak, age thirty-three, no kids of his own, says he might yell at neighborhood kids to scare them off, if they -*rmeeh*, were messing with something that belonged to him, like his durian fruits. Right off, they'd run away, he says; he wouldn't hit them. Long of 'Icek, age thirty-one, three children, says he might pretend to hit them with a stick but wouldn't actually hit them; I've seen this sort of physical threat several times. In 1992, two old friends from Mncaak, Saiyah and Kin-Sima, discussed haranguing, *lesnees*, and swatting, *ptnvt*, children when one is angry, -*bl'aal*:

> **Saiyah:** When I'm angry at kids, I harangue them. When I harangue them [remaining seated, she makes a little jump forward to show how she harangues them], I don't swat them [shoving away gesture with both hands].
>
> **Boy, age seven:** When she harangues, she talks a lot.
>
> **Kin-Sima:** You know, if you're always angry at your child, the child gets angry. If you always harangue them, they'll harangue you back.

Caweh, a twenty-year-old married woman from Sungkeey, said much the same thing: "We think that if you speak harshly to your children, they'll become harsh."

Behavioral scientists mostly agree, so strong is the process of identification with the oppressor. Harsh or corporal punishment produces children more prone to violence than other kids are, even when the parents are punishing violence by the children. Although the children's interpretation of the punishment modifies this effect, it does not erase it. Spanking and other forms of beating also have bad effects on other aspects of a child's life, especially for children younger than two years or for adolescents. Semai say you shouldn't punish children under two because, not being able to talk, they don't know they're doing anything wrong. And you shouldn't punish *litaaw* or *mnaleeh* because they are no longer children. I have never seen anyone hurt a child in those age-groups, nor has the richly inventive and often malicious system of gossip brought any instance to my attention.

I have seen (or, more often, overheard) some instances of corporal punishment in the 1990s. I don't want to say that Semai always follow their own rules in raising children. Who does? But, still, few traditional Semai children *see* any physical violence except the overwhelming violence of thundersqualls and floods, although they hear about violence all the time. Even nowadays, except when people have been drinking, there seems to be little spousal abuse to give children a model for beating people up. Klip of 'Icek, age fifty, with ten kids, says, "If you *-kòòd sngii' ha knah*, hold a resentment toward your wife, it's like starting a little fire that may burn down your whole house."

The Semai context, in which adults do not punish children violently and expect children to be "soft" and "timid" rather than violent, is the one in which children are least likely to use physical violence, although it doesn't render them incapable of violent action (Dentan 1978; Sampson et al. 1997). Peoples who punish children physically, do not spend much time with kids, and fear "youth violence" are going to get what they expect.

Education by the State

When Semai children go to government schools, there's a big change (for a general discussion, see Dentan 1993; Juli and Dentan 2008). Teaching impoverished and "culturally deprived" children in Malaysian rural backwaters does not attract qualified teachers. The government's worry about Semai contacts with non-Malay outsiders reportedly discourages idealistic but non-Malay volunteers. In 1998, there were only about seventy Orang Asli teachers in ninety-five Orang Asli schools and forty-seven hostels, and not all of them shared the language or culture of their students. Semai say that Malay teachers are often absent or do little actual teaching. My observations suggest that they are right. In 1976 at one school where my wife taught a class in English for free, the Malay teacher would show up an hour or so late, read his paper for an hour or less, and go home. In one case, the only Malay teacher available was a gardener by training (Juli Edo 1998:254n13).

But even good and dedicated teachers—I've met a few—face another problem. Authoritarian Islamic education of the sort the Malaysian authorities press on Semai kids relies heavily on rote learning; understanding the material is secondary. For example, the assimilationist curriculum has required since 1925 that the children learn Arabic script so that they can read the Quran on their way to becoming Malays. But most kids will not convert. The script, they say, "looks like worm shit" and is about as useful (Juli Edo 1998:129, 174n). But they memorize it.

Semai children along the R'eiis asked us for this sort of education in English. They'd draw up lists of English words for us to test them on. The same thing happened when I visited Cang Kuaa' in 2004. But the idea of actually using English speech except in response to specific arbitrary demands baffled them. The hidden curriculum, for Semai kids, is to familiarize themselves with having a Malay authority coerce them into performing senseless tasks, being obsequious toward their betters, wanting to become like Malays (Juli and Dentan 2008). Semai schoolchildren at 'Icek in 1992 actually put things away after playing with them at our house.

Teaching the children of subordinate peoples "their place" in a hierarchy helps hierarchical peoples keep their hierarchies stable. But Islamic education in general and Malaysian education in particular, at least until recently, also stress "corporal punishment," a polite way of saying that adults, usually the school headmasters, beat children, sometimes with rattan canes, usually on the (sometimes naked) buttocks or on the palms of the hands, where there are lots of nerves. When a Malay father turns his child over to a religious teacher, he ceremonially hands the teacher a cane with which to beat the child, the way traditional Malay parents do. A Malay humorist from Perak recalls,

> My enrollment in the class was made in the traditional way. I can still remember clearly what happened. Dad handed over to Tuan Syed a bowl of glutinous rice, a fee of $1 and a small cane and then said: "Tuan, I am handing over my son to you in the hope that you'd teach him the Koran. Make him as if he is your own child . . . if he is stubborn or naughty don't hesitate to punish him with this cane—as long as it doesn't reach the extent of breaking any of his bones or blinding his eyes." Tuan Syed took the cane and nodded. Thus end[ed] the formality. But I noticed the teacher already had his own cane. (Lat 1977:n.p.)

Interesting, that bit about "blinding his eyes," isn't it? You should worry about your children's eyes, about *maay klooh mat*, the mythical "eye gougers," if you're parents who love their children and are turning them over to a Malay teacher.

Occasional beatings by Malay classmates continue to reinforce this lesson in civility and subordination, as does their practice, which Semai say is common, of putting their book bags on the bus seats and removing them only for other Malay kids so that the Semai children have to stand. Despite their parents' emphasis on not retaliating against the Malay children, some Semai children, of course, try to respond in kind, as the teachers expect them to do and punish them for doing. Caning or milder forms of "discipline" and bullying teach Semai children 1) that powerful people (teachers, Malays, adults) think it's okay to hurt less powerful people (pupils, Semai, kids) physically and 2) that the Semai children themselves can survive violence and even retaliate. Thus, from a situation in which adults do not expect physical violence from children and do not punish the children with physical violence, the children move into one in which violent adults expect them to be violent too.

By the 1990s, in areas as remote as the Waar, little boys dressed up as soldiers. I took some photographs of their elaborate homemade costumes and gave their discarded toy weapons with the photographs to the American Museum of Natural History, where you can see them if you ask. Still most Semai children simply fantasize about the media violence they see, like children elsewhere; it does not legitimize violence, although it glamorizes power. But the violence is inside the children now and coming back out.

8

Juni Gone Astray

LOOKING FOR VIOLENCE

For a couple of decades after my first visit, most ethnographers who worked with Malaysian indigenes wound up studying nonviolence, no matter what "problem" they originally set themselves. That's how salient it was to our Western eyes. But later, as "development" or whatever you call it proceeded, people working in more accessible and less developed areas found nonviolence less salient. And other apparently nonviolent peoples turned out, on restudy, to be quite violent.

So I went back to Malaysia in 1992 and looked for violence among Semai for a year and half. There was more than I remembered. But I'd never thought Semai suffered from a psychological disease, the inability to be violent. I didn't think Semai "repressed" it either. They struck me then as now as a pragmatic and reasonable people who avoided violence most of the time because they thought that, when you had a choice between getting hurt (if only to hurt someone else) and getting out, sensible people got out. Not surprisingly, most violence my survey turned up seemed to happen in circumstances that were rare during my first visit.

What I want to do in this chapter is tell a couple of exemplary stories, a little like the cautionary tales adult Semai tell their kids and each other. The first is about a boy I knew in 1992, in 'Icek, a foothill settlement in Perak state into which the outside world was penetrating but which it had not yet obliterated. The second is about a grown-up who, recent news I get from Malaysia suggests, may represent what the boy will become. Both settlements are along the Teiw R'eiis, "Root River," Malay Sungai

Rias. The Malay name is the homonym of a word that means "banana stem pith," a traditional metaphor for something you can pierce easily. But their name for the river seems to be just a version of the Semai one. It doesn't mean anything, not really.

PART 1: RMPENT GROWING UP

The economic planners . . . envisage the systematic elimination of the peasant. . . . For short term political reasons, they do not use the word elimination but the word modernization. Modernization entails the disappearance of the small peasant (the majority) and the transformation of the remaining minority into totally different social and economic beings. (Berger 1975:209)

Beside the little river runs an all-weather road the British built along an old bullock track that used to carry the north-to-south trade in Perak. Malay and Chinese settlers followed the road into Semai territory. The Sultan of Perak and his British "Advisor on Aborigines," Pat Noone, set up "Sakai Reserves" along the road. In Malay, "Sakai" means something quite like "Nigger." But in this case the colonial dyarchy meant "Semai." Each headman still has a map of his reserve. They know the maps are im-

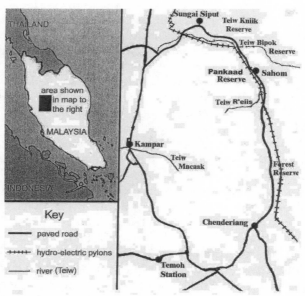

R'eiis-Mncaak Area. Constructed by Michael Wesch (Dentan 2001c:7).

portant (any piece of paper from the outside Powers is important). They keep the maps with their "letters of authority" in little bamboo tubes they tuck into the roof thatch for safekeeping. By 1992, some were pretty ratty. I took the maps to the nearby Chinese market town of Kampar and got several photocopies of each, giving some copies to the headmen and sending others to POASM, the Orang Asli Association, for their records.

But the maps and letters aren't worth much. No one said, back in the 1930s, that they are just pieces of paper designed to "delude" the people into "thinking that they are secure." The British approved a tin-dredging operation on one of those reserves near Pangkaad. Through the reserves, along the road, they set up a huge hydroelectric power line, pylons bestriding the land like skeletal versions of the Thunder Lord. "Reserve" land belonged and belongs to Semai but only until someone else wants it.

Semai think the "Germans" who built the power line buried a murdered human skull beneath each pylon, not a Semai head, but one they got elsewhere. The pylons, like the heads, manifest the immanence of state power, Malay power (see chapter 7).

Later the British built another road to the west, roughly parallel to the old bullock path. Commerce went along the new road, leaving Pangkaad and 'Icek as a relatively undisturbed eddies in the stream of modernization. But Chinese and Malay settlements slowly expanded up the old road. Nowadays, almost all the land west of Pangkaad along the road is in Malay hands, with a few Chinese enclaves. The government has dispossessed and removed most Semai from that area to a "Regroupment Scheme" a few miles away from the road, down a rutted path barely passable to motor vehicles—in order, government spokesmen say, to deliver services more efficiently. The land Semai used to live on went to developers.

In the accumulating wet heat at the bus stop where the path meets the road, you can see two clusters of people waiting for the rackety buses. One group, a little taller maybe, the women a little more likely to have their hair covered, Malays. The other perhaps a bit darker and shorter, but not much, Semai. You wouldn't notice the visible differences if the people talked to each other and didn't stand apart. You can hear the difference: mellifluous Malay, vowel-consonant-vowel-consonant-vowel-consonant, versus staccato Semai, consonant-vowel-consonant, consonant-vowel-consonant. Malays say Semai just squawk and cluck like chickens.

Spewing clouds of particulates and carbon monoxide, the bus rattles and jitters to Kampar, just north of the Semai settlement of Mncaak, where R'eiis people have kinfolk. In the other direction, roughly southward, the road goes to Sahom. There it narrows abruptly as it enters Semai territory before it reaches Pangkaad. Bus service stops there, although people at Pangkaad, looking across the thick, speeding traffic on the superhighway, can see

Sahom in the near distance. The Chinese owners of the local bus company give free rides to Malay schoolchildren. Coming home, Malay kids put their book bags on the seats, so that Semai kids have to stand until the Malay kids get off. The Semai children, who live farther east along the road, have to walk a mile or two or three to catch the bus. Even when they get lifts on kinsmen's motor scooters, they may be drenched by the rainsqualls that

Rmpent helps butcher a wild boar. Rmpent is standing behind and to the right of the older boy who is holding the meat. That boy's father has a shotgun and a small pack of dogs, much larger than traditional Semai dogs, and goes hunting in the Forest Reserve that runs down the banks of the R'eiis River. There are more wild boar now than there used to be because of the slaughter of the great cats that used to eat them. We found traces of only one tiger along the R'eiis when I was there but lots of pig wallows. Icek, 30 March 1992. Photograph by R. K. Dentan.

sweep in from the Indian Ocean, sheets of chilly water shattering as they hit the ground, soaking the children's hair and clothes and papers.

Along the road to Kampar stand telephone poles holding wires along which small groups of red-beaked raucous kingfishers perch in rows four or five birds long, screaming. But telephone and electric wires also stop at Sahom. Semai must use car batteries for electricity, in the shadow of the huge hydroelectric pylons. Their kids run a slight but significant increased risk of cancer as a result of their exposure to the strong electromagnetic fields the wires emit, but most Semai don't know that.

The postal service stops at Sahom too. Semai collect mail at a Malay shop in Sahom. I wrote a letter for them in Malay, to the head of the post office in Kampar, asking very politely and humbly that the service be extended the quarter mile to Pangkaad. But he didn't answer. Every service stops at Sahom, where Semailand begins.

In the early 1990s, the government was blasting the new north-to-south superhighway through orchards belonging to Pangkaad "Sakai Reserve." I spent a month there in 1991 with my longtime mentor Ngah Hari, in a new house his son Sudeew had built of cheap brick-red *brbow* wood, on the rocky refuse from the blasting. He built the house there to stake a claim to the new land before someone from the adjacent Malay settlement registered it as his own property, as Malays often do.

During the day, the house was stifling. Old-fashioned Semai houses are of flattened bamboo or woven attap palm leaves so that the air actually circulates through the walls. The walls themselves don't reach the roof, so breezes can waft through the gap between the two. This house was a prefab box, like a freight car, two doors and one window, no circulation of air. The choice during the day was to swelter or to choke on the construction dust that reddened the children's clothes and hair. People snuffled and coughed constantly because of dust clogging their noses and throats.

From 8:00 A.M. on, huge bulldozers rattled and banged constantly. Every now and then a siren would shriek, there'd be a pause, then a BOOOOOM as the engineers blasted through the limestone tors, followed by a patter and crash of rocks.

You could still look out from the house across the trash-strewn red-mud wasteland of the superhighway and see the forested hills on the other side. In the morning quiet, before the bulldozers arrived, you could still hear the bell-like hoohooing of gibbons. By 1991, the big hardwoods were all gone from the forest, of course, every one, to make salad bowls and knickknacks in Japan and the West. But there were still some huge white *puleey* trees, so big that if you tried to photograph a person standing by one, just to dramatize its size, you couldn't fit both into the same shot without dwarfing the person into invisibility. And you could still feel the drop in temperature like a caress when you entered the woods.

When I came back in 1992, I lived a mile or so farther down the road into Semai territory, at 'Icek, where small children still scattered in flight like sparrows when strangers appeared. The road construction was still just a rumble in the distance, approaching. 'Icek backed against a Forest Reserve, denuded of hardwoods but still home to pigs and tigers and king cobras. But no big animals, no gaurs or rhinos or elephants.

What Rmpent Understood

> Human nature, obstinate and fundamentally rebellious, is in fact represented in the colonies by the bush, by mosquitoes, natives, and fever, and colonization is a success when all this indocile nature has finally been tamed. Railways across the bush, the draining of swamps and a native population which is non-existent politically and economically are in fact one and the same thing. (Fanon 1968:250)

In 1992, Bah Rmpent, age nine, was a witty, energy-packed kid. "Rmpent," his Semai name ("Pent" for short), is the name of a stemless thorny palm with large leaves Semai once used for thatch. It was very common, but now it's a useless weed where it hasn't been exterminated. The Malay registrar, finding the name ludicrous, gave the boy an official Muslim name of the sort that appears on the identity card every Malaysian must carry. Official policy, remember, is to merge Semai into the "Malay mainstream" as impoverished Muslims.

To me, Pent seemed a homely, skinny, sad-looking little boy. Long ago I was a homely, skinny, sad little boy myself. So his looks predisposed me to like him and want to protect him, though he was in most ways quite different from myself as a child. I think about him when I think about Semai. I've written a couple of articles about him (Dentan 1993, 2001b). The account of Pent's life that you're reading now is a version of the 2001 article.

Pent presented himself in the harsh uncompromising way that I've encountered in other young men who were having a hard time. But our next-door neighbor, Kyah Grcaangsmother, presented herself in much the same way. She had a beautiful craggy face, what anthropologists used to call "Australoid": deep eye sockets, prominent brow ridges, red-tinged black wavy hair. She was from the Cameron Highlands, high in the mountains. There, 'Icek people said, everyone talks harshly. And every now and then, her lined face would split with a brilliant warm smile. I enjoyed just hanging around with her, waiting for that smile.

So I don't know that Rmpent was as sad as he looked or as tough as he acted. I doubt I could have persuaded him to talk about how he felt. Semai don't talk much about feelings, and most boys Rmpent's age, in my experience, try to hide their feelings from adults anyway. But I never tried to get him to talk, not wanting to pressure him.

He didn't smile much. He didn't have much to smile about. He wasn't good looking, didn't do well in school, wasn't strong or self-confident. Also, he was a *knòòn prncaa'*, a foster child, a "child for feeding" in the Semai phrase. In the 1960s on the Teiw Tluup, the prevalence of fosterage had made hash of my attempts to collect genealogies. Men and women often split up, and the kids went with the parent they liked best. Many children were living with people biologically not their kin. Indeed, a few older kids adopted us in the sense that they used kinship terms for us and spent more time in our house, eating with us, sleeping on our floor, than they spent "at home." But Malays stress the difference between "real" and foster children, and by the 1990s, people of the R'eiis seemed to have learned to think of adopted kids as somehow significantly different from biological kids. I saw no sign that people treated foster kids worse than others, but maybe the differentiation left a mark.

Rmpent used to come over to our house for fun. He sometimes voluntarily took on the task of teaching me, making it clear to me (as his Malay teachers apparently made clear to him) that teaching stupid, culturally deprived students was a thankless task that would make a saint impatient. He would frown and wave his small forefinger at me, snarling in Malay, "STUPID! STUPID! STUPID!" the way his Malay teachers did to him. Despite his flamboyant dissatisfaction with my performance, however, he persisted in his self-selected task, coming back to try again every few days. Sometimes we'd both just act goofy to amuse each other.

When I was working with someone else, I'd give him some paper and pens, the way I did with other children, so that they could amuse themselves. One day he drew an impression of the superhighway that the Malaysian government was building through a settlement about a mile downstream from him. You can learn something from Rmpent's sketch.

On the near side of the road in his sketch is a betelnut palm. Semai plant this tree in gardens within their settlements, near their houses. Rmpent's rendering is quite accurate. Look at the photo in Ivan Polunin's *Plants and Flowers of Malaysia* (1988:147, pl. 154) if you don't believe me. Kid has a good eye.

Next in the sketch comes the road, unpaved red raw earth at the time, strewn with garbage and plastic scraps the work crews tossed away. Along the road rattles a bulldozer, followed by a truck carrying rock blasted from the steep limestone tors that block the roadway. Semai boys Rmpent's age loved the bulldozers, although the operators made it clear that they did not love the little boys. I have a collection of bulldozers-smashing-things pictures by Rmpent.

Rmpent's sketch.

On the far side of the road in Rmpent's picture is a rubber tree, a rubber tapper sketched in at its base, less detailed than the rest of the picture. The new highway slashed through Semai rubber and durian fruit orchards, separating the trees from the village by half a dozen lanes of what was to be heavy traffic, with no provision for getting safely across. The compensation the builders offered for the destroyed trees was substantially less than the compensation paid Malay communities for the destruction of the same number of trees of the same species. Sudeew, my Semai *mnaang*, younger brother, said the builders probably figured Semai were too stupid or timid to protest or that they were too used to being cheated. "Happens all the time," he said.

Above the tree, by the bulldozer, the blobby mass represents an explosion, blasting loose the rock. The other pictures Rmpent drew regularly were of warplanes bombing and destroying, helicopters blasting away at people. Same blobby explosions.

Rmpent attends a Malay school. Kyah Grcaangsmother, his neighbor, says bullying there sometimes make her *-lees*, angrily harangue people. For example,

> If the kids don't go to school, if [my husband] doesn't take them [to school on his motorbike, since it's a mile to the Sahom terminus of Malay settlement and bus service], if he doesn't chew them out, I'll *-lees* him. They get in trouble if they don't go to school.

If the kids pick fights with their friends, I tell them, "Don't mess with your friends, be good to your friends. [If you don't], you'll be sorry. If you're a bad friend, people won't like you."

I -*lees* about the Malay school kids in Sahom. They bully Semai kids all the time. They hit them, they take their books and papers. "Malay kids are bad," I say. "They'll pick fights with you, don't you hit them back, you'll just get in trouble."

But Rmpent hasn't learned much else in school. His Malay, the language of instruction, is adequate, not good. Neither is his Semai. He doesn't know the names of local plants and animals or of the divisions of Malaysia. He is ignorant in two languages and two cultures. Again, let me say I don't know that he was sad. Children have a capacity for joy that escapes us as we age. A situation has to be unbearable for them to be sad all the time, and Pent's day-to-day life wasn't that bad. Still, he was just a little boy when I knew him, and already his future seemed set.

PART 2: TRANSITION: "GET THE FUCKING JOB DONE"

At present violence isn't a problem here. By 2020 [when the Malaysian government plans for the country to be "developed" and industrialized] the Humans will probably turn violent. We're not violent now because we're still *primitif*. We still have places to flee to now, but by then we'll be shut out of all those places. We don't want to fight, but when we have no alternative, no place to flee to, we'll be forced to. (Nudiysfather, the shaman, 13 March 1991)

The government's motives in setting up Regroupment Areas like Teiw Kniik may be good but their effect is bad for our way of life. When people are crowded together like that, you need private property lines and that makes people take sides. Also being given things to plant, like rubber and oil palms, increases dependency and in the long run works against people's becoming progressive in their thinking. ("Busu," Semai leader, 8 May 1992)

Still, speed, mobility, gratification of the will; those were good things, modern things. . . . That was all that really mattered . . . get the fucking job done. . . . Regrets, consequences, disappointments; to hell with them all. (Mason 1990:39, 40)

Preface: Traditional Violence and Erotic Love

Even in a society as casual about sexual relations between *litaaw* and *mnaleeh* as Semai used to be, the loss of people you love can make you so sad that you go crazy or kill yourself (see chapter 6; Dentan 2000a). This sort of pain can also lead to murder. Frustration in erotic love is the main

cause of violence among most foragers and "simple swiddeners" like traditional Semai. "In olden days," people say, or "in the mountains," that is,
at some place and time distant from their own, disputes over women
could lead to murder. The only two cases of murder I know about from
the "olden days" before the emergency of the 1950s both involved such
quarrels. Here they are.

An old Waar River man said his mother's father killed her first husband, some time before World War II, probably the 1920s. This is the
story his mom told him. Since the early 1900s, Semai near the Tapah-
Cameron Highlands road have grown *btaar* trees commercially. The
trees are up to 150 feet tall, with smooth bark. The only way to get to the
beans is to tie a pole a few inches thick to the trunk. You do that by
wrapping a circle of rattan around the pole and the trunk, adding another circle a yard or so higher up, then another a yard or so above that
and so on. On either side of the pole a short arc of the rattan circle is a
few inches from the trunk. You use these arcs as rungs of a ladder to
climb up to the canopy where the beans are. The jealous suitor weakened a rung with his machete, so that when the husband climbed his
tree he broke through and fell to his death. (The name of the rival,
Nyuup Crgòòh, Vanish Cause-to-Pray, suggests that the mom may have
been telling a cautionary tale rather than a factual history or that the
narrator, a witty man, might have been putting me on. So does the motive that the mother and her lover wanted to avoid the messiness of a divorce since traditional Semai divorces were usually informal and un-
problematic). On the other hand, this sort of indirect violence would be
characteristic of Semai, both affording a moral "out" ["I didn't make
him climb the tree, he did that on his own, and died of the fall, the *yn-
gnòòng*, not by my hand"] and illustrating Ngah Hari's remark that
"We're not as nice as you think we are, just sneakier."

The other incident comes from the field notes of Clayton Robarchek
from Lngkuuk, high up the Tapah-Cameron Highlands Road, 19 and 29
October, 1974, which he shared with me, generous as always. This summary is mine:

> Ataak (not his real name) was born at Skòòp on the Tapah-Cameron High-
> lands Road. One of his kinsmen "stole" the wife of a man from Gòòl (Tapah,
> in Perak state). Gòòl people then killed the man, his wife and his *jaa'*, grand-
> mother or woman in her generation. The "big headman" who lived at Mile
> Three (or Mile Eight) sent machetes to the quarrelling groups and summoned
> them to his headquarters to talk. This official was the "raja darat," a Malay
> term for "king of the hinterland" [the Malay-appointed Semai headman
> whom Ngah Hari describes in chapter 6].
>
> He told the groups to stop the killing and sent Ataak's family to Bòòt, near
> where the road crosses the Waar. Eventually they moved to Lngkuuk, far up

the road. For other versions of this story, see Gomes (2004) and Juli, Williams-Hunt, and Dentan (2008).

Litaaw Violence

In 1992, 'Apel, "Apple," age thirty-three, a small unmarried Mncaak man whom I've known and liked since he was a newborn, usually dressed all in black, long-sleeved shirt, and long pants. Cool. He didn't have a steady job but was a good blowpipe hunter. His skill let him contribute to the household of the Pangkaad headman, his kinsman, with whom he stays sometimes. One of the clearest images in my memory of the R'eiis is little 'Apel in his cool black outfit, blowpipe on his shoulder, walking across the enormous hot bright red devastation of the expressway the government was building, heading off toward the dark green shade of the wounded rain forest, looking small but indomitable. One day in the headman's house, we talked about 'Apel's fighting history:

> Yes, I've hit people, not Semai. Once when I'd been drinking, a Tamil who called me "Sakai." And once sober, a Chinese guy on a bus who was bugging a woman from Sungkeey, yelling "Sakai! Sakai!" at her.
>
> Bah Panda' from Steit once tried to start a fight with me when he was drunk, but I backed away from it [-*sabar*] and his buddies held him back. When he drinks, he thinks he's Samson.
>
> *Ki-kawbooy*, acts like a cowboy, wants to take everybody on.
>
> I heard there was a fight in Sahom. Bah Jimin [in his thirties] and Bah 'Idris [forty] got into a fight with Malays, and *we* had to call the police. . . .
>
> [But if someone threatened me], that's his problem, I don't care about that. Hey, it's something we're against. We don't get hot *ruwaay* [lose our tempers].

Many *litaaw* still don't fight back. Long, age thirty-two, a married man with one child, says that three Malay men with whom he was working on a housing project in the local city -*tumbuh nlaak*, ganged up on him and beat him up, threatening him with knives. "No reason," he says, "they just felt like it." If anyone -*haay*, harasses, you, he says, "Run away! If you can't run away you'll have to fight. Fighting is pointless."

Media

Violent media images now permeate Semai life, on *tiwi'* (TV) sets when people can afford to buy and run them, at the movies, but also on the walls of most Semai houses. *Litaaw* pin up clippings or posters of muscle-bound weight lifters, action movie stars like Sylvester Stallone and Arnold Schwarzenegger, and World Wrestling Federation (WWF) stars

like Hulk Hogan: black S&M leather, bulging biceps. Even on the relatively remote upper Waar, a *litaaw*, age fifteen, said he'd watched Rambo
on TV and asked, with a big grin, whether I knew "WWF." The *litaaw*
draw pictures of men with enormous muscles. Really hip *litaaw* wear
headbanger, heavy metal, or death rock T-shirts, featuring skulls and gore
against a black background. Not much hidden significance to the symbolism, I think, just the obsession to be strong and hip that afflicts young
men everywhere, particularly in the presence of young women. Whenever I dressed up to go to town, people would tease me: "Oh, you look
like a *litaaw*." The young men wear long hair, rouge and lipstick, too, the
way *litaaw* in "olden days" wore their hair and painted their faces. They
bridle when you make the comparison, though. Most *litaaw* nowadays
want to be *modun*, "modern," hoping the girls will find them as attractive
as they find Malay men.

Alcohol

Development brings alcohol, which Semai drink particularly at *ronggeng*
parties:

> A man ran amok in Kluni', near Slim River [in southernmost Perak], at a
> *ronggeng* (dance party). People were drinking. The *mnaang* [younger brother]
> got drunk and obnoxious, the *tne'* [elder brother] tried to calm him down.
> The *mnaang* grabbed a machete and began waving it around [-*main yoid*, "fool
> around with a knife"]. The *tne'* grabbed at the knife, cutting the palm of his
> own hand. Seeing his own blood made him blood-crazy [-*gila' bhiip*, cf. -*buul
> bhiip*]. He began hitting at things with the machete, cars and such. Eventually
> he ran off into the woods until he felt safe and calmed down. He wasn't
> drunk himself. ("Langiid," 4 June 1992, Kampar)

Alcohol may also fuel marital quarrels::

> Usually we get over -*bl'aal* [anger, resentment] in a day. Drunks might quar-
> rel but *bi-sabar ya maay*, other people would calm them down. The headman
> and elders would intervene. You don't hit grown-ups. When my wife and I
> quarrel, we take our quarrel to the headman. I've taken her and she's taken
> me. We quarrel over my drinking sometimes. That's probably what we quar-
> rel over most. My wife harangues me [-*lees*]: "You've got ten children!"
> ("Klip," fifty-year-old Methodist Semai man, 17 March 1992)

Gender

Other Malaysians' relatively patriarchal attitudes make Semai women targets for quick contemptuous sex. Traditional Semai gender equality and

casualness about sex feeds into the cross-culturally common sense that relatively poor and powerless women are "just begging for it" simply by existing. Outsiders who rape Semai women can usually settle by confessing and paying what is for them a small fee, meeting the *bicaraa'* requirements for fines. But outsiders who abuse Semai women anger Semai men.

Semai Methodist missionaries say that joining the Senoi Praak ("War Humans"), a special Malay-run but Asli-manned paramilitary police unit, fosters promiscuity and drinking. Apparently, being outside one's community with other *litaaw* facilitates quarrels, as it does everywhere else in the world.

I talked about that with Long, age thirty-one, a married adept with six children, on 6 April 1992, the usual hot sticky kind of day. We were in the main room of his house, where he keeps the herbs and other love potions he sells Malays, especially Malay women. I don't know him well, but I sat in on one of his consultations, with a middle-class Malay woman from Ipoh. Her husband was sleeping around with another woman, and instead of yelling at him, walking out, or lapsing into depression, as most Semai women would, she wanted something to put in his food to bring him back to her. Long, noncommittal about the efficacy of his drugs, warned that love takes more than potions and that it might be better just to accept reality, but she wanted the potion and perhaps the caresses that go with medication. The woman's husband may still have been on his mind when he talked with me:

> [I] never hit anybody, never. I see some guy coming out of my house, maybe I ask what's he doing. Some people might hit their wives. Usually they just *dee' ku i' sngii*, keep it in mind as a resentment. Next time your wife did it, you might look for another woman. I've never *-kah-kuuh*, hit, my wife, or sent her home, nothing like that. That's dumb.
>
> Never got into fights at *ronggeng* either. I don't drink, and, hey, there's *lots* of women. Only time I hit anybody was I got into a fistfight when I was in the Senoi Praak in Bidor.
>
> The other Semai guys there were bugging me [Malay "usik"].
>
> Badmouthing me.

Sitting cross-legged on the floor in the kitchen of her house at 'Icek, a middle-aged friend, Panda', with her, helping her chop hot little green bird peppers to eat with salt and rice for lunch, Grcaangsmother, Rmpent's and my neighbor, talked about violence with me:

> **Kyah:** No, [I] never [hit anyone]. What would I hit someone for? [grins] I never got into a fight with anyone, except maybe for a minute when I was a kid. We women don't fight, don't hit people. There's no point in hitting people. If you work, there's a point to it, you eat [gestures, pointing with her

knife]. Fighting and war, no point to that. . . . People want to live. Me too. I never heard of Humans [Semai] killing anybody. Maybe some other district. People from different places think differently, you know? We, we'd be afraid, we never kill people.

Panda': We maybe fight a little, but not till someone dies.

Kyah: Right, we fight to the life, not to the death [grins].

But Kyah herself fools around outdoors with her chum and admirer, Wa' Yah, a plump pretty *mnaleeh*, seventeen, ambitious but aware that she's not nearly as smart as Kyah. Yah has just finished mushing some henna leaves to make the yellow dye with which the women will anoint their fingernails, Malay-Arabic style. Kyah is sitting on my houseladder.

Kyah: Go get me some betelnut.

Yah: [Feints at Kyah's head with the butt of the pestle, as with a spear. You shouldn't order people around that way, but Cameron Highlands people like Kyah are pretty gruff and assertive].

Kyah: [to RKD]. She's trying to kill me. Well, that makes me *-bl'aal*, get angry.

Yah: [Flounces off and gets dishes from her house to wash at the village water tap, sashaying nose up past Kyah. Yah washes the dishes and fills some plastic water bottles, taking maybe five minutes, then takes the dishes and bottles back to her house. Finally, still ostentatiously not looking at Kyah, flounces downhill toward the nearest betelnut palm, about 100 meters away].

Kyah: [loudly, so that Yah will hear] *O, ki-bl'aal*, she's angry.

Yah: [In Malay, as she plods back up the hill with the betelnut] I'm gonna to get you, 'm gonna hit you, 'm gonna pound on you, 'm gonna kill you, I'm comin' for you . . . [gives Kyah the betelnut]

Kyah: But she still wants to beat me up.

Yah: [Grinning widely, feigns a quick one-two punch, left-right, to Kyah's stomach].

PART 3: JUNY: THE BOY GROWN UP

Gradually [the indigenes] succumbed to our vices. . . . And to that the conquered gave the label of "modernization" which was actually integral to their enslavement. (Tacitus A.D. 98:chapter 21:1–2, Dentan tr.)

The story I'm going to try to tell now may be about how love leads to violence. Several people interpreted what happened in those terms, familiar to Semai. But people in a position to know said the motive was something else, not the *litaaw* love of women but the capitalist love of money, a new, modern passion.

Here's Juny

> pain loneliness deceit and vanity
>
> —From Michael Ondaatje, "Tin Roof" (1997:691)

I first met Juny, not his real name, by the R'eiis in 1992. He was in his forties, with a squarish lined face and slightly hollow cheeks, high cheekbones, and slightly more pronounced epicanthic folds in his eyelids than most Semai. His grandfather was a Chinese man who'd taken a Semai concubine, a by-product of increased contact between Semai and outsiders. Juny was bigger and more energetic than most Pangkaad people. He had many projects and worked hard at them, although he often took time off. He spoke some English, what he called "broken English," not enough to sustain a conversation but enough to clarify ambiguous points or at least to help arrive at a helpful Malay word. Few Semai back then spoke any English. Juny had learned English, he said, from associating with Englishmen. He was vague about where. He wanted to work with me, he said, unlike most R'eiis people, who preferred keeping their distance, not knowing me personally, the usual Semai pattern. He wanted to write me stories after I returned home, he said, and he did write me a couple of useful texts while I was in Malaysia. He was interested in preserving Semai culture, he said, as I was. He saw Ngah Hari as a rival and belittled him when he had the chance. Semai do that with rivals, backbiting, not confronting.

Juny was living with his wife's father, the house where 'Apel stayed when he was in Pangkaad, next to my kid brother Sudeew's house: the same sort of house, built there for the same reasons. The explosions and clattering of the heavy construction machinery made it hard to talk in this house. Juny's kids were another problem. Unlike most Semai children, they often intruded themselves into adult conversation. The behavior of the youngest, age two, the age when Semai kids move from coddled infancy into ignored childhood, gave me reason to learn Semai words for "throwing a tantrum" (*-laac*, cf. *trlaac*) and "fly into a rage" (*-b-riic noos*, eaten-up heart, cf. *ceep riic*, small munia birds large flocks of which can wipe out a paddy crop). That's the first betrayal Semai feel, that abandonment by adults, and it heightens their sensitivity to the death of loved people or betrayal by them (Dentan 2000a). The four-year-old repeated everything we said IN A VERY LOUD VOICE. The eldest children, girls, hung around looking pretty but were more retiring. Then Juny broke his foot in a motorbike accident and could not work elsewhere, so we couldn't work together.

Juny described himself as peace loving. If someone hit him, he said,

> I'd beg his pardon. The second time, I might get a little hot: "What's your *problem*? Why did you hit me?" If he answers he has a sore heart with me, I'd want to work things out. But if he keeps it up [hitting me] and I can fight back, I will. If not, I'll run away. . . . When I was a kid long ago I'd be drinking Guinness, I'd hear people saying [mean things about me], I'd get hot, if someone hit me, I'd hit him. But since I got married I don't drink or quarrel, I don't run around to *ronggeng*, dances, I mind my own business.

Juny's wife "Umi" was plump and bucolic-looking woman, also clearly intelligent although less verbally facile. At least when I was around, Juny deferred to her more than most Semai husbands do to their wives. For example, when I asked what he'd do if he got angry, *-bl'aal*, he missed the point and said that *salah paham*, Malay for "misunderstandings," sometimes caused anger or disputes over where your garden starts and mine stops. His wife understood the question better: "We *-ra'roo'*," she said, lecture each other. "Or we fix it, *-pr-bòr bali'* [saying] *he' hal he'*, *egn hal egn*, *pe' ma*, you mind your business, I'll mind mine, no problem." Asked if he ever harangues (*-lees*) people, Juny says he *-ajar*, disciplines his wife:

> After that I don't hold a resentment. As long as when I tell her to cook she cooks, there's no hassle. I don't want hassles.

Other people say he beats her, and that's a connotation of the Malay word *ajar* as Semai use it.

Juny doesn't drink, he says. Talking about running amok, he says that Malay amoks slash at everything, are angry (*-bl'aal*), don't worry about consequences. A guy who drinks alcohol, he's like that, Juny says, he could chop at trees, he's like partly crazy (using the Malay word "gila," crazy and violent). His heart is, you know, clenched.

Juny is an entertaining storyteller. He told me with great verve, for example, about a lowland Semai couple in their eighties who fight all the time. The man will come home from work, and she won't *-gap teh*, boil water for tea, right away as lowland women are supposed to today. So he'll take a swipe at her, but she'll hit him right back, so he'll grab her ear, like that. One time they fought so hard they fell out of the house and ripped each other's clothes off. He laughed a lot during the story, as did his wife.

Juny's Crime: A Pastiche

'Ahmad (a pseudonym) was a quiet, humorous, and intelligent man in his late forties. He believed that, for Semai to survive as a people, they should stop drinking and have more children. He himself converted to Islam, partly as a buffer against alcoholism, and fathered a dozen kids, some of whom married Malays. I've known him since 1963. He was the one who first told me about Juny on the bus coming back from Kampar where we'd gone to buy groceries. On the seat in front of us an old man from Pangkaad listened in to the story, twisted around with his elbows on the back of his seat, nodding occasionally to confirm details as the bus rocked through the desolate sun-drenched scrubland and Malay settlements on its way to the bus stop, a couple of miles from the Semai settlement, where people have to get off for the trek home.

'**Ahmad:** That Juny business was in the 1970s, right?

Old man: [Nods].

'**Ahmad:** That'd make Juny a *litaaw*, about eighteen. He and a little boy, Kubooy, right?

Old man: [Nods, *right*].

'**Ahmad:** He and this eight-year-old boy beat a Chinese man badly.

Old man: With a machete.

'**Ahmad:** With a machete. They took his motorbike. Juny rode the motorbike around for about a month afterwards [taps the side of his head, indicating stupidity or craziness]. Then he ran off into the jungle. He hid there until Mat Ariff came to get him. Mat Ariff said some Malay spells over him [-*jampi'*]. It made him a little less crazy, so he gave himself up. He was the first Semai ever arrested for murder in Perak, so the authorities went easy on him. So, they put him in jail for ten years.

RKD: Any Semai arrested for murder in another state?

'**Ahmad:** Not that I know of.

Old man: [Shakes his head, *no*].

RKD: Why'd he do it?

'**Ahmad:** Who knows? [usual Semai answer to questions about motive]. He's part Chinese. His father's father was Chinese. Juny's father kept to himself. They didn't mix with the rest of us. They wanted to mix with Chinese. Juny's like that too.

(I was surprised. I wasn't surprised that I hadn't heard about it earlier. I was new to R'eiis, and no one trusted me. Semai don't look for trouble, and talking about murder could attract trouble. But I was surprised that I'd already talked with the killer, several times. 'Ahmad knew that. He wanted to be sure I knew who I was dealing with. Without making a big deal about it.)

James was the younger of two Semai Methodist men, Langiid the elder. They talked to me at the Misi Senoi, Senoi Mission, in Kampar:

James: Juny's from a bad family. His grandfather was Chinese. His heart's Chinese. The family didn't participate in Semai life.

Langiid: Juny was working as a night watchman for Chinese at a tin mine. The Chinese quarreled about something. They told him to kill a Chinese man from Jeram. He stole the Chinese man's motorbike, then ran away into the hills. His father brought him back to town. The sentence was life imprisonment, but he got out after four years.

James: Bad blood, that Chinese blood.

Langiid: He learned English in jail. Worked on improving himself [smiles].

In 1992, Saad (a pseudonym) was a witty man in his sixties, with close-cropped white hair. He rarely spoke without irony. Life had treated him badly. He worked with the British when they were recruiting Semai during the Communist uprising of the 1950s. Asked if he'd ever hurt or killed anyone, he said his unit killed a couple of Chinese "Communist Terrorists," but, since it was during a shootout, nobody could tell who killed whom. He earned a pension that the Malay-dominated government won't pay now. He reached a position of authority in the JHEOA, from which the postindependence Malay regime removed him. Saad was a de facto headman but without bureaucratic status or "letter of authority." People respected his intelligence and leadership ability but didn't like or trust him. Verbal facility like Saad's, Semai say, is dangerous: glib people can persuade you to do things that work against your own best interests. Saad's sense of how the world works was a lot like mine, and I liked him.

But Ngah Hari was uncomfortable with Saad's constant *snabuh*, suspicion and bad-mouthing. Saad was one of the few people I talked with about violence who said Semai used slow-acting poisons the way both Malays and Semai say that Malays do. "There's no evidence," no *sah*, Ngah Hari says. "If Saad didn't talk about his suspicions all the time, he wouldn't *-bl'aal*, get angry, hold a resentment. If he *-bl'aal* long enough, maybe he'd do something like get some old people to help him generate *pnalii' snabuh*. Snabuh can make your *sngii'*, mind, "hot." You search out someone who can cause *pnalii'snabuh*. Then everybody gets sick: red eyes, shooting chest pains as if you were being stabbed, can't draw breath. Many of us would die. It can wipe out a whole settlement if we don't flee. But don't let's talk about it. If you talk about it, it'll happen later, the *pnalii'*, the demon. . . . [The sorcerers are] *maay ngraa' MANAH*, really really ANCIENT people, most dead now. Maybe there're still some sorcerers among *maay jknuuk*, the woman-stealing slavers in the mountains.

Saad: A *mnaleeh* [nubile young woman] was involved. You know what *litaaw* are like [grin]. Juny and a Chinese man were both in love with a Chinese *mnaleeh* who worked as a cook. Juny was working as a guard at a tin mine back then. Who knows what the *mnaleeh* was thinking? The quarrel got out of hand. They got into some kind of stupid fight on the street. I don't know how or why; they were by themselves. Stupid thing to do. He waylaid the Chinese, killed him, and rode the man's motorbike back to Kniik, left it under his house [grins, shakes his head]. He finally ran away into the forest when he heard the police were after him. His father looked after him for a while but finally turned him over to the police. He was sentenced to hang, but they figured his criminal career was over, he'd been brainwashed by the Chinese. Sixteen years they jailed him. Aaaay, kids. Got no brains.

Ngah Hari hadn't heard Juny's story until Saad told me about it. Listening, he wrapped his arms around himself as Semai do when something upsets them. He kept glancing around, afraid someone would overhear the narration.

After Saad left, we talked about why Ngah Hari hadn't heard the story before, although his wife comes from Juny's settlement, his adopted son Sudeew has a house there, and he visits often. Maybe they were afraid the Chinese would be angry at them and retaliate. They could run people off the road with their trucks. Or maybe they were just ashamed.

Later he told me some details he had learned. Before the killing Juny had a wife, a woman from Prgvvb. He used to beat her. They had a child who died at age nine, before Juny was jailed. They were divorced before Juny went to jail.

The Cowardice of the Ethnographer

Knowing these stories meant I had to interview Juny again. But there's a moment, just before the naked force of a monsoonal thundersquall bursts over your little house, when the world lies paralyzed before its imminence. Drops of water tremble on the pointed tips of the huge leaves. Faint currents of demonic chilliness seep into the hot stagnant oppressive air. The blackening sky sucks the color from the variegated greens of the rain forest, leaving a slaty greenish darkness. The impending interview weighed on my imagination like that.

In the United States, I've worked with murderers in voluntary prison programs that New York State once allowed the American Studies Department to run, before political concerns led the university to purge the department. I've had murderers as advisees and never felt particularly uncomfortable. But I never talked with the murderers directly about the killing. I hang around sometimes with people who study violence for a living. It doesn't seem to bother them, not personally. But it bothers me.

It was harder for me to raise the topic with Juny and Arifin (the other Semai murderer I talked to [Dentan 2007]) than I'd anticipated. I was scared, I think. Violence scares me, scares me so badly I can't even let myself feel the fear but just have to guess it's there by the way I act. Along the R'eiis, with my wife and little girl in a fragile house in the rain forest, disturbed rain forest but still deep and dark, with tigers still leaving their tracks in the mud and spitting cobras in the tall grass of our yard, the fear seemed reasonable. But it didn't go away with Arifin when I talked with him in Pudu Prison either, when there was no chance at all of violence.

I suspect that the essentialism that drenches U.S. folk notions of violence is in my head too, making me think *once a murderer always a murderer*, as if murderers were different from the rest of us in some fundamental way, the way Lombroso thought a century ago (e.g., 1911). Semai don't think like that, I suspect. Juny has a *muh nicneec*, bad name/reputation, among people who know what he did, although they don't discuss it with outsiders. Most of them don't think of criminals as a different breed from ordinary people, the way so many Americans do. So there's none of the postpunishment punishment Americans inflict on people who have committed crimes, the public humiliation and ostracism. But intellectually I think that sort of essentialism is foolish: Juny has kids, I have kids; Juny has a wife, I have a wife. We're more alike than different.

Back in America on the cusp of the millennium, chewing over my vacillation, I concluded I wasn't spiritually ready for this investigation. I talked with the American murderers about academic and bureaucratic problems, the weather, the Buffalo Bills, things both of us wanted to talk about, things that manifested our common humanity.

But, back then, I had to talk with someone I already knew a little, so I couldn't hide in the comfortable role of social scientist, couldn't think *this person is nothing, this person is a bug, this person is a research subject.* And we didn't know each other well enough that the topic could come up casually. And, to me, the topic is *dirty.* I'd be asking about intimate uncleanness, ripping away at scabs of denial and selective inattention. *Hi! How ya doin'? Let me interrogate you about your hemorrhoids, about what you do with your semen after you masturbate, about how your father sexually molested you. Okay?*

By the time I'd steeled myself to talk with Juny's father-in-law, a village elder who was one of the few R'eiis people to retain any traditional Semai woods lore, I was so jumpy that he became nervous too. He'd known I was interested in violence but hadn't mentioned Juny's homicide. We avoided talking about his silence, but I suspect that also made us nervous. I was too uneasy to take notes, fearing to inhibit him, so this statement is even more a reconstruction than usual.

Juny's Father-in-Law: We folks [Semai] don't do that sort of thing. We never do that sort of thing. Yes, my son-in-law did kill a Chinese man. It was in Shrimp River [pseudonym for a Malay-Chinese town built in an area that was Semai country as late as 1950]. They jailed him in Tapah, for maybe a year. Not for very long, because we Humans never never kill anybody, never steal things, and they know that. His own family turned him in, persuaded him to turn himself in. We don't kill people. It was because he was living in Shrimp River, hanging around with Chinese, working as a night watchman. Maybe they put him up to it. It's not the sort of thing we do. We don't kill people. We don't steal or kill. We'd be afraid to.

When I first heard Juny's story, I asked Colin Nicholas to check it out. He's a Malaysian anthropologist who has written extensively about current Semai problems (e.g., Nicholas 1990, 1994; Nicholas et al. 2003). The next two entries are lightly edited versions of a memo Colin sent me, dated 24 July 1992.

Mahak: [Mahak, not his real name, was in secondary school when the crime happened. He went to the trial with Bah Akeh, whose story I retell next.] Bah Juny was *nicneec*, bad. Nobody was surprised to hear he killed somebody. The story goes that Bah Juny treated his wife badly, beating her a lot. Once, while she was pregnant, he beat her so badly that she miscarried.

Bah Akeh Gadong: [In the 1970s, Akeh worked for the Tapah branch of the Perak JHEOA. Akeh was the court interpreter in Juny's case, so his version of what happened carries more authority than others.] Bah Juny's heart was *nicneec*, evil. Back then—1972, maybe 1974—Bah Juny was working at a tin mine as a day laborer, typical Semai job. He was about thirty-five then. He married, but he'd get married and then get divorced, get married and get divorced. Just like his father.

Bah Juny was in love with a Chinese *mnaleeh* who also worked at the mine. She had a boyfriend [call him Ah Cau] another worker at the tin mine. They had gone steady for almost a year and were planning to get married in a couple of months. Juny was jealous. He thought that, if he got rid of Ah Cau, the girl would fall for him.

So, on that day, he went to see the girl and found out that she was expecting Ah Cau to come courting. Juny recruited a Semai boy to be a lookout while Juny waited in ambush. When Ah Cau came along on his Vespa [motorbike], the boy tipped Juny off. Juny came down and blocked the victim's path. They talked for a minute or so, then Juny beat him to death with a club. He dumped the corpse in a sand pit nearby. He took the victim's Vespa and rode straight home. There he changed the license plate. Then he rode the Vespa to the Semai settlement at the nineteenth milestone on the Tapah-Cameron Highlands Road and hid the bike in the bushes.

The Chinese *mnaleeh* suspected Juny had done something to her fiancé because of the strange way he had acted when he visited her just before the crime. The body of the victim was discovered the day after the murder. The police went to Juny's house and, not finding him there, took his father into custody. They beat the father [as Semai say cops routinely do when Semai come to the police station], until he told them where Juny was hiding. Twelve days later Juny was in the prison at Taiping, in south Perak.

The case was heard in the High Court in Ipoh, the capital of Perak. While Juny was awaiting trial, his wife left him. He was found guilty and sentenced to four years' imprisonment. Bah Akeh pleaded for leniency: Juny had children to care for, and so on. The sentence was reduced to two years. But he only served a year and half because of good behavior.

The reason Juny did it is that he isn't really Semai. His grandfather was half Chinese. His father was an illegitimate child.

What Juny Said

The closer I got to confronting Juny about the murder, the more nervous I got, the more difficult raising the issue seemed. I convinced myself I needed to see him alone, so as not to shame him I told myself, not to underline the *muh nicneec*, evil reputation, that serious misbehavior brings Semai. And, since Semai are rarely alone, that consideration served to rationalize my cowardice and procrastination for a couple of months. I only had about four months in the community, and it had taken a month or so to find out about Juny, so I managed to wait until almost the last minute.

But early one morning, walking down the road to talk with Ngah Hari, I encountered Juny alone, busy as usual, bulky cast on his leg still slowing him down, clearing a taro patch where the bad drainage caused by the highway construction had created a new little swamp. I stopped walking, my back to the Forest Reserve on the north side of the road. It had been stripped of its valuable hardwoods, damaged badly, raped really. Behind me was the little path that led to the small stream where people washed their clothes and defecated. Plastic trash draped the plants along the path, even the little Crinum lilies that are important in Semai cleansing rituals. The stream itself, a foot or two wide, was usually awash in turds and soapsuds because the highway crews used it too, so the current was overburdened. But still, when you hunkered down to defecate, baby rock turtles would flee to bury themselves in the sand of the pools, the butterflies came to drink and the dragonflies to kill, and the shady forest remained much cooler than the dazzling caustic dust-laden sunlight that drenched Juny as he worked, where nothing but sharp-leaved sedge and elephant ear grew. Behind him a yellow dog was rolling on its back in the dust.

Feeling unclean and stifled, *Mòng edn*, "I'm here," I said. Standard greeting. Juny paused in his work, leaning on his dibble, favoring his injured leg.

Mòng he', "There you are." Standard reply. Two little girls and a boy, maybe six to nine years old, passed by, carrying bright red plastic buckets. In the buckets were squirming giant black millipedes the children would sell to Chinese middlemen, who pass them on to a lab in the state capital. Sometimes they catch big black scorpions instead. The Chinese mount them in plastic and sell them to Japanese tourists. I waited till the kids were out of earshot, though they probably couldn't have heard us over the clatter-crash of the bulldozers.

"I heard you killed someone," I blurted. "A Chinese person."

His face twisted into an expression I could not read, partly because he was backlit by the dense sunlit haze and sizzle of the solar rain so that his face was in darkness. He spoke emphatically and bitterly, deepening his voice so it was almost easy to hear him over the sounds of destruction behind him.

Juny: I didn't do the actual killing. That was the Chinese. It wasn't my idea. I was working at a tin mine with three Chinese from Sarawak. They pretended to be my friends. We'd eat and drink together. They wanted to rob the towkay [Chinese businessman]. They persuaded me to go along with it. They lay in wait for him and ambushed him. When they found out he didn't have any money they killed him. They ran off to Sarawak. They left me to take the blame. You understand. Chinese are THE WORST PEOPLE IN THE WORLD. Their mouths are sweet but their hearts are rotten. Their thoughts don't follow a straight path. You can't trust them. You can't be friends with them. They're very smart, look who controls all the economy in this country, but they'll betray you. I didn't do the killing, I didn't even take part in it, but the police had to arrest somebody. I was the only person they could nail.

And that didn't actually contradict what he'd said to me a month earlier when I asked him if he'd ever killed anyone.

I never have. I wouldn't say I couldn't, but I never have. In the olden days, the storie go, people got shot with blowguns.

If ther was a quarrel about a woman or something there'd be a feud. But I personally never encountered that, so it's hard for me to say.

Not Clarity but the Sense of Shift

> The beautiful formed things caught at the wrong moment
> so they are shapeless, awkward
> moving to the clear
>
> —Heading and epigraph from Michael Ondaatje,
> "The Gate in His Head" (1997:610)

What happened to make Juny a killer? Well, he chose to be one, of course. In flat silhouette his crime is depressingly familiar. A greedy jealous young man, not born stupid but stupidified by circumstance, commits a stupid brutal crime of passion and greed.

Happens all the time. The two Semai murderers I talked with were both *litaaw*, the Semai label for young men between puberty and maturity, say between twelve and thirty years old. Mature people mock *litaaw*, as footloose, vain, irresponsible. They dress up like Malay punk rockers, who dress up like Boy George, because the Islamic government won't let them dress up like headbangers or heavy metal or death rockers. It's all self-indulgent illusion about being who you aren't. And when the illusion shatters, reality rushes in, and there can be terrible trouble, terror and rage.

"Identification with the oppressor" in Malaysia, where the dominant peoples are patriarchal Malays and Chinese, casts *litaaw* resistance to subordination in terms of manhood. In that code what would otherwise be just an insult becomes an insult to one's manliness. Semai boys learn the Malaysian "boy code" from the mass media and in school. Following their parents' advice—"don't fight back"—gets them picked on by other boys whose own background paints bullying as better than being bullied. The two murderers had consciously decided not to be Semai any more. That happens a lot to minority kids in that position, even in America (e.g., Hansen 1966:258–59).

And many *litaaw* are bellicose, though undisciplined. Here's how they talk:

Yahyah, twenty-four: There wouldn't be any fights at our *ronggeng* [Malay-style dance parties, with lots of flirting and drinking] if it wasn't for outsiders [*maay*]. Everybody comes to our *ronggeng*—Malays, Chinese, Tamils, everybody.

Sarip, twenty-eight, his covillager: We fight Malays because they molest our women. The Police Field Force [Malay parapolice] kidnapped a woman from near our place and kept her naked for days and days while they gang-raped her. . . . [The case was "settled," he said, using the English word. Nobody went to jail. Not for raping a Semai woman. Just paid a few dollars. The usual. You know.]

Yahyah: Listen, we're not *maay manah ntum*, old-time people. Somebody knocks us down, what're we supposed to do? Just lie there and grin? [laughs].

Sarip: Hey, if we had weapons, we'd drive the Malays off our land [aims an imaginary rifle, squinting and grinning]. We're not *maay manah ntum*.

A Litaaw Reverie. Like boys in their early teens elsewhere, in 1993, Grcaang, the elder brother of Rmpent's buddy Tkooy, laced the deserts of schooling with fantasy. He was good looking and knew it. He seemed to be enjoying his young manhood, fishing with a homemade fish spear, beginning to hunt with the grown-ups, thinking about girls, and taking his ease. He shared this page from his school notebook with me.

The first line is apparently Malay and about making money. The next says, also in Malay, "I like Wa' Kiaw." The next refers to another mnaleeh. *The fourth is unclear but may be in Semai and refer to another* litaaw, *Rohman. Then come the Malay word for "voyage" and the statement "Amy = Isobella." The Malay sentence " I like to eat rice" (= I'm hungry) is on the side and a bearded (European) figure in a tricornered hat on the other.*

But the centerpiece is the figure of litaaw *cool as of 1993: long hair, sunglasses, and an inverted peace symbol forming the "O" in the thrice-repeated word "ROCK." In the early 1990s, it was hard to find any Semai* litaaw *who did not look up to Malay pop rockers. Acoustic guitars were everywhere. What young man anywhere does not want to be popular and admired, hip and free, rich and powerful? (For a photo of Grcaang in 1993, see the cover of the* Journal of Anthropology and Humanism *26, no. 1 [2001].)*

Should we condemn them, or our own *litaaw*, for being who they are, for their slightly embarrassed insecure bravado, their hollow desperate pretensions? The same feelings make them capable of great loyalty and courage, too, compassion and startling selflessness. We should judge young men deed by deed, not by essence. Their vices and virtues commingle inextricably. Their unformed young maleness flows into the hollows and channels the rest of us leave open for them. Whether what young men do is valuable, or dangerous, is up to us as much as to them:

After all, very few *litaaw* actually rape and murder. The Semai murderers

> had once been boys with intelligent eyes and brightly innocent mouths, unafraid and loving creatures eager to please and be pleased. What had turned them into the embittered brutes they had become? (Banks 1989:322)

That's the serious issue, not testosterone.

And there were constraints on Juny's choice of violence. His family was as "dysfunctional," full of brutality and betrayal, as his young manhood. Many people commented how stupid he had been: killing was stupid, keeping the motorbike was stupid, fleeing into the rain forest was stupid. All *litaaw* are "brainless," says Saad. Their passions and posturing make them act stupid. But while *litaaw* do almost all the fighting, they don't normally kill people. To understand Juny's "brainlessness," consider his other options.

Talking about "oppression" is out of fashion (Graeber 2007b). Everybody knows it happens, and almost everybody is against it, in principle. But it's like pederasty among Arabs; there's a "will not to know" (Murray 1997). Oppression is pervasive in my country, but you don't mention it. Every now and then some egregious case makes the evening news, there's a chorus of condemnation of the bad guys, and the issue drops out of sight again. And griping about particular instances is okay, as long as it stays on a semijocular or academic level. But no serious, possibly consequential discussion, please.

Even among intellectuals, with the passing of the Soviet Union and the emergence of hitherto "submerged" voices into academic discourse, the brief vogue of talking about oppression has subsided into occasional murmurs about "subalterns." These are "postcolonial" times. We put quotation marks around words like "oppression" because we don't want to "privilege" particular sorts of "victim status." *Everybody is oppressed*, we say, quite rightly I think, but many academics carry that thought into absurdity. If everyone is a victim, no one is a victim, not really. In a society that relentlessly, compulsively stresses that the glass is half *full*, to say everyone is a victim is to say everyone is "okay."

Maybe talking about it would make us conscious of the pervasive chronic fear of violence on which oppression ultimately depends. We have enough fear of violence in our consciousness already, terrorists, pedophiles, bosses, our rulers. We can look away from our fears, "dissociate" or "deny" them as the psychologists say, when they get too painful. And the ubiquity of oppression in our lives helps. The limitations it puts on our freedoms are so familiar that we don't notice them until we stumble off the straight-and-narrow path and fall.

We learn that quiet desperation, early, as children. Human children know that they are inferior to adults in terms of any sort of power. Not long ago, only a few centuries, English speakers used to talk about "fearing" one's parents as forthrightly as Semai do. But nowadays, because we Americans love our children or think we should, we have become mealymouthed about teaching them to fear us. We know we do that: but it runs up against our "will not to know." This mystification of how adults use their strength to ensure the mindless subordination of children occludes our understanding of other forms of oppression (Juli and Dentan 2007).

We fail to understand, for example, why oppressed peoples like Semai often seem to trust and even love their oppressors, never wondering why our children often seem to trust and love us. Feminists are disturbed that Sudanese women defend the custom of mutilating women's genitals. But they don't find it odd that children who have been hit may say that they deserved it, though the fact that these children often go on to beat their own children may make them ill at ease. The mystification of arbitrary power facilitates this acceptance of subordination, of course, the "ideological hegemony" that instructs women that they need an operation to smooth and refine their genitals, to constrain their lust—which teaches children that they need punishment to learn to "be good."

You can make quite powerful arguments in favor of infibulation or spanking. People do all the time. But the subalterns don't accept these arguments just intellectually. They acquiesce emotionally, too. I don't mean that people don't resist. They do, all the time. Indeed, you can think of the acquiescence as a form of resistance. No normal creature likes being subordinate. This insubordination is an instance of the Premack principle, named after the libertarian psychologist Walter Premack, who claims to have demonstrated experimentally that, the rewards being equal, any organism will chose rewarding itself over being rewarded by a "caretaking organism" like a human experimenter. Subalterns want freedom. But in a hierarchical and oppressive society, as the Marquis de Sade points out compulsively, my freedom depends on your oppression. The desire for freedom and the desire to take the oppressor's place are closer kin than Americans find comfortable. Why would Juny want to identify with *maay miskin*, poor and pathetic people (Geh 1993), when his mixed parentage let him identify with the relatively rich and powerful Chinese?

Most subalterns have no chance of replacing their bosses. That's why they're subalterns. Children can't dominate their parents until it's too late to do the children any good. But they can imagine how to do it: by acting like their parents until ultimately they become like them. That's what I was talking about in the introduction to this book when I was talking about "identification" as how anthropologists try to understand other people. People learn who they and others are by comparing themselves with other people, especially more powerful ones. And people don't like the bad news about being oppressed, which runs up against their "will not to know." They do like the emotional lift that the possibility of freedom gives them and so find it easier to identify with more powerful people than with less powerful ones. That's what "identification with the oppressor" is about. It even makes people want to be involved in "development" and "modernization" in quite horrible ways.

That was the worst thing that happened to Juny, I think. He wanted to be Chinese so badly and feared being Semai so much that the choice of Chinese, any Chinese, as his reference group was really no choice at all. I bet it felt good to be seen in public with his Chinese buddies, with their rough masculine swagger, their brash assertive sexuality, their unnuanced conviction of their ethnic superiority over all other Malaysian peoples. But I also imagine that he sometimes felt, maybe without being aware enough to word it to himself, that he had slipped out of their rhythm, came in half a beat late, missed what their exchange of glances meant. His identification with Chinese did not bring identity. And his denial that he was Semai, like any "will not to know," made him stupid. Even if you're willing not to be who you are, what you are, even if you want to be different, it's hard.

Then the whole painstaking construction of himself as Chinese collapsed. He thought he was Chinese, almost, but the Chinese who used him didn't think he was. They'd patronize him, the way you patronize a child acting too grown-up for its years, making him a sort of mascot, peripheral to their group, as other Malaysian peoples were peripheral to China, Zhongguo, the Central Country. On good days, they would see his Semai ancestry as a sort of developmental disability, not his fault really but incapacitating. He got lost in the web of connections, *guanxi* Chinese call it, which his brutal pals understood so thoroughly.

So they let him make himself a patsy for them and played him for a fool. The harshest punishment he received was learning that his foul companions rejected him and betrayed him. He responded, eventually, by rejecting them, angrily, by becoming not only Semai but an expert on Semai, a man capable (after discreet consultation with his father-in-law) of instructing a foreign anthropologist about Semai culture. And there was some identification with the oppressor in that relationship too.

Flight and Bardo

> . . . we pass
> through each other
> like pure arrows
> or fade into rumor

> —From Michael Ondaatje, "Rock Bottom" (1997:711)

But the story doesn't end with the murder, right? You could cast the next part of the story as a traditional Semai cautionary tale: alluring Chinese with their privileged access to the beautiful things formed by the "developed" world metamorphose into betrayers, shape-shifting demons camouflaged in "modernization." I think that, until that betrayal, Juny floated on the surface of life like a water strider, blown around by the slightest breeze, never understanding how fragile the surface tension that supported him was, how cold and dark it was beneath the surface, until he broke though. His terror was great enough that he needed shamanic medical treatment before he could come out. His flight, I imagine, marked his entry into his bardo, the ambiguous transitional spiritual state the *Tibetan Book of the Dead* discusses.

I see him in my imagination after the murder, eyes darting from side to side like the eyes of Semai in the old slaving days, "like a deer tied to a post" as Malays say, looking behind him into the unfathomable flickering shadows to see what's following him, right hand resting on one of the flayed trees along the path rattan cutters follow. Rattan cutters amuse themselves by slashing away at the undergrowth as they trudge uphill, even slashing the great boles of the trees. On the shattered ligaments of a white branch parallel to the path I imagine a little flying lizard tenses, the tiny gray-green bellows of its sides pulsing in and out, preparing to leap and glide away, leaving the terrified murderous human behind. The rippling water of a small stream far below catches a wandering ray of light. Beyond the stream the huge hydroelectric towers stalk through the doomed inhuman grandeur of the forest.

He knows the vague narrow path he's followed runs precariously along the edge of a cliff, but the vegetation on the precipice side is so thick that you can't actually see the edge. Your knowledge is intellectual merely, your eyes tell you you're safe from falling, but if you fell, you'd just fall and fall, leafy branches careening past, uncaring green canopy wheeling above you.

He finds himself a place to sleep, maybe, sheltered between two great buttress roots that prop up an unscalable, unthinkably white *puleey* tree. Above this place where light and kindness never reach loom the lattice-work of vines, the straight vertical gray-green tree trunks. Stunned by fear, he can hear the monsoonal wind, perhaps, sweeping down through the leaves at him like time to come, the first blast speeding by him and the rest still coming, buffeting the enormous leaves, making the bamboos clack together. He sits hugging himself, keeping himself from coming apart, everything once clear having slipped away from him, afraid that if he opens his eyes, he will disintegrate, waiting for the brilliant ancient darkness.

He can remember the clarity outside from whose menace he now flees: the bright pastel heat, shiny expensive cars, beautiful Chinese *mnaleeh*, money, knowledge, respect. *I used to be happy*, he thinks; but that was never true. Police, poverty, ignorance, scorn, no love at all. A sour mouth-ful of crippled hopes, fear ripping at his heart.

In traditional Semai cautionary tales, ambiguities move into clarity: most stories end with the phrase "if you are Human, be humane; if Mon-ster, be monstrous." But Juny's choices were never so clear.

You'd be surprised at how much even a dishonest brutal stupid person can hurt.

9

Inconclusion

PRELUDE: SUMMARY INTERPRETATION

I would fain advance naught but substantiated facts. But after embat-
tling his facts, an advocate who should wholly suppress a not unrea-
sonable surmise, which might tell eloquently upon his cause—such an
advocate, would he not be blameworthy?

—Melville (1989:113)

Here I need, like some nineteenth-century novelist, to "crave the
reader's indulgence." Ethnography grows out of the way ethnographers make sense of their experiences with a particular set of people. People mostly make sense out of experiences by referring back to other experiences they've had or read about, organizing the total in a way that
makes sense according to the narrative style of their friends and associ-
ates. I think people make narratives out of their recollections of the more
or less random neuronal discharges that constitute the raw stuff of
dreams in pretty much the same way (Dentan 1988). Experiences don't
make sense: we make sense out of them.

The original version of this book included specific details from life in
America, and experiences that seemed to clarify what Semai did and said.
They took up too much space for this book, though they're on the accom-
panying website (http://www.rowmanlittlefield.com/isbn/0742553302).
Still, to know enough to retrace how I came to my current understanding
of Semai peaceability, you need to know a little of my personal history,
just enough to gauge how much it colored my analysis. It was, after all, a

failure to attend to history as much as any other facet of my ignorance, that led me to misunderstand Semai in the first place. I had to meet a lot of other people and undergo some uncomfortable changes myself before the Semai achievement seemed more than odd and exotic, admirable perhaps, but quaint and, well, primitive.

1960s: Intellectual Errors

> [O]ur contact with another is not accomplished through analysis. Rather, we apprehend him in his entirety. From the outset, we can sketch our view of him using an outline of symbolic detail, which contains a whole in itself, and evokes the true form of his being. The latter is what escapes us if we approach our fellow creature using only the categories of our intellect. (Leenhardt 1937:2)

When I first visited Semai, in the early 1960s, I wasn't ready professionally or spiritually to understand Semai nonviolence. I suffered the delusion that I could approach other humans using only the categories of my intellect even after, on a personal level, it was clear I couldn't do that while living with Semai. People just won't sit still for that. But back home, writing up my "field experience," I tried to replay that delusion, the way I had learned to in grad school. For example, I presented the "ceremonies of innocence" (chapter 5) as "taboos" that originated in horror of violence, a Semai notion of themselves as "nonviolent people." Several people tried to explain these customs to me, but, since Semai lacks a sophisticated vocabulary of probability and a word for "stress," I didn't understand that the various words I translated as "taboo" or "forbidden act" might refer to stress and stressors. I was thinking about bestial demons and glittering flying souls, the filigrees with which Semai explain these notions to themselves. The concreteness of the examples they gave ("Tiger'll eat her") misled me. When I asked, people would say, "Well, maybe once in a hundred [or thousand] times," and add some other possible misfortune, like falling and getting hurt. What they meant, I should have understood, was that stressed-out people are likely to get upset or depressed and become distracted and accident prone. Back then, my own people didn't understand stress as subtly as Semai did, so perhaps, I tell myself, it wasn't only youthful arrogance and ethnocentrism that clouded my understanding, but also cultural deprivation.

1970s: Academic "Radicalism"

> Since any and all events can be lifted by men of bad faith out of their normal contexts and projected onto others and thus consequently condemned, since one's thoughts can be interpreted in terms of such extreme implications as to reduce them to absurdity or subversion, obviously a mere declaration of good faith is not enough. In an all-pervading climate of intellectual evasion or dishonesty, everything becomes dishonest. . . . To imagine straight com-

munication is no longer possible is to declare that the world we seek to defend is no longer worth defending, that the battle for human freedom is already lost. . . . Have you taken your passions, your illusions, your time, and your circumstances into account? . . . More than that no reasonable man of good will can demand. (Wright 1993:428–29)

The first revisionary experience came during "the sixties," most of which happened in the 1970s. George Appell, a scholar-activist who had worked in Malaysian Borneo, was the first to link my work with the study of nonviolence, not my concern until my thesis (on food restrictions) and first book were complete: he suggested the subtitle "a nonviolent people of Malaya" for the book. Working with colleagues in a "radical" academic department—gay and lesbian activist, Marxist feminists, Native American traditionalists, Puerto Rican activists, and the like—forced me to consider power and "oppression" as general phenomena: what brought these disparate people together as often touchy and uneasy allies? Departmental activism and focus on oppression was to lead to the eventual dissolution of the department and its reconstitution in a form less politically troublesome to the academy; but not before I came to see the similarities between the Semai/Malay relationship and the Native American/European or African American/European one. The dynamics of other forms of oppression suggested several avenues to explore.

For example, Malaysian histories of the time ignored Malaysian indigenes like Semai. Combating the invisibility of "subaltern" peoples was a major concern of my historian colleagues. I'd read early accounts of Semai for ethnographic data but not as causally relevant to the present. Scholarly analyses of histories of "submerged" peoples, by people like Vine Deloria and W. E. B. Du Bois, helped inform my rereading of the early accounts. I began to pay more attention to the inequality between Semai and other Malaysians. Most other Malaysians, for example, had never heard of Semai, just as most New Yorkers in the 1970s didn't know the state had a large Native American population. Invisibility was part of their submersion. One reason Malaysian indigenes generally do not share the aversion of, say, Native Americans to anthropologists is that in Malaysia (as Bah Tony said to me in the 1970s), "You made us *known*."

I hadn't thought about the effect of slaving on people. Most accounts I had read treated it as a deplorable but abstract condition, discussion of which was too embarrassing to the former perpetrators to be proper "liberal" academic discourse. The then rising generation of indigenous Malaysian activist scholars, notably Tan Chee Beng, Colin Nicholas and Alberto Gomes, sharpened my perceptions of Semai history and current predicament. Slavocratic terrorism seemed to have something to do with the widespread nineteenth- and early twentieth-century reports of Semai "timidity" in the presence of outsiders. That avoidance of conflict, I thought, might evolve into general nonviolence. The first couple of chapters in the book attempt to clarify the documented Semai historical experience as experience rather than abstraction.

Finally, Marxist-feminist "deconstruction" of "hegemonic discourse" pointed up unwitting biases in my work. In the academy, that insight ultimately devolved into an extreme cultural relativism that deconstructed Marxism and feminism as well in the process delegitimizing ideas like "oppression" (Graeber 2007b). It also so valued "resistance," broadly construed, that just talking about accommodation with, resignation to, or identification with oppressors seemed like betraying the people with whom you'd worked. I couldn't integrate into my analysis wry phrases like "Lime [as body paint] you sweat off; Malays, what are you gonna do?" (*Kòp hi pluh, Gòp haroo' hi-ha-bvh?*). But I still think power differences determine great swatches of human behavior so that surrender to the greater power of the Malay state and rejection of subordination are what gives Semai life its distinctive flavor. Totalizing relativism, by contrast, takes the old Italian proverb *traduttore traditore*, translators are traitors, to such an extreme that we reject any understanding of each other on the grounds that all understanding is biased and imperfect. What I learned is what Richard Wright asserted in defiance of McCarthyite attack in the passage that opens this section. We should produce biased accounts that state our biases as honestly as we can because that's the best we can do. Perfection is beyond us: but imperfect communication beats no communication at all. We're not going to get to "final accounts" but we'll get better as long as we keep talking with each other.

Hence this brief confessional.

1980s: Surrendering

> Why should they care about the plots, the hatred and heroism, of the world?
> Their deep core is the love of a soul guide. (Rumi 2001:162)

I don't know if Semai would use their word *guniik* to gloss the word that Rumi's wonderful translator Englishes as "soul guide" or how they would construe the terminological similarity between the Roman Catholic litany *Sanguis Christi, inebria me* (Christ's blood, intoxicate me) and their own *blnuul bhiip*, "blood drunkenness." But by the end of the 1970s, I needed spiritual guidance of the sort these epigraphs seem to be talking about. My multiple chemical addictions had become a vortex that was swallowing all the rest of my life. I tried all the ways of controlling them that I'd heard of except suicide, which I thought about a lot. Utterly disabled and more terrified than I've ever been before or since, I finally sought refuge in Alcoholics Anonymous (AA). At the time, I regarded AA as a society of Holy Rollers, losers, not a program of any potential use to me. But by 1980, there was nothing else left to try. That experience of terror and powerlessness, accepting which is essential to successful AA praxis, gave me new insight into the terror that seemed to overwhelm Semai during violent thundersqualls, flash floods, and landslips: I too no longer felt safe, felt everything I valued slipping away. And I began to wonder whether there was a connection between my "bottom" (as AAs call that experience), slavocratic terrorism (chapter 2), and the terror of being overpowered by the stupid violent Thunder Lord (chapter 3). Was a sense of being overwhelmed part of the ethos, the emotional background, of Semai life?

Now, AA social and political structure is a lot like that of rain-forest foraging bands and of "simple" Southeast Asian swiddeners like Semai. I won't belabor the similarities here since I've done so elsewhere (Dentan 1992, 1994). Thomas Lechner (2003) has written a definitive study of AA as an egalitarian "band." The point relevant here is that the AA program for surviving sobriety involves accepting one's powerlessness over addiction and eventually "in all our affairs." The sensation is not of an effortful controlling of one's urges. It's just relief: "I don't have to try to do *that* any more. Whew!" Stressful lives get much easier if you take things as they come, not as you'd like them to be. *Ma ha-'uuy?* ask Semai in Perak state, *jaluu' hem-bvvh?* in Pahang: "What you gonna do?" Meaning: there's nothing *to* do. *To' ma i ma,* "no matter." Give up, move on.

That's not an unusual response to relative powerlessness. Impoverished Malay peasants say much the same thing: *apa nak buat?* for "what you gonna do?" and *tidak apa* for "no matter." Malay "tidak apathy" frustrated colonialist British efforts to introduce capitalism. As one old Malay fisherman told me over coffee, with a shrug and a smile, *Kita orang melayu tak berapa rajin,* "We Malay people don't spend a lot of energy [on moneymaking]." Max Weber noticed similar behavior among medieval European peasants; it led him to sketch capitalist insatiability for money as a theologically induced obsessive-compulsive disorder.

Semai say explicitly that too much concern with wealth makes you unhappy and undermines *slamaad,* serenity, peace, social harmony. From an egalitarian viewpoint like that of Semai, making money isn't worth subordinating yourself to cold contemptuous outlanders, at least no longer than you need to. For Btsisi', another Aslian people, "work" (a Malay word) is what you do on someone else's plantation; what you do on your own is "playing."

No one who has ever watched Semai or Malay peasants working would call them lazy or apathetic. They work hard at tasks they choose. Indeed, there is a Semai epic about how they learned to work hard and submit to the cycle of time (Dentan 2006). But since they usually don't work to earn more money than they need to be comfortable, they strike outsiders as indolent—a word whose Latin root means "not suffering." Refusal to suffer and an aversion to subordination makes coercive "economic development" difficult, even when you relocate the people into rows of mutually identical stifling tin-roofed houses (chapter 8).

Another similarity between AA and Semai traditions is that, rather like the first three Steps of AA, Semai séances involve embracing terror, a skill they say they learned from the violent Thunder Lord. Usually Semai don't remember much about the trances, but afterward, they say, life goes more smoothly, with fewer quarrels and demonic attacks. It's a relief, like "letting go" in AA.

In their séances, Semai temporarily reject violence—killing, wounding, mockery—and instead love and nurture their demonic spirit guides, of whom Thunder Lord is the greatest. The Perak word for séance, *n'asik*, remember, comes from an Arabic word for erotic surrender and thus for the Sufi surrender to the God of Love that Rumi celebrates. The original plan for AA was to culminate in a similar mystical experience of the sort William James describes, a surrender to a more or less Christian God. There are significant "cultural" differences between Sufi *asyik*, Christian mysticism, and Semai *n'asik*, of course. But the second historically derives from the first, in the waning days of El 'Andalus, and Semai, Sufi missionaries, or both saw enough mutual similarity between each other's rituals to give them the same name. That perception and my own needs led me into the literature of mysticism, which I had theretofore found unintelligible and repellent.

One apparent difference between AA and Semai ideology is that Semai imagine that, as they surrender to the demonic powers, those powers surrender to them (chapter 4). I'm not sure the difference is important. Who is the Lover and who the Beloved in Sufism and Catholic Christianity is also pretty ambiguous. In the end, they're the same. The difference in emphasis may reflect Semai stress on individual autonomy and rejection of subordination.

But again, participation in AA social structure is explicitly individualistic and egalitarian. Mutual aid and identification with the fellowship are important values in AA, as among Semai, but neither group has any mechanism other than peer pressure for coercing conformity (chapter 6). The identity between people and *guniik* is always transient. Individual autonomy always reasserts itself.

1990s: Children

What the children hadn't learned to do was to modulate or translate, their thoughts into the refined, socially coded answers of adults. It was true that their moral logic was occasionally skewed, but their opinions were still considered. And I wanted to know what they thought. (Hooper 2002:51–52)

An interest in the notion of relief by surrender to what overwhelms you with pain and terror began to lead me into unfamiliar territory. For one thing, I began to think about children. I hadn't paid much intellectual attention to Semai children. They were always around, in my house, sometimes on my lap while I was trying to work, but not of any significance, you know, more like the chicks whose constant omnipresent peeppeeppeeppeep turned my tape recordings into baby chicken soundscapes. Early on, I had been struck by Semai indifference to obedience and their horror at the idea of corporal punishment. "We don't *ajar* our kids," one man explained, using a Malay word that means *teach, instruct; advise, correct and guide; scold, beat.* "We don't hit our kids. Malays are always hitting hitting hitting their kids. That's why our kids are strong and healthy, and Malay kids are like baby rats." His wife expressed shock at the very idea of corporal punishment: "Suppose you hit your child and it DIED?" Very different from my childhood. But I mentally dismissed noncoercive child rearing, as a facet of a nonviolent and egalitarian ethos, ignoring the way Semai taught their children to fear strangers and seek solace from adults they knew.

By the 1990s, though, I had become more interested in children. Americans were beginning an intense and obsessive concern with child abuse. The corporate media began to feature stories about child sexual abuse by strangers, as Semai child rearing featured the fear of kidnapping and mutilation by strangers, although the people most likely to hurt children are everywhere their kinsmen and neighbors. But "conservatives" in America also began to advocate increasingly severe forms of corporal punishment for children, giving rise to a brisk cottage industry in guides to "discipline" and instruments like whips and paddles. The idea that caressing children is evil and beating them good seemed almost the opposite of Semai praxis (Dentan 2001a).

I should have paid attention to children earlier, of course. The relationship between children and adults seems to be a "natural metaphor" for power relations in most societies (Juli and Dentan 2008). The invisibility of children to me in the 1960s and 1970s was an instance of the invisibility of "subalterns" to their fellow citizens. The way Semai treated and thought about children and the way children learned to be Semai began to seem increasingly important aspects of Semai peaceability (Dentan 2001a). I began to pay intellectual attention to ideas of child rearing in the abstract and to children in my neighborhood, my children's friends in particular. The kids' consequent affection and shared analyses of their lives helped me personally and professionally.

Talking with the kids, I began to see that children are almost always overwhelmed. Almost half a dozen of them lived in situations that seemed to me in some ways abusive. The kids swore me to secrecy: better the familiar and painful than life among strangers. Bruno Bettelheim's insight into the phenomenon of "identification with the oppressor," the Stockholm syndrome, as a response to intense terror, seemed disturbingly relevant to some of the kids' experiences and to their responses. Such identification, said Anna Freud, was a fundamental ego defense mechanism, the way children learn who they are and so escape condemnation and punishment by adults. It seemed also to explain the less stark response of "social identification" that social psychologists talk about in which people in the lower strata of society identify with their "betters." Like several other researchers, I had been surprised by Semai "double consciousness," their way of seeing the world not only through their own eyes but simultaneously through what they conceived the Malay view to be. Now it seemed to make sense.

And the kids' problems reminded me of my own response to beatings, which I hadn't thought about for years. There comes a point during a prolonged beating when you stop struggling, your muscles relax, and you enter a detachment that feels like floating in a pale yellow void, the color I suppose from the blood in your eyelids, aware of the pain but somehow not involved, indifferent. Surrender, letting-go, see?

But even identification with the oppressor, the most complete surrender imaginable, need not lead to subordination (Lechner 2003). Max Weber suggests that a concern with obedience emerges in human societies only after the development of militarism. In the United States, advocates of corporal punishment sometimes talk about the importance of "discipline" in producing "Christian soldiers." That's what Semai see as *n'ajar* and reject, perhaps because they lack a militaristic tradition.

Recently

> People are, after all, capable of bellicose behavior. But bellicosity, although it may be an asset for warriors, only hampers soldiers, whose primary virtues are discipline and obedience. However uncomfortable the terminology has become in recent decades, primitive warfare really is distinct from civilized warfare, and the difference between bellicosity and obedience is crucial. . . . Armies are complex, hierarchical, and disciplined social organizations of soldiers, not ephemeral gatherings of more-or-less independent warriors. (Hacker 2004:153)

Finally, in time of war, I've recently become more sympathetic with the plight of young men. It's easy not to like them. They are everywhere prone to bellicosity, more likely to commit acts of brutality than any other age cohort. It's hard not to imagine that they have chromosomal, hormonal, or neurological predispositions, if not to physical violence, then to uncontrolled energy and the resulting wild behavior that prompt American authorities to drug so many of their boy-children with amphetamines like

Lang with submachine gun. Just entering his teens, Lang was like most litaaw, indeed like most young men everywhere, anxious to be as cool and hip as imaginable. In early 1992, he and a couple of other boys carved themselves an array of weapons from the soft, light, and easily shaped wood of a giant puleey tree (Alstonia sp.), which Semai traditionally use for disposable ritual utensils like the sickness figures some subgroups use during séances. The paraphernalia of violent oppression is glamorous for litaaw. That's what social psychologists mean when they talk about "identification with the oppressor/ aggressor" (just as in the hairdo of the mnaleeh in illustration 2.1). AK-47s and Nikes, what a vision! River Waar, 1992. Photograph by R. K. Dentan.

Ritalin, and to jail so many others. It's easy to blame young men for their disconnectedness, their irresponsibility. Semai and Americans do it routinely. Young men are an affliction in most societies. Social pathologies flourish among them: violence, suicide, the dark pestilence of addictions. "Testosterone crazed," say Americans. "No brains," say Semai, and mock their preening and self-importance.

Semai are just beginning to reward belligerence the way we do. Young men, *litaaw*, are just beginning to join complex, hierarchical, and disciplined social organizations of soldiers. It's there, say Semai, that violence and drunkenness flourish. The discipline, *n'ajar*, that Max Weber says stems from such organization is not yet a salient part of child rearing, though the battering that accompanies it is beginning to appear, facilitated by drinking alcohol. But in the old days, this belligerence was focused on hunting and its spiritual equivalent, trancing, *n'asik*.

WHAT CAN "WE" LEARN FROM SEMAI?

> It's a mutual joint-stock world, in all meridians. We cannibals must help these Christians. (Melville 1989:72)

Theory

> In summary, what may most usefully be said of the Semai is that they do not deny human nature, but do their very best to hobble it wherever necessary, in the interest of balance and human welfare. Their utopian solution, however, is a poor competitor in the open market. And as all ideas, all mutations, in the end all species, must be judged on their success in competing with others of their kind, the Semai experiment has to be judged a noble failure. (Watson 1995:157)

Lyall Watson's assessment of the Semai adaptation to violence is unusually generous. Most physical anthropologists dismiss them as "losers," as if "losing" were an unusual and vaguely shameful experience for human beings and not an environmental stress like other environmental stresses to which people need to adapt. I suspect that this dismissal comes out of social Darwinism, not Darwinian evolutionary theory. It reflects 1) capitalist values, which, as Weber argues, construe riches as a measure of Divine favor and the market as the universal measure of worth, and 2) macho militaristic inegalitarianism, according to which beaten people should (and do) feel unworthy and ashamed. But temporary defeat in war or economic struggle is not the same as extinction or even relative lack of fitness. What Darwin says in this matter is that

Today, ethnographers come from all over to learn about West
Malaysian indigenous peoples. The back-and-forth with the
publisher somehow led to the disappearance of the names of
this set of ethnographers, of the young Burmese refugee artist
who sketched them, and of the Japanese ethnographer who took
this picture, but perhaps it's as well that we all remain generic.
We descended on the restaurant, where no one spoke Malay or
English, none of us able to speak Burmese, but with many gestures and a lot of goodwill on all sides were able to communi-
cate well enough that we could all congratulate ourselves on our
abilities in that area. From left to right in the sketch we are (bald
bespectacled) American, (dress-wearing) Semelai (a people related to Semai), Malay (with head scarf), and Japanese (with
camera). The isolation has broken in which apolitical terrorists
flourished and peaceful ways of life could sustain themselves,
making new forms of community possible, at least in theory.

at all times throughout the world tribes have supplanted other tribes; and as morality is one element in their success, the standard of morality and the number of well-endowed men will thus everywhere tend to rise and increase. (quoted in de Waal 1996:23)

Computer modeling suggests, in fact, that among egalitarian peoples like Semai and most pre-Neolithic societies (except for specialized big-game hunters), violence and feuding reduce survival rates and, for surviving populations, replace hunger as the second-leading cause of death after old age. Excluding large segments of the population from violence and revenge significantly improves survival rates. So does nonviolent conflict resolution. Flight from known aggressors enhances the survival of the total population at the cost of social cohesion (Dentan 2008; Younger 2005). The model, in other words, reproduces a segment of Semai history as, in evolutionary terms, a success (cf. Dentan 1992).

And there's a certain parochialism in assuming that stratified militaristic states are, in the same terms, successful. Depending on how you define "human," you can measure human evolution in millions, hundreds of thousands, or, at least, tens of thousands of years. For such states to be demonstrably successful, a conservative would want them to last, say, 50,000 years, the minimum estimate of how long egalitarian human societies have lasted. There are some indications, indeed, that stratified militaristic states threaten the survival of the human species, let alone of statist social organization, and that's after only 6,000 years or so. Maybe states will be the "noble failure."

> Cultural adaptation involves changes of all sorts that continually affect our relationship to our environment. It results in changes that can never be ideal, as the environment itself is constantly changing. No adaptation or response is a perfect or final solution . . . each carries with it certain costs and hazards.
>
> Adaptation is always opportunistic: We take advantage of whatever resources are available to us at a particular time. . . . Adaptation is at once the solution of a particular problem and the source of unanticipated changes and, inevitably, new problems. (Bates 1998:9)

The good news, if there is good news in such a prospect, is that, in the ruins of state societies, people, even children, often spontaneously create new societies on the egalitarian sharing model of societies like Semai. As I've pointed out, these humane inventions usually get short shrift from statist conflict resolution specialists (chapter 6). The wiring seems built in, at least as much as the wiring for violence. Like all other adaptations, including violence, it works when conditions are right and not when they aren't.

Practice

Readers have a right to expect authors to make sense of what they have forced on the readers. I've indicated how tentative I feel about doing that, how inadequate, how much I fear what Arthur Kleinman (1985) awkwardly calls "delegitimating" individual Semai experience. But I'm a dutiful type. So what can we learn—and from now on by "we," I mean "we in the bosom of industrialized states"—what can we learn by reading about Semai?

We need to set aside some prejudices. In America, now, it is a truism that violence not only works but works better under any circumstances than anything else. One of the most appealing things about violence is that it *feels* like a simplification, especially with frustrating "impossible" problems. When your children are being "impossible," you "pop 'em one"—just to "get their attention"—*That'll learn ya*. Confronted with the impossibly complex Gordian knot, Alexander the Great, that model soldier, cuts it in two. Indiana Jones, faced with an menacing Arab warrior demonstrating *silat*, the complex and beautiful Arab martial art, shoots him. "How can we tell heretics from Christians?" asks the captain. "Kill 'em all," says the despicable Simon de Montfort. "God'll sort 'em out." At the Army-Navy store downtown, you can buy T-shirts with that as a slogan. When you do yield to the simplifying impulse, even when you read anecdotes like these, you get a little gasp of (sometimes guilty) relief and pleasure.

I suspect that little rush of relief, often denied almost as soon as felt, underlies the old learning theorists' postulate that "aggression" always came from "frustration." Turns out that's not true. Not universally, anyway. There's an apocryphal story that at the Battle of Manila in 1898, Admiral Dewey rebuked his sailors for cheering as a Spanish battleship sank: "Don't cheer, boys. Those poor fellows are *dying*." I hope he said that. But the joy that made the American sailors cheer was mostly from the warriors' prayer: *they die, not us*. Power feels good. Violence unchecked, pure force, "raw power," as we say: hey, that's *real* power. It's the terrorists' creed: "Only violence is pure and uncorrupted and uncompromising" (Dingley 2001:453).

The justifications and rationalizations come later: they're animals, she's sleeping around, he asked for it, it's my kid. I remember reading a slaver's diary: he said he didn't doubt that Africans were the intellectual equals of Europeans, that he had carried Socrates or Plato in the holds of his ships. But, he said, it made no difference to him one way or the other. He was just making a buck, right? On *In the Life*, a PBS series, a young man who had killed a gay man for no special reason said, in effect, "Tell the truth, it sort of slipped my mind. I don't mean it wasn't a big deal or anything.

But I didn't think about it." Once the victims are available, in the chilling Malay simile, "it's like killing ants."

To think that we can ward off violence and the chaos it causes by *reading about it* is as pathetic as to think we can accomplish the same end by eating meat off different plates from fish. The mid-twentieth-century Marxist Adorno says that exercises like this book constitute the knee-jerk ideological response of the capitalist state to the threat of proletarian unrest, which capitalism constructs as chaotic violence. The cure would be "scientific management" of conflict, coupled with "social engineering" to eliminate the injustices that feed violence (e.g., Luke 1998:57–63). Conservatives could embrace the former, liberals the latter. Who could object? It's all so *zweckrational*, "instrumentally reasonable," as bureaucracy should be.

We don't have stateless societies any more. If the people are on this planet and have no state, they're in a "failed state." Restore order (by force if necessary), ship in the conflict-resolution mavens, we can bring "peace" by the use of violence or the threat of violence: "*Potentially, war can be eliminated and replaced by effective and just conflict management procedures and institutions*" (Fry 2006:262; italics in the original).

But then you need a bureaucracy with enforcement powers. That's where reactionary capitalist America and neofeudal capitalist Malaysia agree and even the old social fascist Soviet Union. And intellectuals like myself rush, as Benedict Anderson and Max Weber said we would, to provide the information that will strengthen the hand of the *zweckrational* bureaucrats. If people like Semai, from whose ranks administrators hardly ever arise, should object? "Scientific managers" and social engineers have, at their backs and out of sight, willy-not-to-know-nilly, the threat of violence.

Most would-be managers and social engineers are fundamentally decent folk. Douglas Fry, who advocates a bureaucratic Final Solution to violence, is one of the most fundamentally decent people I know. People like this, mostly from the post-Christian Western bourgeoisie, don't believe in violence as a disciplinary measure. Most grown-ups, even nasty ones and patriarchal Abrahamic fundamentalists, are not consistently cruel to children. Usually, we're indifferent or even kind. We're not *that* hard to love and trust. But it's not *zweckrational* to let one's subordinates gum up the program, is it? To let children throw snits or "act out" when they need to do or learn what adults know is good for them? When appeals to gentle reason fail, what else is there to do but cause a little pain? Lovingly, maybe. They'll thank you for it later.

So violence ultimately isn't the problem, is it? As two longtime students of violence declare, people hurt each other "because they can" (Gelles and Straus 1988: 17–51). You don't need to have been an abused child to be-

come an abuser. All you need is 1) to be a little stressed out, 2) to have people less powerful than you are *available*, and 3) to be unaware of more
powerful disapproving people watching. Rationalizations, justifications,
and obfuscations help make violence happen, but it happens without
them, too.

The problem is letting some people be more powerful than others. Semai know that: it's stupid to hurt others when you can get hurt doing so.
For thousands of years, almost all human societies recognized the danger
of letting some people have more power than others and took active steps
to maintain equality. Semai still did that in the 1960s. The danger, of
course, comes from the calculus of violence: people are much more likely
to resort to violence when they are the powerful ones because the consequences are much less likely to hurt them. They will tend to reject conflict
resolution techniques, however sophisticated. Inequality breeds violence.
Any schoolchild can tell you that. That's the paradox inherent in bureaucratic "solutions" to violence.

The more or less simultaneous rise of the state, state religion and capitalist mercantilism (the "globalization" of the Neolithic) was a social disaster for most people. Inequality became the rule. Instead of coordination,
you had subordination and superordination. Only marginalized people,
people like Semai, could maintain anything like the old freedoms. For
millennia, peasant revolutionaries in Europe strove to overthrow the ever-
strengthening hierarchies, hearkening back to a vaguely remembered,
idealized, egalitarian past:

> When Adam delved
> And Eve span,
> Who was then
> The gentle-man?

The problem with violent revolution, however, is that it mostly fails, and
when it succeeds, it succeeds only in creating new inequalities. In America today, egalitarians seek to "empower" the oppressed. But all these
struggles reek of "identification with the aggressor." The State is a kind of
cancer that spreads itself everywhere by imperialism or by reproducing itself among previously state-free peoples, whom we now call "failed
states." Overthrowing the State, one state at a time, is impossible. And
states don't "wither away."

Recruitment into the lowest stratum of the state, subjection to alien impersonal institutions of justice, corrodes egalitarianism (chapter 6; Juli,
Williams-Hunt, and Dentan 2008). Competition with other Semai for
scarce resources (like land, which outsider landgrabs make scarce) erodes
community solidarity. The loss of refugia to which one may flee from

quarrels with neighbors or from outside oppression eliminates a safety valve:

> In the past, peasant response to undue exactions or injustice had been flight, but there was no refuge in a peninsula dominated by a single colonial power. (Andaya and Andaya 1982:202)

Flight, the traditional Semai response to oppression, now works against formal local institutions like the *bicaraa'*; for one can flee from Semai society itself, physically or spiritually (chapter 6). Alcohol potentiates violence. Religion, despised by one's non-Semai neighbors, loses its power. The outside world is indifferent now, not murderous. Peaceability falters and fails (chapter 8; Dentan 1995, 2007; Dentan and Williams-Hunt 1999).

Life on the margins of the state, traditional Semai-style society, becomes impossible. Whatever the origins of Semai peaceability, its maintenance depended on a pervasive egalitarianism that was possible only to the degree that Semai could keep away from outsiders and outsiders were willing to let them do so. People can—and probably should—create self-marginalized peaceable enclaves in which egalitarianism can flourish as long as it doesn't threaten state or monied interests, though. It takes a lot of attention to maintaining boundaries (Dentan 1994; Lechner 2003; Niman 1997), and outsiders will always be hostile (Niman 2008)

To minimize violence, protect potential abusers from stress and keep people as equal as you can. Of course, the transition would be rough: as economic change brings some power to women in impoverished and often patriarchal societies, men become more likely to beat them, trying to terrorize them back into traditional deferent submissive behavior (e.g., McClusky 2001). Under egalitarian conditions, frustration in sexual love was the only motive that was likely to motivate Semai to risk the formal and informal penalties that violence could bring, to lose the love of their peers.

What Semai can teach us, if anything, is that "surrender" in the sense I am using the word can be a successful adaptation to the imperialism of the state, state religion, and capitalist globalizing. Caring for children and fostering one's friends also "work" in evolutionary terms: "love" we used to call that before "love" became a four-letter word.

Freedom, I suspect, is utterly negative. Kliy and Melville's Bartleby had it right. If you can't flee, you can at least withdraw your consent. Power depends on consent. The consequences of saying "I prefer not to" can be vicious. Differential power permits, indeed encourages, viciousness. But if you can accept whatever consequences follow your actions or inactions, then you can be free. I think that's how traditional Semai freedom worked. People would act to accomplish their ends, knowing all the time—and *accepting*—that success was not under their control. That's what I've been calling a "surrendered" attitude.

It would help if people would treat striving for power with the fear and contempt it deserves, as Semai do. But the opposite tendency seems to hold in industrialized societies today, nurtured by the constant capitalist generation of new unfulfilled desires and, paradoxically, by the increasing powerlessness of the mass of the people. Instead of rebuilding America's decaying schools, the powers-that-be install surveillance cameras and metal detectors; instead of fostering their children, parents turn the family itself into a "power struggle." Everything is about the bottom line: "winning" and "losing." This obsession is not good for us. It makes it hard for us to learn anything from Semai. And it doesn't make us happy.

So I'm not optimistic:

> I read something once, in the public library, up in St. Charles. It said . . . in your life you end up back where you started, maybe way back when you were little. The difference is you understand it the second time around. But it don't do you no good. (Burke 1996:142)

(Dis)Respect

> Official sources conspire to assure us that everything is OK, that ours is, in fact, the best of all possible worlds, and that it is getting better all the time. . . . Nothing is wrong; the threat has been dealt with; there is nothing to see. . . . What is avoided is the radical price paid (usually by others, willy nilly) in order that those of us who are privileged with the status of participants may go about solving the world's problems. (Redding 1998:21)

But the theory isn't what I'm interested in here. Theories come and go in anthropology. Young scholars seeking jobs have to trash the theories of their elders and peddle new ones, and then along comes another generation to do the same to the new hegemonic ideas. The cumulative part of anthropology so far is not theory but facts, ethnography. Despite the biases in all ethnographic accounts, like the ones I've tried to sketch in this one, we can still learn from old accounts, though we curse the old authors for omitting facts that seem crucial to our new minds, as our heirs will curse us. We can still learn interesting and important things about Scythians from Herodotus and Britons and Germans from Tacitus and about Mongols from Juvaini and Marco Polo. The mere documented existence of peaceable peoples like Semai undermines theories of human nature congenial to American lives (Fry 2004). Ethnographies are mountains and endure; theories are mayflies and don't.

And the basic rule in writing or reading ethnography is "humility," a word cognate with "humus" and "human," from Sanskrit *bhumi*, earth.

We're mud, we humans, earthen wetware. We need to recognize that we're all just mudpeople, that we must not dismiss anyone's life as unworthy of our attention. No one is so despicable or stupid or depraved or pathetic that paying attention to what that person has to say and what that person does "wastes" our time. What we can learn from Semai depends on how willing we are to learn. We needn't claim to be completely open minded. Nobody is, and nobody would believe us. But we need to remember that, as Senator Pat Moynihan used to say, "Nobody knows everything. But everybody knows something."

But being willing isn't hard. I love primary sources, I love listening to people, I love ethnography: that's where you learn things the way you learned as a child, semiconsciously, in context, holistically (to use a much overused word), observations just heaping up until they overwhelm your intellectual categories and you have to admit to yourself that you got everything utterly wrong and have to start sorting and resorting again.

Semai do not exist to teach "us" moral lessons. If we, whoever "we" are, are to draw any lessons from their lives, which are as variegated and ever changing as our own, we must treat them with the same respect we owe each other, as complex individuals joined to each other in complex ways. The simple statement that they traditionally committed fewer acts of physical violence than we do opens the door to layers and layers of complexity. If you're interested in understanding violence and peaceability, you need to take Semai seriously, not as comic-strip primitives. I've tried to do that in this book.

The Semai Achievement

Let's pause a moment and consider the magnitude of the Semai achievement. The title of this book is ambiguous, on purpose. You can read the "overwhelming" as gerund or participle, as grammarians say. Overwhelmed by terrorism, Semai overwhelmed terror. This was a society in which people defined "violence" so broadly that they did not allow themselves the cheap, shrouded cruelties that pervade most people's lives. It was a place where people were ashamed to commit what they defined as "violence," which for them included disrespect, abandonment, and betrayal.

That doesn't mean that they never did commit violence or that they were crucially different from other peoples. The stunning achievement of Semai is not that they worked with better building materials than most people have available nor that they lived in Edenic isolation from the horrors that form the backdrop of most human lives. On the contrary, they took those horrors; added concepts from a stark proto-Saivist religion in which God was brutal, incontinent, and stupid; and transmuted the result into a triumph for the guile and wit of ordinary decent people. And, of course, their solution didn't and doesn't always work.

That's part of what this book is about, how the system of peaceability worked, how it failed, what the stresses were in the system, what the personal costs were. Semai are people as imperfect as you find anywhere, and Semai life is not a quick fix for the problems of violence. Their achievement deserves the more respect because they are *not* "essentially" nonviolent, not better people than anyone else, and still they made the sacrifices that led to peace. One of the great barriers to creating a peaceable society in the Euroamerican world is the attempt to have everything perfect and free. Perfectionism is a sickness, and peace will cost you.

Most Semai don't respect their achievement. It's too closely associated with poverty, misery, terror, and insult. Most Malaysians have never even heard of Semai and accord them therefore the disrespect of ignorance. Of those who have heard of them, most think of them as "naked savages," the Chinese Malaysian phrase for them. To this "naked savagery," people respond according to their personal biases, with pity, contempt, or paternalism. Most Malaysians who know anything about Semai see a backward and pitiful people, living "unprogressive" (*kurang maju*) lives, needing to be awakened (*di-bangunkan*) by state or private developers. There's some contempt in this attitude, and for some people the contempt is all there is. And finally there are a few who see them through the eyes of the environmental movement, as Rousseauvian Noble Savages, an illusion that serious intimacy with the people will destroy. Of the peaceability, all these outsiders see is the timidity and weakness.

And there are Semai with all these attitudes, of course. That's how "double consciousness" and "identification with the oppressor" work. They shield people like Semai from feeling the poverty, misery, terror, and insult. But let's not blame Malays or "Malay culture" for the violent trauma in which Semai nonviolence seems to have originated nor for the more genial violation in which it is ending. Colonialism, internal or external, makes its own demands on peoples, on colonialists and their prey. The ways they respond are similar, everywhere and at all times (Dentan 1997). Their responses aren't morally edifying, but responses to power rarely are. The first thing we humans need to say to ourselves, wherever we live, is what Alain Resnais says of the Nazis at the end of *Night and Fog*, his 1955 documentary, as the camera pans slowly around the wintry death camp at Auschwitz:

> Are their faces different from ours? . . . There are those who sincerely look on these ruins today as if the monster was dead and buried beneath them; those who feign taking hope again as the image fades, as if there were a cure for the

sickness of these camps; those who pretend to believe that all this happened only once, at a certain time and in a certain place; those who refuse to see; who are deaf to the endless cry. (Dentan tr.)

But you, reader, have enough vignettes and information to form your own opinion, the way you would form your opinion of that family that lives across the street. I don't have any suggestion about how you should evaluate the Semai way of life: just that you should be respectful.

CODA

The era of directed change is happening everywhere, jungle and primary forest are becoming targets of the development projects that mankind is launching, directed change will happen, and happen fast, because mankind is always looking for ways to fulfill the needs of their lifestyle. (Blurb on the cover of *Nong Pai* ["New Path"], the house organ of the Jabatan Hal Ehwal Orang Asli, #2, 1991)

This *Nong Pai* text accompanies two pictures, one of an old-style Semai settlement, with scattered houses of various types surrounded by green fields and forests, the other of a "relocation scheme," with a line of look-alike government-issue houses surrounded by mud bulldozed into featurelessness, the landscape of Nkuu' the Destroyer. You want to agree with Kathe Koja (1994:204), the horror writer: "Things can always get worse; and they do." But that would be wrong. Partly.

I don't have anything else to say about Semai peace and violence, I think. The system itself grew out of injustice, and in some ways things are better now. The slave raids have stopped. The old system is falling apart so that it's hard to gather more information about it. Nothing endures, right? Not the earth itself. It's time for a different story. But we can remember, as the Chinese remembered for thousands of years, that

> Once upon a time
> people who knew the Way
> were subtle, spiritual, mysterious, penetrating,
> unfathomable.
>
> Since they're inexplicable
> I can only say what they seemed like:
> Cautious, oh yes, as if wading through a winter river.
> Alert, as if afraid of the neighbors.
> Polite and quiet, like houseguests.
> Elusive, like melting ice. (Laozi, quoted in Le Guin 1997:20)

A collapsing star falls into itself until it reaches a critical diameter called the Schwartzchild radius. At this point, the star can transmit no more information, though the collapse continues, we think. But to an observer, the star appears frozen at the point just before the final descent into what astronomers call a naked singularity.

Writing this, I think of evenings in Malaysia, the sun just gone down, sitting on my house ladder, looking across the valley at the rain forest in the gathering darkness, greens mutating into rich blackness, hearing its white noise, insectile chirrr modulating into something harsher and more staccato, knowing that if I went in, I would be lost:

> We are safe here the war
> is somewhere else the war is
> in our heads but we are safe.
> Safe. The banks open and close
> and open: we are saved. (from "We Know," Goodman 1989:33)

Glossary

Traduttore Traditore (Translators = Traitors)

APPROXIMATE PRONUNCIATION

Semai has many more vowels than English, almost as many as Finnish, so that any approximation of spelling that uses English orthography is merely a rough-and-ready approximation of what Semai sounds like. Moreover, there are over 40 dialects of Semai, so that selection of any particular dialect would be arbitrary. Since this book involves several dialect zones, I have settled on the approximation of spelling that best fits the dialect of the area from which most examples of a particular word come. Thus, because most of the discussion of Nkuu' concerns people on the Tluup, I've chosen that spelling instead of the Perak pronunciation, Ngkuu'. Conversely, because most of the discussion of demons concerns Perak peoples, I've approximated their pronunciation *nyanii'* rather than the Tluup pronunciation, *janii'*.

Stress is on the last syllable. Vowel length is phonemic, also as in Finnish, so that *mnhar* means "meat" and *mnhaar*, "generous." Confusingly, Semai uses similar-sounding but distinct words to refer to similar but distinct categories of things, particularly sounds and smells (with the result that the classification of sounds and odors is so much more complex and nuanced than English that it is almost impossible to translate accurately). As a result, Semai stories—and even conversations—are full of untranslatable wordplay like the Italian axiom that serves as epigraph to this glossary.

a, as in f*a*ther

o, as in r*o*pe but a little shorter

i, as *ee* in s*ee*k

ò, as *ou* in *ou*ght

e, as in b*e*t

u, as *u* in p*u*t; (uu as *oo* in b*oo*t)

v, as *e* in th*e*. (omitted in unstressed [=non-final] syllables)

c, as *tch* in pi*tch*.

apostrophes (') stand for glottal stops, as in Brooklynese "l'il" or "-" in co-operate."

Final –w, as "o" but finishing by closing the lips. Thus, *litaaw* sounds like "leet-OW!"

WORDS AND ACRONYMS OCCURRING OFTEN IN THE TEXT

Asli   See Orang Asli.

Aslian   Pertaining to languages spoken by Orang Asli, q.v.

Bicaraa', becharaa   Noun. From Sanskrit-Malay bicara, "discussion, quarrel, trial," in this book glossed as "town meeting." Familiar in the peace-anthropological literature as *becharaa'*, the spelling adopted by Clayton Robarchek (1979, 1997), who first described the Semai version of this conflict-resolving institution. Semai in the area of formal *bicaraa'* and many peace-anthropologists (e.g., Fry 2000:341–43) regard *bicaraa'* as crucial to Semai peaceability, although Semai outside the *bicaraa'* area seem to live as peaceably as Semai inside. *Bicaraa'* were part of the institutional incorporation of a large set of Semai into the sultanate of Perak at the beginning of the twentieth century (Juli, Williams-Hunt, and Dentan 2009). Like the imposition of conflict-resolution techniques on egalitarian acephalous ("anarchic") societies elsewhere, in other words, whether or not *bicaraa'* improved peaceability, they did facilitate (in this case British) imperialist and (in this case Malay) internal colonialist penetration of lands thitherto belonging to free peoples (in this case Semai). The "pacification" may have been as illusory as the "pacification" by police riot of a group of pacifist anarchists, reported in my hometown newspaper (Niman 2008).

Department of Aborigines   Department set up to control Orang Asli so that they would not support the Communist rebels during the mid-twentieth-century Malaysian Emergency.

Emergency, The. Insurgency, largely by Maoist Chinese, 1948–1960, during which both sides actively terrorized and/or recruited Orang Asli (Dentan 1995; Leary 1995). See also Senoi Praak.

[G]nghaanh   See *tnghaan'*.

Jabatan Hal Ehwal Orang Asli Malay, "Department of Orang Asli Affairs." A renaming of the JOA, which makes it clear that the department runs Orang Asli, not the other way around. It used to control every aspect of Orang Asli life but failed so egregiously at providing education that that function was shifted to other government agencies. After Independence, the Directors General traditionally were Malays from Kelantan, a state associated with radical Muslim ideas, and Islamic missionizing is a major function of the department (Nobuta 2008). Assimilation to the Malay population is its overriding goal. Semai call it, snarkily, *Jual Orang Asli*, "Sell Out Indigenous Peoples" (Nicholas 2000:171), or *Pejabat Gòp*, "the Malay Bureau." Other Orang Asli call it Jabatan Haiwan Orang Asli, *haiwan* being a Malay word for "beasts" (Nobuta 2008:269).

Jabatan Orang Asli. Malay, "Department of Orang Asli"   New name for the Department of Aborigines following Malaysian independence.

JHEOA   *Jabatan Hal Ehwal Orang Asli.*

JOA   See *Jabatan Orang Asli.*

Litaaw   Noun. Nubile pubescent young man without children old enough that the community can be fairly sure that they, and their parents' marriage, will survive. Usually between ten and thirty years old. Stereotypically, vain, irresponsible, oversexed, "daring" (Malay *berani*), and willing to defend Semai women from insult or attack by outsiders (*maay*, q.v.) The title *Bah* is appropriate for *litaaw* and littler boys, although the issuance of identity cards has frozen it in place for many now mature people. To address someone as *Bah* So-and-so suggests that you don't take him very seriously. It is the address form of *mnah*, parent's younger brother (or younger male cousin in the parents generation).[1]

Maay   Noun, pronoun. Generic for "folk," by which I mean entities (including other humans) who live in various dimensions of the cosmos (= have territories, *Inggri'*), and there have their own languages and houses and even assume human form. Thus, "underground folk," *maay kròm tei'*, include as ideal type, the dragon; as subtypes, the regal python, the crocodile, and the giant monitor lizard, *Varanus salvator*; and generically all snakes and lizards (for ideal types in Semai thinking, see Dentan 1970). Together with a geographical feature or ethnonym, *maay* identifies types of people: *maay sraa'*, "hinterland folk" like Semai; *maay Gòp*, Malays (the ethnonym may come from an old word for " enemy"); *maay Tluup*, "Telom River folks." The term connotes people other than oneself and those close to you, people whose concerns don't involve you, so that *hal maay*, "other people's affair," is a phrase people use to dismiss something as of no interest to them. The term "Semai," an "exonym," name given to a people by outsiders, might be cognate.

Mnaleeh Noun. From *'aleeh*, "little girl." Nubile pubescent young woman without children old enough that the community can be fairly sure that they, and their parents' marriage, will survive. Usually between ten and thirty years old. Stereotypically, vain, irresponsible, and over-sexed. The title *Wa'* is appropriate for *mnaleeh* and littler girls, although the issuance of identity cards has frozen it in place for many now mature people. It is the address form of *una'*, parent's younger sister (or younger female cousin in one's parents' generation).*

Orang Asli From Malay, "Aboriginal People." The official generic ethnonym for the indigenous peoples of peninsular Malaysia, most of whom speak or used to speak languages of the Aslian subgroup of the Mon-Khmer branch of Austroasiatic.

Pnalii', pnali' Noun. From Sanskrit-Malay *pali*, "sacred," *pemali*, "taboo" at all times, as opposed to only under certain circumstances. The primary meaning concerns mixing categories, especially of foods, and the cataclysmic cosmic collapse that results (Dentan 1970). It's the Semai equivalent of keeping kosher. See also *rawuuc*. Semai may also use the term in the generic sense of "disgusting" or "ritually dangerous," like *punan* and *trlaac*, q.v.

Punan Noun. In Malay the cognate word, *kempunan*, can mean a tight place, a snare; hence a dilemma or choice of evils; but elsewhere in Malaysia and Indonesia, among people who speak Austronesian (Malayo-Polynesian) languages related to Malay, it refers primarily to re-fusing to share with others, particularly food, and the bad consequences such a refusal brings. The idea is that everyone who is living in a particu-lar area has a right to the local resources: not accepting your share, or not sharing your surplus, puts the "social capital" of the community at risk. Recent studies of the effects of stress (which *punan* could induce or raise) suggest that those predictions are statistically accurate (Dentan 2004). The term may also be used in the generic sense of "taboo" or "ritually defil-ing," like *pnalii'*, q.v.

Raban Malay. "Incoherent," as of drunken speech. Perak Semai some-times use the term to express the Tluup notion of *rawuuc*, q.v.

Rawan Malay. "Mixed," as of rice mixed with vegetables and other sidedishes. Perak Semai sometimes use the term to express the Tluup no-tion of *rawuuc*, q.v.

Rawuuc "Without guidelines, wandering, mistaken, astray." Equivalent to Malay *ta'tentu*, q.v. It may be etymologically connected with Malay *ra-ban* and *rawan*, q.v., and shares some meanings with Malay *tak tentu*, q.v., all words that Perak people tend to use to express the basic idea of *rawuuc*, one of the words that expresses Semai unease about disorderly behavior that seems conducive to cosmic chaos. To get lost and wander around in-stead of staying on the safe path is to walk *rawuuc*. To mix incompatible categories of food and risk *pnalii'* (Dentan 1970) is to eat *rawuuc*. Drunken babbling, which most Semai do not find amusing, is talking *rawuuc*. The word has strongly negative connotations. Also *rawooc*.

Senoi Praak. Sen'oi Praaq From Temiar *sn'ooy praak*, "People of war." Temiar are northern neighbors of Semai; their word for "war" comes from Malay *perang*. Paramilitary group founded in 1957 during the Emergency (q.v.) by then "Adviser on Aborigines" R.O.D. Noone, to recruit Orang Asli as allies in the armed struggle against Maoist insurgents (Jumper 2001; Miller 1960; Mohd. Tap 1990:217; Nobuta 2008:29, 194, 268n17). This grouping played an important part in forming an "Orang Asli" ethnic identity (q.v.) for the diverse and complex indigenous peoples of peninsular Malaysia. It has also been a hotbed of drunkenness, violence, and sexual promiscuity. For example, one of the first murders of the new millennium was by a young *litaaw* (q.v.) who killed a Senoi Praak member who had boasted that he had killed the young man's father by using Malay black magic.

Slamaad Perak Semai. From Arabic-Malay *selamat*, "[God-]blessed, peaceful" Safety, peaceability, calm, quiet, order, clarity, conceived of as the ideal conditions for a happy community. People can maintain *slamaad* by sharing freely; maintaining self-control and a calm demeanor; shunning greed, ambition, envy, and backbiting; and generally behaving in a mutually tolerant and orderly manner. Any offense that upsets the community is also an offense against *slamaad* and may thus incur a separate fine at a town meeting (see *bicaraa'*).

-Sngòòh Verb, Fear, respect.

Snngòòh Noun. From *Sngòòh*, q.v. Fear, fright, caution.

-Srloo' Verb. To put in the right place, thus, for a hunter, to hunt down and kill. [The structure implies a root word *-sloo'*, with which I am not acquainted.]

Srngloo' Noun. The process of *-srloo'*, q.v. A *knah srngloo'* is a "hunting wife," the cool luckiness that allows a hunter to locate and kill game, visualized as a demon lover attracted to the hunter's body; for the relationship to work, both parties must be kept "cool" (a special form of the *halaa'-guniik* relationship). Letting someone down, notably by not showing up for an appointment, is also *srngloo'*, possibly fatal, in the same way that *punan* may be metaphorically a sort of fatal trap.

-Srngòòh Verb. From *Sngòòh*, q.v. Frighten, teach to respect. An important tactic in Semai child rearing, as a way of making children mistrust strangers (*maay*, q.v.) and stick close to home, Teaching "stranger danger" in North America runs along similar lines.

Srnngòòh Noun. The process of *-srngòòh*, q.v.

Ta' tentu Malay. "Not certain, unclear." Semai sometimes use this term as a synonym for *rawuuc*, q.v.

Tnghaan' From Sanskrit *tanha*, "desire, lust." I suspect that [g]*ng-haanh*, q.v., a term I heard far less often, is a dialect variant. Perhaps the term entered Semai from the old Hindu-Buddhist Khmer colony around Bernam in Perak (Bernam = Khmer "Phnom"). On the Tluup, people use it rarely, if ever. The word refers to offenses against social solidarity and *slamaad*, q.v., like failing to share food or failure to mourn the dead. Aside from the fact that the word is of Sanskrit origin, the fact that punitive consequences affect the perpetrator rather than the victim, unlike other Semai prohibitions (*pnalii'*, *srn[g]loo'*, *punan*, q.v.), suggests that the idea originated outside Semai culture, like *tolah*, q.v.

Tolah Noun. From Malay *tulah*. Disrespect and its supposed consequences. For Malays the word occurs mostly in the context of deferring to one's social and political superiors. In the relative egalitarianism of Semai ideology, it pertains mostly to deferring to one's elders and especially to opposite-sexed in-laws in ascending generations. Semai tend to regard respecting one's older biological kinsmen and neighbors as less problematic, perhaps because Semai child rearing involves so much *srnngòòh* by them. But, before they become kinfolk by marriage, one's in-laws are *maay*, q.v., and therefore potentially quite tricky to approach. Tluup people imagine this trickiness largely in sexual terms (as do Malays). You get too intimate with people, you might have sex with them. The Tluup solution is to forbid any contact or to mandate sexual horseplay, so that whatever happens is socialized and thus acceptable. The imagined penalties are also sexualized: vaginal prolapse, inguinal hernia, or genital filiariasis, all of which have the effect of making one's genitals swell to enormous size, not a bad way of representing what happens in one's imagination when one fails to exercise erotic self-control. Aside from the fact that the word is Malay, the fact that punitive consequences affect the violator rather than the victim, unlike other Semai prohibitions (*pnalii'*, *srn[g]loo'*, *punan*, q.v.), suggests that the idea originated outside Semai culture, like *tnghaan'*, q.v.

-Trlaac Verb. From –*lic-laac*, "to wreak devastation, wipe something out, throw a hissy fit"? To bring about cosmic collapse by uproariously losing self-control, as children stereotypically do, so that when children are playing outside, screaming, and laughing, adults (often laughing themselves) will cry, "*Trlaac! Trlaac!*" The adults may attribute the violence of a tropical cyclone to children's stereotypical boisterousness. The term may also be used in the generic sense of "disgusting" or "ritually dangerous," like *pnalii'*, q.v.

Bibliography

Akiya [Mahat Cina]. 2007. *Perang Sangkil*. Batu Caves, Selangor, Malaysia: PTS Fortuna.

Alland, Alexander. 1981 *To Be Human: An Introduction to Anthropology*. New York: John Wiley and Sons.

Anagnost, Ann S. 1994. "The Politics of Ritual Displacement." In *Asian Visions of Authority: Religion and the Modern States of East and Southeast Asia*, edited by Charles F. Keyes, Laurel Kendall, and Helen Hardacre (221–54). Honolulu: University of Hawaii Press.

Andaya, Barbara Watson, and Leonard Y. Andaya. 1982. *A History of Malaysia*. London: Macmillan.

Anonymous. 1908. *Hikayat Hang Tuah*. Singapore: Malay Literature Series.

Arata, Catalina M. 1999. "Coping with Rape: The Roles of Prior Sexual Abuse and Attributions of Blame." *Journal of Interpersonal Violence* 14: 62–78.

Banks, Russell. 1989. *Affliction*. New York: HarperPerennial.

Barks, Coleman, ed. and trans. 2001. *The Glance: Rumi's Songs of Soul Meeting*. New York: Penguin Compass.

Barks, Coleman, John Moyne, A. J. Arberry, and Reynold Nicholson. 1995. *The Essential Rumi*. San Francisco: Harper.

Bates, Daniel G. 1998. *Human Adaptive Strategies: Ecology, Culture, and Politics*. Boston: Allyn and Bacon.

Bateson, Gregory. 1958. *Naven*. Stanford: Stanford University Press.

Belloc, Hilaire. 1950 [1940]. *Selected Cautionary Verses*. Harmondsworth: Penguin.

Berger, John. 1975. "Historical Afterword." In *Pig Earth* (195–213). New York: Pantheon.

Blake, William. 1994. *The Works of William Blake*. Ware: Wordsworth Editions.

Bly, Robert, ed. and trans. 1981. *Selected Poems of Rainer Maria Rilke*. New York: Harper and Row.

Brite, Poppy Z. 1996. "Introduction: The Consolations of Horror." In *The Nightmare Factory*, by Thomas Ligotti. New York: Carroll and Graf.

Brodsky, Joseph. 1997. *On Grief and Reason: Essays*. New York: Farrar, Straus and Giroux.

Brown, C. C. 1989 [1951]. *Malay Sayings*. Singapore: Graham Brash.

Brown, Karen McCarthy. 1991. *Mama Lola: A Voudou Priestess in Brooklyn*. Berkeley: University of California Press.

Burke, Edmund. 1982 [1971]. "Letter to a Member of the National Assembly." In *A Portable Conservative Reader*, edited by Russell Kirk (47–48). Harmondsworth: Viking Penguin.

Burke, James Lee. 1996. *Cadillac Jukebox*. New York: Hyperion.

———. 1999. *Heartwood*. New York: Dell.

Cady, John F. 1964. *Southeast Asia: Its Historical Development*. New York: McGraw-Hill.

Cameron, John. 1865. *Our Tropical Possessions in Malayan India: Being a Descriptive Account of Singapore, Penang, Province Wellesley, and Malacca; Their Peoples, Products, Commerce, and Government*. London: Smith, Elder and Co.

Card, Claudia. 1996. "Rape as a Weapon of War." *Hypatia* 11, no. 4 (special issue on Women and Violence, Bat Ami Bar On, ed.): 5–18.

Carey, Iskander Yusof. 1976. *Orang Asli: The Aboriginal Tribes of Peninsular Malaysia*. Kuala Lumpur: Oxford University Press.

Carper, Thomas. 1991. "Cosmos." In *Fiddle Lane*. Baltimore: Johns Hopkins University Press.

Chua, Lawrence. 1998. *Gold by the Inch*. New York: Grove Press.

Clastres, Pierre. 1989 [1977]. "What Makes Indians Laugh." In *Society and the State: Essays in Political Anthropology*, edited by Pierre Clastres, translated by Robert Hurley and Abe Stern (129–50). New York: Zone Books.

Clemons, Walter. 1993. "Divas to Die For." Review of *The Queen's Throat: Opera, Homosexuality, and the Mystery of Desire*, by Wayne Koestenbaum. *New York Times Book Review*, 28 February, 14.

Cohen, Leonard. 1997. "Closing Time." In *More Best of Leonard Cohen* (Audio CD, Sony).

Cook, Michael, Susan Mineka, Bonnie Wolkenstein, and Karen Laitsch. 1985. "Observational Conditioning of Snake Fear in Unrelated Rhesus Monkeys." *Journal of Abnormal Psychology* 94, no. 4: 591–610.

Danaraj, A. G. S. 1964. *Mysticism in Malaya*. Singapore: Asian Publishing.

de Waal, Frans. 1996. *Good Natured: The Origins of Right and Wrong in Humans*. Cambridge, Mass.: Harvard University Press.

Dentan, Robert Knox. 1967. "The Response to Intellectual Impairment among the Semai." *American Journal of Mental Deficiency* 71: 764–66.

———. 1968. "Semai Response to Mental Aberration." *Bijdragen tot de Taal-, Land-, en Volkenkunde* 124: 135–58.

———. 1970. Labels and Rituals in Semai Classification. *Ethnology* 9: 16–25.

———. 1978. "Notes on Childhood in a Nonviolent Context: The Semai Case." In *Learning Nonaggression: The Experience of Non-Literate Societies*, edited by Ashley Montague (94–143). London: Oxford University Press.

———. 1979. *The Semai: A Nonviolent People of Malaya.* New York: Holt, Rinehart and Winston.

———. 1988. "Butterflies and Bug-Hunters: Dreams and Reality, Reality and Dreams." *Psychiatric Journal of the University of Ottawa* 13, no. 2: 51–59.

———. 1989. "How Semai Made Music for Fun." *Echology,* no. 3, 100–120

———. 1992. "The Rise, Maintenance, and Destruction of Peaceable Polity: A Preliminary Essay in Political Ecology." In *Aggression and Peacefulness in Humans and Other Primates,* edited by James Silverberg and Patrick Gray (214–70). New York: Oxford University Press.

———. 1993a. "A Genial Form of Ethnicide." *Daybreak,* autumn, 13, 18–19.

———. 1993b. "A Confessional and Memorial of Orang Asli." In *Orang Asli: An Appreciation,* edited by Hood Salleh, Hassan Mat Nor, and Kamaruddin M. Said. Kuala Lumpur: International Convention Secretariat, Prime Minister's Department.

———. 1994. "Surrendered Men: Peaceable Enclaves in the Post Enlightenment West." In *The Anthropology of Peace and Nonviolence,* edited by Leslie E. Sponsel and Thomas Gregor (69–108). Boulder, Colo.: Lynne Rienner.

———. 1995. "Bad Day at Bukit Pekan." *American Anthropologist* 97: 225–50.

———. 1997. "The Persistence of Received Truth: How the Malaysian Ruling Class Constructs Orang Asli." In *Indigenous Peoples and the State: Politics, Land, and Ethnicity in the Malaysian Peninsula and Borneo,* edited by Robert Winzeler (98–134). Monograph 46, Yale University Southeast Asia Studies. New Haven, Conn.: Yale University Southeast Asia Studies.

———. 1999. "Spotted Doves at War: The Praak Sangkill." *Asian Folklore Studies* 58, no. 2: 397–434.

———. 2000a. "This Is Passion and Where It Goes: Despair and Suicide among Semai, a Nonviolent People of West Malaysia." *Moussons* 101: 31–56.

———. 2000b. "Ceremonies of Innocence and the Lineaments of Ungratified Desire." *Bijdragen tot de Taal-, Land- en Volkenkunde* 156: 193–232.

———. 2001a. "Ambivalence in Child Training by the Semai of Peninsular Malaysia and Other Peoples." *Crossroads: An Interdisciplinary Journal of Southeast Asian Studies* 15: 31–56.

———. 2001b. "Semai-Malay Ethnobotany: Hindu Influences on the Trade in Sacred Plants, Ho Hiang." In *Minority Cultures of Peninsular Malaysia: Survivals of Indigenous Heritage,* edited by Razha Rashid and Wazir Jahan Karim (173–86). Penang: Academy of Social Sciences.

———. 2001c. "A Vision of Modernization: An Article on a Drawing by Bah Rmpent, Child of the Sengoi Semai, a Traditionally Nonviolent People of the Malaysian Peninsula." *Journal of Anthropology and Humanism* 26, no. 1: 1–12.

———. 2002a. "Against the Kingdom of the Beast: An Introduction to Semai Theology, Pre-Aryan Religion and the Dynamics of Abjection." In *Tribal Communities in the Malay World: Historical, Cultural and Social Perspectives,* edited by Geoffrey Benjamin and Cynthia Lau (206–36). Leiden: International Institute for Asian Studies and Singapore: Institute of Southeast Asian Studies.

———. 2002b. "Disreputable Magicians, the Dark Destroyer, and the Trickster Lord." *Asian Anthropology* 1: 153–94.

———. 2004. "Cautious, Alert, Polite, and Elusive: The Semai of Central Peninsular Malaysia." in *Keeping the Peace: Conflict Resolution and Peaceful Societies around the World*, edited by Graham Kemp and Douglas P. Fry (167–84). New York: Routledge.

———. 2006. "How the Androgynous Bird God Brought Agriculture to Semai of West Malaysia: Discipline, Hard Work and Subordination to the Cycle of Time." In *Les Messagers divins/Aspects esthétiques et symboliques des oiseaux en Asie du Sud-Est. Divine Messengers/Bird Symbolism and Aesthetics in Southeast Asia*, edited by Pierre Le Roux and Bernard Sellato (295–355). Aix-en-Provence: Presse de l'Universite de Provence; Paris: Editions Seven Orients.

———. 2007. "Arifin in the Iron Cap." In *Southeast Asian Lives: Personal Narratives and Historical Experience*, edited by Roxana Helen Waterson (181–220). Singapore: Singapore University Press; Athens: Ohio University Press.

———. 2008. "Recent Studies on Violence: What's In and What's Out." *Reviews in Anthropology* 37, no. 1: 1–27.

Dentan, Robert Knox, and Ong Hean Chooi. 1995. "Stewards of the Green and Beautiful World: A Preliminary Report on Semai Arboriculture and Its Policy Implications." In *Dimensions of Tradition and Development in Malaysia*, edited by Rokiah Talib and Tan Chee Beng (53–124). Petaling Jaya: Pelanduk.

Dentan, Robert Knox, Kirk Michael Endicott, Alberto G. Gomes, and M. Barry Hooker. 1997. *Malaysia and the Original People: A Case Study of the Impact of Development on Indigenous Peoples*. Boston: Allyn and Bacon.

Dentan, Robert Knox, and Anthony Williams-Hunt. 1999. "Untransfiguring Death: A Case Study of Rape, Drunkedness, Development and Homicide in an Apprehensive Void." *RIMA: Review of Indonesian and Malaysian Affairs* 33, no. 1: 17–65.

Devahuti, D. 1965. *India and Ancient Malaya (from the Earliest Times to circa A.D. 1400)*. Singapore: Eastern Universities Press.

Dingley, James. 2001. "The Bombing of Omagh, 15 August 1998: The Bombers, Their Tactics, Strategy, and Purpose behind the Incident." *Studies in Conflict and Terrorism* 24, no. 6: 451–65.

DiPiero, W. S. 1990. "Gulls on Dumps." In *The Dog Star*. Amherst: University of Massachusetts Press, 1990.

Donne, John. 1947 [1624]. "Meditations XVII (from Devotions upon Emergent Occasions)." In *The Literature of England: An Anthology and a History*, vol. 1, edited by George B. Woods, Homer A. Watt, and George K. Anderson (592–93). Chicago: Scott, Foresman.

Douglas, Sheila, ed. 1987. *The King of the Black Art and Other Folk Tales*. Aberdeen: Aberdeen University Press.

Du Bois, W. E. B. 1979 [1903]. *The Souls of Black Folk: Essays and Sketches*. New York: Dodd.

———. 1992 [1935]. *Black Reconstruction in America*. New York: Atheneum.

Dunn, Stephen. 2004. *The Insistence of Beauty: Poems*. New York: Norton.

Dutton, Don, and Susan Painter. 1981. "Traumatic Bonding: The Development of Emotional Attachments in Battered Women and Other Relationships of Intermittent Abuse." *Victimology* 6, no. 1: 139–55.

Edmondson, Aimee. 2001. "Spare the Rod? Not Here, Most Agree." *The Commercial Appeal* (Memphis, Tenn.), June 3.

Elsass, Peter. 1992. *Strategies for Survival: The Psychology of Cultural Relations in Ethnic Minorities*. Translated by Fran Hopenwasser. New York: New York University Press.

Evans, Ivor H. N. 1923. *Studies in Religion, Folk-Lore and Custom in British North Borneo and the Malay Peninsula*. London: Frank Cass.

Fanon, Frantz. 1968 [1961]. *The Wretched of the Earth*. New York: Grove Press,.

Fei, Hsiao-Tung (Xiaotong). 1980. "Ethnic Identification in China." *Social Sciences in China* 1: 94–107.

Feiffer, Jules. 1995. *Introduction to Franz Kafka and Peter Kuper, Give It Up! and Other Short Stories*. New York: Comics Lit.

Feldman, Allen. 1991. *Formations of Violence: The Narrative of the Body and Political Terror in Northern Ireland*. Chicago: University of Chicago Press.

Forbes, Henry O. 1885. *A Naturalist's Wanderings in the Eastern Archipelago: A Narrative of Travel and Exploration from 1878 to 1883*. New York: Harper and Brothers.

Freeman, Derek. 1968. "Thunder, Blood and the Nicknaming of God's Creatures." *Psychoanalytic Quarterly* 37, no. 3: 353–99.

Fry, Douglas P. 2000. "Conflict Management in Cross-Cultural Perspective." In *Natural Conflict Resolution*, edited by Filippo Aureli and Frans B. M. de Waal (334–51). Berkeley: University of California Press.

———. 2004. "Conclusion: Learning from Peaceful Societies." In *Keeping the Peace: Conflict Resolution and Peaceful Societies around the World*, edited by Graham Kemp and Douglas Fry (185–204). New York: Routledge.

———. 2006. *The Human Potential for Peace: An Anthropological Challenge to Assumptions about War and Violence*. New York: Oxford University Press.

Geh, Lida. 1993. "No More Than Tenants at Will?" *Sunday Star*, June 20.

Gelles, Richard J., and Murray A. Straus. 1998. *Intimate Violence*. New York: Simon and Schuster.

Gellner, Ernest. 1988. "Trust, Cohesion and Social Order." In *Trust: Making and Breaking Cooperative Relations*, edited by Diego Gambetta (142–57). London: Blackwell.

Gomes, Alberto. 2004. *Looking for Money: Capitalism and Modernity in an Orang Asli Village*. Subang Jaya, Malaysia: Center for Orang Asli Concerns and Melbourne: Trans Pacific Press.

Gonda, J. 1952. *Sanskrit in Indonesia*. The Hague: Oriental Bookshop.

Goodman, Mitchell. 1989. *More Light: Selected Poems*. Brunswick, Me.: Dog Ear Press.

Goonan, Kathleen Ann. 1994. *Queen City Jazz*. New York: Tor.

Graeber, David. 2007a. "Turning Modes of Production Inside Out: Or, Why Capitalism Is a Transformation of Slavery (Short Version)." In *Possibilities: Essays on Hierarchy, Rebellion, and Desire*, by David Graeber (85–112). Oakland, Calif.: AK Press.

———. 2007b. "Oppression." In *Possibilities: Essays on Hierarchy, Rebellion, and Desire*, by David Graeber (255–98). Oakland, Calif.: AK Press.

Grossman, David. 2001. "Living under the Threat: How Fear Kills the Soul." *The Age* (Melbourne), September 27.

Gray, John. 1998. *False Dawn: The Delusions of Global Capitalism.* New York: New Press.

Hacker, Barton C. 2004. "Fortunes of War: From Primitive Warfare to Nuclear Policy in Anthropological Thought." In *Cultural Shaping of Violence: Victimization, Escalation, Response,* edited by Myrdene Anderson (147–64). West Lafayette, Ind.: Purdue University Press.

Hansen, Marcus Lee. 1966 [1938]. "The Third Generation." In *Children of the Uprooted,* edited by Oscar Handlin (255–71). New York: George Braziller.

Harms, Erik. 2004–2005. "Something's Funny in Saigon: Mr. Westerner, Misrecognition and the Missed Joke." An Anthropological Comedy of Errors. Cornell: *South East Asia Program Bulletin,* winter/spring, 12–15.

Harrison, H. S. 1929. *War and the Chase: A Handbook of the Collection of Weapons of Savage, Barbaric and Civilised Peoples* (2nd ed.). London: London City Council.

Hasan Mat Nor. 1989. "Pengumpulan Semula Orang Asli di Betau: Satu Penelitian Regkas." *Akademika* 35: 97–112.

Hooper, Chloe. 2002. *A Child's Book of True Crime.* New York: Scribner.

Hoskins, Janet. 1996. "Introduction." In *Headhunting and the Sociological Imagination in Southeast Asia* (1–49). Stanford, Calif.: Stanford University Press.

Inglis, Fred. 1993. *Cultural Studies.* Oxford: Blackwell.

James, William. 1997 [1902]. "The Varieties of Religious Experience." In *Selected Writings,* edited by Robert Coles (23–549). New York: Book of the Month Club.

Juli Edo. 1990. "Tradisi Lisan Masyarakat Semai." *Monograf Fakulti Sains Kemasyarakatan dan Kemanusiaan* 16. Bangi: Universiti Kebangsaan Malaysia.

———. 1998. "Claiming Our Ancestors' Land: An Ethnohistorical Study of Seng-oi Land Rights in Perak Malaysia." PhD diss., Australian National University.

———. 2007. "Indigenous Laws and Decision-Making among the Orang Asli of Malaysia." Paper presented at the annual meeting of the American Anthropological Association, Washington, D.C., 28 November.

Juli Edo and R. K. Dentan. 2008. "Schooling vs. Education, Hidden vs. Overt Curricula: Ways of Thinking about Schools, Economic Development and Putting the Children of the Poor to Work." *Moussons* 12 (in press).

Juli Edo, Anthony Williams-Hunt, and R. K. Dentan. 2009. "Surrender, Peace-keeping and Internal Colonialism." *Bijdragen tot de Taal-, Land- en Volkenkunde* 165, no. 1 (in press).

Jumper, Roy Davis Linville. 1997. *Power and Politics: The Story of Malaysia's Orang Asli.* Lanham, Md.: University Press of America.

———. 2001. *Death Waits in the Dark: The Senoi Praaq, Malaysia's Killer Elite.* London: Greenwood Press.

Karim, Wazir Jahan. 2001. "Constructing Emotions and World of the Orang Asli." In *Minority Cultures of Peninsular Malaysia: Survivals of Indigenous Heritage,* edited by Razha Rashid and Wazir Jahan Karim (13–26). Penang: Academy of Social Sciences.

Khoo Boo Teik. 2008a. "Conquering and Vulnerable." *Aliran Monthly* 28, no. 5: 2, 4–6.

———. 2008b. "Anwar Ibrahim and the Experience of Defeat." *Aliran Monthly* 28, no. 5: 7–11.

Kleinman, Arthur, and Byron Goods, eds. 1985. *Culture and Depression: Studies in the Anthropology and Cross-Cultural Psychiatry of Affect and Disorder*. Berkeley: University of California Press.

Koja, Kathe. 1991. *The Cipher*. New York: Dell.

———. 1994. *Strange Angels*. New York: Bantam Doubleday Dell.

———. 1996. *Kink: A Novel*. New York: Holt.

Kozol, Jonathan. 1995. *Amazing Grace: The Lives of Children and the Conscience of a Nation*. New York: HarperCollins.

Kristeva, Julia. 1982. *Powers of Horror: An Essay on Abjection*. Translated by Leon S. Roudiez. New York: Columbia University Press.

Kristofferson, Kris. 2004. "Me and Bobby Magee." *The Essential Kris Kristofferson*. Sony.

Kronman, Anthony T. 1995. "Amor Fati (The Love of Fate)." *University of Toronto Law Journal* 45: 163–78.

Laderman, Carol. 1994. "The Embodiment of Symbols and the Acculturation of the Anthropologist." In *Embodiment and Experience: The Existential Ground of Culture and Self* (183–97). Cambridge Studies in Medical Anthropology, no. 2. Cambridge: Cambridge University Press.

Larkin, Philip. 1974. "This Be the Verse." In *High Windows*. New York: Farrar, Straus and Giroux.

Lat. 1977. *Lots of Lat*. Kuala Lumpur: Berita Publishing.

Leary, John D. 1995 *Violence and the Dream People: The Orang Asli in the Malayan Emergency, 1948–1960*. Athens: Ohio University Center for International Studies.

Le Guin, Ursula K. (1998) *Lao Tzu Tao Te Ching: A New English Version*. Boston: Shambhala.

Lechner, Thomas M. 2003. "Surrender without Subordination: Peace and Equality in Alcoholics Anonymous." PhD diss., State University of New York at Buffalo. http://sites.google.com/site/drthomaslechner.

Leenhardt, G. 1937. *Do Kamo*. Paris: Gallimard.

Luke, Brian. 1998. "Violent Love: Hunting, Heterosexuality and the Erotics of Men's Predation." *Feminist Studies* 2, no. 3: 627–53.

Lye Tuck-Po. 2004. *Changing Pathways: Forest Degradation and the Batek of Pahang, Malaysia*. Lanham, Md.: Rowman & Littlefield.

Macdonald, Charles J.-H. 2008. "Order against Harmony: Are Humans Always Social?" *Anthropologi: Journal of the Finnish Anthropological Society* 33, no. 2: 5–21.

Mason, Lisa. 1990. *Arachne*. New York: Avon.

Maxwell, Allen R. 1996. "Headtaking and the Consolidation of Political Power in the Early Brunei State." In *Headhunting and the Social Imagination in Southeast Asia*, edited by Janet Hoskins (92–126). Stanford, Calif.: Stanford University Press.

McClusky, Laura J. 2001."*Here, Our Culture Is Hard*": *Stories of Domestic Violence from a Mayan Community in Belize*. Austin: University of Texas Press.

McElwee, Patricia. 2004. "Becoming Socialist or Becoming Kinh? Government Policies for Ethnic Minorities in the Socialist Republic of Vietnam." In *Civilizing the*

Margins: Southeast Asian Government Policies for the Development of Minorities, edited by Christopher R. Duncan (182–213). Ithaca, N.Y.: Cornell University Press.

McGarrell, Edmund F., Andrew L. Giacomazzi, and Quint C. Thurman. 1997. "Neighborhood Disorder, Integration and the Fear of Crime." *Justice Quarterly* 14, no. 3: 479–500.

McNair, J. F. A. 1972. *Perak and the Malays*. Kuala Lumpur: Oxford University Press.

Means, Gordon P., ed. N.d. *The Sengoi: An Aboriginal Tribe of the Malay Peninsula*. Unpublished videocassette (http://www.keene.edu/library/orangasli.cfm).

Miller, Harry. 1960. "The Fighting Senoi." *Straits Times Annual for 1960*, 17–19.

Melville, Herman. 1974 [1853]. "Bartleby the Scrivener." In *The American Tradition in Literature*, edited by Sculley Bradley, Richard Croom Beatty, G. Hudson Long, and George Perkins (901–33). New York: Grosset and Dunlap.

———. 1989 [1851]. *Moby Dick*. Pleasantville, N.Y.: Reader's Digest.

Mills, L. A. 1925. "British Malaya 1824–67." *Journal of the Malayan Branch, Royal Asiatic Society* 33, no. 3: 1–424.

Mineka, Susan, M. Davidson, Michael Cook, and R. Keir. 1984. "Observational Conditioning of Snake Fear in Rhesus Monkeys." *Journal of Abnormal Psychology* 93: 355–72.

Mohd. Tap bin Salleh. 1990. "An Examination of Development Planning among the Rural Orang Asli of West Malaysia." PhD diss., University of Bath.

Morgenstern, Naomi. 1997. "Mother's Milk and Sister's Blood: Trauma and the Neoslave Narrative." *Differences: A Journal of Feminist Cultural Studies* 8, no. 2: 101–26.

Mosby, Steve. 2003. *The Third Person: A Journey into the Heart of Darkness*. London: Orion Books.

Moyne, John, and Coleman Barks, eds. and trans. 1984. *Open Secret: Versions of Rumi*. Putney, Vt.: Threshold Books.

———. 1986. *Unseen Rain: Rubais of Rumi*. Putney, Vt.: Threshold Books.

Murray, Stephen O. 1997. "The Will Not to Know: Islamic Accommodations to Male Homosexuality." In *Islamic Homosexualities: Culture, History and Literature*, edited by Will Roscoe and Stephen O. Murray (14–54). New York: New York University Press.

Nagata, Shuichi. 1995. "Decline of Rituals among the Orang Asli of a Resettlement Community of Kedah, Malaysia." Paper presented at the annual meeting of the American Anthropological Association, Washington, D.C., 19 November.

———. 2004. "Leadership in a Resettlement Village of the Orang Asli in Kedah, Malaysia." In *Leadership, Justice and Politics at the Grassroots*, edited by A. R. Walker. *Contributions to Southeast Asian Ethnography* 9: 95–126.

Nah, Alice. 2004 "Negotiating Orang Asli Identity in Postcolonial Malaysia: Beyond Being 'Not Quite/Not Malay.'" *Social Identities* 9: 511–34.

Nicholas, Colin. 1990. "In the Name of the Semai? The State and Semai Society in Peninsular Malaysia." In *Tribal Peoples and Development in Southeast Asia*, edited by Lim Teck Ghee and Alberto G. Gomes (12–36). Kuala Lumpur: Jabatan Anthropologi dan Sosiologi, Universiti Malaya.

———. 1993. "We Need to Reciprocate." In *Orang Asli: An Appreciation*, edited by Hood Sellah, Hassan Mat Nor, and Kamruddin M. Said (41–48). Kuala Lumpur: International Convention Secretariat, Prime Minister's Department.

———. 1994. "Pathway to Dependence: Commodity Relations and the Dissolution of Semai Society." *Monash Papers on Southeast Asia*, no. 33. Clayton, Victoria: Centre of Southeast Asian Studies, Monash Studies.

———. 2000. *The Orang Asli and the Contest for Resources: Indigenous Politics, Development and Identity in Peninsular Malaysia*. Kuala Lumpur: Center for Orang Asli Concerns [COAC] and International Work Group for Indigenous Affairs [IWGIA].

Nicholas, Colin, Sevan Doraisamy, Rizuan Tempeh, Tijah Yok Chopil, and Ali Kuchi. 2003. *The Orang Asli and Local Government: History, Present Situation and Suggestions for Improvement*. Subang Jaya: Center for Orang Asli Concerns.

Niman, Michael. 1997. *People of the Rainbow: A Nomadic Utopia*. Knoxville: University of Tennessee Press.

———. 2008. "Getting a Grip. Weirdos Riot: What's Wrong with the Buffalo News?" *Artvoice* 7, no. 29: 4–5.

Nobuta Toshihiro. 2008. *Living on the Periphery: Development and Islamization among the Orang Asli*. Kyoto: Kyoto University Press; Melbourne: Trans Pacific Press.

Noone, R. O. D. 1961. *Communist Subversion of the Hill Tribes (Lessons Learned during the Emergency in Malaya)*. Mimeograph, HQ Senoi Pra'ak.

Noor, Farish A. 1999. "Hobbes' Leviathan Revisited: An Analysis of Power and Authority in the Framework of the Centralized Malaysian State." *The Framework of the Centralized Malaysian State* (http://www.freemalaysia.com), 4 March.

———. 2002. "Feudalism's Economy of Excessive Violence." In *The Other Malaysia: Writings on Malaysia's Subaltern History* (115–18). Kuala Lumpur: Silverfish.

Nordstrom, Carolyn. 1997. *A Different Kind of War Story*. Philadelphia: University of Pennsylvania Press.

———. 2004. *Shadows of War: Violence, Power and International Profiteering in the Twenty-First Century*. Berkeley: University of California Press.

Norton, G. Ron, Bryan Harrison, Jean Hauch, and Linda Rhodes. 1985. "Characteristics of People with Infrequent Panic Attacks." *Journal of Abnormal Psychology* 94, no. 2: 216–21.

Oates, Joyce Carol. 1978. "Happy Birthday." In *Women Whose Lives Are Food, Men Whose Lives Are Money: Poems of Joyce Carol Oates* (53). Baton Rouge: Louisiana University Press.

———. 1989. *American Appetites*. New York: E. P. Dutton.

Ondaatje, Michael. 1997. *The Collected Works of Billy the Kid; Running in the Family; In the Skin of a Lion; The Cinnamon Peeler*. New York: Quality Paperback Book Club.

Otterbein, Keith O. 2004. *How War Began*. College Station: Texas A&M University Press.

"Pak Sanno." 1998. "UMNO—Unfettered Materialism New Oligarchy?" E-mail correspondence, 24 December.

Parry, Richard Lyon. 1998. "What Young Men Do." *Granta* 62: 83–123.

Peluso, Nancy Lee. 1996. "Fruit Trees and Family Trees in an Anthropogenic For-
    est: Ethics of Access, Property Zones, and Environmental Change in Indonesia."
    Comparative Studies in Society and History 38: 510–48.
Peterson, Christopher, Steven F. Maier, and Martin P. Seligman 1993. *Learned Help-
    lessness: A Theory for the Age of Personal Control*. New York: Oxford University
    Press.
Pollock, Donald. 1993. "Review of *Desire and Craving: A Cultural Theory of Alco-
    holism*, by Pertii A. Lasuutari." *Social Science and Medicine* 38, no. 10: 1471–73.
Pollack, William. 1999. *Real Boys: Rescuing Our Sons from the Myths of Boyhood*. New
    York: Henry Holt.
Polunin, Ivan. 1988. *Plants and Flowers of Malaysia*. Singapore: Times Editions.
Prosser, Maria. 2000. "'It's Only Someone Who's Been through It That Under-
    stands': Social Constructions and Personal Realities of Domestic Violence."
    Master's thesis, State University of New York at Buffalo.
Razha Rashid. 1995. "Introduction." In *Indigenous Minorities of Peninsular Malaysia:
    Selected Issues and Ethnographies*, edited by Razha Rashid and Wazir Jahan Karim
    (1–17). Kuala Lumpur: Intersocietal and Scientific Sdn. Bhd.
Razha Rashid and Wazir Jahan Karim, eds. 1995. *Indigenous Minorities of Peninsu-
    lar Malaysia: Selected Issues and Ethnographies*. Kuala Lumpur: Intersocietal and
    Scientific Sdn. Bhd.
———. 2001. *Minority Cultures of Peninsular Malaysia: Survivals of Indigenous Her-
    itage*. Penang: Academy of Social Sciences (AKASS).
Redding, Arthur F. 1998. *Raids on Human Consciousness: Writing, Anarchism and Vi-
    olence*. Columbia: University of South Carolina Press.
Resnais, Alain, director. 1955. *Night and Fog*.
Rice, Stan. 1995. *Fear Itself*. New York: Knopf.
Rilke, Rainer Maria. 1960. *Sonnets to Orpheus*. Translated by C. F. MacIntyre. Berke-
    ley: University of California Press.
Robarchek, Clayton A. 1977. "Frustration, Aggression and the Nonviolent Semai."
    American Ethnologist 4, no. 4: 762–79.
———. 1979. "Conflict, Emotion, and Abreaction: Resolution of Conflict among the
    Semai Senoi." *Ethos* 7: 104–23.
———. 1997. "A Community of Interests: Semai Conflict Resolution." In *Cultural
    Variation in Conflict Resolution: Alternatives to Violence*, edited by D. P. Fry and K.
    Björkvist (51–58). Mahwah, N.J.: Lawrence Erlbaum Associates.
Robarchek, Clayton A., and Carole J. Robarchek. 1995. "'They Who Eat Our
    Souls': Animism and Ethics in Semai Religion." Paper presented at the annual
    meeting of the American Anthropological Association, Washington, D.C., No-
    vember.
Rosenthal, M. L., ed. 1962. *Selected Poems and Two Plays of William Butler Yeats*. New
    York: Macmillan.
Royce, J. N.d. "Play in Violent and Non-Violent Cultures." Unpublished manu-
    script.
Rumi, Jalaludin. 2001. *The Soul of Rumi: A New Collection of Ecstatic Poems*. Transla-
    tions, introductions, and notes by Coleman Barks et al. New York: Harper-
    Collins.

Sampson, Robert J., Stephen W. Raudenbush, and Felton Earls. 1997. "Neighbor-hoods and Violent Crime: A Multilevel Study of Collective Efficacy." *Science* 227: 918–24.

Schelling, Andrew. 1991. *Dropping the Bow: Poems from Ancient India.* Seattle: Broken Moon Press.

Shorto, H. L. 1971. *A Dictionary of the Mon Inscriptions from the Sixth to the Sixteenth Century Incorporating Materials Collected by the late C.O. Blagden.* London Oriental Series 24. London: Oxford University Press.

Skeat, Walter William. 1900. *Malay Magic.* London: Macmillan.

Skeat, Walter William, and Charles Otto Blagden. 1906. *Pagan Races of the Malay Peninsula.* London: Frank Cass.

Steinmetz, Suzanne K. 1971. "Occupation and Physical Punishment: A Response to Straus." *Journal of Marriage and Family* 2: 664-665.

Straits Times. 1998. "Teachers Fight Shy of Schools for Orang Asli." *New Straits Times,* 4 July.

Straub, Peter. 2004. *In the Night Room.* New York: HarperCollins.

Swettenham, Frank A. 1880. "From Perak to Slim and down the Slim and Bernam Rivers." *Journal of the Straits Branch of the Royal Asiatic Society* 5: 51–68.

Tacitus. A.D. 98. *Agricola.* Manuscript.

Tarn, Nathaniel. 1991. *Views from the Weaving Mountain: Selected Essays in Poetics and Anthropology,* Albuquerque: College of Arts and Sciences, University of New Mexico.

Thompson, Edward Palmer. 1993. *Witness against the Beast: William Blake and the Moral Law.* New York: New Press.

Thucydides. 1951. *History of the Peloponnesian War.* Translated by Charles Smith. Cambridge Mass.: Harvard University Press.

Watson, Lyall. 1995. *Dark Nature: A Natural History of Evil.* New York: HarperCollins.

Wilkinson, Richard J. 1971a [1920]. "Notes on Negri Sembilan." In *Papers on Malay Subjects,* edited by R. J. Wilkinson (227–321). Kuala Lumpur: Oxford University Press.

———. 1971b [1911]. "A History of the Peninsular Malays, with Chapters on Perak and Selangor." In *Papers on Malay Subjects,* 3rd rev. ed., edited by R. J. Wilkinson (13–151). Kuala Lumpur: Oxford University Press.

Williams, Charles Kenneth. 1972. *I Am the Bitter Name.* Boston: Houghton Mifflin.

Williams-Hunt, Anthony Peter (Bah Tony). 1985. "Land Conflicts: Orang Asli Ancestral Laws and State Policies." In *Indigenous Minorities of Peninsular Malaysia: Selected Issues and Ethnographies,* edited by Razha Rashid (36–47). Kuala Lumpur: Intersocietal and Scientific Sdn. Bhd.

———. 2007. "Semai Customary Land Law." Paper presented at the annual meeting of the American Anthropological Association, Washington, D.C., 28 November.

———. 2008. E-mail to rkdentan@buffalo.edu (29 May).

Williams-Hunt, Peter D. R. (Bah Janggut). 1952. *An Introduction to the Malayan Aborigines.* Kuala Lumpur: Government Press.

Wilson, Peter Lamborn. 1988. *Scandals: Essays in Islamic Heresy.* New York: Autonomedia.

Wittgenstein, Ludwig. 1974 [1921]. *Tractatus Logico-Philosophicus*. Translated by D. F. Pears and B. F. McGuiness. London: Routledge and Kegan Paul.

Worthman, Carol M. 1999. "Emotions: You Can Feel the Difference." In *Biocultural Approaches to the Emotions*, edited by Alexander Laban Hinton (41–74). Cambridge: Cambridge University Press.

Wright, Richard. 1993 [1957]. "Tradition and Industrialization: The Historical Meaning of the Plight of the Tragic Elite in Asia and Africa." In *Speech and Power: The African-American Essay and Its Cultural Content from Polemics to Pulpit*, vol. 2, edited by Gerald Early (427–42). New York: Ecco Press.

Wright, Stephen. 1994. *Going Native*. New York: Delta.

Yeats, William Butler. 1962 [1939]. "The Circus Animals' Desertion." In *Selected Poems and Two Plays of William Butler Yeats*, edited by M. L. Rosenthal (184–85). New York: Collier.

Younger, Stephen M. 2005. *Violence and Revenge in Egalitarian Societies*. Los Alamos, N.M.: Los Alamos National Laboratory.

Yusoff, Muhamed Nasir. 1987. "Fostering a Brighter Future for Asli Kids." *The Star*, 27 March.

Index

abjection, 79–80
adept-familiar relationships, 4–5, 39, 88–93, 182, 193
adepts: demon lovers of, 4–5, 39, 88–93, 182; gender of, 91–92; illness, curing, 4–5, 89, 94–95, 133, 182; the Lord's gift of power to, 73, 83–84, 111; role of, 93; seduced by power, stories of, 94–108. *See also* séances
age grade system, 4
agriculture, traditional, 2, 142, 143
Alcoholics Anonymous, 111, 234–36
alcohol intoxication, 118, 136, 165, 211, 212
animals: dogs, treatment of, 135–36; hunting, 126–27; mocking, 71, 73, 118, 134–35; Semai concept of, 4; souls of, 4, 71

bathing, ritual, 5, 133, 191
the Beast God, 68. *See also* Nkuu', the Lord
blood intoxication, 15, 28, 78, 84, 109–10
Btsisi' ("Mah Meri"), 22, 35–36, 235
bullying, 115–16, 140, 198–99, 204
Bureau of Aboriginal Affairs, 171

"camping", 132
capitalism, effect on Semai, 146
chaos, 77–80, 114–15, 118, 133–40, 182
child abuse: learned helplessness with, 78–80, 110; physical, 38–41, 137, 190–92, 196–97; in schools, 137, 196–97; sexual, 92, 192, 195; surrender of the child to, 92
child rearing: comforting in, 190; discipline practices, 179, 196–97; examples of, 100–101, 129; frightening used in, 179–81, 189; noncoercive, 4, 196–97, 237; in the shadow of slaving, 178–79; shame used in, 145; stories role in, 74, 80–81, 179–83; tantrums, responding to, 193–94
children: bullying by, 204, 209; differentiation of the self in, 79–80; education by the state, 67, 197–99, 208–9; enslavement of, 2–3, 7, 34–35, 37, 185–87; foster-age program for, 186–87; fostering of, 207; ignoring the rules, 135–36; kidnapping of, 185–87; subordination of, 227; violence against, 137, 190–92, 195–97,

refuse, consequences of, 167–71, 174–75; surrender and, 92, 110–12, 173, 246–47
friendships, 97–98, 121–24, 174
frontiersmen, defined, 7

ghost stories, 180
globalization, 143, 182
God of the Dark, 67, 68–70, 83. *See also* Nkuu', the Lord
Golden Bridge program, 182
Great Britain, 2, 19–22
greed, 146, 235

harangues, 145, 196
headhunting, 183–87
helplessness, love in dissolving, 111–12. *See also* learned helplessness
Hinduism, 66, 109
historians, objectivity of, 1
homophobia, 91
horror literature, 80–83, 180
housing, 146–47, 159–60, 205
hunters' violence, 124–27
hunting, 88–93, 204
hunting wives, 5, 73, 78, 89, 166

illness: adepts for curing, 4–5, 89, 94–95, 133, 182; demonic infection, 94–95; enforced conformity as cause of, 142; ritual bathing to cure, 5, 133, 191; social capital and, 114; stress and, 138–40; Thunder Lord and, 4

joking relationships, 130–31, 151

kidnapping, 185–87
K-reproductive strategy, 177

land development, 146, 153, 203, 205, 250
language: of age and respect, 131; of deception, 125–26; hostility in conversation, 135; Orang Asli, 2; Semai vs. Malay, 203; of violence, 117

laughter and horror, 81–82
leadership roles, 4, 18
learned helplessness: child abuse and, 78–80, 110; origin of, 188; persistence in post-traumatic events, 177; requirements for, 65–66; Semai response of, 66–67, 87; stress and, 139; surrender compared, 78–79; teaching children, 179
literacy, 209
the Lord: disease and, 4; fear of, 68–70; gender of, 4; gift of shamanism, 78, 83, 88, 111; Lord of the Dance, 95; Semai on, 72–74; shaming/humiliating, 111, 145; surrendering to, 110–11; violence of, 67–70, 73, 83–84, 134, 235–36
love: conflict resulting from, 142, 145–46; fear transformed through, 88, 94–95; helplessness dissolved in, 111–12; hunting and, 88–93; violence and frustration in erotic, 145, 209–11
love potions, 213
Ludat, people of the forest, 73

Mah Meri. *See* Btsisi'
Malay: fear of, 34, 178; feudal society, 6–7, 34–37, 66–67; marriage to Semai, 59, 182; narrative traditions, 38; Semai, attitude toward, 249; society, rules of polite, 85; theology of violence, 66–67; trait of acquisition, 27–28; women, attitudes toward, 154, 212–13
Malay-Semai relationship, 182
Malay justice, 171
Malay state: colonialism of the, 9, 32, 143, 236, 249; education of Semai children, 178, 197–99, 208–9; Golden Bridge program, 182; land development, 146, 153, 203, 205, 250; nineteenth-century sultan wars, 19–20; Regroupment Schemes, 2, 95–96, 116, 173, 203,

About the Author

Robert Knox Dentan received his Ph.D. in anthropology from Yale University in the lower Paleolithic. Most of his ethnographic work has been with Semai, with whom he lived off and on for several years since 1962. The remarkable peacefulness of their daily routine has given him by association a reputation of expertise on nonviolence and, thus, of expertise on violence. Go figure. He is emeritus professor at the State University of New York, where he retains an e-mail address, rkdentan@buffalo.edu. His two best-known books are *The Semai: A Nonviolent People of Malaya* (2nd ed., 1979) and *Malaysia and the Original People: A Case Study of the Impact of Development on Indigenous Peoples* (with Kirk Michael Endicott, Alberto G. Gomes, and M. Barry Hooker, 1997).